Changes in the Life Insurance Industry: Efficiency, Technology and Risk Management

INNOVATIONS IN FINANCIAL MARKETS AND INSTITUTIONS

Editor:

Mark J. Flannery
University of Florida
Gainesville, Florida, U.S.A.

Changes in the Life Insurance Industry: Efficiency, Technology and Risk Management

edited by
J. David Cummins
Department of Insurance and Risk Management
The Wharton School
The University of Pennsylvania

Anthony M. Santomero
Department of Finance
The Wharton School
The University of Pennsylvania

Kluwer Academic Publishers
Boston/Dordrecht/London

Distributors for North, Central and South America:
Kluwer Academic Publishers
101 Philip Drive
Assinippi Park
Norwell, Massachusetts 02061 USA
Telephone (781) 871-6600
Fax (781) 871-6528
E-Mail <kluwer@wkap.com>

Distributors for all other countries:
Kluwer Academic Publishers Group
Distribution Centre
Post Office Box 322
3300 AH Dordrecht, THE NETHERLANDS
Telephone 31 78 6392 392
Fax 31 78 6546 474
E-Mail <services@wkap.nl>

 Electronic Services <http://www.wkap.nl>

Library of Congress Cataloging-in-Publication Data
Changes in the life insurance industry: efficiency, technology,
and risk management / edited by J. David Cummins and Anthony M.
Santomero.
    p. cm. -- (Innovations in financial markets and institutions)
  The findings of a multi-year study initiated by the Wharton
Financial Institutions Center in 1995, and reported in 10 chapters
by the editors and other researchers.
  Includes bibliographical references.
  ISBN 0-7923-8535-7
  1. Insurance, Life -- United States. I. Cummins, J. David. II.
Santomero, Anthony M. III. Series.
  HG8951 . C477 1999
  368.32'00973 -- dc21
                                    99-30333
                                       CIP

Contents

About the Authors

David F. Babbel joined the Wharton School faculty in 1984 and currently is professor of insurance and finance. He teaches in the graduate program primarily in the areas of insurance finance and investment management. Prior to joining Wharton, he was on the finance faculty for seven years at the University of California at Berkeley, where he taught principally in the areas of international financial management, corporate finance and investments.

A former vice president and director of research in the pension and insurance department of Goldman, Sachs & Co., and economist at the World Bank, he is a financial consultant for several of the largest financial institutions. He has published prolifically in academic and professional literature on asset/liability management, insurance, fixed income investments, and foreign exchange risk management. He is co-author of a 1996 monograph, "Valuation of Interest-Sensitive Financial Instruments."

He received his undergraduate training in economics at Brigham Young University, and his graduate training at the University of Florida in finance. His postdoctoral education in insurance was undertaken at the University of Pennsylvania's Wharton School.

Peter Cappelli is a professor of management at the Wharton School and director of the Center for Human Resources, University of Pennsylvania. He received a DPhil at the University of Oxford in 1983 and a B.S. degree from Cornell University in 1978.

He has been the chairperson of the management department at the Wharton School and currently serves as co-director of the U.S. Department of Education National Center on the Educational Quality of the Workforce at the University of Pennsylvania.

Before joining the Wharton School faculty in 1985, he held appointments at the University of California at Berkeley, University of Illinois, and Massachusetts Institute of Technology.

His primary areas of research are human resource compensation issues, labor economics and union-management relations. Currently he is completing a major study of the changing employment contract in the Unite State.

Roderick M. Carr has been the deputy governor of the Reserve Bank of New Zealand since July 1998. In this role, he is responsible for the Reserve Bank's operations, payments systems operation and financial system oversight, and is a member of the Reserve Bank's Board of Directors.

Prior to joining the Reserve Bank, he held senior management positions in the global payments area of the National Australia Bank in Melbourne. From 1994 to 1997, while completing his doctoral studies, he was Research Fellow and a Project Director at the Wharton Financial Institutions Center in Philadelphia.

Previously, he served as chairman and manager of the Ministerial Committee on the Funding and Provision of Health Services for the New Zealand government. He was chief manager of retail financial services and general manager of BNZ Life Insurance Ltd. before going overseas.

He holds a Ph.D. and M.A. from the Wharton School, University of Pennsylvania, an M.B.A. from Columbia University's Graduate School of Business in New York, and an L.L.B. (Hons) from the University of Otago.

J. David Cummins is the Harry J. Loman Professor of Insurance and Risk Management at the Wharton School of the University of Pennsylvania and Executive Director of the S.S. Huebner Foundation for Insurance Education. His fields of specialization include financial risk management of insurance firms and the economic analysis of efficiency and productivity. Dr. Cummins has written or edited fifteen books and published more than fifty refereed journal articles in publications such as the *Journal of Business*, *Journal of Finance*, *Management Science*, the *Journal of Banking and Finance*, the *Journal of Financial Intermediation*, the *Journal of Economic Perspectives*, the *Journal of Risk and Insurance*, the *Journal of Risk and Uncertainty*, the *Journal of Productivity Analysis*, and the *Astin Bulletin*. He has received eighteen prizes for his journal articles including the prize as best financial paper at the Centennial Meeting of the International Actuarial Association, Brussels, Belgium, in 1995, the Brian Hey Prize for best financial paper by the Institute of Actuaries (U.K.), in 1998, Alpha Kappa Psi-Spangler Prize, the Robert C. Witt Award, and several *Journal of Risk and Insurance* articles awards. Dr. Cummins has served as consultant to numerous business and governmental organizations including IBM, CIGNA, Liberty Mutual, the National Association of Insurance Commissioners, the Alliance of American Insurers, the U.S. Department of Justice, and the Internal Revenue Service. He is a past-president of the American Risk and Insurance Association, has served as editor of the *Journal of Risk and Insurance* and as Visiting Scholar at the Federal Reserve Banks of Atlanta and Philadelphia, and currently is Associate Editor of seven refereed journals.

He received his Ph.D. from the University of Pennsylvania in 1972, M.A. from the University of Pennsylvania in 1971, and B.A. from the University of Nebraska in 1968.

Lorin M. Hitt is assistant professor of operations and information management at the Wharton School, University of Pennsylvania. He received a Ph.D. from Massachusetts Institute of Technology, 1996, an M.S. from Brown University in 1989, and an Sc.B. from Brown University in 1988. He joined the Wharton School faculty in 1996.

His primary research areas include information technology and productivity, information systems and organization, economics of information, and applied econometrics. Presently, he is engaged in contract structure for IS outsourcing and in measuring the productivity effects of information systems.

He is currently involved in an empirical investigation on the relationship between organizational practices, information technology, and productivity. He is investigating the role of firm structure on the value of information systems investments, and optimal contract structure for IS outsourcing arrangements.

Craig Merrill is an assistant professor of finance and the Grant Taggart Fellow of Insurance and Risk management at the Marriott School of Management at Brigham Young University. He received his Ph.D. in insurance from the Wharton School of the University of Pennsylvania.

His primary area of academic research and publication is the valuation of interestrate contingent securities with applications to derivative pricing, modeling of default risk, and valuation of insurance liabilities. One of his monographs on financial valuation models was commissioned and published by the Society of Actuaries, and is used in their certification exams. Others of his papers, on financial valuation models for life insurers, which he has co-authored with David Babbel, are a key part of the effort of the American Academy of Actuaries' efforts to implement a unified valuation system for life insurers. He has also conducted research and published on investment strategy and loss distribution models.

His consulting assignments (AIG, Goldman Sachs, Lazard Freres, Winkelvoss & Associates, New York Life, and others) have involved such projects as a two-factor bond pricing model, multi-asset return simulation models, compiling a database of intraday Treasury security prices based on the GovPX data feeds, and development of international interest-rate and exchange-rate simulation models. He has also presented professional seminars on risk management, mathematical finance, and financial pricing of insurance liabilities.

James F. Moore is a senior research fellow with the Wharton Financial Institutions Center and a consultant to Enhance Financial Services. His research spans a wide variety of insurance related topics including retirement savings behavior, pricing of catastrophic risk, and the role of insurers as financial intermediaries. He currently is exploring parallels between pricing and risk analysis in the catastrophic and credit risk arenas. Prior to pursuing graduate study, he worked for William M. Mercer where he focused on asset-liability management for pension plans and post-retirement medical plans. He has a Ph.D. and M.A. from the Wharton School of the University of Pennsylvania and a B.S. from Brown University.

Laureen Regan is an assistant professor in the department of risk management and insurance at the Fox School of Business in Temple University. Her research interests are in property-liability insurance industry market structure. She earned her Ph.D. from the Wharton School in December 1993, and has published articles in the *Journal of Risk and Insurance*, and the *Journal of Law and Economics*.

Anthony M. Santomero is the Richard K. Mellon professor of finance and the director of the Financial Institutions Center at the Wharton School of the University of Pennsylvania. He is a leading authority on financial institution risk management and financial structure and a recognized consultant to major financial institutions and regulatory agencies throughout North America, Europe, and the Far East. His studies into the effects of capital regulation have influenced the way regulators around the world control the industry, and his examination of risk management systems continues to pioneer new approaches and techniques in this area as well.

As a consultant for leading financial institutions in the Unite State and abroad, he has addressed issues of financial risk management procedures, the pricing of risk of various kinds, and credit risk evaluation and management. He has advised the Federal Reserve Board of Governors, the FDIC and the General Accounting Office on a wide range of issues relating to capital regulation and structural reform. Internationally, he has been a consultant to the European Economic Community in Brussels, the Inter-American Development Bank, the Kingdom of Sweden, the Ministry of Finance of Japan, the Treasury of New Zealand, the Bank of Israel, the National Housing Bank of India, the Saudi Arabian Monetary Agency, and the Capital Markets Board of Turkey. In addition, he currently serves as a permanent Advisor to the Swedish Central Bank.

He is associate editor of seven academic journals, including the *Journal of Money, Credit and Banking, Journal of Financial Services Research*, and *Journal of Banking and Finance*. He has written more than 100 articles and monographs on financial sector regulation and economic performance, including one of the first studies to analyze the behavior of banks in Japan.

He received his A.B. in economics from Fordham University in 1968, his Ph.D. in economics from Brown in 1971, and received an honorary doctorate from the Stockholm School of Economics in 1992.

Sharon Tennyson is associate professor of policy analysis and management at Cornell University. She holds a Ph.D. degree in economics from Northwestern University with a specialization in industrial organization and public policy, and was previously on the faculty of the department of insurance and risk management at the Wharton School of the University of Pennsylvania. Her professional career has focused on economic and policy issues in insurance markets, most notably automobile insurance regulation, insurance fraud, and insurance distribution. Her work has been published in economics, insurance and finance journals, and she has received research funding from a variety of sources. Her current research initiatives include claiming behavior and claims payment practices in automobile insurance, the impact of institutional arrangements on insurance regulatory outcomes, and consumer shopping and purchase behaviors in insurance markets.

Michael R. Tuohy is managing director of Tillinghast Towers-Perrin. He joined the firm in 1973 to establish the London office. In 1977, he became head of the Atlanta office's life insurance consulting operations. In 1984, he moved from Atlanta to head up the firm's New York offices. In 1988, he was chosen to lead the firm's joint venture with Towers Perrin's general management practice. In October 1989, he became head of Tillinghast-Towers Perrin's life insurance practice. He was appointed the firm's managing director in March 1991.

He has extensive experience not only in the United States and the United Kingdom, but also in Australia, Canada, South Africa, and several European countries. His consulting background includes work in the areas of life insurance company acquisitions, strategic planning, product development, and financial reporting and measurement, with particular emphasis on the creation of meaningful reports to management.

He received a B.A. from Oxford University. He is a Fellow of the Institute of Actuaries, an Associate of the Society of Actuaries, a member of the American Academy of Actuaries and a Fellow of the Conference of Consulting Actuaries.

Changes in the Life Insurance Industry: Efficiency, Technology and Risk Management

1 LIFE INSURANCE: THE STATE OF THE INDUSTRY

Anthony M. Santomero

1. Introduction

The life insurance industry in the United States is at a point of dramatic evolutionary change. Some would argue the factors that have altered the industry in the past will accelerate its transformation in the future. The past several decades have been a time of fundamental change in terms of the environment that is facing firms in this industry, the expectations of its customers, and an ever-shifting product line, including substantial proliferation and innovations in product offerings. Shifting attention from the past to the future and gazing into the next century, we can see this transformation accelerating. The confluence of three factors has contributed to movement in this industry: 1) the technological revolution that has been transforming the financial sector; 2) the demographic shift that is part and parcel of the aging of the baby boom generation; and, 3) the constant, indeed ever-increasing, competition in the market for financial services. Together, these features of the life insurance market lead to heightened expectation of change for the industry as a whole, and shifting firm-specific fortunes over the next decade and beyond.

Of course, this assessment and prediction may not be unique to the life insurance industry; it can be asserted for any number of industries in general, and for the entire financial service industry in particular. Indeed, some of the factors driving change here apply to broad classes of firms in many industries.

The changing role of computers and information technology, for example, has dramatically changed the way we conduct our daily lives. Their impact is omnipresent in how we choose all our service providers, and how we interact with everyone from our bookstore to our broker. In turn, technology gives the service provider many new options for marketing products to us. However, these factors listed above have effects that are unique or at least more palpable to life insurers and financial service providers in general. Technology really has altered the financial service industry in a way that is substantially different from other industries.

Demographic changes and their impact on the product mix of insurers are also readily apparent in their substantial impact upon the life insurance industry and its future. As a result, today, the largest business segment for life insurers is not life insurance. The single largest share of life insurance premiums is attributable to annuity sales to a generation that is, at least currently, more concerned about protecting income than bequests. This dependence on annuities has not always been the case. If we look back to 1945 and the end of World War II, life insurance premiums were roughly nine times annuity contributions to premium income.[1] While demographic changes may have affected all areas of the economy, it is unlikely that it has had such a profound effect anywhere else. Because of demographic shifts, dresses may be a bit longer and cars a bit bigger, but no other industry's revenues have been completely transformed by the shift in the size of age cohorts and the impact of their "dollar votes."

Competition, too, is a common theme throughout the economy, and in this respect, the changes to the life insurance sector may appear to be no different than others have experienced. Nonetheless, the changes here have been particularly profound. The once staid exclusive arena of insurance, maintained by overly zealous state regulation, has seen competition from other financial service firms, and insurers entering from their own jurisdictions and from around the world. If this is not unique, it is at least a case study of the perils of competition and the effect it has on a market.

Where does this leave the industry and its senior management? How should they react to this environment and what is the road to success? These are the questions that are asked in the current volume, as researchers from the Wharton Financial Institutions Center investigated the industry, its past, its present, and its future. The results are not reassuring. What emerges is an industry in flux with well-defined problems and challenges, and a wide variation of proposed solutions.

This situation, in fact, may not be all bad. As an industry in flux, challenges are often opportunities, and some strategies for success will fare better than others. Management choice becomes a key determinant of success, rather than general economic trends or industry growth. In fact, in sectors subject to the forces of change, the value and importance of management capability is at its highest. Success will be achieved by those that confront today's challenges and remedy today's maladies. Failure or extinction will be the fate of others.

To set the context for this study of the life insurance industry, this initial chapter will review the key challenges facing the industry and describe how the volume addresses them in subsequent contributions by the research team. It ends at the beginning of our journey to understand the determinants of success. It outlines the ways we address key future challenges to the industry for maintaining its position as a major segment of the broader financial service sector.

2. The Changing Nature of Financial Sector Institutions

The past two decades have ushered in a revolution in the nature of financial institutions. The traditional distinctions between commercial banks, thrifts, investment banks, investment management companies, and insurance firms have blurred, and in some cases disappeared. The reasons for this transformation, viz., the enablement of technology and the erosion of the regulation that had preserved these separate sub-industries, are unique to each group's history.

For the banking sector, product market segmentation that was assured by the passage of the Banking Act of 1933, especially those segments normally referred to as the Glass Steagall Act, achieved the separation of banking from underwriting. However, over time, much of the substance of Glass Steagall has been put aside by permissive regulatory rulings and the deregulation wave of the 1980s. The McCarran Ferguson Act of 1945 effectively relegated the full authority to regulate insurance activities to the states. However, insurance distribution by banking institutions is increasing everywhere. Add to this the recent decision of the Comptroller to permit federally chartered institutions to offer insurance products when they are domiciled in towns of under 5,000 inhabitants, and the result is to significantly reduce the effect of that statute. The recent regulatory approval of the Travelers Citicorp merger in 1998, albeit subject to subsequent legislation, suggests that such product expansion will not be relegated to smaller institutions. Notwithstanding the continued reluctance of Congress to pass financial reform legislation, the banking sector is moving inexorably toward product expansion and universal banking.

The same could be said of the thrift industry. This once staid industry of local savings and loan associations and mutual savings banks has gone through a roller coaster ride over the past 25 years. From expansion to collapse, the number of these banking institutions shrank by two-thirds and their demise was widely forecast. Over the intervening period, however, the survivors have been transformed into direct competitors for the retail banking segment, and a significant provider of life insurance and annuity products to their customers. While these entities are unlikely to emerge as major competitors of any magnitude when compared to the larger financial service giants, the leaders here have ample regulatory leeway to compete and thrive in this sector.

For their part, the investment banking firms are not waiting, nor wanting, for competitive challenges. These traditionally aggressive competitors have used the financial boom of the last two decades along with the increasing interest in capital market investments by the baby boom generation to expand their size and influence to unprecedented levels. Industry participants that have chosen a wide product range have broadened both their focus and their influence throughout the financial sector. Names like Morgan Stanley, long associated with wholesale underwriting, have become mass-market distributors through, in part, their acquisition of Dean Witter. Merrill Lynch has transformed its retail brokerage franchise into a full-service global financial giant that is capable of large scale underwriting, asset management, brokerage services, and the offering of standard insurance products. In fact, the industry has seen a movement, more generally, to asset management and the related businesses associated with retirement savings spawned by the deinstitutionalization of pension funds and the trend away from defined benefit plans. While more will be said of this later, it is important to recognize that these firms have long managed corporate pension assets. The evolution to greater personal asset accumulation for both retirement and bequest has increased the industry's interest in the insurance market and led to its entrance into insurance products or close substitutes over the last decade. While this move presents regulatory hurdles, they have not been roadblocks to their increasing market presence.

Finally, no review of the financial service landscape would be complete without recognizing the emergence of investment management companies. These entities, most recognized for their lead product, open-end mutual funds, have been a phenomenon of the 1990s. Not since their early days in the 1950s have they seen their rapid growth in size and their importance to average retail and wholesale customers recognized by both the public and the press. This increased visibility is warranted. The once stagnant industry has seen its assets grow to over $3.4 trillion[2], a figure that rivals the asset size of the banking or life insurance industries. Leading firms have seen considerable growth at the expense of both these latter industries, as consumers have seen mutual fund products as close substitutes to both bank savings vehicles and the retirement asset offerings of the life insurance industry.

This, then, leads to the discussion of the insurance industry itself. Here, the picture is one of change and separation. The industry once was regulated and behaved like a relatively homogeneous sector. Distinctions across states, while relevant, were not fundamental, and distinctions across firms were of equal disinterest. Organizational form was the most relevant difference, as mutual and stock firms coexisted, with broadly similar product arrays. However, the advent of specialized firms and specialized products, supported by separate fund accounting rather than the general fund, began the process of innovation. The move to specialization and focus meant traditional competitors followed different paths, with some emphasizing health coverage, others simple life, and still others products aimed at more general asset accumulation. These differences became evident in distribution approaches as well, with some retaining exclusive career agents, others focusing on broker distribution, and still others increasingly dependent on bank and/or broker channels. As some moved toward asset accumulation, they found themselves in direct competition with other parts of the industry. Firms like USAA accepted the challenge and now compete directly in the mutual fund and consumer credit arena. Others have remained in life products, even as they have shifted more generally from simple life to universal life and annuity products.

The net result is that the once separate segments of the financial service industry are all converging by both design and marketing happenstance. Seeking new dollars and a larger customer base, the passage of time has caused a convergence in the financial industry in which institutions are looking more alike. Allowable activity for each segment has overlapped and this overlap is accelerating. Geography, once a barrier to entry or at least an obvious regulatory limit, has been connected by wires, computers, and faxes as never before.

Where does this leave the fate of individual institutions operating in this new world? Will they all converge, offering an identical array of products that span the entire market? This is unlikely. Rather, firms and whole industries (though to a lesser extent) must define their value-added niche in the market and focus their product offerings accordingly. This creates some critical challenges for management. Similarity does not necessarily lead to success. Rather, each firm must find its own unique array of products and services. The operative strategy is likely to be affected by their historical roots and the strengths that have been built over decades. And, as we will see in the surveys that have been answered by leaders of the insurance industry, today there are markedly different perceptions of strengths and weaknesses in the life insurance industry. It is management's challenge to harness the firm's unique capabilities and adapt them to this changing, increasingly competitive market.

Yet, the life insurance industry has at least one unique advantage common to all of its members: it has a long history and reputation in the single most desirable financial market segment, the market for retirement assets. To understand the future of the life insurance industry, one must understand the shift in both the demographics of the United States and the method used to provide for retirement benefits. It is to this that we now turn.

3. The Changing Nature of the Retirement Asset Market

It is a recognized fact that the nature of asset accumulation for retirement is undergoing a virtual revolution in the United States and many other countries as well. Since the advent of social security in the 1930s and the slow but sure increased dependence of salaried workers on company-provided pensions, the current generation of retirees learned to expect that their retirement wealth was in the hands of others. Whether it was the government, as in the case for social security, or a defined benefit, a vested pension offered through an employer and guaranteed by the government through PBGC, the concern for financial welfare was a concern that was beyond the average worker's kin and responsibility. With the graying of the baby boomers, however, the assurance of the same relative benefits from both of these post-retirement annuity sources seems less likely. Savvy workers, therefore, have begun to reassess their plans for retirement and their exclusive dependency on vested pension programs.

There is reason for concern. Both the government and the corporate providers of pension coverage have been reassessing their own capability to credibly represent their financial capacity to sustain current benefit levels with existing premiums. This concern has led the government to establish a federal commission to consider changes in the federal program, even as employers have begun to shift the burden of retirement coverage to employees. The former is well known and will not be discussed here. The latter is perhaps less recognized but no less dramatic. As the current generation has moved from consumption to saving, they have begun to observe an unmistakable push by employers away from standard deferred benefit programs and toward less guarantees of life-long income made by the corporate sector. Clearly, there has been a shift toward greater personal responsibility for retirement financial planning and greater dependence upon one's own resources to sustain current lifestyles.

This, in turn, has caused consumers to shift their personal financial portfolio choices from standard savings and bequest products to asset accumulation and annuity-type products. The effect on the financial market, in general, has been extraordinary and the effect on the relative importance of annuity and standard life insurance products to the life insurance industry has been nothing short of revolutionary.

As recently as 1985, the share of total premiums to the industry was 38.6% for life insurance products versus 34.6% for annuity products, with health insurance premiums comprising the balance. At the end of 1995, the tally was 29.2% for life insurance premiums versus 47.1% for annuity considerations. Interestingly, annuities have not cannibalized the life insurance marketplace; they simply have been the group of products showing substantially higher growth rates over the recent past. Looking back to 1945, the annualized growth rate in annuities has been 11.5%. For life insurance premiums, it was 6.3%. Over the last 10 years of the period (1985–1995), annuities maintained their long-term growth rate, growing at 11.9% per annum. At the same time, industry life insurance premiums grew at an annualized rate of 1.9% for the decade and an anemic .6% per year for the first half of the 1990s.

Demographic change has played a major role in this transformation on a number of fronts. First, the boomers will be the first group to retire en masse with defined contribution account balances, instead of the annual defined benefit annuity payments alluded to above. In addition, this generation is expected to live longer than past generations. This is a double-edged sword for life insurers. Life insurance protects the policyholder's family against his/her untimely, i.e., *early* death, while an annuity protects the policyholder against his own untimely, i.e., *late* death. As we live longer, the relative value of these insurance mechanisms changes. The likelihood of dying prematurely decreases and so the cost of this coverage declines. On the other hand, as we have more time to provide for ourselves in our golden years, the cost of doing so rises.

Second, changes in our social structure, such as the increasing preponderance of dual-earner households, compounds the shift. Traditionally, and still to some extent today, life insurance is purchased by the husband to provide for the wife and children in case of the loss of his income. A working wife acts as a built-in hedge against her husband's early death. If she is able to generate sufficient income to provide for herself and the children, then if the husband dies life insurance needs are less. On the other hand, if the couple decides to retire at the same point in time, this exacerbates the need for old-age income protection. With neither spouse working, there are no earnings coming in and two mouths to feed—mouths used to consuming that which two incomes can provide.

The third demographic factor is the sheer size of the current post-World War II cohort in particular—"the baby boom." Our timing of the current study is particularly apropos when viewed with this generation as a backdrop. The baby boom started in 1945 with the close of World War II, and boomers are now turning 50. Fifty is not only significant because it marks the age of membership eligibility for AARP membership, but also because it marks a milestone age for many, when the financial planning focus shifts from the current needs of the family to the future needs of retirement. For those fortunate few who have been preparing diligently for a number of years this may mean an intensification of prior efforts, but for many more it comes as a rude awakening.

To insurers, these three demographic features all converge and lead to large pools of liquid wealth, followed by an associated need for programmed withdrawal. For those retiring with defined contribution balances as their sole pension wealth, their social security benefits represent their only source of annuitized wealth and guaranteed income stream. Yet even social security may not be immune from change. Many of the reform proposals targeting social security would remake this cornerstone of retirement planning in the image of today's 401(k)s. To the extent that America's retirement wealth is liquid and not pre-annuitized, there is and will be a growing opportunity for life insurers to increase the market for annuities and utilize their actuarial skills in mortality risk pooling.

However, the majority of annuities sold today are not immediate annuities. They are deferred annuities—tax-preferred savings vehicles with provisions for annuitization at some future date. For those households that cannot utilize other tax-preferred vehicles such as Individual Retirement Accounts (IRAs) or 401(k)s because they are unavailable, or because they have been contributed to up to the extent the law allows, these may be useful savings mechanisms. Yet, the insurance company is in competition with those companies who have grown to dominate the turf for tax-preferred savings, viz. the mutual fund companies.

4. Financial Service Competition and the Future Challenges to Life Insurers

The changing nature of the customer product choice has had a profound impact on the money management industry, which will have spillover effects for the life insurance industry in the years to come. The decline in whole life has reduced the attractiveness of its distribution by agents and independent brokers, even while the term products have become commoditized. Together, these trends have meant that the industry's capacity to support and grow its agent networks is limited. The lament associated with the high cost of distribution has become louder as volumes have shrunk and difficulties have arisen for some of the vanishing premium products that have taken the place of simple whole life. In short, the delivery cost issues arise anew because of recent product evolution and consumer demand.

In the area of retirement asset opportunities, recent trends offer their own set of issues to be addressed. Many of these relate to the changing nature of customer interaction and its associated operating challenges. When the defined benefit plan was king, the assets in the plan were not dedicated to individual accounts. They could be managed as large pools with the trustees of the plan doling differing amounts out to various money mangers to invest as they saw fit under a master trust. In the defined contribution world, assets are generally dedicated to individual employee accounts, where the individual employees have discretion over how the money is invested. The issues associated with managing a pool of customers differ dramatically.

In the defined benefit plan, there is a single individual or small group of individuals determining how that money is invested. In an extreme case, the funds may be divided among several asset managers. Additional contributions are made quarterly (if made at all) and disbursements are made monthly. For the modern defined contribution plan, by contrast, each individual makes decisions, generally investing in any number of funds. Inflows may be as frequent as weekly, outflows are sporadic, and asset allocations for any or all accounts in some cases can change daily. The demands and resources required to respond to these needs differ tremendously.

In the early days of defined contribution accounts, many of which were managed in part by life insurers, the plan sponsor or an outside consultant handled the administrative and record-keeping functions. The actual money management function was handled similar to that for defined benefit plans. In the late 1980s and early 1990s, companies began to outsource these operations. Mutual funds already had similar operations in place and the move to modern defined-contribution record keeping and administration simply meant expanding the capacity of existing operations. Therefore, growth of the 401(k) as the dominant means of private sector retirement wealth provision has been a windfall to the mutual fund industry and has dramatically increased its relative share of the retirement asset marketplace.[3] Recent increases in eligibility for traditional IRA contributions as well as the establishment of the Roth IRA are additional changes that play to the mutual fund industry's strengths.

Whereas a decade ago defined contribution plan participants knew their employer as the overseer of the plan, today they see the mutual fund family in that role. In the event an employee leaves his employer, he is still able to keep the money where it is, whether this is an insurance firm or a mutual fund family. This presence in the mind of the consumer is a natural foothold from which to expand. If the initial provider is a mutual fund company, it attempts to keep and expand its management services for these clients as much as possible. The next logical progression has been for the mutual fund families to establish affiliated insurers. These sister companies underwrite annuities and receive a fee for bearing actuarial risk, but leave the invested assets with the mutual fund. Recent data suggest that these affiliated firms have been some of the fastest growing entities in the life insurance business.

On the other hand, if the initial provider is an insurer, the affiliation here too can extend beyond the initial pension period and beyond the initial pension product. This has led some members of the industry to offer proprietary funds to industry clients and market their services to a wider array of customers through a wider array of products.

Beyond this, mutual funds and pension products are not the only marriage to be made. Insurers give both commercial and investment banks the ability to offer a full range of tax-favored financial products through their distribution outlets, which include bank branches and retail brokers. The theme is that there are gains to be made from consolidation and alliances, but members of the insurance industry must look beyond both their standard products and their traditional distribution channels to grow and expand with the market.

In addition, the recent view is that to be successful, you must be big. This perspective is not alien to the life insurance industry, which has seen its share of consolidation in the past few years. The number of life insurers in the United States decreased by one-fourth between 1989 and 1995.[4] This represents consolidation at all levels—some insurers have grown by acquiring many small entities, but there have been notable pairings at the top of the industry as well. This mirrors current activities in other insurance realms as well with dramatic consolidation in property-casualty, reinsurance, and the brokerage industries.

Probably of most importance is the emergence of cross-industry mergers, most significantly identified with the pairing of The Travelers and Citicorp. The combined colossus, Citigroup, will be a force to be reckoned with in the areas of insurance, commercial banking, and investment banking. While these multi-headed financial beasts are new and strange to the American financial service landscape, they are old news in the rest of the world. The financial service landscapes in Europe and Asia are accustomed to such diverse financial services providers. These American integrators contend that they are playing catch-up on the global stage and are being hamstrung by outdated Depression-era legislation.

The degree to which future consolidation can and will take place is still to be determined. The review and possible repeal of existing laws will govern the extent of consolidation. One additional complication for insurers is really 50 additional complications. In the United States insurance regulation is primarily the purview of state-level entities. This poses an additional burden and cost associated with any merger.

Another feature of the bigness story, and a unique issue within the insurance industry, is the growing trend toward de-mutualization. Many of the country's largest life insurance companies have operated under mutual ownership structures in which policyholders are in effect the firm's equity holders. Increasingly, this ownership structure is being seen as a disadvantage to a consolidating industry. Firms are converting to public ownership where access to external capital and the ability to use one's own equity currency to finance the acquisition of insurance and other financial service businesses is viewed as critical to maintain competitive position.

What does cross-industry merger provide an insurer that merging with another insurer does not? Better information is clearly one answer. Typically, an insurer has little knowledge of a customer beyond which insurance products he buys. The data on individual customers may include the value of those products, monthly payments, and some details on medical status. However, generally these pieces of information are scattered across various computer systems in various departments—marketing, payment processing, claims processing, and underwriting. Only recently have insurers made inroads to link these various pieces of information. Historically, insurance record keeping has been product focused. In the new world of financial services, databases are client focused.

A bank has a wealth of customer financial information at one site. It knows if a customer deposits his paycheck to his checking account, has an outstanding mortgage, automobile loan, or credit card as well. The bank may have access to detailed information on this customer's income, debts, and spending habits. This information is invaluable for marketing purposes. Similarly, the mutual fund that oversees this individual's 401(k) account has information on his or her income, and, given the individual's choices for asset allocation, can make inferences on risk tolerance and investment behavior. If these data from the bank and mutual fund are combined, they make for a very powerful marketing and sales tool.

Banks and their providers also offer attractive means to distribute a broad array of products. In addition, the advent and growth of technologies such as direct deposit, phone, and Internet banking create opportunities to interact with customers. The automatic teller machine (ATM) and the living, breathing teller at a branch present opportunities to sell insurance. This may be through signage at the branch, a query from a teller, or a message flashed on the screen while data are being processed.

Here, relying on the mass marketing ability of existing bank, brokerage, and mutual fund firms may prove fruitful as low-cost distribution and marketing opportunities to reach a broader audience. A flier stuffed with every monthly account statement touting the benefits of insurance and annuities in financial planning is less costly than a sales call by an agent to each of these households, or even a fraction of them. To many of these households, such generic products that are cheap to manufacture may best meet their needs.

This is not to say that the traditionally profitable path of catering to the wealthiest will be forgotten. Catering to the wealthy and their needs presents an insurer with a different set of demands than does selling to the mass market. For customers purchasing generic products, standard service levels may be good enough. The mass-market customer wants prompt, courteous, and informed answers to his other questions, but is willing to accept them over the phone from an anonymous voice on the other end of an 800 number. These customers are familiar with the "do it yourself" culture of self-help manuals and Home Depots. Educate them and provide them with the resources to answer their own questions—automated 800 numbers and websites—but let them do most of the work themselves.

The wealthy consumer purchasing custom-tailored products demands custom-tailored service. His or her insurance needs are more specialized and must be met by an array of products that take into account specific needs and incorporate existing portfolio composition, tax, and estate planning. This customer demands hand-holding and should be willing to pay the service cost. The ability to provide these services requires a fleet of extensively trained agents or other service personnel that have a broad spectrum of knowledge covering many existing fields and products—traditional insurance, investment management and asset allocation, tax and estate law.

What does this mean for existing distribution channels? Clearly, there has already been some sorting, based on past distribution and current marketing strategies. Some companies that are focused on direct marketing strategies have been devoting less resources to relationships with field agents. These firms are already aligning with banks or mutual funds to target the mass market. The resources that they have developed—direct marketing experience, development of centralized call centers—are essentially back office skills that are transferable and may be applied to underwriting activities under a number of different names. These skills are product focused and do not entail an extensive commitment of time to get to know and understand the minutia of the individual customer. These skills, integrated with marketing data provided by an affiliated bank or group of banks, allow for broad sales of products. In cases where the direct marketer does not have a household name, co-branding with the affiliated bank(s) has provided a level of comfort to customers. This may be an especially advantageous mechanism in rural areas or other places where banks are small and franchises are regional in nature.

A bigger adjustment will be necessary for insurers with traditional agency operations. They have substantial resources already dedicated to the training and bonding of existing agents. Maintaining and growing these operations are difficult and expensive. Insurers in these situations face a tough choice. Either they make significant changes to their distribution models and become leaner, focusing on the mass market and competing with already lean organizations, or they cater to the high end of the market. Catering to the high end will require significant investment in existing as well as new agents to ensure that they have the knowledge and skills to meet the diverse needs of the wealthy. Some firms have already made this commitment and have found some success. Firms in this category can most likely point to some factor that gives them a strategic advantage with the wealthy, such as a top credit or claims-paying rating for which they can demand the higher premia that more personal service demands.

The paradigm here can be examined on a two-coordinate axis with four quadrants. On the x-axis is the relative premium level the insurer can charge. The y-axis gives the relative operating cost of the insurer. Firms with *justifiable* high operating costs that relate to service quality or safety may be able to recoup them through higher premia (northeast quadrant), and more logically would cater to the high end of the market.

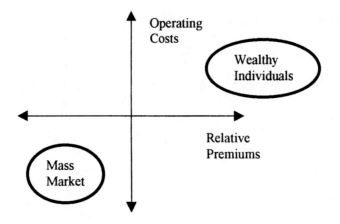

Those firms that are more streamlined and efficient with lower justifiable operating costs (southwest quadrant), should target the mass market. Firms with high operating costs that cannot justify high premiums in the marketplace will not last long.

5. Finding a Strategy for Success

Success, then, will involve choices. These include product array, distribution channel or channels, cost structure, and key customer franchise. Not all firms can or should operate in every area of the market and it is the responsibility of management to find the right place within the continuum.

In this volume, we investigate the choices management has made in the past and their results. We do so in many ways to offer a series of perspectives on the state of the industry, the successes and failures that it has had in competing for customer attention, and to examine the challenges ahead. It is the result of several years' effort, which included two major field-based studies, numerical analyses of industry trends, and interaction with both the industry itself and its consulting community.

The effort began in 1995 when the Wharton Financial Institutions Center, with the benefit of generous support from the Sloan Foundation, began two parallel studies of the industry. The first study involved a collaboration with Tillinghast Towers-Perrin for the development of interviews and a broad-based questionnaire that was sent to the industry to identify key concerns, drivers of performance, and its sense of threats and opportunities. The study also requested extensive data on technology and human resource practices, areas where industry concerns have long centered. This effort was advised by an industry working group, to whom the researchers reported and discussed both their methodologies and early findings. Added to this data was the National Association of Insurance Commissioners (NAIC) data on industry-wide measures of costs and returns, so that results could be cross-correlated with issues that centered around more quantifiable measures, such as efficiency ratios, and these could be investigated in greater depth. We report on the analysis of relative costs, performance levels, and integration re-engineering, using not only survey data but also the rich NAIC data that are available for the industry as a whole. In fact, some of the most interesting results are obtained by contrasting and comparing survey statements with the more standardized data available across the industry.

The second source of information for this volume is a parallel study of financial risk management systems that was begun about the same time by a second research group at the Center. In this work, researchers conducted a field-based investigation of the exact systems employed by the industry to manage the financial and actuarial risks of the firm. Through on-site visits, they interviewed key executives and examined actuarial models that estimated liability exposure and the financial management systems devoted to asset management. Further, they investigated the extent to which these two sides of the balance sheet were coordinated in firm-level risk management, commonly known as asset-liability management.

6. An Outline of Things to Come

The following chapters report the results obtained in our effort to investigate the industry in these many ways. The book covers the challenges facing insurers in the dynamically changing financial sector as gleaned from our major survey of the industry. It also offers an analysis of the industry's cost structure and how management is using the key drivers of performance, namely technology and labor. The volume also will analyze pricing and risk management issues, and strategic choices for the future.

The book is organized in independent but related chapters authored by the leading researchers engaged in the project.

- Chapter 1 has reviewed the landscape of the financial service industry and the changing role of insurance within this context. It points to the challenges and opportunities faced by these firms and the key determinants of success or failure.

- Chapter 2, authored by James F. Moore and Anthony M. Santomero, will report on the survey conducted by the Wharton Financial Institutions Center during 1996/97 in detail. Participants in the survey include the major industry players and, in aggregate, account for a majority of the insurance coverage and premiums in the industry. The survey opens up a number of different areas of inquiry. It begins with an analysis of the threats and opportunities facing the industry, as seen by market participants. Then, it surveys the range of current product offerings, distribution channels in use, strategic choices being made by participating firms, the current use of technology, human resource practices, and efficiency standards. The results offer a clear image of a diverse industry.

- J. David Cummins, in Chapter 3, examines the relative cost efficiency of firms within the industry and examines more closely those firms that were part of our sample group. The approach used, a class of benchmarking methods known as frontier efficiency methodologies, pioneered in his earlier work, permits the researcher to examine the level of firm efficiency distinct from scale and scope economies. As such, it permits the researcher to determine best-practice cost structures and to estimate firm losses associated with operational inefficiency.

- Chapter 4 by Roderick M. Carr, J. David Cummins, and Laureen Regan is best summarized by its title, "Efficiency and Competitiveness in the U.S. Life Insurance Industry." It should be clear that determining lost opportunities and relative inefficiency across firms is merely a first step in the remediation process that should be aimed at achieving best practice. This chapter is a step in this direction, as it looks into the sample of participating firms to try to determine what causes this relative efficiency or inefficiency. It cross correlates firm-specific characteristics with relative efficiency scores. The messages here are of substantial importance in redressing performance gap and for beginning a process of reengineering.

- Chapter 5 by J. David Cummins, Sharon Tennyson, and Mary A. Weiss examines firms that have been active mergers and acquisition participants to see if their relative inefficiency is related to their consolidation efforts in either a negative or positive way. In insurance, as in other parts of the financial sector, merger activity has been substantial as noted above. It is well known that such consolidation results in operating inefficiencies, at least temporarily. Only if best practices are transferred across the new entity will such consolidations improve efficiency. This chapter tries to shed some light on which firms succeed in attaining cost efficiencies and which do not. The results are both interesting and important.

- Peter Cappelli and Clint Chadwick look at human resource practices in the industry and evaluate them relative to other parts of the service sector in Chapter 6. The recurrent theme in insurance circles is that operating costs within the industry are the result of high broker commissions and high labor costs. The authors show us what can be learned from this and from other service sectors. They discuss how aligning human resource systems with firm strategy, and preserving relationships with employees during downsizing, can pay off for firms in the long run.

- Chapter 7 is devoted to technology and its use in the industry. In this chapter, Lorin M. Hitt displays a wealth of knowledge of the appropriate and productive use of technology to insurance. As we have noted, technology is transforming the entire service sector and this is clearly true in the financial services industry. In this chapter, this researcher, who has engaged in the broader industry efforts on the use of technology for competitive advantage, evaluates the life insurance industry's use of this strategic tool. The researchers' goal is to explore this relationship among information technology practices within the organization and their contributions to the efficiency of firms as a whole.

- Chapter 8 transitions from costs to revenues with the contribution of David F. Babbel and Craig Merrill. As the authors note, in the final analysis, insurance product pricing will be a central determinant of success or failure for firms within the industry. Prices must be sufficient to carry operating costs, no matter what their level. However, product pricing must be done accurately in order to cover actuarial risk and the financial risk inherent in the product design. This chapter looks at the pricing challenges and how they are being met by the industry.

- "An Analysis of the Financial Risk Management Process Used by Life Insurers" by David F. Babbel and Anthony M. Santomero is the focus of Chapter 9. Traditionally, risk has been understood to be actuarial risk in most parts of the insurance industry. Yet, the financial risk associated with asset returns and asset-liability management has recently been recognized as a critical issue in these turbulent times. These researchers have recently completed a best-practices study of financial risk management systems for the financial sector, in general, and the life industry, in particular. This chapter reports and updates their findings.

- Michael R. Tuohy has the last word in Chapter 10. Appropriately titled, "Challenges and Issues for Growth," this chapter looks forward with the benefit of all that has been reported here. The author directly addresses where this analysis of the state of the industry leaves management and what executives should do to react and profit from the observed trends. Armed with the results of this study and Tillinghast Towers-Perrin's Annual CEO survey, this industry-thought leader and veteran looks ahead to challenges and opportunities, and focuses the reader on the future, not the past.

It is hoped that the new perspectives offered in this book on the changing industry will be helpful to contemplate the future.

Notes

1. Data for life insurance and annuity considerations is from ACLI (1996).
2. Federal Reserve Bulletin (1998), Table 1.47.
3. See Santomero and Hoffman (1998).
4. See ACLI (1996).

References

American Council of Life Insurance (ACLI). *Life Insurance Fact Book*, 1996.
Board of Governors, Federal Reserve System. *Federal Reserve Bulletin*, November 1998.
Santomero, Anthony M. and Paul Hoffman. "Life Insurance Firms in the Retirement Market: Is the News All Bad?" *Journal of the American Society of CLU and ChFC*, July 1998.

2 THE INDUSTRY SPEAKS: RESULTS OF THE WFIC INSURANCE SURVEY

James F. Moore and Anthony M. Santomero

1. Introduction and Overview

This chapter will report on the results of the 1996 Wharton Financial Institutions Center survey of the retail U.S. life insurance industry. The purpose of the survey was to ask leading market participants to determine the drivers of relative firm efficiency and to query the industry concerning future trends. Specifically, the survey focuses on what set or sets of individual practices and strategies contribute to efficiency gains and lead to competitive advantage in this marketplace. While these questions are not new, the current circumstances in which the industry finds itself are certainly changing.

Over the past 20 years, the industry has moved from a focus on traditional insurance protection products, e.g. ordinary life, to more reliance on products. In doing so, the distinction between life insurance firms and various other forms of financial intermediaries has become less precise. In addition, the marketplace itself is evolving with changes in products, product characteristics, and competitors. The net result is that whereas 20 years ago our survey participants were competing almost exclusively with each other, now they count banks and mutual fund companies as direct competitors. This changing playing field leads to differences in how to play the game and how to keep score, and, consequently, leads to the need for different measurements for who is winning and who is losing.

An initial objective of the study was to expand on previous work that examined the productivity and efficiency of the life insurance industry. The majority of the previous work in this field focused on "macro" firm factors.[1] Data used for these studies are generally public information contained in annual filings with regulators, collected by A.M. Best or the National Association of Insurance Commissioners (NAIC). Inputs and outputs are taken from these filings and include such factors as premium volume, incurred benefits, assets, reserves, product mix, and various operational costs. Additional factors such as choice of distribution systems and organizational form (mutual or stock) are also included.

These measures, while informative, provide an incomplete picture of the insurance operation. They leave out much of the individuality that differentiates one insurer from the next. The macro data present a snapshot of one point in time, or, if linked together over a number of years, a historical vignette of how the industry has changed. It answers questions such as: Who has gotten bigger? More competitive? More efficient? What mix of products has proved most profitable? While the answers to these questions are important, many questions are left unanswered: the "why" and the "what's next."

An insurance company is a collection of decision-makers and procedures as is any company. Many decisions are made daily. Others are made less frequently, but all have impacts that will shape the firm for years to come. Some are financial: How much should we pay underwriters? Agents? Claims processing personnel? How much should we spend on technology? Some are operational: How should we allocate our technology spending? What role should technology play in our underwriting process? Our claims processing? Customer service? Others are strategic: What product markets should we focus on? What customer segments do we wish to target? How has our industry changed and, more importantly, how will it change in the future? The macro-data based studies provide little insight into these questions.

To answer these questions, and others like them, requires "getting inside the black box", i.e., the use of surveys of individual insurers and their key personnel. The first step in creating our survey was to focus on issues that are both important to industry executives and that provide insight into the industry's challenges. To achieve this end, survey questions were designed around two main themes:

1. What do insurers believe are the big issues and challenges facing the retail life insurance industry in the next five to ten years?
2. What are the best practices in place today that can be emulated?

As a starting point, the researchers used a companion study of the retail banking industry completed by a group headed by Harker and Hunter that focused on similar issues in the commercial banking sector.[2] This provided an initial set of questions to work from that focused on operational and managerial questions. For additional insight into current industry-specific concerns, the Wharton researchers partnered with Tillinghast Towers-Perrin, a leading consultant to the insurance industry. These inputs, coupled with site visits to pilot participants, served to shape the surveys, develop the questions, and present the issues in appropriate and familiar terms for all of the individual divisions surveyed— marketing, underwriting, claims processing, information technology, and human resources.

In each case, survey participants completed extensive questionnaires that delved into key issues in the financial services environment that face the insurance sector along with their own perspectives on successful practices that relate to corporate strategy, marketing, distribution channels, under- writing methodology, policyholder service, claims settlement, information technology, and human resources management.

The survey was first completed by a small number of firms that also func- tioned as an advisory group to the project. After completion of the pilot study, 310 insurers (groups and individual firms), were approached to participate. Seventy firms completed all or parts of the survey. Participat- ing firms had total assets in excess of $585 billion and 1995 premiums of approximately $95 billion that could be attributed to their life and health operations. This represented approximately 35% of the industry by assets and 28% of industry premiums. A majority of respondents underwrote business in all 50 states and the District of Columbia.

What is the overarching message that emerges from their responses? One major conclusion is that there are no quick fixes or uniformly-agreed- upon ways in which each and every firm within this industry can compete and succeed in this dynamically changing environment. In short, there are no easy answers. Survey participants present myriad views on how to go about running a successful insurance company. Firms in the sample repre- sent a cross-section of sizes and product focus. This market comprises many sub-markets and, depending on who the survey respondents are and where they focus their efforts, they may or may no find themselves competing with one another. The right strategy for a large insurer with a complete array of products is not necessarily the right strategy for a company that focuses on a single product niche. However, there are some common themes to responses. Accordingly, this review of the survey results will concentrate on six broad themes and the insights obtained from the participants associated with each.

1.1. Theme 1: External Forces will Play an Important Role in the Future of the Retail Life Insurance Sector

For years insurers have been able to exploit the profitability of a tax code that favors life insurance products. With the advent and growth of tax-favored vehicles that are not the sole domain of the insurance industry, such as Individual Retirement Accounts (IRAs) and defined contribution retirement plans, industry participants recognize that there is a growing threat from other financial services firms. Substitutes for annuities and life insurance from "outsiders" threaten existing market share. The ever-present possibility of a change in the tax law threatens the size and scope of traditional product markets.

1.2. Theme 2: Rapid and Efficient Harnessing of Technology is Important for Survival and Growth

While computers have long been important for managing the large amounts of data held by life insurers, how that data are managed and what they are used for is an evolving issue. There is a growing consensus that the organization of data should be focused around the customer rather than around individual products. Properly utilized, emerging technologies for managing that data will increase the efficiency of processing policy applications—from the agent level through underwriting to policyholder services, and eventually to claims payment. Additional advantage goes to firms that can best utilize technology for marketing and to provide information to clients quickly and cheaply. Those firms that move late or make significant missteps in their management of these new technologies will be at tremendous disadvantage. A significant challenge to the industry will be the conversion of historically independent legacy systems to the networked environments that are needed for more comprehensive information management.

1.3. Theme 3: There will be Dramatic Changes in How Life Insurance Products are Distributed

The role of and need for insurance agents to distribute products is diminishing. Advances in technology and the advent of other financial service firms entering the arena have led some firms to abandon agency systems entirely and others to gradually move to other complementary distribution methods. For some insurers, direct marketing or marketing alliances may be a more cost-effective means of selling. Over time some will find the Internet cost effective, even though it is currently only a curiosity. Other firms cannot afford to abandon their agents and start over. Agents can be vital, cost-effective producers for an insurer, but will increasingly be seen as one part of a more complex distribution model.

1.4. Theme 4: For Many Insurers, the Move to More Customer-Driven Strategies will Require a Stronger Marketing-Driven Culture

Perhaps due to the traditional dominance of the decentralized agency system, life insurance has been slow to develop a corporate level marketing competence. For most firms surveyed, information about customers that might be useful in the development of segmentation strategies or cross-selling initiatives exists only at the agency level. Increasingly, firms are building processes and systems to capture relevant customer information at the corporate level as competition from more marketing-focused financial services firms, often outside of insurance, compete for their customers' business.

1.5. Theme 5: Costs Matter Greatly; but Insurers do not Convey an Urgency in Addressing Costs, nor a Consistent Vision in How to Trim Them

The two areas mentioned previously, information technology and agency systems, have significant costs associated with them. As in any financial service firm, personnel and technology are two dominant expense categories. Managing them effectively means maximizing productivity while at the same time keeping costs to a minimum. Insurers are slowly moving to a paradigm that values profitability over absolute size. However, the linkage from that to their own cost-containment initiatives is still slow.

1.6. Theme 6: Life Insurers are Playing with a Defensive Game Plan

The prevailing view is that other financial service firms are moving onto life insurance turf and taking business away from life insurers. Insurers view protecting their installed customer base and market share as the preeminent priority. Next comes leveraging existing buyers and known market segments. Far down the list of priorities are expanding upon existing markets and developing new products to capture more customers to the insurance market. The emphasis seems to be on maintaining the same piece of the pie rather than expanding the size of the pie itself.

The next sections provide a more detailed review of the survey's results, focusing more on the specific answers offered by participating firms. Issues explored are the industry's perception of market environment, appropriate firm strategy, product array, and operational challenges of paramount importance to success. More in-depth details of key issues relevant to the industry are given, but the six themes indicated above are also reinforced. Indeed, these themes come from a distillation of the answers offered to the specific questions enumerated below. The review begins with the participants' view of their environment and moves steadily to the firm's responses to these industry-wide challenges and opportunities.

2. The Financial Environment Facing the Industry

What are the greatest threats to insurers over the next decade? Table 2-1 summarizes respondents' views concerning threats to their companies and to the industry from the new and changing financial marketplace. Respondents ranked the threats on a scale from 1 to 5, with 1 indicating no threat at all and 5 being very threatening. The table presents mean and median scores, and the percent of the sample ranking each threat as very threatening (a score of 5). Rankings were relatively consistent across sort criteria.

The greatest perceived threat listed by respondents comes from more technologically sophisticated competitors. The use of technology as a competitive tool to gain access to the insurance market and its customers has changed drastically over the last decade and encompasses many different areas. Among these are technology-driven distribution and servicing capabilities such as the Internet, call centers, and data mining applications for tailored marketing strategies. Technology is also driving competitive advantage in productivity and quality differentiation in policy

Table 2-1. Financial Environment Risk

	Mean	Rank	Median	Percent Ranking as Very Threatening
More technologically sophisticated competitors	4.05	1	4	34.4
Changes to tax laws	3.89	2	4	32.8
New products from non-insurance financial companies	3.82	3	4	27.9
More cost efficient competitors	3.74	4	4	27.9
More customer service oriented competitors	3.64	5	4	21.3
Agency productivity	3.62	6	4	18.3
Non traditional distribution mechanisms	3.51	7	4	18.0
Federal and state regulators	3.46	8	4	16.4
Non financial service competitors	3.11	9	3	8.2
Volatile investment markets	3.10	10	3	4.9
Better capitalized competitors	3.07	11	3	13.1
Liability for market misrepresentation	3.07	12	3	4.9
Deterioration of financial rating	3.02	13	3	6.6
New products from insurers	2.98	14	3	4.9
Market conduct problems	2.98	15	3	3.3
Existing products from non-insurance financial concerns	2.90	16	3	3.3
Bigger competitors	2.85	17	3	11.5
Smaller/niche competitors	2.70	18	3	3.3
Consumer groups	2.51	19	3	4.9
Existing products from insurers	2.48	20	3	1.6
Foreign companies	2.36	21	2	1.6
Asset quality deterioration	2.10	22	2	1.7

maintenance and claims processing through the use of automated scanning. This involves optical character recognition software to reduce keypunch time and errors, and underwriting with the use of expert systems. While the impact of many of these technology issues is explored in other sections of the survey, taken together they are seen as clearly of paramount importance to the respondents and represent the most immediate threat to future success.

The second most important concern is changes to tax laws. Life insurance policies and annuities enjoy favorable tax treatment for purchasers and, later, to beneficiaries. To the extent that these favorable features are removed from the tax code in the future, life insurers will certainly feel the fallout in reduced premiums from these three principal products. Together with their ranking of federal and state regulators as eighth on the list of threats, it is clear that the whole set of regulatory issues poses real risks in the face of broad deregulation trends in the broader financial services industry.

Tied to this in some measure is threat number three, new products from non-insurance financial companies. If annuities lose some of their tax-advantaged status as accumulation vehicles, their differences from mutual funds narrow. As the regulatory distinctions between insurance and non-insurance financial firms narrow, this becomes an area of increasing concern. It is interesting to note that while insurers perceive the innovation threat from non-insurance financial firms, they do not seem to feel that product innovation and development is an important threat from others within the industry.

Agency productivity and more customer service oriented competitors are viewed as significant threats by a strong majority of the sample. The implications for individual firm strategies though are unclear. Much of this is tied to the emergence of nontraditional competitors and alternative distribution systems. Some insurers see these as the wave of the future. They strategically view themselves as product originators who can outsource the distribution process to banks and brokers who are piggybacking insurance sales on existing marketing mechanisms.

Issues that were not seen as specific threats were deterioration to asset quality, competition from foreign entities, existing products from other insurers, consumer groups, insurers of any particular size, or market conduct issues. While these have been problems in the past for certain individual companies, they are not viewed by the respondents as systemic threats of any real magnitude. Either there is an unwarranted belief that these problems cannot happen among our sample, or the woes of others have brought about internal review of these risks and preemptive mitigation. Some would argue, for example, that the advent of risk-based capital in 1993 has played a major role in causing the industry to address some of these asset quality issues.

Taken together with other results, these findings seem to imply a relatively mature market that is well demarcated with many firms struggling to protect the business they already hold and expanding existing business rather than pursuing new avenues of opportunity.

3. Corporate Objectives and Strategies

Survey participants were asked to indicate the relative importance of various corporate objectives and strategies for future success. This set of questions provides strong indication that there is no unanimity in the direction that surveyed insurers are going. Table 2-2 presents a summary of respondent assessments of the relative value of each objective or strategy. As was done for market threats, survey participants graded each objective or strategy on a scale from 1 to 5, with 5 representing the most important or relevant choice.

Table 2-2.   Corporate Objectives and Strategies

	Mean	Rank	Median	Percent of Sample Ranking Item as a High Strategic Priority (4 or 5)
Focus on client retention	4.42	1	5	92
Concentrate on known geographical or customer groups	4.11	2	4	82
Strong investment in agent training and development	4.05	3	4	76
Target financial planning and security needs of customers	3.84	4	4	73
Focus on customer over products	3.56	5	4	55
Focus on high wealth individuals	3.27	6	3	47
Spend much of resources on marketing	3.25	7	3	44
Provide an extensive and integrated product range	3.24	8	3.5	50
Be a market leader in product innovation	3.19	9	3	47
Seek to be low-cost leaders	2.91	10	3	31
Be a leader in distribution channels and marketing	2.88	11	3	26
Focus on protection rather than savings products	2.84	12	3	29
Spend much of resources on consumer behavior	2.12	13	2	6

Four strategies ranked as dominant among the 13 choices provided. These are 1) to focus on maintenance and enhancement of sales and service systems toward client retention, 2) to concentrate on known geographic or customer groups, 3) to view agents as a customer group and provide substantial investment in their training and development, and 4) to target the financial planning and security needs of customers. Nearly all of those surveyed viewed client retention as the utmost priority. Those few that did not view it as a priority tend to have a strong product orientation toward annuities.

For other objectives, there was far less consensus. Many of the other strategies listed were important to a sizable fraction of the sample, but not to a significant majority. These included focusing on customers over products, targeting wealthy individuals, providing extensive product ranges, and devoting significant resources to marketing. In part, this reflects insurers segmenting into specific niches and clienteles. Some may feel well positioned to cater to the wealthy and devote the necessary resources to maintaining those customer relationships, while others do not feel their position gives them a strategic advantage in this marketplace. Similarly, large multi-product firms may feel it is important to provide a wide array of products to attract customers and leverage existing product sales. Others focusing on specific market niches do not feel this is a strategic priority.

Consistently ranking near the bottom were the choices to either be a low-cost leader or to be an innovator in product development. Apparently respondents view growing the top line of the income statement (revenues) to be a greater source of earnings improvement than that which can be achieved by wringing out additional profits through cost reductions. Respondents may not see great value in product innovation as there is less benefit to being an innovator in the retail segment than in the commercial marketplace. Innovations may be costly and easy to copy, hence reducing the net premium associated with being a market leader. Being a close-follower in product innovation may then be a more appropriate alternative.

Table 2-3a and table 2-3b present the financial and non-financial performance metrics that these firms currently use, as well as those viewed to be important three years earlier and to be important three years in to the future. Survey respondents were asked to rank the top five measures in each category with a 1 for the most important measure. Those without ranking were given a value of 6. The accompanying figures (figures 2-1a and 2-1b) show, for selected measures, the percent of the sample viewing each measure as most important over the three time periods.

The view in terms of financial measures seems to be shifting from a big

Table 2-3a.   Financial Performance Measures

	1993				1996				Estimated 1999			
	Mean	Rank	Percent Ranking No. 1	Rank	Mean	Rank	Percent Ranking No. 1	Rank	Mean	Rank	Percent Ranking No. 1	Rank
GAAP Return on Equity	4.44	3	17.5	2	3.49	2	30.5	1	3.07	1	41.4	1
Growth in Total Sales	2.39	1	40.7	1	2.70	1	28.3	2	3.12	2	20.0	2
Expense Ratio	5.57	11	5.4	5	5.23	6	10.5	3	5.30	7	8.8	3
Earnings per Share	5.19	8	6.9	4	5.43	10	6.9	4	5.69	12	1.7	7
Economic Value	5.60	12	3.4	6	5.29	8	5.1	5	4.75	4	8.5	4
Growth in Total Assets	5.41	9	1.7	8	5.44	11	3.4	6	5.59	10	3.4	5
Investment Yield	5.10	7	1.7	7	5.14	5	1.7	7	5.19	6	1.7	8
Risk Based Capital	4.59	4	1.7	9	4.73	4	1.7	8	4.75	5	1.7	9
Commission Paid	4.08	2	0.0	10	4.12	3	1.7	9	4.22	3	0.0	10
Market Return on Equity	5.03	6	0.0	11	5.23	7	1.7	10	5.30	8	0.0	11
Statutory Return on Equity	5.00	5	6.9	3	5.29	9	0.0	10	5.45	9	0.0	12
Net Growth in Average Premium	5.57	10	0.0	12	5.71	12	0.0	10	5.69	13	0.0	13
Claims Experience	5.96	13	0.0	13	5.93	13	0.0	10	5.67	11	1.7	6

Table 2-3b.   Non-financial Performance Measures

	1993				1996				Estimated 1999			
	Mean	Rank	Percent Ranking No. 1	Rank	Mean	Rank	Percent Ranking No. 1	Rank	Mean	Rank	Percent Ranking No. 1	Rank
Net Growth in Number of Policies	3.36	1	19.6	3	3.25	1	25.0	1	3.77	1	21.4	1
Policy Persistence	3.98	2	21.4	1	4.00	2	25.0	2	4.59	5	17.9	3
Market Share	4.29	3	20.0	2	4.22	3	16.4	3	4.24	2	20.0	2
Number of Agents	5.55	11	3.6	7	5.07	7	8.9	7	4.52	4	7.1	5
Employee Satisfaction	4.34	4	8.9	4	4.64	4	7.1	4	5.36	9	1.8	10
Agent Retention Rates	5.47	9	8.9	5	4.68	5	5.4	5	5.23	7	1.8	9
Net Growth in Number of Policyholders	5.46	8	1.8	8	5.53	10	1.8	6	5.47	11	1.8	8
Agent Recruiting Rates	5.93	15	3.6	6	5.25	8	1.8	7	4.45	3	10.7	4
Development of Alternative Distribution	5.84	13	0.0	15	5.75	13	1.8	8	5.32	8	3.6	7
Products per Household	5.00	6	1.8	9	5.79	14	1.8	9	5.68	14	1.8	12
Lead Generation Levels	5.52	10	1.8	10	4.93	6	0.0	10	5.38	10	0.0	14
Number of Customer Households	5.30	7	0.0	11	5.52	11	0.0	11	5.52	12	0.0	15
Financial Counseling Effectiveness	5.84	12	0.0	12	5.61	12	0.0	12	5.68	15	0.0	16
Customer Satisfaction Surveys	5.88	14	0.0	14	5.73	15	0.0	13	5.14	6	5.4	6
Number of Non-agency Personnel	5.88	5	0.0	13	5.86	15	0.0	15	5.66	13	1.8	11
Lead Conversion Rates	6.00	16	0.0	16	5.89	16	0.0	16	5.71	16	1.8	13

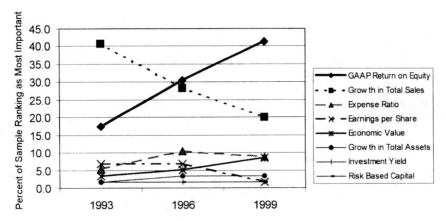

Figure 2-1a.   Financial Performance Measures

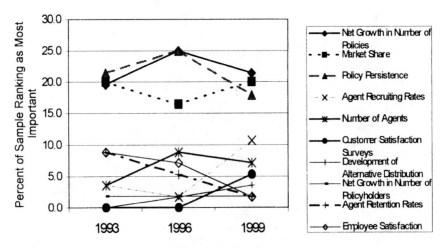

Figure 2-1b.   Non-financial Performance Measures

is good view to a profitability is good mentality. Whereas three years earlier, growth in total sales overwhelmingly would have been the top choice for a yardstick, GAAP return on equity (ROE) is the number one choice for 1996. And for 1999, twice as many respondents picked the profitability measure as the most important financial benchmark over sales growth. These two choices were viewed as clearly more important measures than any other choice given.

Expense Ratio, a traditional benchmark for the insurance industry, was picked as most important by a significant number of firms, but it had a low ranking based on its mean score—indicating that a few firms view it as an important benchmark, but the vast majority do not. A similar story can be told for earnings per share, which is the likely result of the sample that includes both stock insurers, for whom this measure is important and those organized as mutuals, for whom it has little real meaning.

Measures that are increasing in importance are GAAP ROE, as mentioned above, expense ratio, commissions paid to agents and brokers, and economic value added to shareholders. Falling in importance are net growth in average premium, growth in total assets, and both market and statutory return on equity. The latter may indicate a movement to a common accounting-driven ROE benchmark and increasingly, economic value added measures, that better capture true economic performance.

It is puzzling that while profitability measures are seen as important, only 31% of the sample saw cost cutting as a strategic priority. This may be consistent with the strong emphasis on sales growth. Companies seeking revenue growth may also be recognizing the need for commensurate investment. Nevertheless, this finding is somewhat out-of-line with other sectors of the financial service industry where cost cutting has taken on a more prominent role in their business strategies.

Views on non-financial performance measures are summarized in Table 2-3b. While the reliance on bigness may be shrinking, it is not dead. The clear top three choices for all three time periods were net growth in number of policies, policy persistence, and increasing market share. Neither growth in the number of policyholders nor the number of policyholding households were seen as very important, which indicates the perceived value of repeat sales. This may hint at the cost of converting leads to new customers. Once a customer base is established, it appears more cost effective to approach them for repeat business or policy expansion than to generate new policyholders. This may also reflect an increasing recognition of the importance of relationship building as a defense against new competition for household assets.

The importance of development of alternative distribution channel measures rise over time while the importance of agent retention rates is falling. This confirms interview comments from industry executives who broadly anticipate the need to aggressively respond to changing distribution patterns in financial services. The reliance on existing agency systems and agents seems to be diminishing and insurers are striving to lessen their dependence on existing distribution systems that are costly and may not be effective over time. Similarly, the viewed importance of financial counseling effectiveness has fallen and is expected to continue to fall. While somewhat counterintuitive, this may indicate that many insurers view themselves more and more as providers of products and less as broad-based financial service providers.

An additional shift in focus seems to be from the employee morale to customer satisfaction. While the means for employee satisfaction remain relatively high, this measure was the fourth most important non-financial performance measure in 1993, but falls to ninth or tenth by 1999. Concurrently, the importance of customer satisfaction surveys rises from twelfth to sixth in importance, reflecting a shift to more customer-oriented strategies.

4. Perceived Competitors

Although insurers indicated that the predominant source of threats comes from financial service firms outside of the insurance industry, survey participants were asked to name rivals that they felt were most competitive. In the area of life insurance products, Northwestern Mutual Life was cited most frequently and appears at the top of the list for eight survey respondents. Other firms garnering high marks for competitiveness from their peers were Pacific Mutual and American General, which each received top marks on four surveys, and State Farm, which was rated as the most competitive on three responses. The Hartford was the firm appearing as the most competitive in the annuities marketplace, with citations on six surveys. Also receiving kudos from their peers were Jackson National and Nationwide, with four most-competitive votes apiece.

5. Allocation of Discretionary Spending

Given the threats and objectives already detailed, how have insurers chosen to allocate discretionary spending in the past and present, and how do they expect it to be allocated in the future? Table 2-4 gives the past and projected estimates for areas of discretionary spending. Respondents were asked to choose the five most important areas for discretionary spending and ranked them from 1 to 5. Areas not chosen were assigned a value of 6. Figure 2-2 presents these results graphically.

The current and future number one choice for discretionary spending is product development. This seems curious as respondents did not indicate that being a market leader in product development and innovation was not a particularly important goal, nor did they perceive much of a threat from

Table 2-4. Discretionary Spending

	1993				1996				1999			
	Mean	Rank	Percent Ranking No. 1	Rank	Mean	Rank	Percent Ranking No. 1	Rank	Mean	Rank	Percent Ranking No. 1	Rank
Product Development	3.02	1	24.1	2	3.19	2	33.3	1	3.02	1	30.4	1
Distribution Channel Development	3.13	2	1.9	8	2.72	1	22.8	2	3.32	2	23.2	2
Improving Agency Productivity	4.52	3	37.0	1	4.65	4	17.5	3	4.61	3	5.4	6
Development & Implementation of New Administrative Technology	4.80	4	5.6	4	4.53	3	8.8	4	4.66	4	8.9	4
Remediating Portfolio Quality Problems	4.89	5	0.0	10	4.88	5	3.5	5	4.98	5	10.7	3
Replacement of Legacy Systems	5.09	6	3.7	7	5.56	12	3.5	6	5.05	6	8.9	5
Process Reengineering	5.13	7	0.0	10	5.25	7	1.8	7	5.14	7	5.4	7
Point of Sale Technology	5.17	8	11.1	3	5.28	8	1.8	8	5.30	8	3.6	8
Enhance Policyholder Service	5.20	9	5.6	5	5.46	9	1.8	9	5.32	9	0.0	12
Asset Management Skills	5.43	10	0.0	10	5.47	10	1.8	10	5.36	10	0.0	12
Acquisitions	5.67	11	1.9	9	5.53	11	1.8	11	5.48	11	1.8	9
Development & Implementation of New Underwriting Technology	5.70	12	0.0	10	5.75	14	1.8	12	5.52	12	1.8	10
Customer Research/Mkt. Segmentation	5.78	13	5.6	6	5.16	6	0.0	13	5.70	13	0.0	12
Remediating Market Conduct Problems	5.85	14	0.0	10	5.74	13	0.0	14	5.73	14	0.0	12
Management of Alliance	5.91	15	0.0	10	5.82	15	0.0	15	5.82	15	1.8	11

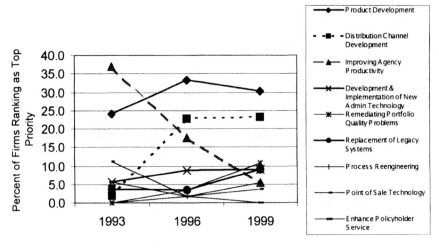

Figure 2-2.   Discretionary Spending

new product development from other insurers. Nevertheless, roughly one-third of the respondents chose product development as the most important area for discretionary spending. This is demonstrated further by the heterogeneity within our sample or it is perhaps an implied statement that while leading-edge innovation is not important, constant attention to product refinement is.

Distribution channel development ranked as the most important area for 23% of respondents. Combined with the number three choice, improvement of agency productivity emphasizes the critical importance placed on distribution systems. There is stark contrast in the projected directions of these two factors. It appears that much of the sample has given up on using large amounts of money to improve agency productivity because its importance fell from the number one priority in 1993, to number 3 in 1996, to number 6 in 1999. This is based on the number of survey respondents who chose it as a top priority in 1993. Distribution channel development has, in contrast, risen from a modest number 8 ranking in 1993 to a strong number 2 in 1996 and 1999. In fact if the mean rankings are examined, distribution channel development rises to number 1 for 1996 as nearly all firms ranked it as an item with priority 4 or greater.

Other uses of discretionary funds vary drastically by firm. There are no other areas getting more than a 10% share as the number one use of discretionary funds, with the exception of some who see potential future portfolio quality issues. Several others can be lumped together as production-related issues—replacement of legacy systems, development of new administrative technologies, and process re-engineering—which, taken together, represent significant investment requirements. Other uses of discretionary funds appear rather modest and consistent over time or are of particular importance to a few insurers. A potentially troubling observation is the low priority placed on customer research/market segmentation. While there is some evidence of a shift to more customer-oriented goals in strategies at the firm level, this does not appear to be translated into investments in the tools needed to develop better customer information. On the other hand, this may also reflect the weighting of those firms intent on a product manufacturing focus and selling through other institutions' customer channels.

6. Premiums and Product Mix

Table 2-5 provides an overview of the products offered by survey participants. For the 54 insurers providing 1995 premium income, the average firm wrote more than $1 billion in premiums, while the median firms premiums totaled roughly $400 million. The average firm would seem to have premium income from a broad range of sources with 60% derived from individual life operations, roughly another third from various annuity products, and the remaining 6% from other sources. Other sources varied by firm and included such things as immediate annuities, single-premium life insurance, long term care, structured settlements, and individual accident and disability insurance. If the dollar weighted averages are examined instead, annuities and other products are seen to comprise a larger share of

Table 2-5.   Source of Premiums

	Mean	Dollar Wtd.	Median	Standard Deviation	Max	N > 0
Total Individual Life and Annuity					7,161,214	
Premiums ($000)	1,168,746		386,757	2,024,182		
Distribution of Business (%)						
Individual Term Life	8	4	3	14	95	42
Individual Ordinary Life	25	20	16	27	100	50
Individual Universal Life	24	15	15	25	83	46
Individual Variable Life	3	5	0	6	35	24
Individual Variable Annuities	14	22	0	25	95	28
Individual Fixed Annuities	19	25	9	24	95	48
Other	6	9	0	17	100	22

premiums—rising from 33% of business to more than 47%, or roughly the overall industry average.

The disparity in these statistics hints at the diversity in the product offerings of participating firms. While traditional core products such as individual ordinary life insurance and fixed annuities were offered by nearly all respondents (50 and 48, respectively), variable life and annuities were offered by fewer firms. The majority of insurers had premium income from three to five source categories. Eighteen insurers were fully diversified in their product offerings and had premiums from six or seven of these categories. Ten firms were specialized to the point of deriving revenue from one or two sources. As indicated by the maximum percentage underwritten in any given category, specialists appeared in nearly all product types save individual variable life.

Table 2-6 shows the percentage of sample insurers offering and manufacturing given products. Here manufacturing indicates that the firm underwrites and retains a substantial piece of the risk associated with the product and is not simply a marketing conduit. While individual term life was seen earlier to comprise a small piece of premiums, it is nearly universally offered

Table 2-6. Products—Percent Offering

	Percent Offer	*Percent Manufacture*
Individual Term Life	90	77
Universal Life	82	74
Immediate Annuities	82	73
Single Premium Deferred Annuities	82	69
Individual Ordinary Life	79	67
Flexible Premium Deferred Annuities	77	64
Second to die Life Ins.	67	53
Single Premium Life Insurance	61	52
Variable Annuities	56	48
Disability Income Insurance	54	27
Variable Life	50	44
First to die Life Ins.	45	35
Long Term Care Ins.	39	17
Individual Health Insurance	27	12
Industrial Life Insurance	3	3

and is manufactured by more than three-quarters of the sample. This may be indicative of its relative simplicity in terms of pricing. Universal life, immediate and deferred annuities, and ordinary life are all offered by more than 70% of survey respondents.

Other individual products, primarily those in the health arena, are offered by a fraction of the sample and manufactured by even fewer firms. Both long term care and individual health insurance are manufactured almost entirely by large firms with substantial group health operations. This is indicative of the difficulty of pricing these risks, both actuarially and economically.

Figure 2-3 shows the number of firms manufacturing or distributing a given number of product categories. No firm distributes or manufactures every product group designated in the survey. Approximately one-fifth of the firms distribute products in 12 or more categories. Less than 5% of the sample manufacture in this many categories. Similarly, roughly a fifth of the sample is specialized to the point of operating in four or fewer product categories. The majority of survey firms distribute and manufacture a varied, but by no means complete array of products.

Respondents were asked to rank four products from the choices given in terms of their relative importantce to their business in terms of revenue generation. Respondents ranked choices based on their importance at the time of the survey (1996), three years earlier (1993), and their expected importance in three years time (1999). Table 2-7 presents the mean rank for each year and the percent of the sample that ranks each choice as the most important product. Figure 2-4 presents graphically the dynamics of the relative importance of the top eight product groups.

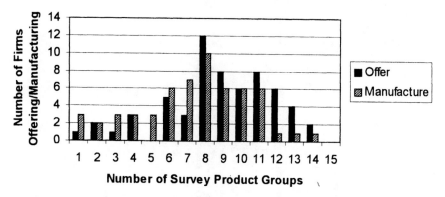

Figure 2-3.   Distribution of Number of Products Offered and Manufactured

Table 2-7. Products—Relative Importance for Revenue Generation

	1993				1996				Estimated 1999			
	Mean	Rank	Percent Ranking No. 1	Rank	Mean	Rank	Percent Ranking No. 1	Rank	Mean	Rank	Percent Ranking No. 1	Rank
Universal Life	2.66	1	25.4	1	2.71	1	32.8	1	2.84	1	27.6	1
Individual Ordinary Life	2.83	2	21.7	2	2.98	2	15.3	3	2.95	2	20.3	3
Variable Annuities	3.45	3	13.3	3	3.25	3	16.9	2	3.02	3	22.0	2
Single Premium Deferred Annuities	3.24	4	11.9	4	3.33	4	5.2	4	3.48	5	6.9	4
Individual Term Life	3.51	5	5.1	5	3.50	5	5.2	5	3.64	6	3.4	6
Variable Life	3.68	13	0.0	13	3.60	6	3.4	7	3.36	4	3.4	5
Flexible Premium Deferred Annuities	3.71	6	5.1	6	3.67	7	5.2	6	3.81	8	1.7	8
Immediate Annuities	3.80	8	1.7	8	3.76	8	1.7	8	3.66	7	1.7	7
Second-to-die Life Ins.	3.83	14	0.0	14	3.81	9	0.0	13	3.84	9	1.7	9
Individual Health Insurance	3.85	7	3.4	7	3.88	10	1.7	9	3.91	11	0.0	12
Disability Income Insurance	3.86	9	1.7	9	3.90	11	0.0	14	3.95	13	0.0	13
Long Term Care Ins.	3.95	12	1.7	12	3.93	12	1.7	12	3.88	10	1.7	11
Single Premium Life Insurance	3.88	10	1.7	10	3.95	13	1.7	10	3.91	12	1.7	10
Industrial Life Insurance	3.95	11	1.7	11	3.95	14	1.7	11	3.97	14	1.7	14
First-to-die Life Ins.	4.00	15	0.0	15	4.00	15	0.0	15	4.00	15	0.0	15

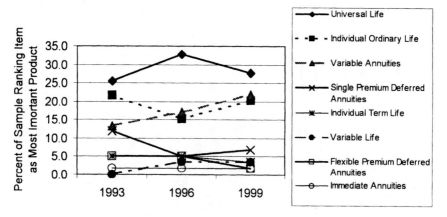

Figure 2-4.   Relative Importance of Life Insurance Products

The first thing to be pointed out is the variety of products that were picked as the most important revenue producer by the sample. No less than 12 of the 15 choices were picked by at least one of the insurers as their leading revenue generator for both 1993 and 1996. For 1999, there were 11 different choices made for most important product. This indicates that although there were a small group of products that were chosen to be important revenue generators for a number of firms, there is substantial heterogeneity in the product mix that produce revenues but no clearly dominant products.

For all three time periods, universal life is seen as the most important product when ranked by both the mean importance ranking and by the number of respondents choosing it as the most important product. However, its relative importance has been shrinking when compared to other products. For both 1993 and 1996, the percentage of respondents choosing universal life as the most important product was roughly twice that of the second choice, ordinary life in 1993 and variable annuities in 1996. For 1999, the margin narrows over variable annuities, the number two choice as most important product, with 28% of respondents expecting universal life to be the dominant product and 22% choosing variable annuities. Rounding out the top five in relative importance are single-premium deferred annuities and individual term life. Variable life sees the largest increase in importance. Other markets expected to be of more importance in the future are second-to-die life insurance, which may have an important role in estate planning for some households and long term care, which may be of growing importance due to the combined impact of longer life expectancy and the maturing of the baby boom generation.

Respondents were asked to rank products as they related to three measures of firm growth—growth to firm-wide gross income, contributions to firm profits, and the value these products added to the company. Results of these questions are present in tables 2-8a–c. In terms of income generation,

Table 2-8a.   Growth Areas—Gross Income

	Mean	Rank	Percent Ranking no. 1
Variable Annuities	2.83	1	25.9
Universal Life	3.10	2	19.0
Variable Life	3.17	3	17.2
Fixed Annuities	3.29	5	12.1
Ordinary Life	3.26	4	10.3
Term Life	3.34	6	5.2
Single Premium Deferred Annuities	3.66	8	5.2
401(k) Annuities and Mutual Funds	3.62	7	3.4

Table 2-8b.   Growth Areas—Contributions to Profits

	Mean	Rank	Percent Ranking no. 1
Variable Life	2.88	2	25.4
Universal Life	2.85	1	23.7
Term Life	3.25	3	15.3
Fixed Annuities	3.32	5	11.9
Ordinary Life	3.29	4	8.5
Variable Annuities	3.61	7	3.4
401(k) Annuities and Mutual Funds	3.53	6	1.7
Single Premium Deferred Annuities	3.78	8	1.7

Table 2-8c.   Value Added to Company

	Mean	Rank	Percent Ranking no. 1
Universal Life	2.79	1	25.0
Term Life	2.80	2	23.2
Variable Annuities	3.20	3	19.6
Ordinary Life	3.38	4	7.1
Fixed Annuities	3.43	5	7.1
Variable Life	3.46	6	5.4
Single Premium Deferred Annuities	3.63	7	3.6
401(k) Annuities and Mutual Funds	3.80	8	3.6

variable annuities, universal life, and variable life rank one through three. Interestingly, while there is a clear order in perceived growth, no product clearly dominates as a number one choice. This may be indicative of survey participants having heterogeneous strategies in terms of product development and marketing orientation.

While variable annuities were picked as number one most frequently in terms of gross revenue generation, their rank is much lower when profits are the benchmark. This may indicate that there are substantial underwriting and administrative expenses associated with the products. There is also the possibility that much of the income they generate is passed back to the annuity-holder. For profits, life insurance products seem to play a greater role. Variable life, universal life, and term life rank one, two, three for contributions to profits. Variable annuities, 401(k) annuities, and single premium deferred annuities rank at the bottom in terms of growth in contribution to profits. This may reflect the greater competition from non-insurance substitutes such as mutual funds or the lack of persistence and the higher turnover among annuity policyholders.

Ranked based on a subjective notion of "value added to company," universal life, term life, and variable life came out as the top three products as measured by both their average ranking and the number of respondents choosing them as the top product group. The category value added to the company served to allow for more flexibility and subjectivity in responses. Suggested measures included the net present value of future premiums or some definition of embedded value—measures intended to capture the long term value of these products to the insurer.

The lack of clearly dominant products by any of these measures underscores the divergence in product focus within our sample. Ordinary life and fixed annuities, while staples of current revenue, would appear to have run their course. Products that offer more flexibility and variability in wealth accumulation or benefit build-up are the choices for the future. Universal life, and variable life and annuities are products that are hybrids of traditional life insurance products and mutual or money-market funds. If these are the products that households truly want, this indicates that there is substantial willingness to bear market risk even when shedding mortality risk.

Interestingly, long term care insurance, while not currently a product from which much revenue is derived, is foreseen by a number of insurers as an area of significant growth. This looks to be an area of tremendous opportunity, but also tremendous risk. The opportunity stems from aging boomers, many of whom will need long term care services. The risk is brought about by the difficulty in forecasting the costs of various medical procedures, not to mention the political climate and state of Medicare decades into the future. Long term care will likely generate great revenue and value to the companies who can price it right and whose underwriting is stringent. It may likely be the downfall of a number of companies who do not.

7. Marketing and Distribution Issues

An issue drawing much attention and debate in the insurance industry is the relative efficiency of various distinctly different distribution systems. Two systems have dominant percentages of the market: exclusive agency systems, where the commissioned agent sells only policies for a single insurer; and non-exclusive agency systems, where an agent may represent a number of different insurers. A third system of increasing importance is direct marketing. Here, in effect, the insurer does away with field agents and relies on telephone sales, direct mailings, affiliated groups, and other means to attract customers.

Each system has its merits and its pitfalls. The direct agent system binds field representatives more tightly to the firms they represent. Champions of this system argue that this enables the agents to have better knowledge of the insurer's products and, because their allegiance is not in question, enables exclusive agents to generate more premium revenue through the sale of additional products and augmented policies. Another point often stressed is that in the exclusive agency system the policyholders are tied to the insurer and not to the agent. Critics contend that because there are substantial costs associated with maintaining a fleet of exclusive agents, other distribution systems that do not bear these costs can make up for the lack of strong insurer-agent ties with additional flexibility and lower distribution costs.

Figure 2-5 presents distribution method by product group (life and annuity) both while products were being sold at the time of the survey in 1996, and also as respondents expected products to be sold by their organization in 1999, three years after the survey. The proportion expected to be sold through non-exclusive agents remained relatively constant, increasing modestly for life products. Survey participants expect roughly 50% of life insurance and 40% of annuity premium revenue to be sold through these channels. The shares attributable to exclusive agents are expected to drop. In the life area, the share attributable to exclusive agents is expected to fall from 35% of sales to 28%. A drop of similar magnitude is foreseen for annuity sales, where the share of premiums from exclusive agents is expected to drop from 32% to 23%.

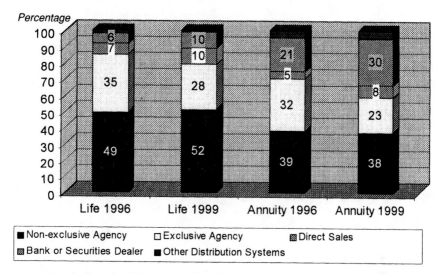

Figure 2-5. Distribution Method

The shortfall from exclusive agent dealing is expected to be made up primarily from increases in direct sales and distribution alliances with banks and securities dealers. The expected growth in direct sales is a modest but significant 3% for both life insurance and annuities. Survey results indicate there are a few niche firms that rely exclusively on direct marketing and a few others that intend to integrate direct marketing to supplement or phase-out existing inefficient distribution channels. The use of banks and securities dealers is expected to increase significantly, with respondents predicting that their distribution of life insurance products through these channels will increase by nearly 50%, from 7% to 10% of sales. These distribution networks have already demonstrated success in marketing wealth accumulation vehicles such as annuities, taking advantage of natural cross-marketing in these other financial intermediaries for certain accountholders. In 1996, one-fifth of annuity premiums for survey respondents were generated by banks or securities dealers. In 1999, that is expected to grow to 30%, which will supplant exclusive agents as the industry's second most important mechanism for distributing annuities. Roughly a half-dozen of the respondents used or expected to use banks or securities dealers to market 90% or more of their annuity products.

Other distribution methods were mentioned by only a few of the participants, with less than 1% of life insurance expected to be sold in 1999 via nontraditional means. Enthusiasm for these distribution methods was slightly greater for annuities, but still amounted to only 4% of revenue.

Distribution vehicles mentioned included unaffiliated broker dealers, third party marketing operations, private label ventures, and membership firms. Curiously, the Internet was mentioned as a viable means of distribution by only one respondent in the 1996 survey.

8. Productivity Issues

Table 2-9 presents aggregate sales productivity broken out by distribution channel. Summary statistics are presented for individual life and annuities disaggregated by the three distribution systems. Of the 55 firms responding to the marketing questionnaires, 32 had exclusive agency systems in place, 20 used exclusive agents, and 3 used a direct marketing approach.

For individual life, the average number of new policies sold per company was roughly 43,700. For annuities, the average sold per company was approximately 16,400. For both product mixes those insurers using exclusive agency networks sold decidedly more policies than those companies using either non-exclusive agents or a direct marketing approach. The averages for exclusive agent firms were some 79,700 new life insurance policies and nearly 22,000 new annuity contracts. The corresponding figures for non-exclusive agents and direct marketers were 22,000 and 36,200 life insurance sales and 13,900 and 8,400 new annuity contracts, respectively. Similar patterns are seen when examining total and per-firm average first year premiums and annuity considerations by distribution system.

This should not lead one to the conclusion that exclusive agencies are necessarily more productive. As previously mentioned, exclusive agency networks tend to have higher fixed costs than other distribution alternatives and are usually associated with larger firms. The number of new sales per firm by distribution system and per-firm premiums is likely a reflection of this size bias.

In fact, if ranked based on average premiums per new policy, non-exclusive agencies and direct marketers fair much better compared to exclusive agent firms. Across all distribution channels the average premium per new life insurance contract sold is $1,834. The average first year annuity consideration is $32,358. For exclusive agent firms, the corresponding averages are $1,405 for new life insurance premiums and $29,863 in average first year annuity considerations. For non-exclusive agents, the corresponding figures are $2,990 and $33,845, respectively. For direct writers the figures are $658 and $47,447. Here, it would appear that on a per-policy basis non-exclusive agents are superior, while for annuity sales direct writers are superior. Of course, such inference is spurious without more information and

Table 2-9. Sales Productivity by Distribution Channel

Individual life	N	Number New Policies			First Year Premiums ($m)			Average Premium per New Policy Sold ($)
		Total	Mean	Standard Deviation	Total	Mean	Standard Deviation	
All Channels	55	2,405,434	43,735	78,925	4,412	79	105	1,834
Non-exclusive Agency	32	702,689	21,959	48,075	2,101	64	90	2,990
Exclusive Agency	20	1,594,195	79,710	107,916	2,239	112	128	1,405
Direct	3	108,550	36,183	33,368	71	24	17	658

Individual annuities	N	Number New Policies			Annuity Consideration ($m)			Average Premium per New Policy Sold ($)
		Total	Mean	Standard Deviation	Total	Mean	Standard Deviation	
All Channels	55	886,364	16,414	25,537	28,681	541	770	32,358
Non-exclusive Agency	32	443,947	13,873	24,335	15,025	501	820	33,845
Exclusive Agency	20	417,169	21,956	28,912	12,458	623	743	29,863
Direct	3	25,248	8,416	9,391	1,198	399	534	47,447

given the relatively small sample of direct underwriters. These figures may reflect market specialization among one or all of the direct underwriters given the skew in average life and annuity premiums.

Other differences across distribution systems are seen when we examine advertising spending. Table 2-10 gives total advertising cost, the average spending by firm, per new policy, and per $1,000 of premium by distribution system. Across all distribution systems there is wide variation in the amount spent on advertising. To some extent this is a function of differences in firm size, but it also reflects differences in advertising policy. The average per firm expenditure on advertising is slightly more than $1 million. Compare this to a median amount of $72,000. For exclusive agency firms, both the mean value and the median are substantially larger, $1.6 million and roughly $500,000, respectively. Spending by non-exclusive agencies and direct writers is considerably less, with a very pronounced disparity between that spent by the mean and median non-exclusive agency insurer, $729,000 vs. $28,500.

The disparity in advertising expenditures between exclusive agencies and non-exclusives and direct firms can partly be attributable to the size of the distribution system discussed earlier. Another factor may be the nature of the advertising done by the different distribution systems. For the exclusive firm, advertising expenditures likely include some local level spending to promote a territory's agent as he is tied to the firm. For the non-exclusive agent, that expenditure is generally the agent's own expense to cover and would not be captured in the advertising expenses of the insurer. This result may also be attributable to the uniqueness of our sample of the industry.

When advertising expenditures are presented per policy or per $1,000 of premium, the same pattern is seen. Exclusive agency firms spend more on advertising than do their non-exclusive and direct writing counterparts. On a per policy basis, the exclusive agencies spend roughly twice their non-exclusive agency counterparts and nearly three times as much as the direct writers ($35 per policy vs. $20 and $12). Per $1,000 of premiums, exclusives spend more than three times as much on advertising as non-exclusives and approximately two and one-half times as much as the direct writers ($7.66 vs. $2.35 and $3.09). Again, the differences in expenditures can be partly explained by different marketing approaches. When asked if they targeted specific customer segments in their market research and advertising, 57% of non-exclusive agency insurers answered that they did, but only 44% for those insurers with defined market research budgets. This compares to 74% for exclusive agency firms and 89% of those with defined market research budgets. It would seem the focus of the advertising done by the

Table 2-10. Advertising Cost of New Business

		All Industry			Per Insurer		
	N	Total Number New Policies	New Life and Annuity Prem ($m)	Total Advertising Spending	Mean Expenditure	Median Expenditure	Standard Deviation
All Channels	56	3,291,798	33,093	57,258,986	1,022,482	72,000	2,176,182
Non-exclusive Agency	33	1,146,636	17,126	24,070,062	729,396	28,500	1,748,543
Exclusive Agency	20	2,011,364	14,697	32,069,539	1,603,477	499,225	2,942,592
Direct	3	133,798	1,269	1,119,385	373,128	150,000	223,763

		Advertising Spending Per New Policy				Advertising Spending Per $1,000 Premium			
	N	Mean	Median	Standard Deviation	Maximum	Mean	Median	Standard Deviation	Maximum
All Channels	48	23.66	6.59	56.58	282.26	3.95	0.85	9.05	55.98
Non-exclusive Agency	31	19.74	5.56	50.89	282.26	2.35	0.65	4.44	16.62
Exclusive Agency	14	34.84	11.54	73.28	282.26	7.66	1.37	15.05	55.98
Direct	3	12.02	6.34	12.77	26.64	3.09	0.73	4.30	8.05

non-exclusive agencies is to promote brand identity and the targeting of sales is left to the agent, while advertising for the exclusive agency firms is more all-encompassing.

Targeted market segments varied dramatically, although not by distribution system. The most commonly sought market segment was high net worth households. Other firms focused on seniors (65+), those households nearing retirement (50–59), baby-boomers, households starting out (25–35), the self-employed and small business owners, minorities, and women. Targeted markets appear to be more closely tied to the insurer's dominant product focus rather than its choice of distribution system.

Certainly, advertising alone does not capture the full cost of attracting new business. Table 2-11 provides the estimated cost for the insurer to acquire new business from a sub-sample of respondents who chose to estimate their costs. Indeed, advertising appears to be a small fraction of the costs. The average acquisition cost across distribution channels is $882 to acquire a new life insurance policy and $360 per new annuity contract. This gives new evidence for the traditional industry perception that "life insurance is sold and not bought."

However, some caution is required here. These data reflect cost per policy and have not been normalized for average premium per policy sold. While costs appear to be higher for exclusive agents than for either non-exclusive agency insurers or direct writers, policies differ and may be systematically different across these three channels. In addition, the strength of these results should be tempered by the small size of each sub-sample.

Table 2-12 summarizes the share of insurers using alliances, affiliations, and other indirect means of distributing products. Parent/affiliate structures

Table 2-11.   Estimated Cost to Acquire a New Policy

Individual Ordinary Life	N	Mean	Median	Standard Deviation
All Channels	15	882	300	1,410
Non-exclusive Agency	8	495	318	511
Exclusive Agency	6	1,508	600	2,098
Direct	1	225	225	na

Individual Annuity	N	Mean	Median	Standard Deviation
All Channels	8	360	73	601
Non-exclusive Agency	4	58	65	33
Exclusive Agency	2	885	885	1,153
Direct	2	437	437	367

Table 2-12.   Distribution Relationships by Principal Channel (%)

	All Channels	Non-exclusive Agency	Exclusive Agency	Direct
Proportion of respondents using parent/affiliate relationship to distribute individual life and annuity	36	33	29	75
Average proportion of premium earned from relationship distribution for those companies involved				
Individual Life Insurance	41	25	51	95
Individual Annuities	48	39	52	85
Proportion of respondents using arrangements with unrelated institution(s) to distribute individual life and annuity	34	34	42	0
Average proportion of premium earned from bank/securities dealer relationship distribution where it exists				
Individual Life Insurance	14	17	10	0
Individual Annuities	42	55	26	0

are most common among direct underwriters and much less so among both exclusive and non-exclusive agency systems and generate a fairly substantial portion of premiums. On the other hand, arrangements with unaffiliated institutions are non-existent for the direct writers and are used in about the same frequency as affiliate relationships by the exclusive and non-exclusive agencies. It is apparent that the proportion of premiums generated by banks and securities brokers is more heavily skewed to annuity products than to life insurance by a factor of roughly 3 to 1. This is reasonable as annuities represent an additional savings vehicle to add to the portfolio of offerings for these institutions, while life insurance can be thought of as a distinctly different sort of financial product.

9. Policy Retention Issues

We have seen some differences in how insurers with different distribution channels go about marketing and advertising their policies. Are there differences in retention of policyholders by distribution system? Table 2-13

Table 2-13.   Policy Persistency: Average Percentage
of Policies Remaining in Force (%)

Term Life	N	After 13 Months	After 4 Years
All Channels	35	87	60
Non-exclusive Agency	19	88	60
Exclusive Agency	14	86	60
Direct	2	84	68
Ordinary Life			
All Channels	33	88	70
Non-exclusive Agency	17	88	68
Exclusive Agency	14	88	73
Direct	2	86	74
Universal Life			
All Channels	36	92	78
Non-exclusive Agency	24	92	77
Exclusive Agency	12	92	79
Direct	0	na	na
Variable Life			
All Channels	9	95	82
Non-exclusive Agency	5	96	85
Exclusive Agency	3	94	78
Direct	1	97	83

examines policy persistence for firms classified by distribution system
for a number of life insurance products. For both term and ordinary life,
roughly 85–90% of policies are still in force one year after the policy
is initiated. After four years, approximately 60% of term and 70–75%
of ordinary life policies are still in force. There is little difference across
distribution system.

For universal and variable life, policies in excess of 90% of policies are
still in force one year after the policies commencement. After four years,
retention of policies is roughly 80% for universal life and 80–85% for variable life policies. Again differences across distribution systems are modest.

Clearly, the evidence is mixed regarding the superiority or inferiority of
any given distribution system. Although the trend seems to be moving away

from reliance on exclusive agents, for those firms that employ this distribution system the change will not happen overnight, nor is such rapid change warranted nor the turmoil associated with it. What are the prevailing issues for existing systems?

10. Agent Management Issues

For insurers with exclusive agents, a major issue is ensuring the exclusivity of those agents. Firms in general view themselves as only moderately successful in ensuring exclusivity. Perhaps this is because of a general weakness in monitoring. Only 29% of those surveyed with exclusive agency systems employ formal audits to ensure exclusivity. A similar 29% rely on anecdotal evidence, and 21% have no review process at all to ensure adherence to exclusivity. A few firms have agents whose life insurance careers are part-time, augmenting another primary job.

Formal reviews of agent performance are conducted quarterly by 40% of exclusive agencies, annually by 20%, and monthly by 25%. Performance reviews are irregular for the remaining 15%. The emphasis seems to be strongly based on gross production. As shown in table 2-14, nearly 70% of evaluation weight is given raw production numbers. Little weight is given to measures of customer service or of profitability of the actual policies sold. Regulatory compliance is given some importance and is likely

Table 2-14.   Criteria for Exclusive Agent Performance Review (%)

	Average Weight
First Year Commissions	30
First Year Life and Annuity Premium	28
Number of Cases Sold	10
Compliance Record	9
Policy Persistency	8
Customer Retention and Satisfaction	4
Product Mix	3
Profitability of New Business	2
Profitability of Renewal Business	2
Renewal Premiums	1
Other	4

ɔn to recent problems faced by some insurers regarding agents' sales tactics.

One major reason for the high cost of an exclusive agency system is high agent turnover. For the average exclusive agency, roughly one-quarter of the field agents were new in any given year. A few firms indicated new agents represent as much as two-thirds of their field staff. There was wide variation in the number of candidates interviewed per hire. The average number across firms was 14, but answers ranged from 2 to 30. Apparently, finding and retaining skilled employees is a difficult process. Table 2-15 indicates that those who were hired as agents were most likely to be new to the business. As the mean percentage of agents without prior experience is substantially below the median, it is apparent that some firms are more successful at recruiting new agents with experience. It is likely that there is a strong hierarchy of firm quality in the minds of agents. Those firms with strong reputations can skim agents from weaker firms. Retention of agents is difficult as well. For the average exclusive agency, less than 3 of every 10 agents hired is with the insurer in four years.

In addition to the cost associated with turnover is the substantial cost of training agents. The average new hire receives 270 hours of formal training. This is generally followed by a period in which a new agent is paired with an experienced agent to show him the ropes in the field. Training does not end there as life insurance is sold on an ever-changing field of regulation and product evolution. The average firm provides roughly 110 hours of annual training for agents with four or more years of service. For this, surviving agents are paid fairly well. The average annual commission income for an agent with 4+ years of service is approximately $35,000.

Retention figures do not appear to be much different for non-exclusive agency firms. For the average non-exclusive agency, roughly 15% of the field agents are new in any given year. A few firms indicated that new agents represent as much as one-third of their field staff. The average firm interviewed six candidates for each addition to their agency force. On average, roughly 50% of the new hires were writing business for the firms a year after hire and 30% were still producing after four years. These figures

Table 2-15. Exclusive Agent Hiring and Retention (%)

	Mean	Median	Standard Deviation
Percentage of New Agents without prior experience	56	72	34
Percentage of New Agents with company in one year	72	75	21
Percentage of New Agents with company in four years	30	22	24

varied dramatically across the sample indicating varied success in retaining agents' services.

Despite similar turnover patterns, the agency distribution systems differ in how they bear costs. A policy sold by an exclusive agent binds the policyholder to the company. If the agent leaves, the policyholder is assigned to another agent for service. The only loss to the company here is its investment in the agent. However, if the non-exclusive agency loses an agent, it may very well lose its customer as here the customer is bound to the agent.

This may be why there is a difference in the criteria used to evaluate non-exclusive agents from that used for exclusive agents. Table 2-16 gives the average weight placed on each factor for the non-exclusive agencies. First year life and annuity premiums are weighed heavily, but the number of cases sold is not given much weight. Policy persistence is given more weight. These different incentives may explain why exclusive agents tend to sell more but smaller policies when compared to their non-exclusive counterparts.

The evidence on turnover for direct marketers is limited given our small sample. Given this caveat, hiring and short-term turnover results are quite similar to those seen for both exclusive and non-exclusive agencies. Approximately one-fifth of the sales representatives for our sample of direct marketing firms are new in a given year. One-half of them have no prior experience with direct insurance sales. Eighty percent are still on the job one year later, but 50% of those hired are still on the job after four years.

Table 2-16. Criteria for Non-exclusive Agent Performance Review (%)

	Average Weight
First Year Life and Annuity Premium	41
First Year Commissions	18
Policy Persistency	11
Compliance Record	8
Number of Cases Sold	6
Customer Retention and Satisfaction	4
Profitability of Renewal Business	4
Profitability of New Business	3
Product Mix	2
Renewal Premiums	2
Other	3

11. Underwriting Challenges

Perhaps the cornerstone of a competitive and profitable insurance operation is its underwriting policy and practices. Here is where insurers determine the fundamental strategy for which policies they will write, how much of the underlying risk they will hold, and against what performance benchmarks they will measure results. Questionnaires focusing on the underwriting practices of the survey participants were sent to each insurer's senior officer in charge of underwriting. Sixty participants returned the underwriting section of the questionnaire.

The first set of questions in the underwriting questionnaire focused on the importance of various factors related to underwriting and its interplay with other aspects in terms of their contribution to achieving underwriting competitiveness. Respondents were given nine factors deemed as potentially important for underwriting competitiveness and asked to rank the importance of each on a scale of 1 to 5, with 1 representing an unimportant factor and 5 indicating a very important factor. A summary of the answers to this set of questions is given in table 2-17.

The factors voted most important were those that maintained close links to the principal decision makers in the underwriting process that were outside of the underwriting department itself—namely, the agents writing policies, the reinsures with whom the underwritten risk would be shared, and the doctors and labs whose analysis would determine a potential policyholder's suitability for coverage. Ranking as less important were issues related to technology, risk retention, and the personnel management of the underwriting department. Advancing underwriting technology through implementation of expert systems was viewed as fairly important, but there

Table 2-17.   Importance for Achieving Competitiveness

	Mean	Rank	Median	Standard Deviation
Close Links to Agents	4.41	1	5	1.18
Close Relationship with Reinsurers	4.04	2	4	1.19
Close Link to Doctors/Labs	3.82	3	4	0.84
Technology/Expert Systems	3.60	4	4	0.90
Higher Retention Limits	3.05	5	3	1.02
Increase Underwriting Staff	2.84	6	3	0.98
Bringing Underwriting in House	2.46	7	2	0.85
Outsourcing Underwriting Services	1.86	8	2	1.15
Lower Retention Limits	1.69	9	2	0.96

seemed to be a lack of consensus among participants as to how to go about improving technology in underwriting and the proper role that technology should play. Decisions on retention limits were viewed as less important. The consensus seemed to be that if an insurer were to do something other than the industry norm, it would be more competitive retaining risk (and foregoing reinsurance premiums) than ceding the risk. Whether underwriting activities should be entirely staffed in-house or farmed out as needed was generally viewed as an issue of secondary importance. However, one respondent did admonish that an insurer should "never outsource such a key function as underwriting."

Respondents were asked to rank their peer companies in terms of underwriting stringency and practice. Northwestern Mutual far and away was named as the insurer with the most stringent underwriting practices with 17 votes of the 37 respondents who chose to rank their peers. Lincoln National was second in being ranked as most stringent with 3 votes. No other firm received more than 2 votes as the most stringent and there was little discernable pattern as to any other ranking.

Although respondents felt little need to change their risk retention strategies, there was little consensus as to what the industry norm for reinsurance purchases should be. Table 2-18 summarizes respondent company practices with regard to use of reinsurance. The average firm retains between $2.75 million and $3.5 million in risk from the life insurance it underwrites. The median value is significantly lower at $500,000 per type of coverage. As indicated by the difference between the mean and median as well as by the standard deviation, minimum, and maximum, there is substantial variation in procedure. Much of the variation can be explained by the size of the insurer writing the business. Big, well-capitalized firms retain more risk per policy. However, this is not always the case. While those firms retaining $1 million or more are very large, there are a number of large

Table 2-18. Use of Reinsurance

	Mean	Median	Standard Deviation	Min	Max
Retention Limit ($000)					
Term Life	2,744	500	7,978	5	50,000
Ordinary Life	2,820	500	7,959	25	50,000
Universal Life	3,455	500	8,837	75	50,000
Percent of Applications with Facultative Re.	4.3	3.0	5.3	0.0	30.0

firms who retain less per policy. These is a significant amount of clustering at the $500,000 level.

Insurers were also asked what percentage of their applications were insured with facultative reinsurance, tied to individual policies as opposed to treaty reinsurance, which covers a book of business. For the average firm, facultative reinsurance was sought for roughly 4% of applications. The relationship as to who is using facultative reinsurance is not simply a function of size. Both large and small insurers were in some instances large users.

12. Technology Use in Underwriting

As in other financial services, the changing role of technology has had an effect on insurers. We used the next section of the questionnaire to solicit responses on how technology has affected the underwriting area of the industry's activity. For underwriting, these are most prominent in two areas—communication with agents and the development of expert systems to facilitate and improve underwriting quality.

Table 2-19 summarizes the primary means of transmittal of applications and communication with agents. By and large, most policy applications are still initially transmitted by mail. Two firms did transmit nearly all forms by air express and a few had the bulk of their application material transmitted from agents electronically, but they were the anomalies. Follow-up communication with brokers and agents tends to be less homogenous. Phone was the most frequently used medium, but other modes were popular as well. Those firms that used real-time computer communication or e-mail for transmittal were of two types—those that used these means almost exclusively, and those who split communications roughly 50–50 between these means and either the telephone or mail. Very few firms had communication spread over more than two or three different means of transmittal. There was no discernable relationship between size and which firms chose to communicate by computer or e-mail.

The other major use of technology in underwriting is the development of expert systems. Based on responses to the survey, it appears that adoption of expert systems is relatively slow in coming to broad acceptance within the industry. Of our sample, only 27% had expert systems in place as of December 31, 1995. Those firms that had expert systems in place tended to be larger than the average sample firm. Table 2-20 provides information on the expert systems and their uses by firms who had them in place at the time of the survey.

For most firms, adoption of these systems was relatively recent with the

Table 2-19.   Means of first application transmittal (%)

	Mean	Median	Standard Deviation	Min	Max
Phone	0.5	0.0	3.3	0.0	25.0
Mail	73.0	85.5	31.6	0.0	100.0
Fax	5.9	1.0	14.6	0.0	100.0
Air Express	14.2	5.0	24.4	0.0	95.0
Computer (batch mode)	2.9	0.0	15.5	0.0	100.0
Computer (real time from agent or client site)	3.9	0.0	16.1	0.0	94.0
Number of Applications Received (000)	65	26	97	2	450

Principal Method of Communication w/Agent or Broker (%)

	Mean	Median	Standard Deviation	Min	Max
Phone	33.7	25.0	24.2	0	89
Mail	24.0	8.5	28.9	0	100
Fax	7.3	5.0	14.4	0	75
Air Express	0.8	0.0	1.7	0	5
Computer (batch mode)	9.2	0.0	23.2	0	100
Computer (real time from agent or client site)	15.4	0.0	24.9	0	90
E-mail	9.3	0.0	24.5	0	100

average adoption occurring in 1992. The earliest adoption was in 1982 and a number of firms had plans to adopt systems after the survey date. Most systems were a combination of products from outside vendors or off-the-shelf systems that were customized to meet the needs of the individual insurer. The systems are rarely used as a substitute for experienced underwriters, but are primarily used to supplement and augment human underwriting activities.

Survey respondents were asked to rank the importance of a number of factors relating to their expert systems on a scale of 1 to 5 indicating the significance of the roles that expert systems were expected to play in the underwriting process and to what extent the systems achieved those goals. A score of 5 indicates that a factor was an extremely significant reason for adoption of the system or that the system has performed beyond expectations in respect to its fulfillment of these goals.

The primary implementation goals of expert systems were to increase

Table 2-20. Expert Underwriting Systems

	Mean	Median/Rank	Standard Deviation	Min	Max
Percent Using Expert Systems	27%				
For Firms Using Them					
Year of Initial Adoption	1992	1992	3.8	1982	1998
Year of Most Recent Major Upgrade	1995	1995	0.8	1994	1997
Percent of Systems Developed In-house	27%				
Percent of Systems Developed by Consultants	14%				
Percent of Systems Purchased from a Vendor	64%				
Percent of Systems Purchased and Modified	33%				
Percent of Underwriting Done Solely by Expert System	14%	10%	12%	0%	35%
Importance in Decision to Adopt Expert Systems					
Increased Speed of Underwriting	4.27	1	0.70		
Improved Underwriting Accuracy	4.07	2	1.10		
Improved Underwriting Consistency	3.93	3	1.03		
Administrative Cost Advantage	3.67	4	1.05		
Increased Efficiency of Policy Issue	3.67	5	1.29		
Enhanced Underwriting Reporting	2.60	6	1.30		
Assist in Underwriter Training	2.40	7	0.99		
Degree Expert Systems Have Achieved Objectives					
Improved Underwriting Consistency	2.71	1	0.91		
Improved Underwriting Accuracy	2.50	2	0.85		
Increased Efficiency of Policy Issue	2.43	3	0.65		
Increased Speed of Underwriting	2.29	4	0.83		
Administrative Cost Advantage	2.21	5	0.70		
Enhanced Underwriting Reporting	2.07	6	1.38		
Assist in Underwriter Training	1.93	7	1.14		

underwriting speed, accuracy, and consistency. Other factors were deemed to be not as important, but were nevertheless significant. Enthusiasm for the effectiveness of the systems is somewhat mixed. Few graded their own systems as stellar. Most felt that they had some value ranking them between a 2, "somewhat effective," and a 3," substantially effective" on average. Those categories scoring the highest were generally the ones for which the systems were put in place—increasing underwriting accuracy and consistency. The systems act as a group of checks and balances for the human underwriters.

What do these systems and procedures add to the cost of a policy? Have they increased efficiency? Table 2-21 shows statistics on the average per policy expenses attributable to underwriting. For the average policy, slightly more than $185 is attributable to underwriting expenses. This figure varies substantially and is more a function of the type of business a firm underwrites than the firm's size. Application turnaround time varied substantially with average application turnaround time fairly evenly split across a number of weeks. There was no apparent relationship between company size and the turnaround time for an application. This is more likely a function of the complexity of the coverage in question, the dollar amount of coverage, and the personal characteristics of the policyholder.

Table 2-21. Underwriting Expenses and Effciency

	Mean (%)	Median (%)	Standard Deviation (%)	Min (%)	Max (%)
Direct Cost per Individual Life Insurance Case	$185.40	$105.00	$351.29	$6.19	$2,400.00
Proportion of Business Written					
Below Standard Rates (Preferred Business)	29	20	29	0	90
At Standard Rates	65	75	29	6	100
At Substandard Rates	9	6	13	0	92
Application Turnaround Time					
same day	5	0	10	0	49
1–5 days	26	18	23	0	95
6–10 days	23	18	18	2	99
11–15 days	18	13	16	0	72
16–20 days	19	12	19	0	81
more than 20 days	27	25	24	0	100

13. Human Resource Issues

Turnover is less of a concern among the underwriting staff than for agents and direct marketing personnel. Approximately one-ninth of the underwriters for the average insurance company are new in a given year and one-quarter were hired within the previous three years. Turnover mirrors replacement—the average firm was neither expanding nor contracting their underwriting staff. Average tenure within an underwriting department (both mean and median) was 10 years. This varies widely across firms—with some firms reporting average tenure of less than five years, and other reporting averages in excess of 20 years. Extremes were more likely among smaller companies, with larger firms exhibiting average tenures closer to the sample average. Promotion from other divisions within the company and hiring experienced underwriters (>5 years) from outside the company were the dominant sources of new underwriters, each contributing roughly 40% of new underwriters. Less common were hiring of junior underwriters (<5 years experience) from outside the company (15%), and hiring of recent college graduates (5%). The average new hire received 100 hours of formal training in the form of classes or seminars and roughly 8 months of supervised on-the-job training in the first year of hire.

The typical pay package for underwriting personnel contained very little in the way of incentive or variable pay beyond the base salary. For the average firm, this amounts to less than 5% of compensation. Perhaps this is because of the difficulty of assessing individual contributions to underwriting since, where variable pay exists, the amount of bonuses or other variable components is usually tied to performance of the underwriting group or the company as a whole.

Respondents also indicated that the most important factors for evaluating underwriters were, in decreasing order of importance, the quality of their relationships with field agents, decision quality audits, the technical knowledge of underwriters, and the turnaround time on underwriting decisions.

14. Policyholder Services

Once a policy is underwritten, it is the responsibility of policyholder services to keep customers happy. Their first task is to anticipate the needs of policyholders. Figure 2-6 presents graphically the means by which insurers define policyholder needs. The figure presents the proportion of the sample using each mechanism to determine policyholder needs. The most common

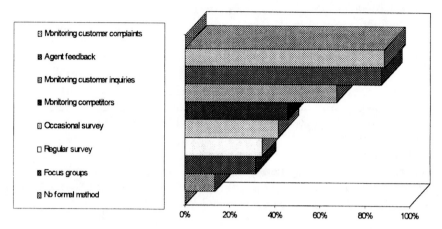

Figure 2-6. Defining Policyholder Service Needs

methods—monitoring customer complaints and getting feedback from agents, are used by nearly 90% of sample firms. The bulk of assessing policyholder needs is passive. Less than half of the firms monitor their competitors' procedures. Forty percent conduct occasional surveys of policyholders. Only one-third conduct focus groups or regular surveys of their policyholders. While the lack of formal customer feedback procedures in place at the time of the survey may be viewed as troubling, this appears to be recognized by the industry with the stated intention of many firms to place more emphasis on customer satisfaction measures in the future.

So what are these policyholders telling insurers that they want? Table 2-22 ranks customer priorities as interpreted by our sample of insurers. Cus-

Table 2-22. Policyholder Service Needs

	Mean	Rank	Median
Prompt Claims Settlement	4.71	1	5
Prompt Loan/Withdrawal Processing	4.35	2	5
Explanation of Policy Terms	4.31	3	5
Prompt Surrender Valuation	3.98	4	4
Timely/Accurate Billing	3.90	5	4
Changes to Policies	3.78	6	4
Change of Address/Ownership	3.67	7	4
Explanation of Premiums	3.66	8	4

tomer service needs are ranked on a 5-point scale with a value of 5 corresponding to the most important need. The single most important service need of policyholders is prompt claims settlement. This was almost universally given a value of 5. Second most important was prompt settlement of policy loans and withdrawals. It seems when customers want their money, they want it fast. All service needs were deemed as at least fairly important. As the means of determining policyholder needs generally stems from complaints, the urgency of those needs is likely made readily apparent by the policyholders.

Respondents were asked to rank their peer companies in terms of the quality in which they handled policyholder services. Northwestern Mutual and USAA Life were both picked as industry leaders in this area by five of their peers. Fidelity Investment Life and Pacific Mutual were both picked as the best in service quality by three respondents. No other firm received more than two votes as having the best policyholder services.

Respondents indicated what uses of technology were in place to aid in policyholder service. Table 2-23 gives the proportion of firms with each technology in place as of the time of the survey. As of 1996, use of toll free numbers and voice mail was almost universal among our insurers. It is likely that usage of other technologies has increased substantially since then, specifically the World Wide Web. It would be hard to imagine that more than a handful have not installed websites in the intervening two years.

Table 2-23.   Technology and Policyholder Service

Technology	Proportion of Respondents with Technology (%)
1–800 toll free for policyholders	92
1–800 toll free for agents	91
Voice mail	90
Automated telephone answering	70
Call monitoring/recording	59
Internet e-mail	29
Relational client database	29
Imaging	29
Voice recognition	10
World wide web	7

15. Claims Settlement

As mentioned previously, prompt and efficient claims settlement is the over-arching desire of policyholders. Table 2-24 gives the distribution of claims settlement times in weeks. Roughly one-fifth of claims are settled extremely promptly, within a week of the claim being filed. On the other hand, nearly 30% take four weeks or longer to settle. The percentage of claims settling in any given time period various substantially among companies as shown by the standard deviation, minimum, and maximum for each designated settle-ment period. This is also show graphically in figure 2-7, which presents the distribution of the average claim settlement time across firms. For the sample, the average claim settlement time is 20 days.

The figure shows that there is a fair amount of clustering in the 16- to 20-day range for average claim settlement, but there is considerable varia-tion about that with five firms requiring 4 days or less to settle an average claim, another five firms generally requiring more than 4 days but less than

Table 2-24.   Claim Settlement Time

	Mean (%)	Median (%)	Standard Deviation (%)	Min (%)	Max (%)
5 days or less	19	5	32	0	100
6–10 days	12	5	15	0	80
11–15 days	15	10	16	0	60
16–20 days	26	20	24	0	95
20+ days	28	10	30	0	97

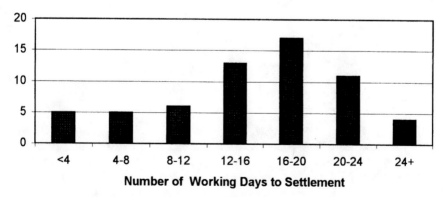

Figure 2-7.   Distribution of Insurers Average Claim Settlement Time

8 days, and another four firms generally taking a month or longer for claims settlement.

The cost associated with claims settlement varied significantly as well. Figure 2-8 gives the distribution of the cost of claims administration per $1,000 of premium. For the vast majority of the sample, claims settlement represented a very small fraction of premiums. The mean figure was $4.57 per $1,000 in claims and the median amount was a scant $1.36 per $1,000 of premium. The average is pulled up by a few insurers writing predominantly specialty lines or by having accidental death and health constitute a large percentage of their business.

Table 2-25 explores claims settlement cost in more detail including the overall cost per insurer, staffing of claims settlement operations, and the costs associated with these staffing levels. The average expenditure associated with claims settlement for our sample was approximately $750,000 per year. This total per insurer figure varies significantly and is largely a function of the size of the insurer. The average firm employed 15 individuals or full-time equivalents (FTEs) to staff their claims settlement operations at an average cost of $55,000 per claims department employee. Those insurers with higher claims department costs per employee tended to be larger in size.

When asked to evaluate the importance of various evaluation criteria for benchmarking claims departments, respondents overwhelmingly cited speed of service as the most important factor. Also ranked as important factors were expenditures by departments relative to budgets. Mortality targets were not deemed especially important for claims departments.

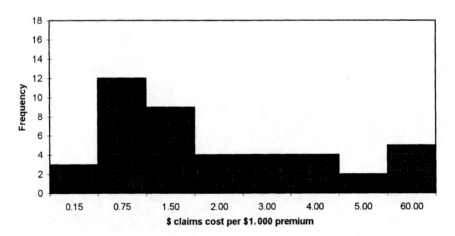

Figure 2-8.   Distribution of Costs of Claims Administration

Table 2-25. Claims Settlement Operations

	Mean	Median	Standard Deviation	Min	Max
Claims department expenditure ($000)	749	359	944	26	5,109
Claims department employee numbers (FTE)	14.6	7.7	21.6	1.6	134.0
Individual life and annuity premium ($)	898,169	386,757	1,268,693	3,000	5,093,200
Claims department cost per claims dept employee ($)	54,946	47,459	30,470	13,750	166,667
Claims cost per $1,000 of premium ($)	4.57	1.36	10.90	—	58.76

Other factors specifically mentioned by individual insurers included the quality and accuracy of claims settlement, number of complaints from policyholder, and responses to beneficiary satisfaction surveys.

16. Information Technology Systems

Insurers, as other financial institutions, are major employers of information technology. Information technology is the glue that holds an insurer together and plays a pivotal role in the strategic thinking and planning for the business. As in other areas of financial services, one dominant theme is the move from large mainframe-based systems to more distributed computing environments. As seen in figure 2-9, this is a change that is moving forward rapidly. Eighty-one percent of respondents rated their companies as users of primarily mainframe systems in 1993. That figure drops to 10% for 1996 and a projected value of 0 for 1999. Over the same period, the share describing their computing strategy as either primarily client server or weighted toward client-server systems rises from 5% to 48%.

With this change in the computing paradigm, we asked survey participants to give us a picture of how they were using information technology (IT), their expectations and priorities with respect to IT, how they went about developing systems, and the costs associated with these activities. Sixty-three participants responded to this portion of the survey in whole or in part. As with many of the other sections of the survey there was considerable variation in the responses obtained (see table 2-26).

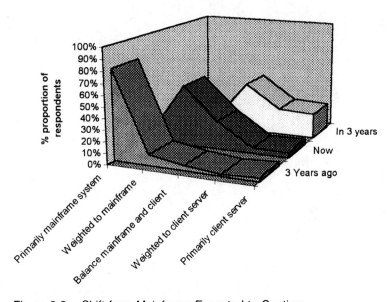

Figure 2-9.   Shift from Mainframe Expected to Continue

Table 2-26.   IT Priorities

	Mean	Rank	Median
New Product Implementation	2.38	1	2
Administration Systems Upgrade	2.95	2	4
New Business Systems	3.21	3	4
Optimization of Existing Systems	3.21	4	4
New IT Planning/Management	3.59	5	4
Implementation of Image Processing	3.64	6	4
Long Range Planning	3.69	7	4
Implementation of Expert Underwriting Systems	3.72	8	4
Implementation of Interactive Voice Response	3.80	9	4

Respondents were asked to rank their top three priorities in their IT operations for a list of given choices or to write in their own priorities if the choices given did not correspond to their priorities. The top choice was given a value of 1, the second a 2, a 3 for third choice, and unchosen priorities were given a value of 4. Only new product implementation was chosen as an IT priority by more than half the sample. Administration systems upgrade and new business systems did score highly among those respondents who selected them as priorities. Write-in priorities were numerous and diverse. A common theme included an orientation toward improvement of customer service support or establishment or upgrade to call centers. Some other priorities can be grouped alone the lines of using and disseminating technology to improve the efficiency and productivity of various operations and field associates.

A major shift in focus in the structuring and management of corporate data is the shift from policy delineated information to a customer focus. This is an area where other financial services are generally seen to be at an advantage. At the time of the survey, only 53% of respondents maintained customer-focused databases that allow the company to access all the policies a household maintains with the company. For 95% of those firms with such databases, records are accessible by home-office marketing personnel. Forty percent of these databases are accessible by agents. Significantly, fully 80% of respondents were unable to tell whether present policyholders held more than one policy. For those having such information, on average approximately one-third of policyholding households had multiple policies in force.

Asked to evaluate their peer companies in terms of their technological sophistication and their perceived success in meeting IT priorities, those firms that were highly regarded by their peers had a familiar ring. Northwestern Mutual Life, USAA, and Fidelity were picked most frequently by their peers. Mass Mutual, with 3 picks, was the only other insurer with more than 2 first-place rankings. There was some bias to the choice of picks by insurer type. Northwestern Mutual and USAA were more likely to be cited by large, diversified underwriters, whereas Fidelity was cited more frequently by firms with a strong annuity focus.

17. New System Development

In implementing systems to meet these needs, insurers go about developing systems in a number of ways. Some systems are developed in-house while others are farmed out to outside consultants and vendors. Table 2-27 presents the distribution of the means insurers use to develop systems and presents the figures for a similar study of the banking sector for comparison. The results are fairly similar with small fractions developing systems entirely in-house or entirely purchasing systems from outside. The bulk of development is done in a blended framework with a skew toward in-house overview and structuring.

Table 2-28 gives the degree to which development, maintenance, and data

Table 2-27.   IT Development Strategies

Retail Banks and Retail Life Insurers	Insurers (%)	Banks (%)
Develop all systems in-house (1)	18	11
Mostly in-house (2)	36	49
Balance of in-house and outsourcing (3)	35	16
Mostly outside (4)	9	16
No in-house development (5)	2	8

Table 2-28.   Percent of Cost Spent in-house

	Development & Enhancement (%)	Information Technology Maintenance (%)	Data Processing (%)
Mean	80	89	89
Median	93	99	100
<=80	29	16	19
80<x<=85	5	2	0
85<x<=90	16	16	5
90<x<=95	16	13	16
95<x<=100	34	53	60

processing are handled in-house on a cost basis. The bulk of IT spending is done internally. Only in the area of system development are outside vendors used to any real extent. In other areas, it is mostly small insurers who use outside sources for information technology maintenance or to handle data processing. Figures 2-10 and 2-11 provide a better look at IT costs for individual life insurance operations. Figure 2-10 shows the distribution associated with employing IT personnel per $1,000 of premium. The majority of the sample spent less $30 per $1,000 of premium on IT personnel although there were some insurers who spent considerably more.

18. Technology HR Practices

Table 2-29 presents summary statistics for turnover and training time spent by IT personnel. Turnover in these areas was similar in scale to that seen in the underwriting area. In all areas about one-sixth of the staff turned over annually on average. Average tenure with individual companies was approximately 12 years for managers and 7–8 years for professional per-

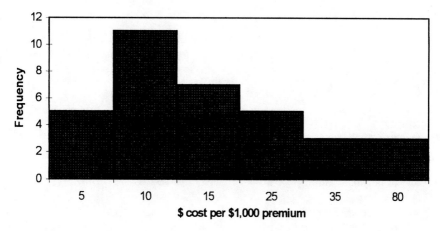

Figure 2-10.   IT Personnel Costs Per $1,000 Premium and Annuity Cosideration, 1995

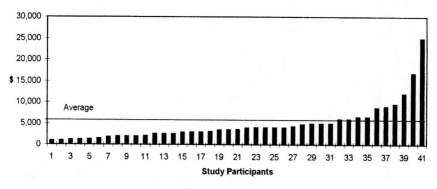

Figure 2-11.   Aggregate Annual Cost Per Personal Computer

sonnel and support staff. Employees spent roughly one week a year in formal training programs after their first year. These figures demonstrate greater success in the life industry in retaining IT personnel than has been seen in other areas of the financial services industry. Other studies demonstrating the high payback from IT personnel investment suggest that the insurers may find themselves comparatively advantaged in this critical area.

The associated cost per personal computer varied widely as shown in figure 2-11. Respondents were asked to provide "the estimated aggregate annual cost per personal computer when support staff, network connections and line costs are included." Estimates ranged from an implausible low of

Table 2-29. IT Personnel Retention and Training

	Managerial Personnel	Programming/ Development Professionals	Technical Support Professionals	Other Support Staff
Percent of Staff New in 1995	11.9%	13.2%	15.8%	18.6%
Percent of Staff Departing in 1995	16.7%	15.0%	18.3%	17.5%
Average Tenure with Company	11.6	8.4	7.1	7.8
Hours of Formal Training in First Year	44	125	57	37
Hours of Formal Training annually After First Year	31	40	39	23

$800, to the astronomic height of $25,000. The mean and median value were a relatively close $4,850 and $3,960, respectively. While some amount of variation is to be expected, the range in values may point to the difficulty respondents had in determining what exactly the cost per personal computer entails. For example, misallocation of the cost of support staff responsible for multiple computer platforms in one way or the other can have major impact on the resulting figures.

19. Conclusions

After sifting through a wealth of data provided by the participating companies, what have we learned? The first thing is that there are no easy answers. There is no unanimity in views among insurers. Each life insurer participates in different subsets of the marketplace. Many face stiffer competition from other financial service firms that are outside the traditional insurance realm than from those inside it. A few specialized insurers face competition from relatively few competitors. The choice of product focus and market focus go a long way in determining the strategic priorities of firms.

   One clear realization by survey respondents is that insurers cannot sit still. The world is changing rapidly around them as seen by their descriptions of perceived threats. Those that survive and thrive must be prepared to either take on or coexist with other financial services that provide the same or complementary products and services. Most of the respondents seem to focus on coexistence. Insurers appear to be most comfortable with a defensive stature protecting the markets they already hold, rather than striking out into markets that are new.

If that is their strategy, what is their best course of action? The answer would seem to be that successful firms will be required to do what they do now, only better, faster, cheaper, and with a smile. Managing a life insurance enterprise is a costly business, with a few areas containing most of the cost. These areas are marketing, distribution, and information technology.

We have seen that exclusive agencies are costly. Whether they justify their costs is difficult to say. On average they do not appear to perform significantly better than either non-exclusive systems or direct marketing. In fact, the results reported in Chapter 4 of this book offer further evidence that this distribution system is relatively costly. Perhaps this is why we are currently seeing a move away from exclusive agencies. It stands to reason that those firms could be dropping this means of distribution as they find it not worth the cost. In the long run, those that retain exclusive agencies will be those for whom the associated costs are worthwhile—those who see real benefit from agents whose productivity is higher than average and whose turnover costs are lower than average.

Information technology is costly, plain and simple. While the cost of computing is dropping precipitously each year, we find we need more of it each year. Increased computing power lets us do individual tasks more rapidly, but also requires we do more tasks in a given amount of time. This added power is advantageous for the consumer who has more choices and more information to draw from when making those choices. The insurers whose technology best empowers its personnel and its customers will be at a strategic advantage. That is, providing computing power and adapting it to existing personnel while making it in line with the objectives of the firm are key challenges facing the industry.

The majority of life insurers indicated that the key products for the next decade are products that are with us today, ones that have been gaining market share within the insurance industry for some time. Variable annuities and universal life have been around since the late 1970s. Variable life insurance dates to the mid-1980s. In an era of skyrocketing stock market prices these products look very attractive compared to their plain-vanilla brethren of years past. This has led the average consumer to move into these products with increasing frequency. Insurers, therefore, must be participants in these areas in order to maintain market share of the growing retirement asset market. Today, managing the underlying funds that govern the value of death benefits or annuity payments probably is of less consequence than in years past. Insurers cannot depend upon their status as traditional providers of actuarial products to retain their market share. Therefore, presence is of paramount importance.[3] The average consumer will likely choose a familiar name and a known association to manage his or her money. Customer knowledge and market segmentation strategies will allow these firms to improve their positions against the broadening range of competitors. The keys to success then are to provide the appropriate products to the right consumers through the most cost efficient distribution alternatives.

It is true, however, that the attractiveness of these asset accumulation products depends crucially on the interplay between stock and bond markets. As long as stocks continue to soar and interest rates are low, these products should grow in their importance. A prolonged downturn in stocks may be disastrous for firms who commit too many resources in these products. In the end, this may prove beneficial to the industry's portfolio that includes not only equity, but also other more stable value vehicles.

Term life is one such staple product. While relatively immune to market downturns, it is truly almost generic. It is widely available and easy to underwrite. Firms that wish to anchor themselves on term life will be those who can keep costs to a minimum.

One product that was mentioned by a few insurers to be of significance in the future, long term care insurance, is indicative of a different path. This is a product that meets a real and growing need, yet it is not in direct competition with mutual fund providers. This represents a path for true product innovation and development. On the other hand, this is a costly path that is not correct for most in the industry. It requires a well-capitalized insurer that can afford the long term development that such a product entails.

Perhaps the best clues about where the future lies is not in the inconsistent answers to individual questions about insurer priorities and focuses, but in the names of the insurers that our survey respondents consistently mentioned as the bests of their peer group. Three names that appeared repeatedly were Northwestern Mutual Life, USAA Life, and Fidelity Investment Life. These three names represent three very different business models.

Northwestern Mutual is one of the oldest and largest mutual insurers in the country. It is an exclusive agency operation. Northwestern is a broad-based marketer that provides a wide range of products, but with a specific emphasis on individual products and life insurance. The company boasts sterling credit and claims-payment ratings and has been very successful in generating policies from high wealth individuals. Its strong credit ratings and the high regard in which its agency force is held for the level of service it provides, should allow Northwestern to continue to be successful in this market segment.

USAA Life is one of a diversified family of insurers created with a special mandate: to provide coverage for military officers and their families. It is a direct marketer with distribution targeted to reach a specific, niche market segment of customers. Life operations and banking services are a follow-on to a larger and older property-casualty operation. USAA is seen as one of the top life insurers in its use of technology and the level of service it provides to policyholders. It too provides a reasonably broad range of products to its customer base.

Fidelity Investment Life Insurance is a part of FMR, the parent company of Fidelity Investments, the world's largest mutual fund family. Fidelity Life was originally created to provide annuity wrappers for existing Fidelity mutual funds. While the vast majority of Fidelity's insurance business is still in the annuity realm, its life insurance operations are growing rapidly.

Three firms, three different backgrounds, three different models—all are seen as among the best in the industry. Remarkably although they started from different points, they are all moving in the same direction—developing diversified financial service families. The old-line insurers are looking more like the mutual fund family. The old guard mutual fund is looking more like the insurers.

Notes

1. See, for example, Cummins and Zi (1999) and Cummins, Tennyson, and Weiss (1999).
2. See Harker and Hunter (1998) or Harker and Zenios (1998) for examples of results from this research project.
3. See Santomero and Hoffman (1998) for a broader discussion of this point.

References

Cummins, J. David and Hongmin Zi. "Comparison of Frontier Efficiency Methods: An Application to the U.S. Life Insurance Industry," *Journal of Productivity Analysis* 10 (1998), 131–152.

Cummins, J. David, Sharon Tennyson and Mary Weiss. "Consolidation and Efficiency In the U.S. Life Insurance Industry," *Journal of Banking and Finance* 23 (1999), 325–357.

Harker, Patrick T. and Larry W. Hunter. "Designing the Future of Banking:

Lessons Learned from the Trenches," Working Paper 98–29, Wharton Financial Institutions Center, Philadelphia, 1998.

Harker, Patrick T. and Stavros A. Zenios. "What Drives the Performance of Financial Institutions?" forthcoming in P.T. Harker and S.A. Zenios (eds.), *Performance of Financial Institutions*, London: Cambridge University Press, 1999.

Santomero, Anthony M. and Paul Hoffman. "Life Insurance Firms in the Retirement Market: Is the News All Bad?" *Journal of the American Society of CLU and ChFC*, July 1998.

3 EFFICIENCY IN THE U.S. LIFE INSURANCE INDUSTRY: ARE INSURERS MINIMIZING COSTS AND MAXIMIZING REVENUES?

J. David Cummins

1. Introduction

Insurers are increasingly using benchmarking techniques to identify operations that need improvement by comparing their performance with other firms in the industry. An important new class of bench-marking methods has been developed called *frontier efficiency methodologies*. The frontier methodologies measure firm performance relative to "best practice" frontiers derived from firms in the industry. Such measures are superior to traditional techniques such as financial ratio analysis because they summarize firm performance in a single statistic that controls for differences among firms using a sophisticated multidimensional framework. Frontiers can be estimated to measure firm success in employing technology (technical efficiency), attaining optimal size (scale efficiency), minimizing costs (cost efficiency), maximizing revenues (revenue efficiency), and maximizing profits (profit efficiency). In this chapter, frontier efficiency analysis is employed to evaluate the efficiency of U.S. life insurance companies. We estimate technical, scale, cost, and revenue efficiency for a sample of insurers that represent 80 percent of industry assets.

Frontier efficiency analysis can be used in a number of ways to assist management in minimizing costs and maximizing revenues. The methodologies enable the firm to evaluate its performance relative to a group of peers. The firm can gauge whether it is performing better or worse than the peer group in terms of technology, scale, cost minimization, and revenue maximization and thus direct management efforts to the areas that most need improvement. Insurers also can use efficiency analysis to identify attractive targets for mergers and acquisitions. And, unlike conventional benchmarking methods, frontier efficiency techniques identify the set of firms in the industry that constitute a given firm's peer group.

Conducting efficiency analysis over time enables management to determine the performance effects of new procedures, strategies, and projects. For example, analyzing efficiency before and after the adoption of a new computer system can help the firm determine whether the new system has been successful in furthering its objectives. Frontier analysis can also be used within the firm to compare the performance of departments, divisions, branches, and agencies. Finally, the results of frontier efficiency analysis can be used in negotiations with regulators concerning mergers, acquisitions, and other types of regulatory issues.

The chapter is organized as follows: In section 2, we provide an intuitive explanation of frontier efficiency techniques, define the various types of efficiency that can be measured, and explain our approach to measuring efficiency in the life insurance industry. Section 3 presents the results of our efficiency estimation and discusses the implications of the results for insurer management and strategy. Finally, section 4 provides our conclusions about efficiency in the industry and discusses the potential for future research.

2. Frontier Efficiency Methodologies

Although efficiency is often used generically as an objective of the firm, there are actually several types of efficiency concepts that convey different information about firm performance. This section introduces the concept of the efficient frontier and defines the principal types of efficiency and their implications for management decision making. We then turn to a discussion of the measurement of inputs and outputs in the life insurance industry. The section concludes with a discussion of the technique we use to estimate the efficiency of life insurers.

2.1. Efficient Frontiers and Efficiency Concepts

The type of frontier that has received the most publicity among financial firms is the efficient investment frontier, which gives the maximum attainable investment portfolio return for each level of risk. The efficient frontiers discussed in this chapter are similar in concept to the efficient investment frontier in that they represent optimal performance according to various criteria. However, the technology used to estimate our frontiers is very different from that used in computing the efficient investment frontier.

2.1.1. The Production Frontier and Technical Efficiency.   Perhaps the most basic type of efficient frontier is the *production frontier*. Firms operating on the production frontier are efficient in the sense that they are using the minimal amount of inputs to produce their outputs. Another way of looking at the production frontier is in terms of technology. Essentially, firms operating on the production frontier are using the optimal technology available to produce their outputs, while firms that are not on the frontier could become more efficient by improving their technology.

Figure 3-1 illustrates the production frontier for a simple case in which a firm uses one type of input to produce one type of output. The quantity of output (Y) produced is measured along the vertical axis and the quantity of inputs consumed (X) is measured along the horizontal axis. The frontier is represented by the line labeled with a V. Firms on the frontier are considered to be efficient in the sense that they are using the minimal amount of input to produce a given level of output. The frontier represents the best performance that can be achieved using the currently available technology.

The concept of *technical efficiency* can be defined with reference to the frontier shown in figure 3-1. Consider firm i operating with input level x_i and output level y_i. This firm is not operating on the frontier and thus is inefficient. The firm's technical efficiency can be measured by reference to its distance from the frontier or, stated another way, in terms of the amount of the input it would use if it were fully efficient compared to the amount of input it is currently using. If the firm were fully efficient, i.e., if it were operating on the frontier, it would use the amount of input represented by the distance $0a$ along the horizontal axis. The amount of input the firm is currently using is represented by the distance $0b$ along the horizontal axis. The firm's technical efficiency can then be defined as follows:

$$Technical\ Efficiency = \frac{Frontier\ Input\ Use}{Actual\ Input\ Use} = \frac{0a}{0b}$$

Technical efficiency ranges between 0 and 1. Firms that are fully efficient have technical efficiency scores of 1, whereas inefficient firms have technical efficiencies less than 1. For an inefficient firm, the difference between 1

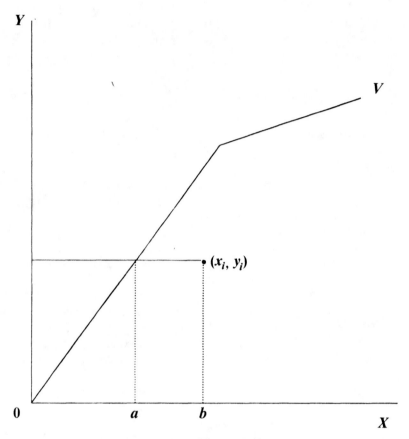

Figure 3-1.   Production Frontier for the Single Input-Single Output Firm

and its technical efficiency score represents the proportion by which input usage could be reduced if the firm were to adopt the most efficient technology, i.e., if it were to operate on the frontier. For example, a firm with a technical efficiency score of 0.75 could reduce its input usage by 25 percent while still producing the same amount of output.

2.1.2. Pure Technical and Scale Efficiency.   Another important efficiency concept that relates to technical efficiency is *scale efficiency*. A firm that is scale efficient has achieved constant returns to scale (CRS). Firms that have not achieved constant returns to scale are operating with either increasing returns to scale (IRS) or decreasing returns to scale (DRS). In terms of the simple production frontier shown in figure 3-1, returns to scale can be conceptualized in terms of the ratio of the quantity of output produced to the quantity of input consumed. A firm in the IRS range could increase its output-to-input ratio by becoming larger (increasing its scale), while a firm in the DRS range could increase the output-to-input ratio by becoming smaller (decreasing its scale). CRS are the ideal, because the ratio of output to input is maximized, i.e., the firm is neither too large nor too small. Thus, one important objective of the firm is to operate with CRS.

A firm's scale efficiency can be measured by decomposing technical efficiency into two components—*pure technical efficiency* and *scale efficiency*. These efficiency concepts are illustrated in figure 3-2. This figure shows two production frontiers, labeled V^c and V^v, again for the simple case of a firm with one output (Y) and one input (X). V^c represents a CRS frontier, i.e., a frontier where the *ratio* of output to input is the same for all levels of input. V^v is a variable returns to scale (VRS) frontier, i.e., a frontier that includes points or regions where returns to scale are increasing, constant, and decreasing. A firm operating on frontier V^v would have IRS for the range of outputs between y_1 and y_2. In this range, the ratio of outputs to inputs increases as the level of output rises. At the output point y_2, the frontier coincides with the CRS frontier and thus CRS is achieved. Then in the output range from y_2 to y_3, the frontier exhibits DRS because the ratio of output to input declines as the amount of output increases.

Pure technical efficiency is measured relative to the VRS frontier, V^v. Consider firm i, operating with input quantity x_i and output quantity y_i. This firm is inefficient in the pure technical sense because it is not operating on the frontier V^v. Its pure technical efficiency is measured by the ratio $0b/0c$. The firm is also scale inefficient because it is not operating on the CRS frontier V^c; and it could further reduce its input usage by moving to this frontier. Its scale inefficiency is the ratio of the amount of input it would use if it operated on the CRS frontier to the amount of input it would use on the VRS frontier, or $0a/0b$. Thus, we have the following relationship:

*Technical Efficiency = Pure Technical Efficiency * Scale Efficiency*

$$= \frac{0b}{0c} * \frac{0a}{0b} = \frac{0a}{0c}$$

Like technical efficiency, pure technical efficiency and scale efficiency range between 0 and 1. An efficiency ratio equal to 1 implies full efficiency, while a score less than 1 implies that the firm is inefficient. To achieve full technical efficiency, a firm must be operating on the CRS frontier (V^c in figure 3-2).

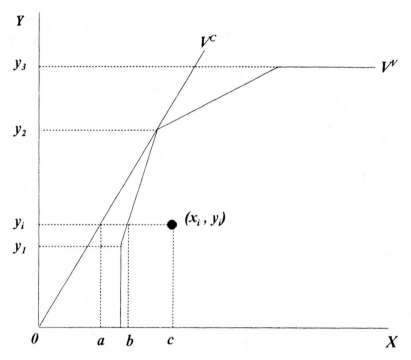

Figure 3-2.   Pure Technical and Scale Efficiency

2.1.3. The Cost Frontier and Cost Efficiency.   Cost efficiency is defined relative to another efficient frontier called the *cost frontier*. The cost frontier gives the minimum costs for producing each level of output. The cost frontier for a single output firm is shown in figure 3-3. In this figure, output is measured along the vertical axis, and costs are measured along the horizontal axis. As in the case of technical efficiency, firms operating on the frontier are fully cost efficient, while firms operating to the right of the frontier are cost inefficient.

To define cost efficiency, consider firm i, which has costs of c_i and output of y_i. This firm could reduce its costs by moving to the frontier. Its cost efficiency thus can be defined by taking the ratio of its potential frontier costs to its actual costs:

$$Cost\ Efficiency = \frac{Frontier\ Costs}{Actual\ Costs} = \frac{0a}{0b}$$

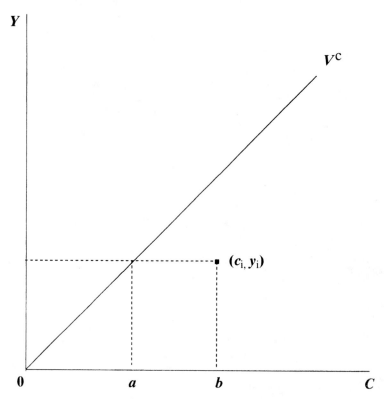

Figure 3-3.   Cost Frontier for a Single Output Firm

Cost efficiency also varies between 0 and 1 with fully efficient firms having cost efficiency ratios equal to 1. Analogously to technical efficiency, the difference between 1 and a firm's cost efficiency represents the proportion by which costs could be reduced while producing no less of the output.

A firm cannot be fully cost efficient if it is not technically efficient. The relationship between cost and technical efficiency is shown in figure 3-4, which also illustrates another type of efficiency known as *allocative efficiency*. Figure 3-4 considers the case of a firm that produces one type of output (Y) using two inputs, x_1 and x_2 (e.g., labor and capital). The firm produces a specified quantity of output Y^*, i.e., unlike figures 3-1 through 3-3, figure 3-4 is applicable to only one specific output quantity. The figure shows that this output quantity can be produced with different combinations of inputs. Specifically, the curved line QQ', known as an *isoquant*, represents

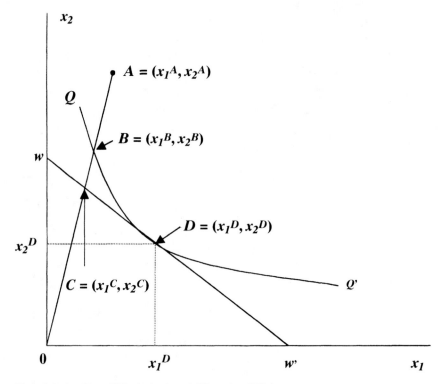

Figure 3-4.   Farrell Technical and Allocative Efficiency

the different combinations of x_1 and x_2 that can produce Y^* using the best technology. Thus, firms operating on the isoquant are considered to be technically efficient.

Also shown in figure 3-4 is a line labeled ww', known as an *isocost* line. The slope of this line is determined by the ratio of the prices of the two inputs used by the firm's production process. Along this line, the firm's total costs are given by $(w_1x_1 + w_2x_2)$, i.e., the price of input 1 multiplied by the quantity of input 1 plus the price of input 2 multiplied by the quantity of input 2. In fact, the line ww' represents the minimum costs attainable by the firm to produce output quantity Y^*. The line is tangent to QQ' at the point D, representing the firm's optimal (i.e., cost minimizing) operating point. Thus, the line ww' also represents the firm's minimum isocost line. A line parallel to ww' but to its left would represent lower costs, because lower quantities of both inputs are used. However, such a line is not feasible for the firm to attain because it is below the curve QQ', representing the best the firm can do in terms of producing Y^* with the best available technology. Thus, the firm minimizes costs by operating at the tangency point between QQ' and ww', i.e., at point D. Operating at point D minimizes costs because the firm will consume the smallest quantity of inputs while producing Y^* using the best technology.

Figure 3-4 illustrates the relationship between cost, technical, and allocative efficiency. Consider a firm operating at point A, i.e., producing Y^* using input combination (x_1^A, x_2^A). This firm exhibits both technical and allocative inefficiency. It is technically inefficient because it is not operating on the best-technology isoquant. Rather, it is using an inferior technology and operating on an isoquant (not shown) to the right of QQ' which requires the firm to use a larger quantity of inputs to produce Y^*. The firm can reduce its input usage by adopting the best technology and thus moving from point A to point B, and the measure of the firm's technical efficiency is the ratio $0B/0A$. One minus $0B/0A$ is the proportion by which the firm could reduce its input usage by adopting the best technology.[1]

This firm also exhibits *allocative inefficiency*. Allocative inefficiency is present because the firm is not using its inputs in the correct proportions, i.e., it is not allocating its resources appropriately when choosing inputs to use in producing Y^*. Specifically, the firm is using too much of input 2 and not enough of input 1. The firm can achieve allocative efficiency by moving along the isoquant from point B to point D. The measure of allocative efficiency is thus the ratio $0C/0B$. Cost efficiency is then defined as follows:

$$Cost\ Efficiency = Technical\ Efficiency * Allocative\ Efficiency$$

$$= \frac{0B}{0A} * \frac{0C}{0B} = \frac{0C}{0A}$$

Cost efficiency varies between 0 and 1 with a fully efficient with efficient firms having cost efficiency equal to 1.

2.1.4. The Revenue Frontier and Revenue Efficiency.   We can also define a *revenue frontier* and measure *revenue efficiency* relative to this frontier. Revenue efficiency is defined as the ratio of a given firm's revenues to the revenues of a fully efficient firm with the same input quantities and output prices. Fully efficient firms have revenue efficiency equal to 1, while inefficient firms have revenue efficiency of less than 1. Revenue efficiency is attained by using the best practice technology and choosing the optimal mix of outputs.

2.2. Outputs and Inputs

2.2.1. Outputs and Output Prices. Insurers are analogous to other firms in the financial sector of the economy in that their outputs consist primarily of services, many of which are intangible. The approach used in most financial institutional efficiency studies is to measure output as the *value added* by the firms in the industry, i.e., the difference between the value of output produced and the value of inputs consumed. Because the outputs are mostly intangible, the general approach for measuring output is to identify variables that correlate highly with the services provided by firms in the industry and result in the creation of value added. In this section, we identify variables that correlate with the value added by insurers. Insurers create value by providing three principal services:

- **Risk-pooling and risk-bearing.** Insurance provides a mechanism for consumers and businesses exposed to insurable contingencies to engage in risk reduction through pooling. Insurers collect premiums from their customers and redistribute most of the funds to those policyholders who sustain losses. The actuarial, underwriting, and related expenses incurred in operating the risk pool are a major component of value added in insurance. Policyholders may also have their risks reduced because some of these risks are borne by shareholders of the insurance company (for stock companies), by previous policyholders whose capital has been left in the company (for mutual organizations), or by other parties holding the debt of the insurance company (for both types of firms). Again, this creates value added by increasing economic security.
- **"Real" financial services relating to insured losses.** Insurers provide a variety of real services for policyholders. In life insurance, these services include financial planning and counseling for individuals and administration of pension and benefit plans for businesses.
- **Intermediation.** Insurers raise funds by issuing insurance policies and annuities and investing the funds until they are withdrawn by policyholders or needed to pay claims. The net interest margin between the rate of return earned on assets and the rate credited to policyholders represents the value added of the intermediation function.

Economists identify the important outputs produced in an industry by looking at operating cost allocations. If an industry is competitive, operating costs represent the amounts that consumers are willing to pay for the goods and services provided by the firms in the industry. The reasoning is that buyers would be unwilling to cover operating costs unless they were receiving some economic value in return. To help identify output variables in life insurance, we briefly consider the operating cost allocations in the industry. About 41% of operating expenses for life insurers represent commissions paid to agents.[2] Agents perform real services such as financial counseling and giving advice on coverages and deductibles. They also collect underwriting information and expand the size and presumably the diversification of the insurer's risk pool, both of which are associated with the risk-pooling function. About 27% of total expenses for life insurers are for personnel costs for functions other than sales and investments. These expenditures are for the underwriters, actuaries, and administrators that operate the insurance risk pool and thus are primarily attributable to the risk-pooling function. Investment expenses account for 9% of total expenses for life (property-liability) insurers. These expenses along with the net interest margin between what insurers earn on their investments and what they credit to policyholders, is a measure of the value added by the intermediation function. Although insurers do not disclose the net interest margin, a rough idea of the potential magnitude of this component of value added can be obtained by observing that a 50 basis point margin on invested assets would be equivalent to 13.6% of total expenses for life insurers. Thus, intermediation is also an important output for insurers.

The variables used in this study to measure life insurance output consist of incurred benefits plus additions to reserves.[3] Incurred benefits represent payments received by policyholders in the current year and thus are expected to be useful proxies for the risk-pooling and risk-bearing functions. Benefits are a measure of the amount of funds pooled by insurers and redistributed to policyholders as compensation for insured events. Most life insurance and annuity products also involve the accumulation of assets, either to pay future death benefits or to be received as income, either in a lump sum or through an annuity. The funds received by insurers that are not needed for benefit payments and expenses are added to policyholder reserves. Reserves in insurance are analogous to bank deposits and also to the bonds and other debt instruments issued by non-financial firms. The funds backing the reserves are invested by insurers in financial instruments. Additions to reserves thus are expected to be highly correlated with the intermediation function performed by life insurers. Both incurred benefits and additions to reserves are correlated with real services provided by insurers, such as benefit administration in the case of health insurance and financial planning in the case of individual life insurance and annuities.

The major lines of insurance offered by life insurers differ in the types of contingent events that are covered and in the relative importance of the risk-pooling/risk-bearing, intermediation, and real service components of output. Thus, we define five output variables, equal to the sum of incurred benefits and additions to reserve for the five major lines of business offered by life insurers—individual life insurance, individual annuities, group life insurance, group annuities, and accident and health insurance.[4]

In keeping with the value-added approach to output measurement, we define the price of each insurance output as the sum of premiums and investment income minus output for the line divided by output.[5] That is,

$$Price = \frac{\begin{array}{c} Premiums + Investment\ Income - \\ Incurred\ Benefits - Additions\ to\ Reserves \end{array}}{Incurred\ Benefits + Additions\ to\ Reserves}$$

The price is a measure of value added because it represents the amount of money spent in providing services in the industry, again under the assumption that the industry is competitive so that buyers receive services commensurate with the funds absorbed by insurers in producing output.

2.2.2. Inputs and Input Prices. We define four insurance inputs—administrative labor, agent labor, business services, and financial capital. We treat home office and agent labor separately because the two types of labor have different prices and are used in different proportions by firms in the industry.[6] Most of the industry's non-labor expenses are for various business services such as legal fees, travel, communications, advertising, and materials. Only a small fraction of expenses are for physical capital such as computers and buildings. Consequently, we do not define physical capital as a separate input but do include it in the business services category.[7] The prices of agent labor, home office labor, and business services are based on survey data on wages compiled by the U.S. Department of Labor.[8] Estimates of the quantity of agent and home office labor are obtained by dividing expenditures on these two expense categories by the agent and home office wage variables. The quantity of business services is similarly defined.

Our final input is financial capital. Financial capital is an important input in insurance, and capital costs represent a significant expense for insurers. Insurers maintain equity capital both to ensure policyholders that they will receive payment even if claims exceed expectations and to satisfy regulatory requirements. The quantity of financial capital is measured as the amount of equity capital reported by the insurer to the National Association of Insurance Commissioners (NAIC).[9]

The cost of capital in the insurance industry is difficult to measure because only a small minority of life insurers are publicly traded. We adopt a three-tier approach to measuring the cost of capital, based on financial ratings assigned by the A.M. Best Company, the leading financial rating firm for insurers. Best's uses a 15-tier letter-coded rating system, ranging from A++ for the strongest insurers to F for insurers currently in liquidation. The three tiers we adopt here consist of the four ratings in the "A" range, the four ratings in the "B" range, and all other rating categories. Based on an examination of the equity cost of capital for traded life insurers, we assign a cost of capital of 12% to the top tier, 15% to the middle tier, and 18% to insurers in the lowest quality-tier.[10]

2.3. Estimating Efficiency

Efficiency is measured by estimating best practice efficient frontiers based on a relevant sample of firms. The firms on the frontier are considered to be the best practice firms in the industry in the sense that their performance is at least as good as that of other firms with similar characteristics. The efficiencies of other firms in the industry are measured in comparison to the efficient frontier.

The method we adopt to study efficiency in the U.S. life insurance industry is called *data envelopment analysis* (DEA).[11] DEA is a mathematical programming methodology that is implemented by solving linear programming problems. DEA efficiency is measured for every firm in our sample of life insurers. The objective in estimating any given firm's efficiency is to define a set of other firms from the industry that dominate the firm in question. For example, in estimating DEA cost efficiency, we are seeking a set of firms that have lower costs than a specific firm while having similar outputs and input prices. The dominating set consists of at least one firm, and the number of firms in a dominating set averages about four. If a dominating set exists, the specific firm's efficiency is measured relative to this set. If no dominating set exists, the firm is considered *self efficient* and given an efficiency score of 1.

3. Efficiency in the Life Insurance Industry

3.1. The Sample

The data used in our study are drawn from the regulatory annual statements filed by insurers with the NAIC. Because all insurers of any

significant size are required to report to the NAIC, our sample initially consisted of virtually the entire industry. We eliminated firms with unusual
characteristics such as zero or negative net worth, zero or negative premiums, and zero or negative input expenditures. We also eliminated firms with
extreme or unusual financial ratios such as very large or very small (negative) returns on equity, expense to asset ratios greater than 75%, and so
forth. Such firms are clearly experiencing financial difficulties and tend to
be non-viable operating entities. The final sample used to estimate efficiency
by year consisted of approximately 750 firms per year, representing about
80% of industry assets.

3.2. Average Efficiencies and Inter-firm Performance

The average efficiencies in the U.S. life insurance industry for the period
1988–1995 are shown in table 3-1. The top panel of the table shows
efficiency averages for the six types of efficiency investigated in this study,

Table 3-1.   Efficiency in the U.S. Life Insurance Industry

Year	Cost	Allocative	Technical	Pure Technical	Scale	Revenue
Averages:						
1988	0.284	0.638	0.469	0.554	0.859	0.301
1989	0.306	0.655	0.491	0.582	0.839	0.311
1990	0.342	0.600	0.578	0.629	0.928	0.244
1991	0.370	0.699	0.544	0.603	0.896	0.376
1992	0.344	0.632	0.556	0.625	0.885	0.366
1993	0.329	0.559	0.599	0.666	0.893	0.355
1994	0.452	0.702	0.647	0.694	0.929	0.371
1995	0.460	0.713	0.649	0.704	0.918	0.321
Standard Deviations:						
1988	0.184	0.209	0.256	0.280	0.173	0.262
1989	0.201	0.222	0.269	0.272	0.192	0.266
1990	0.219	0.209	0.272	0.285	0.119	0.254
1991	0.223	0.204	0.276	0.279	0.147	0.284
1992	0.214	0.204	0.265	0.267	0.152	0.271
1993	0.205	0.208	0.257	0.254	0.144	0.266
1994	0.230	0.202	0.250	0.251	0.102	0.267
1995	0.232	0.205	0.244	0.242	0.114	0.261

while the lower panel shows the standard deviations. The standard deviation is a measure of the heterogeneity of efficiency scores across firms in the industry, with higher standard deviations indicating greater heterogeneity or dispersion of efficiency scores among firms.

Cost efficiency is relatively low in the life insurance industry in comparison with other industries such as property-liability insurance and banking.[12] For example, the average cost efficiency in 1988 is 0.284 or 28.4%, implying that the average firm could reduce costs by 71.6% if it were to operate on the efficient frontier. Revenue efficiency is also relatively low—about 30% in 1988. These results indicate the existence of a very wide gap among the average firms in the industry and the industry leaders, with leadership being defined here as being highly cost and revenue efficient. The low cost and revenue efficiency scores are also indicative of an industry that traditionally has not been subject to much price competition.

One of the most important developments in the life insurance market has been the emergence of *non-traditional competitors* including banks, mutual fund organizations, and securities dealers. Although banks are still barred from insurance underwriting, a number of mechanisms are available that allow banks to market life insurance and annuities. These methods range from purchasing insurance agencies to the sale of "private label" insurance and annuity products in bank branches. These private label products are manufactured by a licensed insurer but sold under the bank's brand name. Mutual fund companies are not subject to federal banking regulation and thus are permitted to underwrite insurance. Accordingly, several of the major fund companies (e.g., Fidelity) own insurance companies that produce products for sale through the funds' marketing networks. Brokerage firms such as Merrill-Lynch also own successful insurance companies.

The non-traditional competitors tend to have much lower product distribution costs than the traditional distribution networks used by most life insurers—exclusive agents and brokers. "Exclusive" agents primarily represent a single insurer, while life insurance brokers represent more than one insurer. Commission rates for agents and brokers have traditionally been much higher than sales commissions in the securities industry. Consequently, many insurers have faced "culture shock" in trying to adapt to the new competitive environment. It is obviously much easier to motivate a securities broker to sell an insurance product for a 5% commission than to convince an agent that the traditional 55% commission for life insurance has to be radically reduced. Many life insurers have still not found a way to compete in the new environment. The likely result will be further consolidation in the industry (see Chapter 5 of this book (Cummins, Tennyson, and Weiss, 1999) for an analysis of consolidation trends) and further loss of market share by inefficient insurers.

The more competitive environment that has steadily developed over our sample period is reflected in the efficiency scores shown in table 3-1. The average scores of life insurers for all six types of efficiency increased between 1988 and 1995. For example, average cost efficiency increased from 28% to 46% and technical efficiency increased from 47% to 65%. The increase in revenue efficiency was more modest, increasing from 30 to 32%, although revenue efficiency was as high as 38% at approximately the midpoint of our sample period. The increases in technical and pure technical efficiency also reflect increased competition as well as dramatic improvements in computing and communications technology. The dispersion of technical, pure technical, and scale efficiency declined during the sample period, indicating a convergence of insurers toward best practices. However, the dispersion in cost efficiency increased, perhaps reflecting the set of insurers being left behind by the insurers that were improving their technologies.

Efficiency scores in the industry vary significantly by insurer size, with larger firms being generally more efficient on average than smaller firms. This is shown in figure 3-5, which tabulates efficiency by size decile, where size is measured by total assets. The figure is based on efficiency averages and average assets over the sample period. Figure 3-5 shows clearly that cost, revenue, technical, and allocative efficiency are highest for firms in the largest-size deciles, and particularly for the tenth decile, which consists of the largest firms in the industry. For example, cost efficiency is about 27% on average for firms in the smallest-size decile and about 55% for firms in the largest size decile. Both technical and allocative efficiency contribute to the higher cost efficiency enjoyed by the largest firms. The differential between the smallest and largest firms is even more pronounced for revenue efficiency, which averages 26% for firms in the smallest decile and 55% for firms in the largest decile.

Because efficiency generally increased over the sample period, we focus our more detailed analysis of efficiency on the results for 1995. The frequency distribution of cost efficiency in 1995 is shown in figure 3-6. The figure shows that cost efficiency among firms in the industry in 1995 ranged from a low of 5% to a maximum of 100%. Two firms had efficiencies of about 5%, whereas 40 firms had cost efficiency scores of 100%. The most common efficiency score among the firms in the industry was 30%. However, the figure again emphasizes the significant dispersion in efficiencies across the industry. As price and product competition continue to

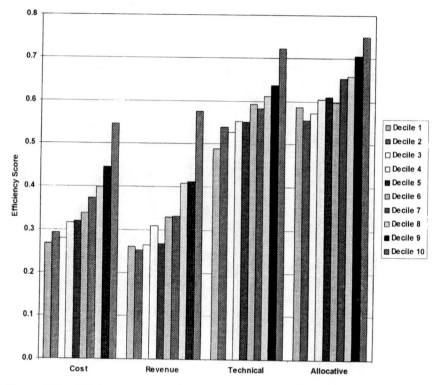

Figure 3-5.   Efficiency by Asset Size Decile

increase in the years to come, the most likely outcome is that average efficiencies will increase and the dispersion in efficiencies will decrease as inefficient firms improve their operations, are acquired, or drop out of the market. These results strongly suggest that the industry is likely to undergo a major restructuring in the near future.

The distribution of allocative efficiencies in the industry is shown in figure 3-7. Allocative efficiencies are generally higher than cost efficiencies, as they must be in view of the fact that cost efficiency is the product of allocative and technical efficiency. However, it is noteworthy that there are few extremely low allocative efficiency scores. The average allocative efficiency score is about 71% and the most common score is in the range of 90 to 95%. Sixty-four firms are fully efficient based on the

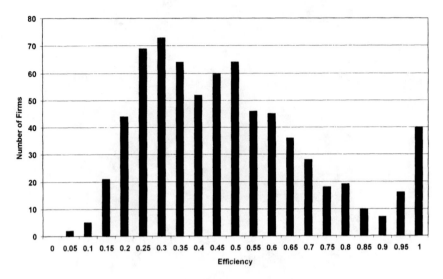

Figure 3-6.   Cost Efficiency: U.S. Life Insurers—1995

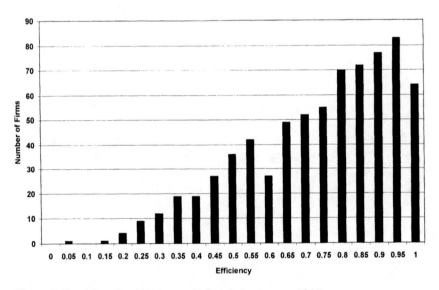

Figure 3-7.   Allocative Efficiency: U.S. Life Insurers—1995

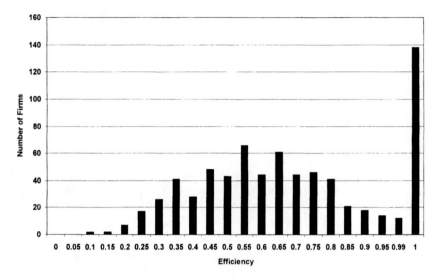

Figure 3-8.   Technical Efficiency: U.S. Life Insurers—1995

allocative efficiency criterion, registering perfect scores of one hundred percent. Allocative efficiency measures the success of firms in choosing the cost-minimizing combination of inputs. Thus, the results suggest that many firms in the industry appear to be quite successful in minimizing costs.

For many insurers with low cost efficiency, the primary reason for their low scores is technical inefficiency. This is shown by figure 3-8, which tabulates the technical efficiency of life insurers in 1995. Thirty % of insurers have technical efficiency scores less than 50%, and 40% have technical efficiencies less than 55%, contrasted with 18% less than 50% and 24% less than 55% for allocative efficiency. Although the number of firms with technical efficiency above 90% is about the same as for allocative efficiency, there are only 80 firms with technical efficiency between 75 and 90%, whereas 219 firms have allocative efficiency between 75 and 90%.

The technical efficiency problems in the U.S. life insurance industry are perhaps not surprising given the rapid advances that have taken place in recent years in computing and communications technology. They are also consistent with our questionnaire results, discussed in Chapter 7 of this book (Hitt, 1999). Our surveys and field research revealed that many insurers are struggling to manage the transition from outdated "legacy" mainframe computer systems toward a distributed computing environment. Insurers are also having difficulty in moving from a policy-focused computing environment that emphasizes record keeping and billing to a customer-focused environment that emphasizes sales and service. Our questionnaires, as well as the technical efficiency scores shown in figure 3-8, suggest that a few firms have succeeded in mastering the new technologies and new approaches to dealing with customers, while most firms have not made very much progress in addressing these challenges.

The distribution of revenue efficiency scores, shown in figure 3-9, reveals that the vast majority of life insurers have a long way to go in achieving the optimal choice of outputs (attaining revenue efficiency). Only about 40 insurers have achieved revenue efficiencies close to 100%, while the most common revenue efficiency score is in the 10 to 15% range. An amazing 81% of insurers have revenue efficiencies less than 50% and 90% have revenue efficiencies less than 75%. There are clearly opportunities for significant improvements in efficiency for firms that are able to master the customer-focused approach to selling and can succeed in withdrawing from unprofitable product lines while developing new products that add value for both customers and shareholders.

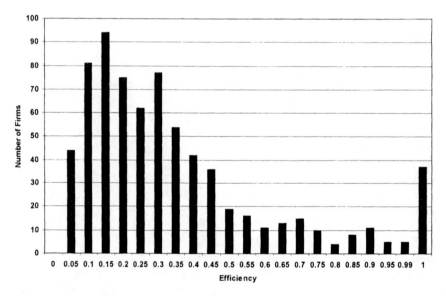

Figure 3-9.   Revenue Efficiency: U.S. Life Insurers—1995

3.3. The Industry's Efficiency Leaders

It is also of interest to consider the leading firms in the industry, as measured by the number of cases where a firm is in the reference or dominating set for other firms in the sample. Recall that the efficiency of each firm in the sample is measured by searching for a set of firms that can be combined mathematically to dominate the particular firm in question. If such a set does not exist, the firm is measured as fully efficient; but if such a set does exist, the firm is inefficient. Thus, one definition of a best practice firm is one that appears in the dominating sets of several other firms in the industry.

The 40 firms appearing in the largest number of dominating sets are shown in table 3-2.[13] All but one of the firms shown in the table have technical efficiency equal to 1.0. The average cost efficiency for the firms in table 3-2 is 84%, compared to 46% for the entire sample; and the average revenue efficiency is 65%, compared to 32% for the sample as a whole. Nearly all of the firms in the top 40 are specializing firms, i.e., they obtain more than half of their revenues from a single line of business. Thus, the solution algorithm tends to pick out specializing firms to replicate or dominate the firms in the industry that are not fully efficient. This result suggests that it is not necessary to diversify across multiple lines in order to succeed, at least in terms of technical and cost efficiency. A variety of distribution systems are employed by the top 40 firms, implying that it is possible to achieve efficiency using virtually any of the industry's current systems.

The top 40 firms in terms of revenue efficiency are shown in table 3-3. The firms are ranked in order of their revenue efficiency scores, and firms with comparable efficiency scores are sorted by asset size. Whereas nearly all of the firms in table 3-2 have technical efficiency equal to 100%, only 13 of the 40 firms in table 3-3 have revenue efficiency of 100%. Thus, it appears to be more difficult to achieve revenue efficiency than to achieve cost or technical efficiency. This result makes sense in economic terms because technical efficiency is primarily under the internal control of the firm, whereas revenue efficiency is more likely to be affected by the actions of competitors or by fluctuations in financial markets. As in the case of technical efficiency, few of the industry's largest firms appear among the top 40 revenue-efficient firms shown in table 3-3. The firms that appear in both table 3-2 and table 3-3 are shown in boldface in table 3-3. Only 15 firms are in the top 40 in both technical and revenue efficiency. Thus, many firms that are among the best practice set according to one type of efficiency criterion may be able to significantly improve their performance by attaining other types of efficiency goals. This result emphasizes the need to evaluate

Table 3-2.   The Top 40—Companies Appearing Most Often in Dominating Sets in 1995

Company	Group	Hits	Distribution System	Distribution of Premium Revenues By Line				
				Percentage of Ordinary Life	Percentage of Group Life	Percentage of Individual Annuities	Percentage of Group Annuities	Percentage of Accident & Health
MBL Life Assurance Corp	MBL Life Assurance Corp	270	Not Available	76.3	2.9	1.3	17.6	1.8
Landmark Life Insurance Co	Landmark Life Insurance Co	220	Agency	100.0	0.0	0.0	0.0	0.0
Gulf Atlantic Life Ins Co	Gulf Atlantic Life Ins Co	198	Broker	0.6	99.4	0.0	0.0	0.0
Foundation Health National	Foundation Health Group	127	Direct	0.4	3.8	0.0	0.0	95.8
Educators Mutual Ins Assoc	Educators Mutual Group	126	Agency	0.0	1.2	0.0	0.0	98.8
Royal Life Ins Co of New York	Royal Insurance Group	113	Agency	20.2	0.0	79.8	0.0	0.0
Federal Kemper Life Assurance	Kemper Group	113	Agency/Broker	59.0	0.0	41.0	0.0	0.0
Dallas General Life Ins Co	Dallas General Life Ins Co	97	Agency	0.9	0.0	0.0	0.0	99.1

Household Life Ins Co	Household International, Inc.	79	Agency	9.4	83.7	0.0	0.0	6.9
Conestoga Life Assurance Co	Conestoga Life Assurance Co	68	Agency	25.3	1.1	0.7	0.0	72.8
Country Investors Life Assur	Country Companies	67	Agency	42.5	0.0	57.5	0.0	0.0
Texas Imperial Life Ins Co	American Capitol Group	65	Agency	95.7	0.0	4.3	0.0	0.0
ITT Hartford Life & Ann	ITT Hartford Insurance Group	65	Not Available	18.5	0.1	80.5	0.4	0.5
American Mayflower Life of NY	First Colony Group	63	Broker	21.8	0.0	78.1	0.1	0.0
Fidelity Investments Life Ins	Fidelity Investments Group	62	Direct/ Broker	0.1	0.0	99.9	0.0	0.0
Connecticut General Life Ins	CIGNA Group	59	Agency/ Broker	20.7	11.9	4.9	46.8	15.8
CareAmerica Life Ins Co	CareAmerica Life Ins Co	59	Broker/ Agency	3.7	5.1	0.0	0.0	91.1
USAA Life Ins Co	USAA Group	59	Direct	32.3	0.3	62.0	0.5	4.9
American International Assur	American International Group	54	Broker/ Agency	2.7	0.6	17.8	76.1	2.9
Ministers Life Ins Co	Minnesota Mutual Group	52	Agency/ Direct	38.7	51.0	3.9	0.0	6.3

Table 3-2. Continued

Company	Group	Hits	Distribution System	Percentage of Ordinary Life	Percentage of Group Life	Percentage of Individual Annuities	Percentage of Group Annuities	Percentage of Accident & Health
Equitable of Colorado Inc	Equitable Group	51	Agency	100.0	0.0	0.0	0.0	0.0
Educators Insurance Company	Educators Mutual Group	41	Agency	0.0	9.8	0.0	0.0	90.2
PacifiCare Life and Health	PacifiCare Life and Health	41	Broker	0.0	2.6	0.4	0.0	97.0
Preferred Life Ins Co of NY	Allianz Insurance Group	41	Mass/Broker	0.0	6.1	84.2	0.0	9.7
John Alden Life Ins Co of NY	John Alden Group	39	Broker	8.9	0.0	90.9	0.0	0.2
American Life Ins Co of NY	Mutual of America Group	34	Mass/Direct	4.1	4.6	81.5	6.6	3.2
Fremont Life Ins Co	Fremont General Corp.	32	Agency	0.0	0.0	98.6	0.0	1.4
EPIC Life Ins Co	EPIC Life Ins Co	32	Agency	0.1	6.6	0.0	0.0	93.3
First Central National of NY	Beneficial Insurance Group	32	Mass	50.1	0.0	2.5	0.0	47.5

Company	Parent		Channel					
First Alexander Hamilton Life	Jefferson-Pilot Corp.	31	Agency/Broker	7.1	0.0	91.1	0.0	1.7
Zale Life Ins Co	Zale Insurance Group	29	Agency	39.6	30.3	0.0	0.0	30.1
Rushmore National Life Ins Co	American Financial Insurance Group	26	Agency	85.3	0.0	14.5	0.0	0.2
Ford Life Ins Co	SunAmerica, Inc.	24	Agency	6.1	0.0	93.9	0.0	0.0
International Life Investors	AEGON USA Inc.	22	Agency	7.7	0.4	61.7	0.0	30.1
Hartford Life Ins Co	ITT Hartford Insurance Group	22	Not Available	20.1	1.8	30.1	47.9	0.0
Merrill Lynch Life Ins Co	Merrill Lynch Ins Group, Inc.	21	Broker	36.3	0.0	38.7	25.0	0.0
Medical Life Insurance Co	Medical Life Group	21	Broker/Direct	1.4	81.3	0.0	0.0	17.4
Key Life Ins Co	Key Life Ins Co	21	Broker/Mass	86.9	6.2	5.0	1.9	0.0
Paragon Life Ins Co	General American Life Group	20	Broker/Direct	8.9	91.1	0.0	0.0	0.0
Empire Fidelity Investments	Fidelity Investments Group	19	Direct/Broker	0.0	0.0	100.0	0.0	0.0
Top 40 Average				25.8	12.5	33.1	5.6	23.0
Industry Average				25.9	6.3	23.1	27.7	17.0

Table 3-3. The Top 40 Companies in Revenue Efficiency

Company	Group	Revenue Efficiency	Distribution System	Distribution of Premium Revenues By Line				
				Percentage of Ordinary Life	Percentage of Group Life	Percentage of Individual Annuities	Percentage of Group Annuities	Percentage of Accident & Health
Employers Life Ins of Wausau	Nationwide Group	1.000	Direct	0.1	0.9	2.0	97.1	0.0
Berkshire Hathaway Life of NE	Berkshire Hathaway Ins Group	1.000	Not Available	0.0	0.0	9.7	90.3	0.0
Fremont Life Ins Co	Fremont General Corp.	1.000	Agency	0.0	0.0	98.6	0.0	1.4
American Partners Life Ins Co	American Express Financial Corp.	1.000	Direct	0.0	0.0	99.2	0.8	0.0
Educators Mutual Ins Assoc	Educators Mutual Group	1.000	Agency	0.0	1.2	0.0	0.0	98.8
Great American Life Assur Co	American Financial Insurance Group	1.000	Agency	55.8	0.0	44.2	0.0	0.0
EPIC Life Ins Co	EPIC Life Ins Co	1.000	Agency	0.1	6.6	0.0	0.0	93.3

Texas Imperial Life Ins Co	American Capitol Group	1.000	Agency	95.7	0.0	4.3	0.0	0.0
United Health & Life of OH	United HealthCare Corporation	1.000	Agency	0.0	2.4	0.0	0.0	97.6
Gulf Atlantic Life Ins Co	Gulf Atlantic Life Ins Co	1.000	Broker	0.6	99.4	0.0	0.0	0.0
National Capital Life Ins Co	National Capital Life Ins Co	1.000	Not Available	62.9	0.1	37.0	0.0	0.0
American Medical Security Ins Co	United Wisconsin Group	1.000	Not Available	0.0	0.0	0.0	0.0	100.0
Educators Insurance Company	Educators Mutual Group	1.000	Agency	0.0	9.8	0.0	0.0	90.2
Centurion Life Ins Co	Centurion Insurance Group	0.977	Direct	73.2	0.6	0.0	2.2	24.0
AIG Life Ins Co	American International Group	0.948	Broker/Agency	76.2	0.6	5.2	14.6	3.4
United Health & Life of IL	United HealthCare Corporation	0.894	Agency	0.0	1.5	0.0	0.0	98.5
USAA Life Ins Co	USAA Group	0.802	Direct	32.3	0.3	62.0	0.5	4.9

Table 3-3. *Continued*

Company	Group	Revenue Efficiency	Distribution System	Distribution of Premium Revenues By Line					
				Percentage of Ordinary Life	Percentage of Group Life	Percentage of Individual Annuities	Percentage of Group Annuities	Percentage of Accident & Health
Old Standard Life Ins Co	Metropolitan Mortgage Group	0.776	Broker	0.0	0.0	100.0	0.0	0.0
Foremost Life Ins Co	Foremost Corp. of America	0.751	Agency	0.0	0.0	0.0	0.0	100.0
First SunAmerica Life Ins Co	SunAmerica, Inc.	0.715	Broker	6.8	0.0	93.2	0.0	0.0
Delta Life and Annuity Company	Delta Life & Annuity Group	0.712	Agency	0.2	0.0	98.1	1.7	0.0
American Enterprise Life Ins	American Express Financial Corp.	0.712	Not Available	0.0	0.0	96.1	3.9	0.0
John Alden Life Ins Co of NY	John Alden Group	0.710	Broker	8.9	0.0	90.9	0.0	0.2
Family Guaranty Life Ins Co	Franklin American Corp.	0.687	Not Available	100.0	0.0	0.0	0.0	0.0

USG Annuity & Life Co	Equitable of Iowa Group	0.675	Broker	8.7	0.0	91.1	0.2	0.0
Anchor National Life Ins Co	SunAmerica, Inc.	0.673	Broker	1.7	0.0	53.6	44.7	0.0
PacifiCare Life and Health	PacifiCare Life and Health	0.661	Broker	0.0	2.6	0.4	0.0	97.0
Sterling Investors Life Ins Co	Sterling Investors Life Ins Co	0.647	Agency	0.0	4.9	0.3	0.0	94.8
Western United Life Assur Co	Metropolitan Mortgage Group	0.626	Broker	2.3	0.0	97.7	0.0	0.0
Preferred Life Ins Co of NY	Allianz Insurance Group	0.622	Mass/ Broker	0.0	6.1	84.2	0.0	9.7
Dallas General Life Ins Co	Dallas General Life Ins Co	0.614	Agency	0.9	0.0	0.0	0.0	99.1
Provident American Ins Co	Provident American Ins Co	0.610	Agency	0.8	0.0	2.1	0.0	97.1
American Life & Casualty Ins	American Life Holdings Group	0.607	Agency/ Broker	7.9	0.0	92.1	0.0	0.0
MBL Life Assurance Corp	MBL Life Assurance Corp	0.606	Not Available	76.3	2.9	1.3	17.6	1.8

Table 3-3. *Continued*

Company	Group	Revenue Efficiency	Distribution System	Percentage of Ordinary Life	Percentage of Group Life	Percentage of Individual Annuities	Percentage of Group Annuities	Percentage of Accident & Health
Royal Life Ins Co of New York	Royal Insurance Group	0.603	Agency	20.2	0.0	79.8	0.0	0.0
National Integrity Life Ins Co	ARM Financial Group	0.598	Broker	2.8	0.0	42.5	54.7	0.0
Paragon Life Ins Co	General American Life Group	0.596	Broker/ Direct	8.9	91.1	0.0	0.0	0.0
First Alexander Hamilton Life	Jefferson-Pilot Corp.	0.584	Agency/ Broker	7.1	0.0	91.1	0.0	1.7
First Fortis Life Ins Co	Fortis, Inc. Group	0.579	Direct/ Broker	1.3	20.8	0.2	0.0	77.7
SunAmerica Life Ins Co	SunAmerica, Inc.	0.570	Broker	3.9	0.0	32.1	64.0	0.0
Top 40 Average		0.789		16.4	4.6	38.9	8.5	30.5
Industry Average		0.321		25.9	6.3	23.1	27.7	17.0

efficiency and performance across multiple dimensions in order to obtain the most comprehensive view of the firm performance.

3.4. Economies of Scale

As mentioned above, an important economic objective of the firm is to operate at CRS. Firms that are not operating at CRS could reduce average costs per unit of output by becoming larger (if operating with IRS) or smaller (if operating with DRS). A firm's returns to scale has implications for operating strategy as well as its policy towards mergers and acquisitions. A firm in the DRS region of the cost curve might consider selling off unprofitable lines of business and subsidiaries, while a firm operating in the IRS region might consider a merger as a possible method for achieving optimal scale. Returns to scale in an industry also have implications for regulatory policy regarding industry consolidation.

Scale economies for U.S. life insurers are shown in figure 3-10, which graphs the percentages of firms operating with IRS, CRS, and DRS in 1995. The graph shows that the majority of firms in the three smallest asset-size

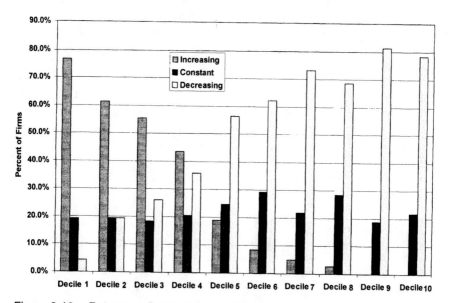

Figure 3-10.   Returns to Scale: U.S. Life Insurers

deciles are operating with IRS, i.e., these firms can reduce average costs by becoming larger. The majority of firms in the six largest asset-size deciles, on the other hand, are operating with DRS. These firms are already "too large" in the economic sense and could reduce average costs by becoming smaller. The percentage of firms that have achieved the economic ideal of operating with CRS is about one-fifth (22%) for the entire sample; and the percentage approaches 30% in size deciles 6 and 8. Somewhat surprisingly, the percentage of CRS firms in the largest size decile is about the same as for the sample as a whole. Thus, it is possible even for large firms to avoid scale diseconomies.

The firms in the largest size decile that operate with CRS are shown in table 3-4. These firms are of interest because further investigation may reveal best practice characteristics that may be adopted by other large firms to improve their scale economies. In comparison with the industry averages, the large CRS firms tend to acquire more of their revenues from asset accumulation products (individual life, individual annuities, and group annuities) than from indemnity products (group life insurance, accident and health insurance). Ninety % of the revenues of the large CRS firms comes from asset accumulation products in comparison with only 77% for the industry as a whole. There also appear to be benefits from specialization— 11 of the 13 firms shown in table 3-4 acquire the majority of their revenues from a single product line. This suggests that product focus strategies are associated with scale efficiency, i.e., large firms that write multiple lines are more likely to encounter DRS. The results also suggest that mergers among most of the largest firms in the industry cannot be justified on the basis of cost efficiency.

Seven of the 13 firms shown in table 3-4 employ mixed distribution systems that consist of brokers and tied agents, four firms rely exclusively either on agents or brokers, and one firm uses the direct distribution channel. Thus, it appears to be possible to achieve scale efficiency using a variety of distribution channels.

3.5. Efficiency by Distribution System

One of the most important issues confronting a life insurer is the choice of a system or combination of systems to distribute its products. A wide variety of distribution systems is available ranging from the traditional agency system to direct distribution through banks or securities dealers. Life insurance distribution systems can be categorized into four major groups:

Table 3-4.   Firms in Largest Asset Size Decile with Constant Returns to Scale

Company	Group	Distribution System	Distribution of Premium Revenues By Line				
			Percentage of Ordinary Life	Percentage of Group Life	Percentage of Individual Annuities	Percentage of Group Annuities	Percentage of Accident & Health
Principal Mutual Life Ins Co	The Principal Financial Group	Agency/ Broker	7.7	2.7	6.6	59.4	23.5
Connecticut General Life Ins	CIGNA Group	Agency/ Broker	20.7	11.9	4.9	46.8	15.8
MBL Life Assurance Corp	MBL Life Assurance Corp	Not Available	76.3	2.9	1.3	17.6	1.8
Western National Life Ins Co	Western National Life Ins Co	Agency	2.6	0.0	67.1	30.3	0.0
SunAmerica Life Ins Co	SunAmerica, Inc.	Broker	3.9	0.0	32.1	64.0	0.0
American General Life & Acc	American General Group	Agency	76.1	0.1	11.3	4.1	8.4
USG Annuity & Life Co	Equitable of Iowa Group	Broker	8.7	0.0	91.1	0.2	0.0
General Electric Capital	GE Capital Corporation Group	Broker/ Agency	15.1	0.0	73.4	11.5	0.0
USAA Life Ins Co	USAA Group	Direct	32.3	0.3	62.0	0.5	4.9
AIG Life Ins Co	American International Group	Broker/ Agency	76.2	0.6	5.2	14.6	3.4
Continental Assurance Co	CNA Insurance Group	Agency/ Broker	7.2	3.2	3.8	44.3	41.5
American Life & Casualty Ins	American Life Holdings Group	Agency/ Broker	7.9	0.0	92.1	0.0	0.0
American International Assur	American International Group	Broker/ Agency	2.7	0.6	17.8	76.1	2.9
	Average: CRTS Firms in Top Decile		26.0	1.7	36.1	28.4	7.9
	Average: Entire Industry		25.9	6.3	23.1	27.7	17.0

1. Agency distribution. The agency distribution system involves the sale of insurance through agents that "exclusively" distribute the insurer's products. Exclusivity has proven difficult for many insurers to enforce, however, so it is perhaps more accurate to characterize the agency system as a network of agencies that *primarily* distribute the insurer's products. Insurers using the agency system tend to devote more resources to training with the objective being the creation of "career agents," who will primarily or exclusively represent the company.

2. Distribution through insurance brokers. Insurers also can choose to distribute their products through insurance brokers that represent several insurers. Insurers generally do not provide much training to brokers but rather enter into contracts with brokers already in the market. Insurers that sell insurance through securities brokers also are classified as using a brokerage system, although insurance brokers and securities brokers often take significantly different approaches to marketing their products.

3. Direct distribution. This system consists of distribution through telephone contact between the customer and a sales representative. Although the representatives must be licensed as insurance agents in order to sell insurance, they are compensated mostly by salary rather than commissions, and, unlike agents, are usually company employees.

4. Mass marketing. Mass marketing insurers generally distribute insurance through the mails. Perhaps the most significant distinction between direct sales and mass marketing is that direct distribution may involve significant telephone counseling by the sales representative. In mass marketing, on the other hand, the buyer may place the order through the mails with little or no contact with company employees.

The average efficiencies by distribution systems are shown in figure 3-11. Companies that primarily use the brokerage distribution system are significantly more efficient than insurers that primarily rely on one of the other three systems for all types of efficiency except allocative efficiency. We believe that there are two major factors that account for the superiority of the brokerage system: 1) The insurer makes little direct investment in entering into a contract with a broker. The amount of training involved is minimal, and the company can exit or terminate the relationship without much cost if the broker's performance is unsatisfactory. In economic terms, dealing with brokers is almost exclusively a *variable cost* activity, i.e., there

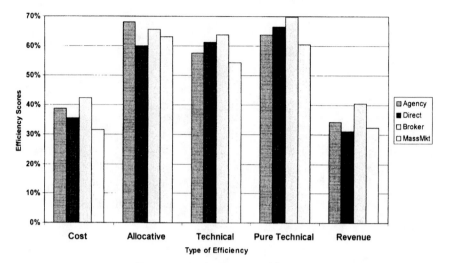

Figure 3-11.   Average Efficiency by Distribution System

is no fixed capital investment that the insurer loses if it decides to terminate the contract. And 2) because brokers have the opportunity to deal with
a wide range of insurers, the insurers who succeed in this marketing channel
have in a sense been "selected" by the brokers as firms that can provide
attractive products and investment yields to policyholders, while still being
able to compete in terms of the commission rates paid to the brokers. Firms
that can accomplish both objective are almost by definition more efficient
than other firms. Exclusive agents and company employees, on the other
hand, are likely to face search costs and transactions costs in switching
insurers, and as a result they are less likely to switch from a poorly
performing to a better performing insurer than are brokers.

     Firms using the agency system are more cost and revenue efficient than
firms using direct sales or mass marketing, but they are less technically
efficient than the direct marketers. The technical efficiency result makes
sense because direct marketing firms have been the leaders in the implementation of customer-focused data banks and sales-interface technologies.
The superiority of agency firms in cost and revenue efficiency is more
difficult to explain but may be attributable to the skill levels of professional
agents in comparison with direct marketing employees and the low "hit
ratios" of mass mailings. Agency insurers are also more allocatively efficient
than insurers using the other three types of distribution systems, i.e., on
average they are more successful at choosing cost-minimizing input

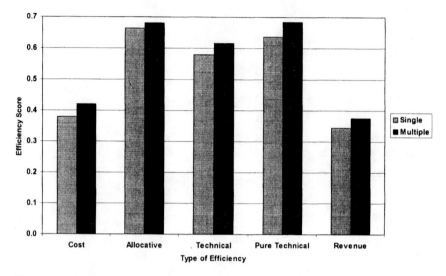

Figure 3-12.   Efficiency of Single versus Multiple Distribution Systems

combinations. Agency firms may be more allocatively efficient than direct or mass marketing firms because they have faced a somewhat less-dynamic environment in terms of changes brought about by technology and thus have had fewer opportunities to make mistakes in overinvesting or underinvesting in new computer or communications systems.

An important trend in the insurance industry over the past decade has been the move away from the use of a single distribution system to the use of multiple distribution systems. The majority of firms still use only one distribution system. However, 26% of firms that report using the agency system as their primary distribution system also report using at least one other system; and the comparable percentages for firms reporting the brokerage, direct, and mass marketing systems as the primary system are 31%, 39%, and 44% respectively.[14]

Figure 3-12 compares the efficiency of insurers that use only the agency system with insurers that are primarily agency insurers but also use at least one other distribution system.[15] Figure 3-12 shows that agency insurers using at least one other system are more efficient than those relying exclusively on the agency system. The efficiency differences, which are statistically significant for each type of efficiency shown in the figure, range from 1.7% for allocative efficiency to 4.7% for pure technical efficiency. Thus, even with the added complexity of a secondary distribution system, the multiple distribution-system firms are significantly more efficient. Of course, we cannot rule out a "self-selection" phenomenon here, i.e., more efficient and competent firms may be the ones that have chosen to launch an additional system or systems to market their products. Even if self-selection is present, however, the results imply that the added complexity of multiple distribution is not sufficient to overcome any efficiency advantage that these firms may have had before adopting secondary distribution systems.

4. Conclusions

Frontier efficiency methods constitute a new class of benchmarking techniques that have been applied to a wide variety of industries worldwide. The frontier approach analyzes the performance of specific firms by comparing them to efficient frontiers consisting of best practice firms in the same industry. This chapter uses the frontier efficiency approach to analyze the efficiency of U.S. life insurers. Five types of efficiency are estimated—pure technical, scale, allocative, cost, and revenue. Technical efficiency is the product of pure technical and scale efficiency, while cost efficiency is the product of technical and allocative efficiency. Efficiency scores range between 0 and 1, with a score of 1 indicating that a firm is fully efficient. Pure technical efficiency measures the success of firms in using the best available technology, and scale efficiency determines whether a firm is operating with IRS, CRS, or DRS. Allocative efficiency measures the firm's success in selecting the cost minimizing combination of inputs, while revenue efficiency gauges the firm's success in choosing the revenue maximizing combination of outputs.

Several important conclusions emerge from our analysis of the U.S. life insurance industry. Efficiency scores are relatively low in comparison with other financial industries such as property-liability insurance and banking. Moreover, the scores are widely dispersed among firms in the industry, with efficiencies ranging from as low as 5% to a high of 100% (full efficiency). The wide dispersion of efficiency scores is indicative of an industry where price competition is low, allowing inefficient firms to survive for extended periods of time. However, this situation is changing rapidly with the entry of nontraditional competitors such as banks, mutual fund companies, and securities brokers into the insurance market. The results of the intensified competition are evident in the efficiency trends in the industry—most types of efficiency, particularly cost and technical efficiency, have risen dramatically over the past several years. All indications are that competition will only continue to increase in the years to come. Thus, inefficient firms must improve their operating performance, merge with more efficient firms, or exit the market.

Most insurance firms are reasonably successful in choosing cost-minimizing combinations of inputs—allocative efficiency scores are highly skewed towards the high end. However, technical efficiency is generally quite low in the industry, leading to low average cost efficiency scores. The relatively low technical efficiency scores are perhaps not surprising, given the insurance industry's problems with outdated, legacy mainframe computers and the general failure of firms in the industry to develop customer-focused information systems technologies. Revenue efficiency is also highly dispersed and very low on the average. These results strongly suggest that the industry can expect a major restructuring in the years to come as competition forces inefficient firms to improve or exit the market.

Most relatively small insurers are operating with IRS, indicating the possibility for efficiency improvements through growth or merger. Most relatively large insurers operate with DRS, indicating that they are too large to produce their outputs efficiently. The fact that most large firms face DRS suggests that mergers in this segment of the industry generally cannot be justified on economic efficiency grounds. However, about 20% of the firms in the industry operate with CRS, including a number of firms in the top two size deciles. Further information on these firms may help to identify best practices that could be adopted by other large firms to improve their efficiency.

The most efficient firms in the industry tend to specialize—the vast majority of the top 40 insurers in terms of both technical and revenue efficiency gain more than half their revenues from a single line of business. Only 15 firms are in the top 40 in both technical and revenue efficiency, suggesting that even firms that score well in one type of efficiency could improve their operations by focusing on other types of efficiency where they do not rank as high.

The analysis of distribution systems reveals that the brokerage system is most efficient on the average. However, all types of distribution systems are represented among firms ranked in the top 40, indicating that it is possible to achieve high efficiency regardless of the choice of distribution system. Finally, a comparison of firms that use only one distribution system with those that use multiple systems reveals that the latter group of firms is more efficient on average. The difference is statistically significant, however, only for multiple distribution system firms that list the agency system as their primary distribution channel.

Additional research is needed to determine the causal factors underlying the efficiency patterns that we observe in our data. This research can be viewed as a search for both best practices that other firms might adopt and worst practices that other firms should avoid. Practices are construed broadly to encompass physical technology choices such as computer and communications systems as well as organizational choices such as management hierarchies, approaches to strategic decision making, human resource practices and related factors. The survey research reported elsewhere in this book provides a wealth of information on these topics, but further research is needed to provide a more complete picture of the drivers of firm efficiency.

Notes

1. This technical efficiency concept is identical to that discussed. It is just illustrated using a different approach.

2. The expense data discussed here is from the National Association of Insurance Commissions data files, which are based on the annual regulatory statements filed by insurers. The data on operating costs are for 1996.

3. In the past, researchers often used premiums as a measure of insurance output. However, this is incorrect, because premiums represent revenues, that is, price times quantity, rather than quantity (Yuengert, 1993).

4. All outputs (assets, benefits, and policy face values) are expressed in real terms by deflating to 1982, using the Consumer Price Index (CPI). To check the sensitivity of the results to the choice of output proxies, we also estimated efficiency for selected years of the sample period using a more highly disaggregated set of output measures. In this set of tests, we use assets to represent the intermediation function and incurred benefits in the five major lines of business, the number of new and existing policies, and the amount of insurance in force for group and individual life insurance to represent the risk-pooling and real service functions performed by insurers. The resulting efficiency scores were highly correlated with the scores obtained using the five outputs defined in the text. We did not use the disaggregated approach throughout the analysis because some of the variables were not reported by insurers for the earlier years of our sample period (1988 and 1989). Thus, we use the five-output approach in order to have a consistent set of output variables for the entire sample period.

5. Insurers are required to allocate investment income by line in their regulatory annual reports, and we use the reported allocations in defining output prices.

6. Some companies rely exclusively on agents to distribute their products, others have no agents and market their products through the mail or using telemarketing, while still others use a combination of agents and other distribution techniques.

7. The price of business services is the average weekly wage in SIC sector 7300, business services. The wage series is deflated to 1982 dollars using the CPI.

8. More specifically, the price of home office labor is defined as the average weekly wages for Standard Industrial Classification (SIC) Class 6311, life insurance companies. The wages for the state in which the company maintains its home office are used in the analysis to proxy for the price of home office labor. The price of agent labor is measured as the average weekly wages for SIC class 6411, insurance agents. A weighted average wage variable is used, with

weights equal to the proportion of an insurer's premiums written in each state. All wage variables are expressed in 1982 dollars by deflating by the CPI.

9. The amount of capital is deflated to 1982 dollars using the CPI.

10. As a robustness check, we also conducted the analysis using the insurers' reported average return on book equity over the three years prior to each sample year. Using this alternative cost of capital measure did not materially affect the results.

11. An alternative approach is to estimate econometric production, cost, revenue, and profit frontiers. The econometric approach differs from DEA in that it involves the use of a specific functional form for the frontiers. DEA, on the other hand, is non-parametric and thus does not require that the analyst specify a functional form. For further discussion and a comparison of the two methods, see Cummins and Zi (1998). We adopt DEA here because it provides an especially convenient method for estimating economies of scale. For more details on the DEA methodology, see Charnes et al. (1994) and Fried, Lovell, and Schmidt (1993).

12. This result is not properly interpreted as saying that banks and property-liability insurers are more efficient than life insurers, because the firms are not being compared to the same frontier. Thus, it does not imply that property-liability insurers could produce life insurance outputs more efficiently than life insurers. What this finding does imply is that the average life insurer is further from the life insurance frontier than the average bank (property-liability) insurer is from the frontiers for the banking industries.

13. The dominating sets are based on technical efficiency.

14. The source of the information on marketing systems is the A.M. Best Company, *Best's Key Rating Guide: Life-Health Edition*, various years.

15. Only agency insurers are shown in figure 3-12 because the efficiency differences between single and multiple distribution system firms are not statistically significant for insurers listing any of the other three major systems as their primary system.

References

Berger, Allen N., J. David Cummins, and Mary A. Weiss. "The Coexistence of Multiple Distribution Systems for Financial Services: The Case of Property-Liability Insurance," *Journal of Business* 70 (1997), 515–546.

Berger, Allen N. and David B. Humphrey. "Measurement and Efficiency Issues in Commercial Banking," in Z. Griliches (ed.), *Output Measurement in the Service Sectors*, National Bureau of Economic Research, Studies in Income and Wealth, Vol. 56. Chicago, IL: University of Chicago Press (1992), 245–79.

Carr, Roderick M. Strategic Choices, Firm Efficiency and Competitiveness in the U.S. Life Insurance Industry. Ph.D. diss. The Wharton School, University of Pennsylvania, Philadelphia, 1997.

Charnes, Abraham, William Cooper, Arie Y. Lewin, and Lawrence M. Seiford. *Data Envelopment Analysis: Theory, Methodology, and Application*, Norwell, MA: Kluwer Academic Publishers, 1994.

Cummins, J. David, Sharon Tennyson, and Mary A. Weiss. "Life Insurance Mergers and Acquisitions," in J.D. Cummins and A. Santomero (eds.), *Changes in the Life Insurance Industry: Efficiency, Technology, and Risk Management*, 1999.

Cummins, J. David and Mary A. Weiss. "Measuring Cost Efficiency in the Property-Liability Insurance Industry," *Journal of Banking and Finance* 17 (1993), 463–481.

Cummins, J. David, M. Weiss, and H. Zi. "Organizational Form and Efficiency: An Analysis of Stock and Mutual Property-Liability Insurers," forthcoming in *Management Science*, 1999.

Cummins, J. David and H. Zi. "Comparison of Frontier Efficiency Methods: An Application To the U.S. Life Insurance Industry," *Journal of Productivity Analysis* 10 (1998), 131–152.

Cummins, J. David., S. Tennyson, and M. Weiss. "Consolidation and Efficiency in the U.S. Life Insurance Industry," *Journal of Banking and Finance* 23 (1999), 325–357.

Farrell, M.J. "The Measurement of Productive Efficiency," *Journal of the Royal Statistical Society* A120 (1957), 253–281.

Fried, H.O., C.A.K. Lovell, and S.S. Schmidt (eds.), *The Measurement of Productive Efficiency*, New York: Oxford University Press, 1993.

Hitt, Lorin M. "The Impact of the Information Technology Management Practices on the Performance of Life Insurance Companies," in J.D. Cummins and A. Santomero (eds.), *Changes in the Life Insurance Industry: Efficiency, Technology, and Risk Management*, 1999.

Meador, Joseph W., Harley E. Ryan, Jr., and Carolin D. Schellhorn. "Product Focus Versus Diversification: Estimates of X-Efficiency for the U.S. Life Insurance Industry," Working paper, Northeastern University, Boston, MA, 1998.

Weiss, Mary A. "Analysis of Productivity at the Firm level: An Application to Life Insurers," *Journal of Risk and Insurance*, (March 1986), 49–83.

Weiss, Mary A. "Macroeconomic Insurance Output Estimation," *Journal of Risk and Insurance*, September, 1987, 582–593.

Yuengert, A. "The Measurement of Efficiency in Life Insurance: Estimates of a Mixed Normal-Gamma Error Model," *Journal of Banking and Finance* 17 (1993), 483–96.

4 EFFICIENCY AND COMPETITIVENESS IN THE U.S. LIFE INSURANCE INDUSTRY: CORPORATE, PRODUCT, AND DISTRIBUTION STRATEGIES

Roderick M. Carr, J. David Cummins,
and Laureen Regan

1. Introduction

The U.S. life insurance industry is facing increasing competition from alternative financial services providers, including banks, mutual funds, and investment firms, as well as from international competition.[1] Insurers traditionally have been sheltered from price competition that has resulted in low average efficiency and a wide dispersion in efficiency among firms in the industry. Although increased competition has resulted in improvements in overall efficiency during the past decade, many firms are still operating at levels of inefficiency that will be unsustainable in the long run. Firms that fail to improve are likely to face declining sales and downward pressure on profit margins, leading to their eventual exit from the market either through merger, insolvency, or voluntary withdrawal. Even firms that are successful in one area, such as in minimizing costs, may be less successful in attaining other objectives, such as maximizing revenues. Thus, the vast majority of firms in the industry can benefit from improvements in their operations; and even the leading firms must continually seek to innovate to maintain their leadership positions.

The purpose of this chapter is to provide guidance for firms seeking to improve their efficiency and operating performance by identifying the best practices that are used by efficient life insurers. Specifically, in this chapter, we focus on best practices in overall business strategy, product and marketing strategies, and information technology investments related to sales and service capabilities. In examining overall business strategies, we seek to determine whether adopting a "generic" strategy such as cost leadership, customer focus, or product differentiation is associated with superior performance. We also examine the relationship between efficiency and the adoption of narrow versus broad product offerings. The objective is to determine whether insurers should choose to specialize and focus on becoming the best in a few products, or to diversify, and offer a broad range of products that appeal to a wider variety of customers. Finally, most insurers have not yet succeeded in adopting customer-focused as opposed to policy-focused information systems, potentially placing them at a severe disadvantage relative to best practice insurers and other types of financial service providers. We investigate whether the capability of performing specific sets of sales and service tasks online is related to firm efficiency.

The most dramatic changes in the market for life insurance have occurred in the area of product distribution systems. The banks, mutual fund companies, and investment advisors that have recently entered the life insurance market generally can distribute insurance products much more cost effectively than traditional life insurers. This has motivated insurers to look beyond the agency system and to modify agency compensation systems in an attempt to compete more effectively. There has also been a proliferation in the use of multiple distribution systems by insurers. We attempt here to provide some evidence on the success of these innovations in improving firm performance.

In evaluating firm performance, we use the concept of economic efficiency. Economic efficiency is computed relative to best practice efficient frontiers, consisting of the dominant firms in the industry. Two major types of efficiency are used in our analysis—*cost efficiency* (the firm's success in minimizing costs) and *revenue efficiency* (the firm's success in maximizing revenues). The economic efficiency approach is superior to conventional measurement techniques such as the analysis of expense ratios and net income because it summarizes the firm's performance in a single statistic that takes into account differences among firms in product and input mix in a sophisticated multidimensional framework.[2]

To measure the association between business strategy and firm performance, we draw from an extensive survey of actual business practices of U.S. life insurers conducted under the auspices of the Wharton Financial

Institutions Center. The survey was developed based on extensive interviews with senior managers at a sample of 12 U.S. life insurers, and then administered to a sample of 66 life insurers differing widely in size, product mix, marketing strategies, and management practices. Responses from this sample of life insurers are used to measure overall strategies more precisely as well as to identify product and distribution system choices that might influence efficiency. The nature and scope of the survey is discussed at length in Chapter 2. In interpreting our findings, we also draw upon the results of extensive interviews with life insurance industry personnel conducted in conjunction with our own survey research.

The approach taken to identify best practices is to correlate the data on business practices obtained from the questionnaires with the efficiency scores obtained from cost and revenue efficient frontiers. The efficient frontiers are estimated using insurer financial data on outputs, inputs, output prices, and input prices. The frontiers are similar in concept to the efficient investment frontier familiar from finance but are estimated using a different mathematical approach, called data envelopment analysis (DEA), which is explained in more detail in Chapter 3 of this book (Cummins, 1999). The efficient cost frontier represents the lowest costs attained by firms in the life insurance industry in producing a given bundle of outputs, and the efficient revenue frontier represents the maximum revenues earned by firms in the industry while consuming a specified amount of inputs. These are best practice frontiers in the sense that they represent the minimum costs and maximum revenues, respectively, actually attained by firms operating in the industry.

In estimating the DEA cost frontier, a mathematical algorithm is used to find a combination of firms operating in the industry that jointly could produce a given insurer's outputs at a lower cost for a given set of input prices. If no such combination can be found, the given insurer is identified as "self efficient" and given an efficiency score of 1.0. If a set of firms can be found that jointly dominates the given insurer, the insurer is identified as being less than fully efficient. Its efficiency score is the ratio of the costs that would have been expended by the dominating combination of firms to the costs the insurer actually expended. The score is between 0 and 1 with higher scores indicating higher efficiency. For example, an efficiency score of 0.75 indicates that the given insurer is operating at 75% of full efficiency, or, equivalently, that it could reduce its costs by 25% while still producing the same level of output if it operated with the level of efficiency attained by the dominating set of firms.

The concept of revenue efficiency is similar to cost efficiency except that the dominating set of firms earns higher revenues for a given level of output production and input usage than the individual firm under analysis. Revenue efficiency is calculated as the ratio of the revenues of the given insurer to the revenues of the dominating set of insurers; and again a score of 1.0 indicates full efficiency. Dominating cost and revenues sets are calculated separately for each insurer in the sample. Thus, a byproduct of the analysis is the mathematical identification of each insurer's peer group of firms in the life insurance industry.

Given the estimates of cost and revenue efficiency, a two-stage analysis is conducted to identify business practices that are related to higher levels of efficiency. In the first stage, the *categorical analysis*, we calculate average efficiencies for firms using various business strategies and combinations of strategies that were identified as potentially efficiency-enhancing in our interviews and surveys. For example, we calculate average efficiencies for firms by distribution system (e.g., exclusive vs. non-exclusive agents) and range of product offerings (e.g., broad vs. narrow). Statistical tests are conducted to determine whether specific combinations of business strategies are more efficient than alternative strategy-combinations. In the second stage of the analysis, we utilize a statistical technique known as *multiple regression analysis* to search for efficient business practices. Multiple regression analysis enables us to identify efficient practices while holding constant other firm characteristics such as size that are likely related to efficiency. This is important because business practices may be related to the firm characteristics that are held constant in the regression analysis. For example, if distribution systems are correlated with firm size, we would not want to conclude that a given distribution system is more efficient than the alternatives when we are actually observing only a size effect. Multiple regression analysis enables us to avoid that type of error.

By way of preview, our categorical analysis reveals that insurers finding the right combinations of business strategies are more likely to be efficient than those choosing sub-optimal combinations of strategies. For example, firms that combine an exclusive or direct distribution system with a broad product range are on average more revenue efficient than firms combining these distribution systems with a narrow range of product offerings; and firms that combine a mass market strategy (rather than a niche market strategy) with a broad product range are more revenue efficient than firms combining a mass market strategy with a narrow product range. A number of important relationships are also identified in our regression analysis. For example, we find that direct writing insurers (those that market insurance through company employees) are more cost efficient than exclusive agency insurers and are more revenue efficient than both exclusive and non-exclusive agency firms. Insurers that write a higher proportion of their revenues in group annuities tend to be more cost efficient than those insurers with less of their business in group annuities. Conversely, writing more individual life insurance tends to have a net negative effect on efficiency. Technology choices also have an important effect on efficiency. For example, having computerized linkages with agents during the underwriting process is significantly related to both cost and revenue efficiency, probably because it results in higher sales-closing rates. Overall, the findings convey a positive message to insurers—choosing and effectively implementing the correct combinations of strategic choices can reduce costs and increase revenues.

The remainder of this chapter is organized as follows: In section 2, we discuss various hypotheses that have been advanced in the management, economics, and insurance literatures about the relationship between strategic choices and success in minimizing costs and maximizing revenues. We consider generic strategies such as those advocated by Porter (1980, 1985) as well as strategies specific to the insurance industry. The analysis in section 2 provides a conceptual framework for the empirical results and allows us to specify hypotheses to be tested using the efficiency and questionnaire data. The results of the hypothesis tests are presented in section 3, and our conclusions are presented in section 4.

2. Strategic Business Practices

Insurer managers continually make decisions regarding overall strategy, product mix, target markets, distribution systems, and information technology. In this section, we examine each of these decisions in turn and discuss their expected effects on life insurer efficiency in the light of the prevailing theories of firm performance that have been advanced in the managerial economics literature. We begin our discussion of strategic practices with an overview of the evolutionary development of corporate strategy concepts.

2.1. Strategic Choices and Performance

Over the past three decades, the emphasis on what constitutes corporate strategy has shifted from a focus on strategy as *long-range financial planning* (mid-1960s to mid-1970s), to a focus on the business environment emphasizing *industry analysis* (mid-1970s to mid-1980s). From the mid-1980s there has been an increasing emphasis on implementation issues with *people* (*human resources*) being the focus. Increasingly, today the focus of business strategy is on the firm, with its *core competencies* being seen as the source of sustainable competitive advantage.

The industry analysis approach to corporate strategy has tended to present firms within an industry as homogeneous. Senior management was seen as envisioning their firms as portfolios of industry exposures, with the role of management focused on forecasting desirable industries and positioning their portfolio to benefit. To a large extent during the 1970s and most of the 1980s, the ability of managers to influence the destiny of the firm was overlooked or denied. Indeed the "population ecology" view of the firm argues strongly that firms are almost incapable of change (Hannan and Freeman, 1977). Population ecologists argue that over time the characteristics of a population of firms change, not because the firms themselves change, but because firms that are not endowed with the necessary characteristics to survive in the changed environment will die out from bankruptcy, merger, or takeover. At any point in time, the more efficient firms are those with the unalterable endowment of resources that best fits the demands of the environment.

By way of example, for a considerable period of time in property and casualty insurance for homeowners and for auto insurance, independent agency companies have consistently and significantly lost market share to the direct writers. Yet, few if any independent agency firms have made the transition to direct writing—a clearly more cost efficient form of distribution for the personal lines. On the other hand, more recent studies provide support for the hypothesis that the higher costs of independent agency firms are attributable to their providing more services, for which they receive additional revenues, leading to insignificant differences in profit efficiency between direct writing and independent agency firms (Berger, Cummins and Weiss, 1997). A similar finding, that independent agents add something to revenue which is not reflected in cost analysis, is also reported by Regan and Tennyson (1996) and Regan (1997). However, these more recent findings too could be interpreted as consistent with population ecology theory. Even though independent agents may be rewarded for providing better services to small and medium size businesses than direct writers or in providing first-line underwriting capabilities for insurers, they are in effect succeeding based on the inherent characteristics of the independent agency system. The fact remains that there is little migration of firms or agents between the two systems.

In the retail life insurance industry, although industry leaders see nontraditional firms such as banks and securities firms as a major threat because of their relative efficiency in distribution, they find it difficult, if not impossible, to substantially reform or abandon their traditional agency-based form of distribution and, to a lesser extent, servicing. An example of a life insurer which has undergone such a radical transformation is Great-West Life. In 1993 Great-West Life moved to entirely replace its career agency system of distribution with an independent distribution organization. The change, initiated by its Canadian parent, amounted to a revolution in which former distribution relationships were abandoned and a new strategy was formed and implemented.

In contrast to the somewhat deterministic perspective of population ecology theory and consistent with the story of radical change at Great-West Life, the *evolutionary* or *resource-based* view of the firm as developed by Nelson and Winter (1985) argues that firms can learn, with difficulty, over time. How firms learn, how knowledge is transferred within and between firms, and the way in which the learning process shapes firms are all elements of a theory that focuses on the internal workings of the firm as the origin of firm differences and as an explanation as to why change occurs and/or why differences persist over time. This resource-based view of the firm differs dramatically from the earlier perceptions of firms as homogeneous entities differentiated only by size. The move by many life insurers to adopt secondary distribution systems can be interpreted as consistent with the evolutionary view.

By the mid-1980s a number of studies had been conducted that supported the resource-based view of the firm by highlighting the extent of heterogeneity in firm performance within industries. Not only do individual firms perform very differently from each other at one particular point in time and over a period of time, but these differences in firm performance seem to persist over extended periods of time in many industries, even industries that appeared to be competitively structured.

In the resource-based view of the firm, the sources of heterogeneity in firm performance are simply the differing resources and competencies of the firm. A *core competency* is a current or potential source of sustainable competitive advantage if there is heterogeneity among resources and technology, some mobility of factors of production, and there are both ex ante and ex post limits to competition. The quest to identify, control, enhance, and exploit the core competencies of the firm is founded on the belief that firms are different and managers can make a difference. Prahalad and Hamel (1990) describe how core competencies, particularly those that involve collective learning and are knowledge-based, are enhanced as they are applied. Such resources may provide both the basis and the direction for the growth of the firm and this may explain why some firms are relatively more efficient than others.

Which of these theories applies to the life insurance industry? It is likely that there are some important messages from all of them. For example, some firms in the industry may not possess the ability to adapt and, thus, are ecologically doomed. Others may be able to evolve with the market by shedding their unsuccessful practices and exploiting their core competencies or by adopting new strategies and products that succeed in the new environment. The analysis of economic efficiency in the life insurance industry (Chapter 3 of this book, Cummins, 1999) clearly supports the view that insurers are extremely heterogeneous in terms of their performance, while our survey research reveals that strategies and management practices in the industry are also diverse. Thus the more astute firms in the industry may be able to succeed in the new environment by evolving to wards a set of best practice approaches that exploit their core competencies.

Two key questions of interest to managers and strategists are: 1) What are the strategic choices managers can make given the fact the firm is established in a particular industry? And 2) how do these choices impact the efficiency and performance of the firm? The remainder of this chapter attempts to cast light on the answers to both of these questions.

2.2. Generic Corporate Strategies

An influential view of corporate strategy is that firms which clearly follow one of three *generic business strategies* will outperform competitors with muddled strategies, or strategies which do not match their business objectives (Porter, 1980, 1985). This argument holds that a firm with a clear focus is one that has carefully identified its strengths and weaknesses within the competitive framework. The three generic strategies are *cost leadership*, *customer focus*, and *product differentiation*. A cost leadership strategy is one in which firms adopt a strategic focus on cost minimization, price leadership, and efficiency. A customer-focused strategy is one in which the firm concentrates on specific geographic or customer groups and is customer-oriented rather than product-oriented. A product-differentiation strategy is more product/service-oriented, with the firm offering an extensive and integrated range of financial services products. The three generic strategies are portrayed in figure 4-1. A firm following a generic strategy is viewed as operating at one of the corners of the strategy triangle in the figure. Such firms are predicted to outperform firms caught in the middle of the strategy space, the "middle ground." If this hypothesis is correct, a firm that follows one of the three strategies is expected to be more efficient than a firm that does not have a clear strategy. Further, it seems likely that a firm

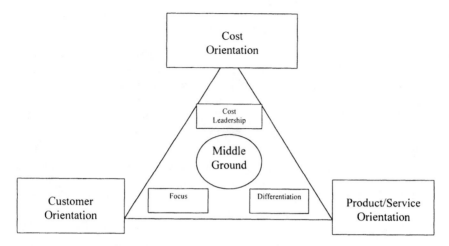

Figure 4-1.   Strategy Space

that adopts a cost leadership strategy will have a higher level of cost efficiency than one which adopts either a customer-focused or product differentiation strategy. However, any of the three strategies, but not the "middle ground" approach, could be associated with revenue efficiency. On the other hand, it is possible that these broadly defined strategies are too generic to apply to an idiosyncratic industry such as life insurance and/or that the generic strategies are dominated by industry-specific strategies, particularly in the important areas of product distribution systems and technology.

In our industry survey, senior executives of life insurance firms were asked to rank a series of statements that define corporate strategy along the dimensions of cost leadership, customer focus, and product differentiation. Firms were then classified in terms of the three generic strategies, and these classifications were used to determine whether differences in efficiency across life insurers were at least partly attributable to differences in strategic focus. If a firm did not adopt one of these strategies, it was assigned to the middle-ground (mixed strategy) class. The classification mechanism is defined in the Appendix.

2.3. Insurance Marketing Strategies

In addition to generic strategies, which take a global view of the objectives of the firm, we also investigate in this chapter a number of industry-specific strategic choices that are available to life insurers. We focus on choices relating to product and distribution strategies as well as information technology capabilities relating to sales and service.

2.3.1. What to Offer. The life insurance industry distributes a broad range of products, many of which are sensitive to mortality and interest rate changes. Longer-term contracts, including whole life insurance and annuities, are more subject to variability in profits because of sudden changes in the underlying environment than are shorter-duration contracts such as term insurance. This is because term insurance premiums can be renegotiated at the renewal date. Furthermore, longer-term contracts expose the insurer to the risk of dis-intermediation. This is a significant risk because it takes several years to recover the initial costs of marketing and administrative expense associated with the sale of a new policy.

Products also vary in complexity, with annuities being less complex than ordinary life insurance and group insurance less complex than individual insurance (Gupta and Westall, 1994). Annuities are generally less complex than ordinary life insurance because annuities are primarily an investment product where yield rates are relatively easy to determine. Ordinary life insurance includes a more significant mortality component as well as several embedded options with the result that prices and investment yields are less transparent. Group insurance is less complex than individual insurance for a number of reasons. First, since there is one master contract, administrative costs are lower. Also, group life contracts generally require little or no individual evidence of insurability, being underwritten on the basis of the group as a unit. Therefore, adverse selection concerns are minimized. Finally, most group insurance is written as yearly renewable term insurance, one of the most standardized insurance products in existence (Black and Skipper, 1994).

More complex products might require more inputs to produce, particularly in underwriting and sales. It seems likely then that the choice of product offerings can result in differences in observed efficiency levels across insurers. This implies that insurers writing proportionally more business in standardized or less complex lines might have higher levels of cost efficiency. Life insurer product mix is measured by a series of variables representing the share of new premiums or annuity consideration generated from ordinary individual life, group life, individual annuities, and group annuities. These are calculated both from the NAIC data and from the survey responses.

2.3.2. Breadth of Product Range. If an insurer concentrates in only one or a few products, investments in human capital, especially in training and experience, are necessarily lower than they would be for a more diverse product range. Increased concentration in a narrower line of products implies potentially greater specialization of skills and technology across a smaller range. Further, technology might be a suitable substitute for some investments in human capital. The number of managers and the layers of management also are likely to increase with the breadth of an insurer's product offerings, potentially increasing coordination costs and costs arising from principal/agent conflicts. Moreover, for a narrowly focused insurer, the potential for internal conflict over priorities and the associated costs of conflict management would likely be lower than for an insurer offering a broader range of products. Thus, it might be expected that more specialized insurers would have higher levels of cost efficiency.

On the other hand, a narrower product range reduces opportunities to benefit from potential scope economies in product distribution and inhibits the ability of the firm to serve a diverse client base. A narrower product range might also expose the insurer to a greater risk that competitors could replicate the firm's products and thus capture market share. Perhaps the most serious risk, however, is that a firm which is very specialized will not be able to serve the diverse financial needs of its existing customers. This seems to be a particular concern in practice as we observe mergers and acquisitions among financial services firms seeking to be one-stop shopping outlets. On the other hand, if life insurance customers primarily shop for products rather than providers, a focus on "being the best" in a selected group of products may be superior to a broader product strategy. Thus, revenue efficiency may be higher or lower for specialized firms, depending on the degree to which the firms is rewarded in the product market for offering a broader range of choices versus gaining a higher degree of expertise in a narrower product range.

To measure the breadth of a firm's product offerings, a firm is defined as narrowly focused if it offered 7 or fewer of the 15 life insurance products from the commonly offered products shown in table 4-1. As shown in figure 4-2, this results in slightly less than one-half of the firms in the sample being classified as offering a narrow product range. Table 4-1 also shows the proportion of insurers in our survey selling and manufacturing each of the 15 products. A firm is defined as manufacturing a product if it is an insurance company and bears the underwriting risk associated with the product. Non-insurers (such as mutual fund companies) offering "private label brand" policies underwritten by an insurer are defined as not being the manufacturers of the products. The most common types of products include various types of annuities, individual term life, universal life, and individual ordinary life insurance.

Table 4-1.   Breadth of Product Range

Companies offering 7 or fewer of the following products are defined as offering a narrow set of products. The variable NARROW = 1 for these firms and = 0 otherwise.

Product	Proportion Offering Product (%)	Proportion Manufacturing Product (%)
Individual term life	90	77
Single premium deferred annuities	82	69
Universal life insurance	82	74
Immediate annuities	82	73
Flexible premium deferred annuities	77	64
Individual ordinary life (whole life)	79	67
Second-to-die life insurance	67	53
Single premium life insurance	61	52
Disability income insurance	54	27
Variable annuities	56	48
Variable life insurance	50	44
First-to-die life insurance	45	35
Long term care insurance	39	17
Individual health insurance	27	12
Industrial life insurance	3%	3%

2.3.3. Target Markets.   Life insurers also make strategic decisions about whether to focus on specific market segments or to market to a broad range of customers. Similar to the argument above, if an insurer focuses on one or a few target markets, it might be likely to use its resources more efficiently. This is particularly so if individual sales to the targeted market segment are larger on average. That is, if an insurer focuses on clients that generate relatively more premium volume per sale (or more insurance in force per contract), then that insurer is likely to have higher levels of efficiency because the fixed costs of product distribution and policy issue are spread over a larger revenue base. In addition, niche marketing insurers have greater opportunity to design their products to serve the specific needs of the target market, potentially increasing customer satisfaction and leading to higher policy retention rates. Firms that adopted a niche strategy were identified from responses to the survey. If a firm indicated that it targeted specific customer segments, and also identified at least two but no more than four specific segments, then it was classified as a niche marketer. If a firm focused on more than four target markets, defined

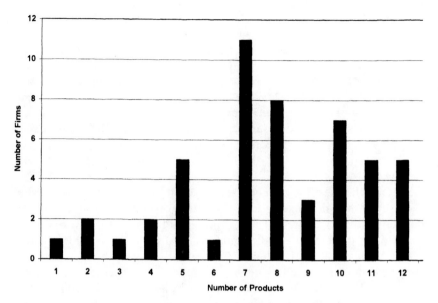

Figure 4-2. Product Range—Frequency Distribution For Survey Firms

markets broadly, or did not target-market at all, then it was classified as a non-niche marketer.

2.3.4. Distribution Strategy. In addition to choosing product offerings and target markets, insurers also face strategic decisions about the way to distribute their products and services. In the retail life insurance industry, where product distribution costs range from 15% of premiums for annuities and deposit type products to 55% of premiums (or even higher) for individual life products, distribution strategy can have a significant impact on efficiency.

The most common method of life insurance distribution is the exclusive agency system. With this method, the company builds its own sales force by recruiting, financing, training, and supervising new agents to exclusively represent it. These functions may be carried out by the insurer directly through company employees or under the insurer's direction through managing general agents appointed by the insurer. Insurers may also distribute products through company employee representatives. Exclusive dealing through agents or employees accounts for approximately 57% of life insurance premium volume.

Life insurance is also sold through brokers, who represent several competing insurers. This system includes insurers using insurance brokers as well as marketing through stockbrokers, mutual fund companies, and banks.[3] Brokerage arrangements account for approximately 40% of life and annuity premium revenue.

Direct response marketing is also used in life insurance. In direct response merchandising arrangements, the insurer targets potential clients and uses mail, telephone, mass market advertising, and, increasingly, the Internet to market products. Direct response may also include mass merchandising where the insurer targets large groups of potential insureds, such as employee groups or members of professional associations. This approach represents less than 2% of total premium volume, but it is expected to grow.[4]

Several theories have been developed to explain the relationship between product mix and optimal distribution strategy choice. One set of theories holds that more efficient firms should be those which optimally match their products with the appropriate distribution strategy. Porter (1980) argues that more standardized, narrowly focused products are more efficiently marketed by tightly controlled employees. This is because employees are not required to exercise much discretion in the sale of these products. However, employees forego the opportunity to cross-sell products when the insurer's offerings are relatively narrow. Therefore, it might more be efficient to market narrowly defined products through non-exclusive channels, where the sales representatives can diversify their own product portfolios.

Transactions cost economics also has been used to model product distribution choice. Transactions cost economics argues that a firm will internalize successive stages of production when the costs of conducting transactions in the open market are higher (Coase, 1937; Williamson, 1979, 1985). In the life insurance product distribution context, this argument implies that more vertically integrated exclusive dealing and employee distribution systems will be more efficient when products are more complex, markets are more subject to uncertainty, and relationship-specific assets are important in the transaction. (The phrase relationship-specific assets or asset specificity refers to the extent to which non-redeployable investments are needed to support an exchange.[5]) When transactions are frequent and supported by relationship-specific investments, vertical integration protects against opportunism that might arise between trading partners. This opportunism becomes more likely and more costly as uncertainty and complexity increase (Williamson, 1985). This implies that more vertically integrated firms should be characterized by higher levels of relationship-specific assets, and specialize in more complex products and markets.[6] Furthermore, because sales representatives of non-exclusive

Table 4-2. Product Range, Distribution Channel and Firm Efficiency (expected relative average efficiency score for firms in each cell)

	Product Range	
Distribution Channel	Narrow* (7 or fewer product offerings)	Broad** (8 or more product offerings)
Non-exclusive agency	DEA_{NN}/DEA_N = higher	DEA_{NB}/DEA_B = lower
Exclusive agency	DEA_{EN}/DEA_N = lower	DEA_{EB}/DEA_B = higher
Direct	DEA_{DN}/DEA_N = higher	DEA_{DB}/DEA_B = lower

Key: DEA_N = average efficiency for all firms with a narrow product range, DEA_{NN} = average efficiency for firms with a narrow product range using brokers (non-exclusive agents), DEA_{EN} = average efficiency for firms with a narrow product range using exclusive agents, DEA_{DN} = average efficiency for firms with a narrow product range using direct selling or mass marketing. DEA_B = average efficiency for all firms with a broad product range, DEA_{NB} = average efficiency for firms with a broad product range using brokers (non-exclusive agents), DEA_{EB} = average efficiency for firms with a broad product range using exclusive agents, DEA_{DB} = average efficiency for firms with a broad product range using direct selling or mass marketing.

dealing insurers can offer the products of competing insurers, insurers with very narrowly focused products are more likely to operate through non-exclusive channels. If this hypothesis is correct for the life insurance market, exclusive dealing and direct writing insurers should offer a broad product range and focus more on individual life insurance, and non-exclusive dealing insurers should be more narrowly focused and specialize in group products and annuities.

For survey respondents, the type of distribution system was determined from questionnaire responses. Exclusive dealing insurers are those using agents who are prohibited or discouraged from selling the products of competitors, while non-exclusive dealing insurers are those using brokers who also offer the products of competitors. Both exclusive agents and brokers are compensated primarily by commission. Direct writing insurers are those offering insurance through salaried company employees, where selling involves in-person or telephone contact between the employee and the customer so that the employee must be a licensed agent. Mass marketing insurers are those selling through the mail, the Internet, or automatic vending machines—channels where person-to-person contacts are minimal.

Based on agency theory and transactions cost economic analysis, table 4-2 sets out the predicted relationship between *fit* and *performance*. Fit is defined as the distribution channel that, at least in theory, mitigates opportunism and transaction costs for a given breadth of product range, leading to relatively superior performance in terms of firm efficiency. Grouping firms by product range/marketing channel, we test for statistically significant differences in the relative efficiency of firms in the different cells after controlling for the fact that the product range is broad or narrow. Insurers distributing products through brokers are expected to be more successful if they focus on a narrower range of products and also if they focus on more standardize products than insurers using agents. Therefore, within all firms classified as having a narrow product range, the efficiency scores of insurers using brokers should be higher than those for exclusive dealing insurers. Conversely, within the class of all insurers offering a broad range of products, efficiency scores for exclusive dealing and direct writing insurers should be higher than those for brokerage insurers.

2.4. Information Technology

It might also be argued that firms using information technology more intensively are more efficient than those which rely less on automation. Insurers invest heavily in technology infrastructure to manage the large volumes of data required to operate efficiently, including actuarial, underwriting, claims, and policyholder account information. These systems may reduce inefficiency by eliminating duplication and speeding communications between client, agent, and insurer. Moreover, technology is likely to be more effective for simpler products, and may be a substitute for human capital. The type of technology investment might also be an important determinant of efficiency. For example, firms that maintain customer-focused rather than product-focused databases might have an efficiency advantage over rivals in lead generation and in maintaining existing customer records.[7]

However, the use of technology to improve underwriting and client service is relatively new in this industry. Therefore, firms that have recently made investments in new technology may take time to develop the skills necessary to realize the value of the investments. While these investments are made with the expectation that efficiency will increase, a negative relationship between high current spending on technology, or a recent major system change, and efficiency might support the idea that initial learning is difficult and costly (Nelson and Winter, 1985).

There is also likely to be a relationship between investments in information technology and an insurer's distribution system. Increases in information technology investments increase the firm-specific knowledge required of employees and agents, which increases training costs. A desire to protect investments in employee skills could lead to the use of a more vertically integrated distribution system. If these investments are made in a non-exclusive relationship, the value may be expropriated by the agent. For example, a broker might access information from the investing insurer and use it to place business on more favorable terms with another insurer. Even in the absence of this type of self-dealing, however, it would take longer for the non-integrated insurer to recover the cost of the investments because it gets only a fraction of the insurance placed by each agency.

One measure of the intensity of technology investments is the ratio of insurer expenditures on information technology (including depreciation and rental cost) to the number of insurance contracts in force. This measure is derived from the NAIC accounting statements. It is expected that efficiency will increase as the firm invests relatively more in technology if technology is an efficient substitute or complement for human resources.

The survey data allow us to measure the uses of technology more precisely and to relate these expenditures to firm efficiency. Respondents were asked whether their employer maintains a relational database that tracks policyholder account and transaction data and makes this information accessible to personnel servicing the account. The existence of a relational policyholder-focused data base is expected to generate an efficiency advantage due to enhanced customer satisfaction and greater success in cross-selling. Executives were also asked if there were electronic communications links between agents, underwriters, customer service representatives, and claims settlement service providers. The expectation is that such links speed communications and result in less duplication and waiting time for services such as policy approval and claims settlement. In addition, computerized linkages between the company and agent during the underwriting process have the potential to reduce the time required to issue policies, which potentially increases the sales closing rate.

Insurers might also invest in expert underwriting systems. These are software systems that make underwriting decisions automatically, based on a set of guidelines developed by underwriting professionals. If the insurance application passes through the system with no problems, it is automatically approved (or declined) and priced. However, if the application does not conform to the guidelines, it is reviewed by a human underwriter. Expert underwriting systems are designed to economize on underwriting expenses for routine applications and to allow underwriters to focus on relatively complex or difficult cases where discretion is required. These systems are relationship-specific investments in the sense that the insurer must invest resources to design and implement the system, and agents and underwriters must also invest time and effort to master the system. Since expert underwriting systems are likely to work most effectively for relatively standardized products, these investments might be more likely for non-exclusive dealing insurers. Our analysis contains an indicator variable set equal to 1 if the insurer uses an expert underwriting system, and 0 otherwise. Expert underwriting systems are expected to be positively associated with efficiency scores.

We also measure the insurer's investment in online communications by examining the number of policy service tasks that can be performed online. One often cited source of inefficiency in the insurance industry is the time it takes to approve policies, make policy changes, issue policy loan approvals, and perform other routine maintenance services. Respondents were asked whether their firm had the ability to perform the following services online:

- premium calculation
- name/address change
- policy issue
- customer profile generation
- policy loan approval
- surrender valuation
- policy cancellation

If these investments do result in an increase in efficiency, then we would expect more insurers to adopt them. Each of these factors is examined individually. Online capability increases with the number of tasks performed online and is expected to be positively associated with efficiency.

2.5. Other Factors Which Might Influence Efficiency

While the strategic decisions discussed above are likely to impact relative firm efficiency, other factors that are less immediately affected by managerial decision making are also likely to play a role in determining efficiency differences across life insurers. Among these are firm size, market share, and growth rate.[8] Each of these is addressed below.

2.5.1. Firm Size. The relationship between firm size and efficiency relates to the economic concept of *economies of scale*. Economies of scale are present when larger firms are able to operate at lower average costs per unit than their smaller rivals. As shown in Chapter 3 of this book (Cummins, 1999), the majority of insurers in the three smallest asset-size deciles (less than $100 million in assets) are operating with increasing returns to scale, i.e., these firms can reduce average costs by becoming larger. The majority of firms in the six largest asset-size deciles (greater than $300 million in assets), on the other hand, are operating with decreasing returns to scale. These firms are already "too large" in the economic sense and could reduce average costs by becoming smaller. The percentage of firms that have achieved the economic ideal of operating with constant returns to scale is about one-fifth (22%) for the entire sample; and the percentage approaches 30% in size deciles 6 and 8. Somewhat surprisingly, the percentage of constant returns to scale firms in the largest size decile is about the same as for the sample as a whole. Thus, it is possible even for large firms to avoid scale diseconomies.

Because of the link between firm size and average costs, it is necessary to control for size effects when measuring the impact of other strategic decisions on efficiency differences. Firm size is measured as the value of firm assets exclusive of separate accounts. Since firms vary widely in size within our sample, the value of assets is transformed by taking the natural logarithm of assets in non-separate accounts.[9]

2.5.2. Market Share. By focusing on a small number of tightly defined markets, a firm might increase its ability to become the dominant player in those markets, even if it is not especially large in absolute terms. Small, focused, lean organizations may have an advantage over larger rivals that pursue a broader marketing strategy either in terms of product offerings or geographical scope of operations. On the other hand, if more efficient firms are more likely to achieve market share gains, we may observe larger firms with broader marketing strategies dominating many markets. In any event, if there is a relationship between market share and firm performance, it must be taken into account when analyzing the other drivers of efficiency.

The most common measures of market share are share of premiums in a state, line of business or national market, or the share of assets held by the firm. Unfortunately, these measures are highly correlated with each other and with firm size. An alternate measure that indicates the insurer's dominance in a particular market is the *market power index*. This measure is developed by averaging the insurer's share of business written in ordinary and group life, individual and group annuities, and accident and health premiums in each of the 50 states and Washington D.C. relative to the dominant insurer in the state.[10] The index ranges from 0 to 1, with the dominant insurer in the state having a market power index value of 1. This value is significantly less correlated with absolute firm size than the firm's share of premiums or assets but does discriminate among insurers on the basis of relative importance across markets.

2.5.3. Growth Rate.   Firms that are growing more rapidly than their competitors might exhibit lower levels of efficiency because costs associated with market research, product development, marketing, and initial sales expenses can adversely impact current earnings. Therefore, a firm that pursues a more rapid growth strategy should expect to have relatively lower levels of efficiency, at least in the short term. To properly identify the drivers of efficiency differences, we need to control for differences among insurers in growth rates. Growth rate is measured by the average annual change in premium volume between 1993 and 1995. Table 4-3 summarizes the strategic and control variables used here as well as the expected relationship between these variables and life insurer efficiency.

3. Results of the Analysis

In this section we explore the relationships between business strategies and efficiency by correlating insurer efficiency scores obtained from an analysis of insurer financial data with the business practices identified in our questionnaire survey. Two principal types of efficiency are examined, *cost efficiency* and *revenue efficiency*. Both are estimated using a mathematical technique known as *data envelopment analysis* (DEA). The technique involves the estimation of efficient cost and revenue frontiers using data on life insurers outputs, inputs, output prices, and input prices. The efficiency of each insurer in the industry is then measured relative to the efficient frontiers. Firms that are fully efficient have efficiency scores equal to 1.0, while those that are not fully efficient have efficiency scores between 0 and 1.0, with higher efficiency scores indicating higher levels of efficiency.

The efficiency scores are correlated with business practices using a two-stage approach. In the first stage, the *categorical analysis*, we compute average efficiencies for insurers with different combinations of product strategies, marketing strategies, and technological capabilities. Life insurers are categorized based on size, business mix, and distribution strategy

Table 4-3. Strategic and Control Variables: Expected Effects on Efficiency

Variable (+/–)	Expected Effect on Efficiency
General Strategy	(+)
Cost Leadership	(+)
Product Differentiation	(+)
Customer Focus	(+)
Mixed	(–)
Lines of Business	
Ordinary Individual Life	(+/–)
Group Life	(+/–)
Individual Annuities	
Group Annuities	
Accident and Health	
Narrow	(+/–)
Niche	(+/–)
Distribution System Choice	
Non-exclusive Dealing	(–)
Exclusive Dealing	(+)
Direct	(+)
Information Technology	
Expenditures per Policy	(+)
Expert Underwriting System	(+)
Electronic Links	(+)
Customer Database	(+)
Online Capability	
premium calculation	(+)
name/address change	(+)
policy issue	(+)
customer profile generation	(+)
policy loan approval	(+)
surrender valuation	(+)
policy cancellation	(+)
Control Variables	
Size	(+)
Market Power	(+)
Growth Rate	(–)

to determine whether significant differences in average efficiency exist across groups. These tests provide evidence on hypotheses concerning combinations of business strategies that are likely to be successful.

The second stage of the analysis examines relationships between business practices and efficiency using a statistical technique known as *multiple regression analysis*. Multiple regression analysis involves the estimation of a linear equation that relates efficiency (the dependent variable in the equation) to a set of strategy and control variables (the independent or explanatory variables).[11] A positive sign on the estimated coefficient of an explanatory variable indicates that higher values of that variable are associated with higher levels of efficiency, and a negative sign implies that higher values of the variable are associated with lower levels of efficiency. Multiple regression analysis enables us to measure the effect of each independent variable on efficiency while holding constant (controlling for) the effects of the other variables included in the equation. Separate equations are estimated for cost and for revenue efficiency.

3.1. Categorical Analysis

Table 4-4 illustrates the relationship between distribution strategy, firm size, and efficiency. Firms are classified into two groups based on assets. Firms with assets of greater than $1.5 billion are classified as large (L), while firms with assets less than $1.5 billion are classified as not large (NL). Because $1.5 billion in assets is approximately the median size in the industry, this classification splits the sample roughly in half.

Survey respondents were asked to identify the primary distribution system used to sell retail life insurance. On the basis of these responses, firms were classified as either non-exclusive (NEX) (using brokers), exclusive (EX), or direct writing (DW). The average cost and revenue efficiency scores for each group are shown in the table.

Significance tests were conducted for differences between the efficiency scores by category. Three separate tests were conducted: 1) The Wilcoxon test, which is a non-parametric test for differences in location (central tendency) across categories; 2) a non-parametric test for differences between medians; and 3) a small-sample t-test for differences between means.

The tests involve the following pairwise comparisons: exclusive versus non-exclusive (EX vs. NEX), large exclusive versus large non-exclusive (LEX vs. LNEX), and not large (small) exclusive versus small, non-exclusive (NLEX vs. NLNEX), small versus large non-exclusive (NLNEX vs. LNEX) and small versus large exclusive (NLEX vs. LEX).

Table 4-4. Efficiency, Size and Distribution Strategy

COST EFFICIENCY

Size		Non-exclusive	Exclusive	Direct	Total	Non-exclusive vs. Exclusive		
						Wilcoxon	Median	t-statistic
Not Large (Assets < $1.5 billion)	Mean	0.5021	0.3590	0.4810	0.4773	0.0680	0.0394	1.493
	Std. Dev.	0.1860	0.0709	na	0.1752			(0.10)
	n	19	4	1	24			
Large (Assets > $1.5 billion)	Mean	0.5928	0.5826	0.6225	0.5938	NS	NS	NS
	Std. Dev.	0.1904	0.2055	0.1662	0.1893			
	n	12	11	2	25			
Total	Mean	0.5372	0.5229	0.6020		NS	NS	NS
	Std. Dev.	0.1899	0.2042	0.1574				
	n	31	15	3				
Not Large vs. Large	Wilcoxon*	NS	0.0430		0.0319			
	Median*	NS	0.0348		0.0336			
	t-statistic	NS	-2.0870		2.2370			
			(.05)		(.01)			

REVENUE EFFICIENCY

Size		Non-exclusive	Exclusive	Direct	Total	Non-exclusive vs. Exclusive		
						Wilcoxon	Median	t-statistic
Not Large (Assets < $1.5 billion)	Mean	0.2571	0.2332	0.4989	0.2632	NS	NS	NS
	Std. Dev.	0.1309	0.1292	na	0.1349			
	n	19	4	1	24			
Large (Assets > $1.5 billion)	Mean	0.4304	0.5707	0.6884	0.5128	NS	NS	NS
	Std. Dev.	0.2299	0.3291	0.4407	0.2915			
	n	12	11	2	25			
Total	Mean	0.3242	0.4807	0.6252		0.0916	NS	2.055
	Std. Dev.	0.1924	0.3238	0.3302				(.025)
	n	31	15	3				
Not Large vs. Large	Wilcoxon*	0.0113	0.0780		0.0009			
	Median*	0.0204	NS		0.0071			
	t-statistic	-2.6800	-1.9600		3.8700			
		(.01)	(.05)		(.01)			

P-values are given for cases where the comparisons are statistically significant at conventional levels (the 10% level or better). *Low P-values* are indicative of statistical significance, e.g., a comparison with a P-value of 0.01 or 1% is more highly significant than a comparison with a P-value of 0.10 or 10%. Comparisons that are not statistically significant are denoted by "NS." Statistical tests involving direct writing insurers were not conducted due to the small sample size. However, the means and standard deviations for the direct writers are reported in the table.

The results generally support the hypothesis that large insurers have an efficiency advantage over smaller competitors. Large insurers are significantly more efficient than not large (smaller) insurers in terms of cost efficiency and revenue efficiency. For example, based on the median tests, large insurers are significantly more cost efficient than smaller firms at the 3.36% level and are significantly more revenue efficient at the 0.71% level.

There are no significant cost efficiency differences between large and small non-exclusive agency firms. However, large exclusive agency firms are significantly more cost efficient than small exclusive agency firms. This result makes sense because there are much greater fixed costs in setting up and operating an exclusive agency system than in running a non-exclusive agency system. Thus, one would expect size and cost efficiency to be related for exclusive agency firms but not necessarily for non-exclusive agency firms. However, size conveys a significant revenue efficiency advantage for both non-exclusive and exclusive agency firms.

To investigate the relationship between distribution system choice, product range, and efficiency, table 4-5 shows the relative efficiency scores for insurers classified by primary distribution system and product range. Recall that transactions cost economics implies that more vertically integrated insurers (exclusive agency firms and direct writers) will offer a broad range of products, whereas non-exclusive dealing insurers will more likely offer a narrow range of products. Also, vertically integrated insurers offering a broad product range are predicted to be more efficient than those offering a narrow product range, with the opposite prediction applying to non-exclusive agency firms (see table 4-2).

The results presented in table 4-5 are consistent with the prediction that insurers with vertically integrated marketing systems are more likely to offer a broad product range whereas non-vertically integrated firms are more likely to offer a narrow product range. The majority (13 of 17) of exclusive agency and direct writing insurers offer a broad product range, and the majority (16 of 29) of non-exclusive agency firms offer a narrow product range.

Table 4-5. Product Range, Distribution Channel and Firm Efficiency

COST EFFICIENCY

Distribution Channel		Product Range		Narrow vs. Broad		
		Narrow (7 or fewer product offerings)	Broad (8 or more product offerings)	Wilcoxon	Median	t-statistic
Non-exclusive Agency	Mean	0.5103	0.5536	NS	NS	NS
	Std. Dev.	0.2086	0.1795			
	n	16	13			
Exclusive Agency and Direct Writing	Mean	0.4260	0.5343	NS	NS	NS
	Std. Dev.	0.1496	0.1628			
	n.	4	13			
Non-exclusive vs. Exclusive						
Wilcoxon		NS	NS			
Median		NS	NS			
t-statistic		NS	NS			

REVENUE EFFICIENCY

Distribution Channel		Product Range		Narrow vs. Broad		
		Narrow (7 or fewer product offerings)	Broad (8 or more product offerings)	Wilcoxon	Median	t-statistic
Non-exclusive Agency	Mean	0.3084	0.3623	NS	NS	NS
	Std. Dev.	0.2307	0.1456			
	n	16	13			
Exclusive Agency and Direct Writing	Mean	0.3704	0.5080	NS	NS	NS
	Std. Dev.	0.3802	0.2867			
	n	4	13			
Non-exclusive vs. Exclusive						
Wilcoxon		NS	NS			
Median		NS	0.0678			
t-statistic		NS	-1.6340 (.10)			

Table 4-5 also provides some support for the transactions cost economics prediction with respect to efficiency. The only statistically significant pairwise comparison in the table supports the hypothesis that among firms offering a broad product range, exclusive and direct writing firms are significantly more revenue efficient than non-exclusive agency firms. The results thus provide evidence that matching distribution system choice with product range has enabled exclusive dealing and direct writing insurers within the survey sample to be more successful in maximizing revenues, but that matching has no significant effect on cost minimization. The suggested net effect is that matching their distribution system with a broad product range has a beneficial effect on profits for exclusive agency and direct firms.

To examine the relationship between product marketing strategy and product range, table 4-6 shows average efficiency scores for firms which adopt niche-market versus mass-market strategies and analyzes the interaction between marketing strategy and product range (narrow vs. broad product offerings). The results support the hypothesis that matching a mass-market strategy with a broad product range is associated with greater success in maximizing revenues. Mass-market firms that offer a broad product range are significantly more revenue efficient than mass-market firms offering a narrow product range (48.7% vs. 30.4%). In addition, among firms offering a broad product range, those following a mass-market strategy are significantly more revenue efficient than those following a niche-market strategy (48.7% vs. 33.2%). Thus, we find evidence that matching product range and marketing strategy contributes to firm performance for mass-market firms and for those offering a broad product range. This makes sense because firms that do not target-market and hence attempt to market to the overall insurance market are likely to need a broad range of products to satisfy the needs of a diverse range of customers.

Table 4-7 illustrates the share of business allocated to each of five major lines for insurers using exclusive versus non-exclusive dealing. The theory above indicates that non-exclusive dealing insurers should specialize in fewer lines of business, and should also be focused on more standardized lines. Among the five lines shown here, annuities are more standardized than ordinary life insurance, and the group market is more standardized, or less complex, than the individual insurance market.

It is clear from table 4-7 that non-exclusive dealing insurers devote proportionally more of their underwriting capacity to the more standardized lines. Based on industry data, non-exclusive dealing insurers write 15% of their business in individual annuities and 11% in group annuities. This compares to 13% in individual annuities and 2.5% in group annuities for exclusive dealing insurers. The percentage of group life premiums to total

Table 4-6. Efficiency and Product Market Strategy

COST EFFICIENCY

		Narrow Product Range (7 or fewer of 15)	Broad Product Range (not narrow)	Total	Narrow vs. Broad Wilcoxon	Median	t-Test
Niche Market	Mean	0.4479	0.5287	0.4954	NS	NS	NS
	n	7	10	17			
Mass market	Mean	0.5271	0.5433	0.5365	NS	NS	NS
	n	11	15	26			
Total	Mean	0.4963	0.5375				
	n	18	25				
Niche vs. Mass	Wilcoxon	NS	NS	NS			
	Median	NS	NS	NS			
	t-Test	NS	NS	NS			

REVENUE EFFICIENCY

		Narrow Product Range (7 or fewer of 15)	Broad Product Range (not narrow)	Total	Narrow vs. Broad Wilcoxon	Median	t-Test
Niche Market	Mean	0.3175	0.3319	0.3260	NS	NS	NS
	n	7	10	17			
Mass Market	Mean	0.3044	0.4874	0.4100	0.0312	0.0516	0.0416
	n	11	15	26			
Total	Mean	0.3095	0.4252				
	n	18	25				
Niche vs. Mass	Wilcoxon	NS	NS	NS			
	Median	NS	NS	NS			
	t-Test	NS	0.0456	NS			

Table 4-7. Distribution System Choice and Concentration by Line of Business (Proportion of Premium Written Allocated to Each Line)

Line	Exclusive (%)	Non-exclusive (%)
Ordinary Life	57.0	35.7
Group Life	7.7	13.9
Individual Annuities	13.4	15.0
Group Annuities	2.5	11.1
Accident and Health	18.5	24.1

Note: These figures measure the average proportion of underwriting capacity devoted to each line of business.

premiums for non-exclusive dealing insurers is about twice that of exclusive dealing insurers. Exclusive dealing insurers write proportionally more business in individual life, with approximately 57% of underwriting capacity devoted to this line, while non-exclusive dealers write approximately 36% of their business in individual life insurance. This allocation is consistent with the expectation that exclusive agency is a more appropriate distribution strategy for more complex lines of business.

Life insurers also make choices about investments in information technology, with the expectation that new investments will ultimately improve firm efficiency. Table 4-8 shows the correlation coefficients between efficiency scores and several variables representing information technology investments and capabilities.

The use of expert underwriting systems is positively and significantly correlated with revenue efficiency. The expert underwriting systems variable is also positively correlated with cost efficiency, but this relationship is not statistically significant. Information technology (IT) expenditures per policy also has a statistically significant positive correlation with revenue efficiency and is not significantly related to cost efficiency, implying a payoff from technology investments for insurers in terms of improved profitability. Having electronic sales and service links with agents has a significant positive correlation with cost efficiency, suggesting that it may be more efficient to communicate electronically than to use more traditional approaches. Having electronic links with agents during underwriting is positively and significantly correlated with both cost and revenue efficiency. Based on our interview evidence, this variable is likely significant because reducing the time required to underwrite a policy leads to higher sales

Table 4-8. Correlation between Efficiency and Technology Measures

Variable		Cost Efficiency	Revenue Efficiency	Percent with Capability
Expert Underwriting	Correlation	0.1020	0.2480	0.2444
System	P-Value	0.5050	0.0979	
	n	45	45	
IT Expenditures	Correlation	−0.0635	0.0870	na
per Policy*	P-Value	0.1212	0.0337	
	n	596	595	
Electronic Sales and	Correlation	0.2623	0.1934	0.2917
Service Links	P-Value	0.0717	0.1877	
with Agents	n	48	48	
Electronic Links with	Correlation	0.3033	0.7963	na
Agents During	P-Value	0.0539	0.0001	
Underwriting	n	41	41	
Customer-focused	Correlation	0.2239	0.2096	0.2777
Database	P-Value	0.1219	0.1483	
	n	49	49	
Online Premium	Correlation	0.0012	−0.2227	0.9130
Calculation	P-Value	0.9935	0.1369	
	n	46	46	
Name & Address	Correlation	−0.1774	−0.0863	0.8936
	P-Value	0.2330	0.5641	
	n	47	47	
Policy Cancellation	Correlation	0.0648	−0.0622	0.8511
	P-Value	0.6654	0.6781	
	n	47	47	
Loan Approval	Correlation	0.0723	−0.1410	0.8298
	P-Value	0.6294	0.3446	
	n	47	47	
Surrender	Correlation	−0.0271	−0.3176	0.8478
Valuation	P-Value	0.8581	0.0315	
	n	46	49	
Proportion of	Correlation	0.0103	−0.1470	na
Standard Functions	P-Value	0.9465	0.3354	
Firm Can Perform	n	45	45	
Online				

*Full sample used rather than survey sample because all data are available from NAIC statements.

closing rates, thus eliminating some wasted effort on the part of agents. These results provide evidence that technology investments improve insurer performance and suggest that technology can be an important competitive advantage in retail life insurance.

Transactions cost economics implies that vertical integration and technological investments are likely to be positively correlated, because such investments tend to create relationship specific assets that are protected from opportunistic exploitation in the vertically integrated firm. We find some support for this hypothesis in our survey data. Vertically integrated insurers (exclusive agency and direct writing firms) have electronic linkages during underwriting in a significantly higher proportion of their underwriting cases than do non-integrated (non-exclusive agency) insurers (32.3% vs. 3.6%). In addition, 38.9% of the vertically integrated insurers have expert underwriting systems, compared to only 14.8% for non-exclusive agency firms. A somewhat puzzling finding is that vertically integrated firms on average can perform fewer of seven standard functions online than non-integrated firms (70.0% vs. 84.1%). A possible explanation for this result is that exclusive agency firms tend to rely more heavily on their agents to perform many customer service functions. In a non-exclusive relationship, it is more difficult to motivate the agent to perform these tasks, so the insurer is more likely to absorb these tasks into a service center with online capabilities.

In summary, the categorical analysis identifies several important relationships between business practices and efficiency. An important overall finding is that *combinations* of business strategies often tend to be correlated with efficiency, i.e., considering strategic choices in combination with other strategic choices is more likely to improve efficiency than considering strategic business practices independently. For example, we find that large exclusive agency firms are more cost efficient than small exclusive agency firms. In addition, firms that combine an exclusive or direct distribution system with a broad product range tend to be more revenue efficient than exclusive or direct firms with a narrow product range. Combining a mass-market strategy (as opposed to a niche-market strategy) with a broad product range is a more revenue efficient strategy than combining a mass-market strategy with a narrow product range. Finally, we find that having an expert underwriting system is positively correlated with cost efficiency and having electronic sales linages with agents during the underwriting process is positively correlated with both cost and revenue efficiency. Thus, insurers have significant opportunities to improve both cost and revenue efficiency by choosing and effectively implementing strategic choices.

3.2. Multiple Regression Analysis

The comparisons above suggest a complex relationship between distribution system choice, marketing strategies technology, and efficiency. Regression analysis enables us to account for complex relationships between firm characteristics and efficiency by measuring the contribution of specific variables to efficiency while controlling for the influence of other firm characteristics that simultaneously affect efficiency. Regression analysis uses a statistical procedure to estimate a linear relationship between a dependent variable (in this case, efficiency) and a set of independent or explanatory variables. The coefficient on any given explanatory variable is interpretable as the effect of this variable on the dependent variable (efficiency) after accounting for the effects of all of the other explanatory variables included in the equation. The two principal types of efficiency, cost and revenue, are used as dependent variables in the analysis.

The estimated regression models are shown in table 4-9. Although a large number of regressions were estimated, we found that we could summarize the results in two cost regressions and two revenue regressions. The number of observations used to estimate the regressions differ across equations because some insurers did not respond to all of the questions in our surveys. Tests were conducted to ensure that differences in results across equations are not due solely to changes in the estimation sample. The sign on each explanatory variable indicates its direction of influence on efficiency, while the significance of the variable indicates whether the variable is an important driver of efficiency differences across insurers. Variables are indicated by asterisks if significant at the 1%, 5%, and 10% levels.

We first discuss the impact on efficiency of overall firm strategy. Recall that firms that adopt one of three generic strategies—cost leadership, product differentiation, or customer focus—are hypothesized to be more efficient than firms that do not adopt a specific strategy but, rather, occupy the middle ground. Further, of the three strategies, a cost leadership strategy is likely to be associated with higher levels of cost efficiency. The counter hypothesis is that the strategies are too generic to have much explanatory power and are likely to be dominated by industry-specific strategies.

Two of the three generic strategies are significantly related to cost efficiency. Adopting a cost leadership strategy is statistically significant at the 1% level with a positive coefficient in the cost efficiency equations. This implies that firms with a cost leadership strategy are significantly more cost efficient than rival firms that do not adopt this strategy. Adopting a customer-focused strategy is also positively related to cost efficiency and is

Table 4-9.   Tobit Regression Analysis: Cost and Revenue Efficiency

Variable Name	Model 1 Parameter Estimate	Model 2 Parameter Estimate	Model 3 Parameter Estimate	Model 4 Parameter Estimate
DEPENDENT VARIABLE (Type of Efficiency)	Cost	Cost	Revenue	Revenue
Intercept	−0.366	−0.113	−1.270***	−0.204
Ordinary individual life premiums as fraction total premiums	0.111*	0.134**	−0.336***	−0.176***
Group annuity premiums as a fraction of total premiums	0.692***	0.758***	0.177	0.218
Dominant distribution type is exclusive	−0.122***	−0.172***	0.077	−0.011
Dominant distribution type is direct	−0.003	−0.073	0.278***	0.176*
Average annual growth in premium and annuity considerations 1993–95	−0.620***	−0.481**		
Offers 7 or less of 15 individual life and health products	0.025	0.022	0.120**	0.012
Log of admitted assets excluding separate accounts	0.036**	0.027*	0.082***	0.027*
Dummy variable = 1 for self-declared cost leadership strategy	0.105**	0.131***		
Dummy Variable = 1 for strategic focus on customers & customer groups	0.106*	0.061		
Real time or batch computer communication during underwriting process	0.001*	0.002***		0.005***
Maintains relational client data base	0.061*	0.051		
Annual voluntary staff turnover rate		−0.006***		
OBSERVATIONS	39	35	46	39
LOG LIKELIHOOD	37.559	36.656	17.887	27.850

Note: *** = significant at the 1% level or better, ** = significant at the 5% level, * = significant at the 10% level.

significant at the 10% level in one of the cost efficiency regression models. This suggests a weaker but still positive relationship between the customer-focus strategy and cost efficiency. The product differentiation strategy was not found to be statistically significant in the cost efficiency regressions, and none of the three generic strategies was significant in the revenue efficiency regressions. Thus, our results provide mixed support for the Porter hypothesis. Nevertheless, it is encouraging that the cost leadership strategy and, to a lesser extent, the customer-focus strategy do appear to offer the opportunity for insurers to generate efficiency gains.

The categorical analysis presented above suggests that strategic choices about product distribution, product mix and focus, and target markets also seem to drive efficiency differences across insurers. The regression models also include variables to measure the importance of these factors. The cost efficiency regressions reveal that exclusive dealing insurers, i.e., those that recruit and train agents that exclusively or primarily represent a single insurer, are significantly less cost efficient than insurers using direct marketing or non-exclusive agents. This finding is consistent with evidence based on our interviews to the effect that the exclusive dealing method is a relatively high cost approach to the distribution of life insurance and is increasingly threatened by non-exclusive and direct sales. Exclusive agency firms were generally believed to be facing the toughest competition from nontraditional competitors such as banks, investment advisors, and fund companies, precisely because of their high cost distribution system.

Our finding that exclusive dealing insurers are less cost efficient appears even more ominous in view of the insignificance of the exclusive dealing variable in the revenue efficiency regressions. The implication is that having an exclusive agency system is associated with higher costs but that it does not generate additional revenues, thus having a net negative effect on profitability. On the other hand, having a direct distribution system (e.g., distributing insurance through company employees rather than agents) has a significant positive effect on revenue efficiency. Thus, direct distributing insurers appear to have a competitive advantage in maximizing revenues over insurers using exclusive or non-exclusive agents and also have a cost advantage over insurers using exclusive agents.

The regression models also test for the effects of adopting a narrow product distribution strategy, as measured by a categorical variable set equal to one for insurers offering 7 or fewer than 15 lines of insurance. This variable has a positive coefficient in the cost efficiency regressions but is not statistically significant. The variable also is positive in the revenue efficiency regressions and is statistically significant in one of the revenue

models. Thus, the models do not support the hypothesis that a narrow
distribution strategy is related to cost efficiency but do provide evidence
that insurers with a narrow distribution strategy are more successful in
maximizing revenues. Thus, it appears that there is a market reward for
specializing in a narrow product range, i.e., "being the best" in a few
products leads to higher revenues. Tests with variables representing a
niche-marketing strategy and interaction variables for having a narrow
product strategy and using non-exclusive agents as well as other product/
distribution combinations did not yield significant results.

The regressions also reveal that product mix is significantly related to
efficiency. The coefficient of the proportion of premiums generated by the
group annuity line of business is positive and significant in both cost
efficiency models, and this variable is positive but not statistically significant
in the revenue efficiency regressions. This means that insurers writing proportionally more business in group annuities are significantly more cost
efficient than insurers specializing in other product lines, holding all other
factors constant. This is reasonable because group annuities are a line with
relatively low complexity, requiring less underwriting, policyholder services,
and sales effort than individual life insurance or annuities. A complementary interpretation is that the group annuity market is relatively price
competitive in comparison with other market segments, leading to higher
market shares for efficient insurers.

Somewhat surprising, the proportion of premiums generated by the individual life line of business is positively and significantly related to cost
efficiency. This is contrary to the evidence obtained in our company interviews, which suggested that the individual life line is relatively inefficient in
comparison with other lines of business. However, this variable is negative
and significant in the revenue efficiency regressions, indicating that insurers with a higher proportion of their business in individual life insurance
are less revenue efficient than other firms. Based on the magnitude of the
coefficients of this variable in the cost and revenue regressions, the net
effect of writing more individual life insurance on profits is likely to be
negative, consistent with the interview evidence. The three-year premium
growth rate is inversely related to cost efficiency. This lends support to the
idea that rapidly growing insurers have to make initial investments in
underwriting, marketing, and administrative costs that are not recovered
immediately, and so decrease efficiency. This variable is not significantly
related to revenue efficiency and was omitted from the final versions of the
revenue efficiency models.

The models also show that larger firms are significantly more cost
and revenue efficient than smaller firms, where size is measured by the

natural logarithm of non-separate account assets. Thus, size appears to convey an advantage in both cost and revenue efficiency. However, after controlling for the other factors considered in the analysis, our market power index did not turn out to be significantly related to either cost or revenue efficiency.

Several variables were tested to assess the influence of information technology on efficiency differences across life insurers. The technology variable that emerged as being consistently most highly related to both cost and revenue efficiency is the proportion of underwriting cases that are processed through computer contact with the agent during the underwriting. As mentioned above, our interview evidence suggests that having computerized contact during the underwriting process tends to reduce the time required to make an underwriting decision and issue policies. This is important because sales closing rates tend to be inversely related to the time lag between the time the application is completed and the policy is issued. Thus, insurers that are able to make decisions promptly and communicate them to the sales force are expected to have higher closing rates and thus to waste less resources on policies that are never accepted by potential buyers. Having a relational client data base is also positively associated with cost efficiency and is significant in one of the cost efficiency models. This variable was positive but not statistically significant in several revenue efficiency models. Thus, the regressions also provide some evidence that relational client data bases are associated with superior performance.

Other technology-related variables tested include the presence of an expert underwriting system, the ability to perform various functions online, and information technology expenditures per policy in force. None of these variables was significantly related to either cost or revenue efficiency in the regression analysis. The fact that information technology expenditures per policy is not statistically significant is encouraging in that it implies that technology expenditures do not lead to reductions in efficiency even though they increase insurer costs. Thus, technology expenditures seem to pay for themselves in terms of efficiency, while giving the insurer improved capabilities in sales and policyholder services. This might mean that some types of technology spending are an efficient substitute for, or aid to, human capital and provides further evidence that information technology investments can pay off for insurers.

The final variable included in the regression models is that insurer's annual voluntary staff turnover rate. Having a higher employee turnover rate is expected to be inversely related to efficiency because insurers with higher turnover rates are expected to incur higher training expenses and to have less experienced employees on average. This expectation is borne out in the cost efficiency analysis, which shows that the turnover rate is significantly and inversely related to cost efficiency. Thus, insurers with relatively high turnover rates have an opportunity to improve their performance by adopting better personnel management procedures. Some suggestions in that regard are provided in Chapter 6 of this book (Chadwick and Cappelli, 1999). The turnover rate was not found to be significantly related to revenue efficiency.

4. Conclusion

This chapter has sought to establish whether there are significant differences in life insurer efficiency attributable to firm choices about overall strategy, product distribution, product mix, target marketing, and information technology. The objective of this detailed analysis is to contribute to a better understanding of the best practices associated with life insurer efficiency.

One of the significant findings of this study is that distribution system choice plays an important role in relative efficiency across insurers. The weight of the evidence suggests that the exclusive dealing insurers within our sample are significantly less cost efficient than either non-exclusive dealing or direct writing insurers. This finding is consistent with our interview evidence to the effect that exclusive dealing insurers are viewed as relatively inefficient due to the high training costs and high agent turnover rates associated with the exclusive agency system. We also find that direct writing insurers are more revenue efficient than either exclusive or non-exclusive agency insurers. Thus, direct writers have a revenue efficiency advantage over insurers using agents and have a cost efficiency advantage over firms using exclusive agents.

We also find some support for the transactions cost hypothesis that non-exclusive dealing insurers should focus on fewer product lines—the majority of vertically integrated insurers offer a broad range of products and the majority of non-vertically integrated firms offer a narrow range of products. The results also show that matching a broad product range with an exclusive-dealing distribution system leads to higher revenue efficiency. Matching a mass-market (rather than niche-market) approach with a broad product range also is positively associated with revenue efficiency. Thus, strategic-fit appears to play a role in determining the performance of life insurers.

We provide some evidence in support of the Porter (1980) hypothesis that firms which adopt one of three generic strategies (cost, customer focus, and product differentiation) are more efficient than rivals that fail to adopt one of these strategies. Firms in our sample following the cost leadership strategy are significantly more cost efficient than firms not following this strategy, and firms adopting a customer-focused strategy also appear to be more cost efficient. None of the three generic strategies is associated with revenue efficiency, a result that we attribute to the dominance of industry-specific strategies involving product distribution, business mix, and technology. Overall, the results suggest a more complex relationship between overall strategic management and business outcomes than presupposed by the generic strategy hypothesis.

Our results provide evidence that having computerized linkages with the agent during the underwriting process and having a relational client data base are significantly related to efficiency. Coupled with the finding that expenditures on technology per policy are *not* associated with cost inefficiency, the findings suggest that technology expenditures tend to pay for themselves while giving insurers better capabilities to perform policy sales and service functions.

Our findings show that size appears to convey advantages in both cost and revenue efficiency. This is consistent with the findings for the entire industry presented in Chapter 3 which indicate that the majority of small insurers are operating with increasing returns to scale. Although the majority of the largest insurers operate with decreasing returns to scale, even in the largest size group a significant proportion of insurers have achieved constant returns to scale. Thus, for appropriately managed insurers, size can provide a competitive advantage and lead to higher profitability. Size plays a more important role for exclusive agency and direct writing insurers than for non-exclusive agency insurers, because of the substantial investment required to create a vertically integrated marketing operation. Relative efficiency levels of insurers are also determined in part by line of business focus. An insurer writing proportionally more business in group annuity products is significantly more efficient than one which concentrates in other, more complex lines, or in lines where price competition is less intense.

An overall conclusion is that insurers can significantly improve their operating performance by making the appropriate strategic choices. While some characteristics such as the insurer's primary distribution system are obviously difficult to change, at least in the short-run, evidence presented elsewhere in this book suggests that more feasible strategies, such as adopting a secondary distribution system, can improve firm performance. In addition, choices related to technology and the strategic fit between an insurer's marketing strategy and distribution system also can make a difference. Insurers with superior management capabilities may be able to make additional gains from acquiring less efficient firms and implementing best practices to improve the efficiency of the acquired firm, thus increasing net worth by more than the purchase price. There are ample opportunities for firms with superior management to succeed in the years ahead.

Notes

1. Although the Glass-Steagall Act prevents banks from underwriting insurance, banks can distribute the products of a non-affiliated insurers. Further, proposed Federal financial services deregulation would remove this barrier to bank and insurer competition.

2. The frontier efficiency measurement approach is discussed in more detail in Chapter 3 of this book (Cummins, 1999).

3. Here, personal producing general agents (PPGAs) are included in the brokerage category. These producers are responsible for hiring and training selling agents, and receive additional compensation in the form of override commissions. (Overrides are the difference between what the PPGA receives from the insurer and what is paid to the producing agent.)

4. These market share statistics are from Peterson, et al. (1994).

5. A personal computer, for example, is not a relationship-specific asset because it can be used to serve multiple purposes. A software system designed to link a computer to a specific-insurer's data base, on the other hand, is relationship-specific because it is likely to be useless in linkages with other insurers.

6. Note that this theory has been applied to distribution system choice for property-liability insurers. However, because of ownership of the expirations list by independent agents in that industry, transaction cost analysis predicts that non-exclusive dealing (independent agency) insurers should focus on more complex product lines and markets (Regan, 1997).

7. A customer-focused data base is one in which all transactions relating to a single customer are organized together and are available online to employees providing service to the customer, including underwriting, claims, and marketing personnel.

8. Although life insurers also adopt different ownership structures, our analysis indicated no significant effect of stock versus mutual ownership form on differences in efficiency. A similar finding is reported in Cummins and Zi (1998). Therefore, we do not discuss the role of ownership structure here.

9. This transformation has the effect of retaining the relative ordering of firms in terms of size but reduces the influence of any extremely large or small firms.

10. Formally, the market power index is equal of P_{ijk}/P_{xjk}, where P_{ijk} = premiums of company i in product line j in state k, and P_{xjk} = premiums of the market leader (x) in line j, state k. Averaging all of a company's product market shares gives the market power index.

11. Because the dependent variable in our regression equations (DEA efficiency estimates for the insurers in the sample) is bounded by 0 and 1, the appropriate estimation technique is Tobit regression.

References

Berger, Allen N., J. David Cummins, and Mary A. Weiss. "The Coexistence of Multiple Distribution Systems for Financial Services: The Case of Property-Liability Insurance," *The Journal of Business* 70 (1997), 515–546.

Black, Kenneth and Harold D. Skipper. *Life Insurance,* Englewood Cliffs, NJ: Prentice-Hall, 1994.

Coase, Ronald H. "The Nature of the Firm," reprinted in *The Firm, The Market, and The Law* Chicago, IL: University of Chicago Press, 1988.

Chadwick, Clint and Peter Cappelli. "Strategy, Human Resource Management, and the Performance of Life Insurance Firms," in J.D. Cummins and A. Santomero (eds.), *Changes in the Life Insurance Industry: Efficiency, Technology, and Risk Management,* 1999.

Carr, Roderick M. 1997. "Strategic Choices, Firm Efficiency and Competitiveness in the U.S. Life Insurance Industry," Ph.D. diss., The Wharton School, University of Pennsylvania, Philadelphia.

Carr, Roderick M., J. David Cummins, and Laureen Regan. "Strategic Choices and Efficiency in the U.S. Life Insurance Industry: A Transactions Cost Analysis," working paper, Wharton Financial Institutions Center, Philadelphia, PA, 1998.

Charnes, A., W.W. Cooper, A. Lewin, and L. Seiford (eds.), *Data Envelopment Analysis: Theory, Methodology, and Applications,* Norwell, MA: Kluwer Academic Publishers, 1994.

Cummins, J. David. "Efficiency in the U.S. Life Insurance Industry: Are Insurers Minimizing Costs and Maximizing Revenues?" in J.D. Cummins and A. Santomero (eds.), *Changes in the Life Insurance Industry: Efficiency, Technology, and Risk Management,* 1999.

Cummins, J. David and Hongmin Zi. "Comparison of Frontier Efficiency Methods: An Application to the U.S. Life Insurance Industry," *Journal of Productivity Analysis* 10 (1998), 131–152.

Gardner, Lisa and Martin L. Grace. "X-inefficiency in the U.S. Life Insurance Industry," *Journal of Banking and Finance* 17 (1993), 497–510.

Grace, Martin F. and Stephen G. Timme. "An Examination of Cost Economies in the United States Life Insurance Industry," *Journal of Risk and Insurance* 59 (1992), 72–103.

Gupta, A.K. and G. Westall. Distribution of Financial Services, *Transactions of the Faculty of Actuaries* 44 (1994), 24–63.

Hannan, Michael T. and John Freeman. "The Population Ecology of Organizations," *American Journal of Sociology* 82 (1977), 929–964.

Nelson, Richard R. and Sidney G. Winter. *An Evolutionary Theory of Economic Change* Cambridge, MA: Harvard University Press, 1985.

Peterson, Michael B., Walter H. Zultowski, Archer L. Edgar, and Ram S. Gopalan. "Life Insurance Marketing," in Edward E. Graves and Lynn Hayes (eds.), *McGill's Life Insurance,* The American College, Bryn Mawr, PA, 1994.

Porter, Michael E. *Competitive Strategy*. New York: The Free Press, 1980.

Porter, Michael E. *Competitive Advantage: Creating and Sustaining Superior Performance*, New York: The Free Press, 1985.

Prahalad, C.K. and Gary Hamel. "The Core Competence of the Corporation," *Harvard Business Review*, (May–June 1990), 79–91.

Regan, Laureen. "Vertical Integration in the Property-Liability Insurance Industry: A Transaction cost Approach," *Journal of Risk and Insurance* 6 (1997), 41–62.

Regan, Laureen and Sharon Tennyson. "Agent Discretion and the Choice of Insurance Marketing System," *Journal of Law and Economics* 39 (1996), 637–666.

Williamson, Oliver. "Transaction-cost Economics: The Governance of Contractual Relations," *Journal of Law and Economics* 22 (1979), 3–61.

Williamson, Oliver. *The Economic Institutions of Capitalism: Firms, Markets, and Relational Contracting*. New York: The Free Press, 1985.

Yuengert, Andrew M. "The Measurement of Efficiency in Life Insurance: Estimates of a Mixed Normal-Gamma Error Model," *Journal of Banking and Finance* 17 (1993), 483–496.

Appendix: Definition of Porter General Strategy Variables

Customer Focused.   An indicator variable that is assigned a value of 1 if a firm answers the questions below in such a way as to indicate that it pursues a customer-focused strategy. Otherwise, the insurer is assigned a value of 0 for this variable.

We try to concentrate on geographic and customer groups we already know
We spend a large amount of resources on marketing
We spend a lot of resources on monitoring consumer behavior
We target the financial planning and security needs of our customers
We focus on clients who have accumulated wealth which requires investing, rather than clients who have accumulated little wealth
We are customer focused rather than product focused

Product Differentiation.   An indicator variable that is assigned a value of 1 if a firm answers the questions below in such a way as to indicate that it pursues a product-focused strategy. Otherwise, the insurer is assigned a value of 0 for this variable.

We try to be "first in" with new or additional distribution channels and marketing concepts
We try to be "first in" with innovative products
We seek to be focused on providing and extensive and integrated range of financial services products

We focus on providing protection rather than savings products
We seek to maintain and enhance the value of our sales and service system to win and retain clients
We recognize our agents as an important customer group and invest in training and technology to meet their needs

Cost Leadership.   An indicator variable that is assigned a value of 1 if a firm answers the questions below in such a way as to indicate that it pursues a cost leadership strategy. Otherwise, the insurer is assigned a value of 0 for this variable.

We seek to be low cost leaders.

5 LIFE INSURANCE MERGERS AND ACQUISITIONS*

J. David Cummins, Sharon Tennyson, and Mary A. Weiss

1. Introduction

The life insurance industry worldwide is undergoing profound change. The increasing integration of financial services institutions and the globalization of insurance markets have greatly intensified competition in this mature industry. Increasing competition has produced pressures for product innovation, distribution system development, greater cost efficiency in operations, more effective use of technology, and a larger capital base.

One potential response to pressures for rapid change is to seek competitive advantage through reorganization. This strategic response appears to be prevalent in the life insurance industry. During the past decade, the U.S. life insurance industry has experienced an unprecedented wave of merger and acquisition activity. Among the merger and acquisition motives most commonly cited are that size is essential to compete in the global market for financial services and that a focus on core businesses is essential to improving efficiency and increasing profits. While these two motives offer different perspectives on competitive strategy, size is thought to be increasingly important even within niche markets.[1]

These developments suggest that the quest for scale economies and efficiency gains provide a major motivation for the recent consolidation activity in the life insurance industry. Thus, an important open question for the industry is whether mergers and acquisitions actually succeed in attaining these objectives. This chapter investigates the question by examining the scale economies and efficiency characteristics of recent life insurance acquisition targets and comparing the efficiency improvements of acquired firms to those of the non-acquired firms in the industry. We also examine the effects of acquisitions on the acquiring firms.

In evaluating firm performance, we use the concept of economic efficiency. Economic efficiency is computed relative to "best practice" efficient frontiers, consisting of the dominant firms in the industry. Two major types of efficiency are used in our analysis—*cost efficiency* (the firm's success in minimizing costs) and *revenue efficiency* (the firm's success in maximizing revenues). The efficient cost frontier represents the lowest costs attained by firms in the life insurance industry to produce a given bundle of outputs, and the efficient revenue frontier represents the maximum revenues earned by firms in the industry with a given amount of inputs. These are best practice frontiers in the sense that they represent the minimum costs and maximum revenues, respectively, actually attained by firms operating in the industry.

The technique used to estimate the efficient frontiers is *data envelopment analysis* (DEA), which is explained in more detail in Chapter 3 of this book (Cummins, 1999). In estimating the DEA cost frontier, a mathematical algorithm is used to find a combination of firms operating in the industry that jointly could produce a given insurer's outputs at a lower cost for a given set of input prices. If no such combination can be found, the given insurer is identified as "self efficient" and given an efficiency score of 1.0. If a set of firms can be found that jointly dominate the given insurer, the insurer is identified as being less than fully efficient. It's efficiency score is the ratio of the costs that would have been expended by the dominating combination of firms to the costs the insurer actually expended. The score is between 0 and 1 with higher scores indicating higher efficiency. For example, an efficiency score of 0.75 indicates that the given insurer is operating at 75% of full efficiency, or, equivalently, that it could reduce its costs by 25% while still producing the same level of output if it operated with the level of efficiency attained by the dominating set of firms.

To identify the factors driving cost efficiency, we decompose cost efficiency into *technical efficiency* and *allocative efficiency*. Technical efficiency measures the firm's success in producing the maximum quantity of output for the amount of inputs (e.g., capital and labor) consumed, and allocative efficiency measures the firm's success in minimizing operating costs by choosing the optimal mix of inputs. Technical efficiency is further decomposed into *pure technical efficiency* and *scale efficiency*. Pure technical efficiency measures the firm's success in using state-of-the-art technology, and scale efficiency indicates whether the firm is operating with increasing, decreasing, or constant returns to scale. The economic ideal is to operate with constant returns to scale, because the costs of producing one unit of output cannot be reduced by becoming larger or smaller if constant returns to scale are attained.

The concept of revenue efficiency is similar to cost efficiency except that the dominating set of firms earns higher revenues for a given level of output production and input usage than the individual firm under analysis. Revenue efficiency is calculated as the ratio of the revenues of the given insurer to the revenues of the dominating set of insurers; and again a score of 1.0 indicates full efficiency. Dominating cost and revenues sets are calculated separately for each insurer in the sample.

The overall objective of the analysis is to determine whether mergers and acquisitions in the life insurance industry have been economically beneficial in the sense of leading to increases in efficiency. We accomplish the objective by conducting two primary statistical analyses. The first part of the analysis investigates the characteristics of firms that are acquisition targets. The purpose is to determine whether acquisitions in the life insurance industry seem to make sense economically in terms of the types of firms that are acquired. In the second part of the analysis, we examine changes in efficiency for insurers that are acquisition targets as well as for non-target firms over the five-year window extending from two years prior to the acquisition to two years following the acquisition. We also examine changes in efficiency over matching periods for firms not involved in acquisitions. A separate five-year analysis is conducted for acquiring firms.

By way of preview, we find evidence that the factors driving life insurance acquisitions are for the most part economically sound, For example, we find that firms operating with non-decreasing (increasing or constant) returns to scale are more likely to be acquisition targets than firms operating with decreasing returns to scale and we also find evidence that relatively efficient firms are more likely to be acquired than relatively inefficient firms. Financially vulnerable firms are more like to be acquired than stronger insurers, suggesting that mergers and acquisitions have reduced the overall level of insolvency risk in the industry. In the five-year window phase of the analysis, we find that acquisition targets experienced larger cost and revenue efficiency gains than non-targets. The cost efficiency gains were primarily due to gains in technical efficiency, reinforcing the importance of technology as a performance correlate in the insurance industry. Acquiring firms also realized larger efficiency gains than firms not involved in merger and acquisition activity. Thus, we conclude that mergers and acquisitions in the life insurance industry are driven for the most part by economically viable objectives and have had a beneficial effect on efficiency in the industry.

The chapter is organized as follows: section 2 presents an overview of recent merger and acquisition activity in the industry and trends in industry market structure and concentration, section 3 discusses specific motives that have been proposed for mergers in the life insurance industry, and their predicted relationship to efficiency and economies of scale, section 4 discusses the sample of firms used in our more in-depth analysis of merger motives and efficiency effects and presents the results of this analysis. The final section of the chapter discusses the implications of our findings for the industry.

2. Merger and Acquisition Activity and the U.S. Life Insurance Industry

2.1. Merger and Acquisition Activity

There is no single authoritative source for information on merger and acquisition (M&A) activity in the life insurance industry. One must search a number of different sources to arrive at an accurate accounting of merger and acquisition activity in the industry. One generally reliable source of information, however, are the reports of Conning and Company, an investment banking and management consulting firm specializing in the insurance industry. This source represents the best estimate of the overall scope and volume of mergers and acquisitions activity that is available over a lengthy time period.[2]

Conning and Company's compilation of the annual number and estimated value of M&A transactions in the U.S. life insurance industry over the time period 1989–1997 is shown in figure 5-1. The figure shows a general upward trend in both the number and value of life insurance M&A over this time period. The number of mergers peaked at 83 in 1994, but the volume of merger transactions has continued to increase in recent years, climbing to over $12 billion in 1997. This does not appear to be the peak of M&A activity in the industry, however; Conning and Company reports that there were 23 transactions for a value of over $7 billion in the first half of 1998 alone (Conning and Company, 1998).

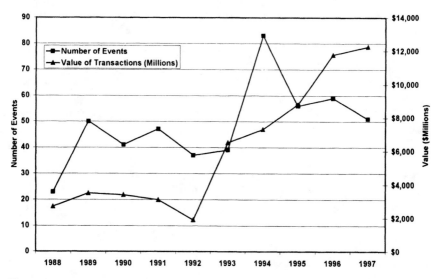

Figure 5-1.   Merger and Acquistion Activity in the Life Insurance Industry

Table 5-1.   Merger and Acquisition Transactions By Type—U.S. Life Insurance Industry

Transaction Type	1989	1990	1991	1992	1993	1994	1995	1996	1997	Total
Acquisition or Merger	44	32	37	29	36	69	49	48	49	393
Partial Acquisition	1	4	6	0	2	1	3	3	0	20
Acquisition of Line of Business	5	5	4	8	1	13	4	8	2	50
Total Transactions	50	41	47	37	39	83	56	59	51	463
Foreign Buyer	5	3	9	3	0	8	0	0	0	28
Foreign Seller or Target	1	1	1	0	6	7	1	0	1	18

Source: Authors' compilations from Conning and Company reports, various years.

The M&A transactions by year over the period 1989–1997 are shown in more detail in table 5-1. The table shows the number of transactions reported by Conning that involved the merger or acquisition of a life insurance company, acquisition of a partial interest in a life insurance company, and acquisition of a book of business or a division of a life insurance company. Of the 463 transactions over this time period, 393 represent the acquisition or merger of a life insurer, 20 represent the purchase of a partial interest in a life insurer, and 50 represent the purchase of only a particular book or line of business from a life insurer.

While no strong trends are apparent in the data, in general it appears that restructuring of company activities via acquisition of a book of business represents a larger fraction of total acquisitions activities in the first half of the period than in the second half. This pattern is consistent with the idea that the merger wave was sparked in part by the desire for rapid change in activities or focus in some companies.

Table 5-1 also shows the numbers of transactions reported by Conning that involved a non-U.S. company. In total, 28 transactions involved non-U.S. companies that bought U.S. life insurance concerns and 18 transactions involved U.S. life insurance companies that bought non-U.S. life insurance concerns. Notice that in the first half of the time period, non-U.S. firms were more prevalent as buyers, while in the second half of the period the pattern reversed and non-U.S. firms were more prevalent as sellers. This pattern is consistent with the fact that interest in life insurance industry restructuring in Europe and elsewhere preceded the restructuring in the domestic U.S. industry.

What is the impact of this wave of consolidation on the structure of the U.S. life insurance industry? While the number of transactions is large relative to past experience, and large relative to activities in many other industries, the number of firms acquired or merged is small relative to the total number of firms in the industry (see the discussion below). Moreover, many firms that are acquired remain separate companies rather than being merged or retired. Thus, it is unclear to what extent M&A activity has changed the competitive structure of the industry. Additionally, other forces such as entry, exit, and insolvency have impacted the industry structure during the same time period, either offsetting or complementing the changes due to M&A.

2.2. Trends in Industry Structure

To gain some insight into these questions, we provide a brief statistical overview of the evolution of the life insurance industry over the period 1988 through 1995. This overview is important in providing the backdrop for analysis of the implications of merger activity in the industry. The data sources for this analysis are the annual accounting reports filed by insurers with the National Association of Insurance Commissioners (NAIC).

The annual numbers of insurers with meaningful data reported to the NAIC are shown in table 5-2. The table shows the total number of compa-

Table 5-2. Number of Firms in the U.S. Life Insurance Industry

Year	Number of Groups	Affiliated Companies	Unaffiliated Companies	Total Companies	Total DMUs*	Total Premiums**
1988	379	891	334	1,225	713	$224,733
1989	379	907	337	1,244	716	$244,196
1990	379	916	341	1,257	720	$266,381
1991	381	941	363	1,304	744	$270,026
1992	381	936	352	1,288	733	$285,034
1993	369	902	339	1,241	708	$315,872
1994	357	899	334	1,233	691	$336,665
1995	341	884	303	1,187	644	$350,238

Source: Authors' construction from NAIC data.
* DMUs = decision making units = number of groups + number of unaffiliated companies.
** Premiums are in millions of current dollars.

nies, the total number of groups and the total number of unaffiliated companies, as well as total annual life insurance premium volume. Most insurance companies are members of groups consisting of several companies under common ownership. The total number of companies in the industry declined during this period, from 1,225 to 1,187. The number of companies affiliated with a group remained relatively constant during this time period, at just under 900. This decrease is evident primarily among the unaffiliated companies, whose number decreased about 10% over the period, from 334 to 303.

The number of life insurance groups also declined around 10% over this time period, from 379 to 341. These parallel trends in the numbers of groups and unaffiliated companies led to a 10% decrease in the total number of decision-making units (DMUs) in the industry (groups plus unaffiliated companies) over this time period, from 713 to 644. Given the growth in premium volume over the period from $225 billion to $350 billion in a period of low inflation, this represents a significant consolidation trend in the industry.

Table 5-3 shows the distribution of premiums and trends in annual premium growth in the major lines of business underwritten by life insurers, and figure 5-2 graphs the percentage distribution of premium revenues by major line of business in 1995. Both the table and the figure show the importance of annuity markets for insurers—group annuities accounted for 24% of premium revenues in 1995 and individual annuities accounted for 22%. Another asset accumulation product, individual life insurance, accounted for another 25% of premium revenues. Group life and accident and health insurance, which are mainly indemnity rather than asset

Table 5-3. Distribution of Premiums in the U.S. Life Insurance Industry

Year	Individual Life	Individual Annuities	Group Life	Group Annuities	Accident and Health	Total
1988	60,643	38,668	15,586	56,702	53,135	224,733
1989	61,082	45,394	16,119	64,197	57,405	244,196
1990	63,422	51,077	17,478	74,236	60,168	266,381
1991	65,450	51,187	17,140	70,960	65,290	270,026
1992	70,028	59,208	19,080	70,354	66,337	285,034
1993	78,818	69,650	20,668	74,377	72,359	315,872
1994	83,051	79,167	23,399	73,758	77,290	336,665
1995	86,102	75,825	24,443	82,597	81,271	350,238
Average Annual Growth Rate:	5.1%	10.1%	6.6%	5.5%	6.3%	6.6%

Source: Authors' compilations from NAIC data.
Note: Premiums are in millions of current dollars. Average annual growth rate is calculated as (Prem95/Prem88)^(1/7).

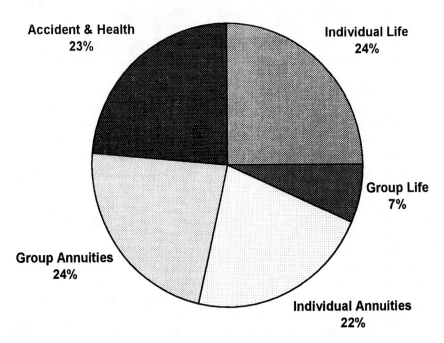

Figure 5-2. Life Insurance Industry Premium Revenues by Line In 1995

accumulation lines, accounted for the remaining 30% of revenues. Because insurers make most of their profits from the margin between the invest-ment yield earned on assets and the rate credited to policyholders on asset accumulation products, the asset accumulation products generate an even higher proportion of profits than their share of revenues would suggest. This is particularly noteworthy because it is in the asset accumulation markets that insurers face the most vigorous competition from banks, mutual fund companies, and investment advisory firms.

The annual growth rate in total life insurance premiums and annuity con-siderations was 6.6% over this time period, but growth varied considerably across lines of business (see table 5-3). The individual annuity business had the highest annual growth rate, averaging 10.1% per year. This far exceeds the growth rate of the indemnity lines, group life and accident and health, which grew at an annual rate of 6.6% and 6.3%, respectively. Group annu-ities and individual life insurance experienced the slowest annual rates of growth, at 5.5% and 5.1%, respectively.

Table 5-4 shows the fraction of total premiums in each line of business that was underwritten by insurance groups for each year in the time period 1988–1995 (the balance is written by unaffiliated companies). For all lines combined, insurers that are members of groups account for 94% to 95% of revenues, and this share has remained nearly constant over the sample period. However, in the individual annuities line, groups gained significant market share over the period—the percentage of revenues underwritten by insurers affiliated with groups increased from 84.1% in 1988 to 91.7% in 1995. The percentage of group annuity revenues written by insurers affiliated with groups remained relatively constant at about 98% during the sample period. Similarly, the share of accident and health premiums written

Table 5-4. Percentage of Premiums Written by Insurance Groups (Percent)

Year	Individual Life	Individual Annuities	Group Life	Group Annuities	Accident and Health	Total
1988	95.1	84.1	95.4	98.8	95.8	94.3
1989	95.0	87.3	95.1	98.6	95.3	94.6
1990	95.3	90.0	95.2	99.1	94.9	95.3
1991	93.4	88.2	94.6	98.7	94.7	94.2
1992	95.3	90.8	94.8	98.6	94.8	95.1
1993	95.4	92.1	93.9	98.6	93.2	94.8
1994	94.7	92.7	93.8	98.3	93.1	94.6
1995	92.9	91.7	93.6	97.8	95.1	94.4

by insurance groups remained constant at around 95%. The group affiliates' share of individual and group life insurance declined slightly over the period, from 95.1% to 92.9% in individual life and from 95.4% to 93.6% in group life.

Concentration trends in the industry are shown in table 5-5, which reports the annual four, eight, and twenty-firm concentration ratios for the industry for 1988 through 1995. These indices represent the share of premiums underwritten by the largest four, eight, or twenty firms in the industry, respectively, and are calculated at the level of decision-making unit (groups and unaffiliated companies). The table shows that asset concentration decreased noticeably over the time period, e.g., the four-firm asset concentration ratio declined from 27.4 to 21.4% between 1988 and 1995. However, the proportions of total premiums written by the largest four, eight, and twenty firms remained relatively constant over the time period, at approximately 20%, 30% and 45%, respectively.

Asset concentration declined due to a loss of market share by the largest insurers in the asset accumulation products resulting from market share gains by the insurer affiliates/partners of nontraditional competitors such as banks, mutual funds, and investment advisors. Premium concentration did not decline in parallel because the largest insurers gained market share in the indemnity lines (group life, and accident and health), partially offsetting the loss in the asset accumulation products. The market share gains in the asset accumulation products by banks, mutual funds, and investment advisory firms (via their insurance affiliates or partners) are most likely attributable to the advantage these firms enjoy over most insurers in product distribution costs.

The market share gains by the top insurers (particularly the top four) in the group life insurance market over the sample period are most likely attributable to scale economies. Group life is a highly competitive market with knowledgeable, cost-conscious buyers (business firms), many of whom have the alternative of self-insuring. Group life insurers thus compete in terms of the efficiency with which they can administer programs for the buyers, resulting in very low expense ratios and profit margins. Being able to spread the fixed costs of operating in the group life insurance business over a broader customer base is thus likely to be a major competitive advantage in this market.

Taken together, the trends in industry structure shown in tables 5-2 through 5-5 and in figure 5-1 are generally consistent with the view that restructuring in the insurance industry primarily involves strategic realignment rather than changes in overall size or market power of particular firms. The percentage of revenues in individual annuities—the fastest growing

LIFE INSURANCE MERGERS AND ACQUISITIONS

Table 5-5. Concentration Ratios for the U.S. Life Insurance Industry (Percent)

	Assets			Total Premiums			Individual Life Premiums			Individual Annuity Premiums		
N=	4	8	20	4	8	20	4	8	20	4	8	20
Year												
88	27.4	39.4	56.5	21.0	29.8	45.0	23.3	31.5	47.9	19.0	29.8	51.1
89	26.2	37.9	55.2	22.2	31.1	46.6	24.3	34.6	51.6	17.7	28.8	49.4
90	24.7	36.4	53.9	23.8	32.6	49.4	26.3	35.4	52.1	19.7	32.7	51.1
91	24.4	35.7	53.9	23.1	33.0	50.1	26.6	35.8	51.8	20.3	33.9	51.9
92	23.6	34.4	52.9	22.4	31.7	48.7	27.1	37.0	53.9	19.8	31.8	49.4
93	22.8	33.3	51.9	20.6	29.7	47.5	26.2	37.3	54.8	17.7	28.8	51.0
94	21.9	31.8	50.9	19.9	29.1	46.1	25.3	35.7	52.0	16.2	27.9	47.9
95	21.4	31.4	51.1	19.6	29.0	45.7	24.8	35.5	52.7	16.2	28.2	49.1

	Group Life Premiums			Group Annuity Premiums			Accident and Health Premiums		
N=	4	8	20	4	8	20	4	8	20
Year									
88	36.6	47.7	61.7	37.0	54.8	77.4	20.0	31.8	52.3
89	37.8	49.6	63.1	37.2	53.8	77.0	21.4	33.1	52.1
90	41.4	52.4	65.7	40.1	57.1	78.4	20.6	34.0	52.9
91	42.7	54.2	67.2	39.4	58.1	81.1	21.0	33.5	54.0
92	45.5	55.8	68.7	37.9	56.5	78.3	22.1	34.5	53.6
93	43.0	52.7	68.2	33.8	52.9	75.9	22.4	33.9	53.7
94	45.4	54.0	69.4	33.2	52.6	75.5	22.1	33.1	53.0
95	46.8	56.1	70.6	29.8	48.5	73.2	22.3	32.9	51.4

segment of the life insurance market—controlled by insurance groups has increased markedly over the last decade. Yet the market shares of the very largest insurers have declined noticeably in both this line and in group annuities. In contrast, concentration in group life insurance has increased significantly over the period, due to the efficiencies associated with economies of scale. Despite these realignments in the market, the overall market share of insurance groups and the overall revenue concentration indices in the market have remained virtually constant.

3. Motivations for Mergers and Acquisitions

Mergers or acquisitions are often motivated by perceived opportunities to improve firm operating performance. In such circumstances, a merger or acquisition may be expected to enhance the efficiency of the target firm and/or the combined post-merger entity. Merger may enhance a firm's efficiency by affecting cost efficiency, revenue efficiency, or both. Firms achieve cost efficiency by adopting the best practice technology (technological efficiency) and by adopting the optimal mix of production inputs (allocative efficiency), taking as given output levels and input prices. In addition, costs can be reduced by attaining the optimal scale—through increasing firm size if the firm is below optimal scale or reducing firm size if the firm is larger than the optimal size. Revenue efficiency is attained by employing the best practice technology and choosing the optimal mix of outputs, holding constant input quantities and output prices. Firms accomplish the economic goal of profit maximization by achieving both cost and revenue efficiency.

There are a number of reasons that merger or acquisition can permit a firm to operate more efficiently. The predominant form of organization in the life insurance industry is the insurance group. Adding a new member to the group has the potential to improve the efficiency of the new group member and of the entire group. While individual companies in a group often operate independently in terms of marketing, a number of important operations are usually undertaken centrally. These include information systems management, investment management, and policyholder services. Spreading the fixed costs of these operations over a broader base has the potential to improve cost efficiency. Revenue efficiency of the group may also be improved if consolidation facilitates cross-selling, improves customer satisfaction, and otherwise enhances the group's ability to produce revenues.

Another rationale for M&A is earnings diversification. Earnings diversification may provide a particularly strong motivation for mergers in the insurance industry. By increasing the breadth of the policyholder pool and entering into loss sharing arrangements among members of an insurance group, losses become more predictable and underwriting earnings volatility is reduced. This potentially gives the insurer the opportunity to take on more risky and higher yielding investments, thus increasing revenues for a given level of overall risk. This reasoning provides another argument for expecting that acquired firms may show revenue efficiency gains as a result of acquisition.

Opportunities for post-merger performance improvements may be greater for acquisitions of firms that are currently relatively inefficient. For example, if the managers of the acquiring group are more capable than those of the target, efficiency gains may occur within the target if the original management is replaced or retrained after acquisition. This reasoning would imply that relatively *inefficient* firms should be more attractive as acquisitions targets than firms that are already relatively efficient.

However, in the life insurance industry there also are reasons to believe that relatively *efficient* firms also might be attractive as acquisition targets. One rationale is provided by the importance of technology. The life insurance industry is undergoing significant technological change; and advances in computer technology offer opportunities for insurers to gain competitive advantages and market share, potentially reducing average costs and increasing revenues. One way to make technology gains quickly is to acquire another firm with better technological capabilities. This suggests that firms with higher technical efficiency may be attractive acquisition targets. Another objective frequently given for M&A is to strengthen a firm's core lines of business or to diversify into new markets or products. Under these objectives as well, firms with higher (cost or revenue) efficiency may be more attractive acquisition or merger targets.

The desire to achieve economies of scale is another common rationale for M&A. Thus, firms operating with non-decreasing (i.e., increasing or constant) returns to scale are likely to be viewed as attractive acquisition targets because they are currently operating in the optimal size range (in the case of constant returns to scale) or have the opportunity to become more efficient through growth (in the case of increasing returns to scale). Firms operating with decreasing returns to scale may be less-attractive acquisition targets because they would have to be reduced in size to achieve optimum scale. Although it is possible to acquire a firm and shed unprofitable operations or lines of business to achieve optimum scale, it is likely to be less costly to acquire a firm that is already scale efficient and hence does not need significant post-merger restructuring. It is also possible that optimal scale can be achieved by combining firms that are operating with increasing returns to scale, providing another reason why firms in the increasing returns to scale range may be relatively attractive as acquisition targets.

Life insurance mergers and acquisitions also may be motivated by regulatory considerations. Following a sharp increase in insolvencies during the 1980s, the NAIC adopted a "solvency policing agenda," including a risk-based capital (RBC) system adopted in 1993. The objectives of the RBC system are to raise capital standards in the industry and to give regulators stronger authority to take action against financially troubled insurers. The existence of the RBC system raises the expected regulatory costs for relatively weak insurers.

Although many insurers restructured their asset portfolios and made other changes to improve their RBC ratios, the weaker insurers in the industry still face the prospect of having to raise additional equity capital to avoid incurring significant restructuring or regulatory costs. Raising capital is difficult for many insurers because the industry contains many mutuals and closely held stock companies. Both of these organizational forms are more limited than widely held stock insurers in their ability to raise new capital. Moreover, information asymmetries with respect to the quality of an insurer's assets and the accuracy of its reserve estimates may raise the costs of external capital, making this source of capital unattractive to many insurers (Chamberlain and Tennyson, 1998). Insurers facing regulatory costs and capital constraints may be likely to favor affiliating with a stronger insurance firm, since information asymmetries between firms within the same industry are likely to be less than those between the target and the general capital markets. Financially weak insurers may be attractive acquisition targets to other insurance firms, particularly if they are efficient and/or operating with favorable returns to scale.

With regard to mergers for the purpose of strengthening capital, unaffiliated single companies are more likely to be acquired than members of an insurance group, as single companies should face greater constraints to capital-raising due to lack of opportunity for capital infusions from the parent concern (Chamberlain and Tennyson, 1998). However, with regard to mergers to achieve optimal restructuring objectives, unaffiliated single companies may be significantly less likely to be acquisitions targets. Managers of insurance groups are likely to view the purchase and sale of individual companies as important components of their strategic arsenal and as potentially enhancing rather than threatening their personal economic value. However, the managers of an unaffiliated company face an uncertain future if their firm is acquired by another firm. This is especially true for top management, the group that has the most control over whether the acquisition takes place. Given this risk to their job security, managers of unaffiliated insurance firms may be more likely to resist takeover offers than managers of insurance groups.

This discussion of the potential motivations for life insurance M&A leads to several predictions regarding the patterns and effects of merger activity in the industry, if acquisition targets are chosen in accordance with these motives. These are summarized in table 5-6. The first prediction is that acquisitions should tend to lead to efficiency improvements for the acquired firm, since consolidation appears to be driven by pressures to compete more effectively. We also can make several predictions regarding which firms will most likely be acquired. First, we predict that firms with non-decreasing returns to scale will be more attractive acquisition targets than firms with decreasing returns to scale. The second prediction is that, because rapid improvements are needed under vigorous competition, more efficient firms will more likely be acquired than inefficient firms. Third, we predict that members of insurance groups will more likely be acquired than unaffiliated single insurers, based on the argument that most acquisitions activity is driven by the desire to optimally restructure. Finally, due to regulatory considerations, we predict that financially vulnerable firms will more likely be acquired than stronger firms.

If our beliefs about the motivating forces underlying M&A in the life insurance industry are correct, the above predictions should be borne out in a majority of the M&A transactions in the industry. To investigate whether this is the case, we undertake an in-depth examination of the characteristics of M&A transactions in the industry. Our analysis utilizes data at the level of the individual firm and compares the characteristics of firms that were acquisitions targets to those that were not. We discuss

Table 5-6. Summary of Predictions About Life Insurance Mergers and Acquisitions

Prediction 1:	Acquisitions will lead to efficiency improvements for the acquired firm.
Prediction 2:	Firms operating with non-decreasing returns to scale are more likely to be acquired.
Prediction 3:	More efficient firms are more likely to be acquired.
Prediction 4:	Firms that are members of insurance groups are more likely to be acquired.
Prediction 5:	Firms that are financially vulnerable are more likely to be acquired.

our data and methodology, and present the results of the analysis in the next section.

4. Analysis of Merger Activity in the Life Insurance Industry

4.1. The Sample and Data

We examine M&A activity in the U.S. life insurance industry during the time period 1989 through 1994. The list of transactions was identified from Conning and Company reports, *Mergers and Acquisitions* magazine, *Best's Review* annual summary of ownership changes, and *Best's Insurance Reports* annual summary of life insurance group composition. Each transaction identified in these sources was then further investigated in the company discussions of *Best's Insurance Reports* to make certain it met our primary criterion of representing a change in the control of a life insurance company. Specifically, we include in our analysis only complete acquisitions and acquisitions of a majority interest that were characterized by *Best's Insurance Reports* as resulting in a change in control. We exclude acquisitions of a minority interest and acquisitions of lines of business from our set of transactions. We also exclude all transactions that represented the internal restructuring of an existing insurance group. Transactions that did not meet these criteria or those that could no be verified in *Best's Insurance Reports* were excluded from our list of transactions.

Our primary objective is to analyze the economic efficiency and certain other characteristics of target firms, and the effects of acquisition on the efficiency of acquisition targets. We also provide an analysis of the efficiency of acquiring firms. However, as explained in more detail below, the analysis of acquiring firms is necessarily less complete than the analysis of acquisition targets as the result of a smaller sample size.

Estimating the efficiency of a firm requires data on firm inputs and input prices, and outputs and output prices.[3] The data used in our study are drawn from the regulatory accounting statements filed by insurers annually with the NAIC. Accordingly, we include in our analysis only those firms for which data reported to the NAIC are available and are a meaningful representation of firm production activities.

To obtain the set of target firms included in the analysis, we omit from our analysis any target firm that was a shell company, in run-off, or inactive prior to the acquisition. In addition, we include only those target firms for which there is a two-year time horizon, both prior to and following their acquisition, in which they are free of other merger and acquisition activity. We also exclude from the sample firms that were merged, retired, or put into run-off or liquidation within two years after acquisition. Imposing these criteria for inclusion in our sample greatly reduces the number of target firms in our analysis but ensures that the results of the analysis are meaningful. Our final sample consists of 106 target firms for which we are able to carry out this in-depth analysis.[4]

4.2. Methodology

We estimate efficiency using data envelopment analysis (DEA) (Charnes et al, 1994), which is described in more detail in Chapter 3 of this book (Cummins, 1999). DEA is a non-parametric approach that computes an efficient best practice frontier for the industry based on convex combinations of firms in the industry. The efficiency of each firm in the sample is calculated relative to this frontier. Fully efficient firms are those that are operating on this best practice frontier. Because all insurers of any significant size are required to report to the NAIC, our data base for determining the industry best practice frontier consists of nearly the entire industry.[5]

In this analysis, we investigate both cost and revenue efficiency. Cost efficiency for a specific firm is defined as the ratio of the costs of a fully efficient firm with the same output quantities and input prices to the given firm's actual costs. Cost efficiency varies between 0 and 1, with a fully efficient firm having cost efficiency equal to 1. One minus a firm's efficiency ratio provides a measure of the proportion by which costs could be reduced if the firm were operating on the cost frontier. Revenue efficiency is defined as the ratio of a given firm's revenues to the revenues of a fully efficient firm with the same input quantities and output prices. Fully efficient firms have revenue efficiency equal to 1 while inefficient firms have revenue efficiency less than 1.

As described more fully in Chapter 3 of this volume, cost efficiency includes both technical and allocative efficiency. That is, a firm can have higher costs than represented by the best practice cost frontier because it is not using the most efficient technology (technical inefficiency) and/or because it is not using the optimal (cost-minimizing) mix of inputs (allocative inefficiency).

Technical efficiency can be further broken down into two components— scale efficiency and pure technical efficiency. A firm that is scale efficient exhibits constant returns to scale (CRS), which means simply that it cannot increase its ratio of output produced to inputs used by changing the quantity of output it produces. Firms that exhibit either decreasing or increasing returns to scale (DRS or IRS) could achieve a greater output-to-input ratio by becoming smaller or larger, respectively, and hence are scale inefficient. A firm must be operating at CRS to achieve full technical efficiency.

Pure technical efficiency measures the firm's efficiency relative to that component of the efficient frontier defined by its "peer group" of firms. If a firm is fully scale efficient, its pure technical efficiency is measured relative to a peer group occupying the CRS segment of the frontier. Such a firm is fully scale efficient but could improve its efficiency in the pure technical sense if it is not currently operating on the CRS segment of the frontier. If the firm's peer group is operating with DRS (IRS), the firm's pure technical efficiency is measured relative to the DRS (IRS) segment of the frontier. Firms operating with DRS (IRS) could improve their efficiency in the pure technical sense if they are not currently operating on the DRS (IRS) segment of the frontier by moving to the frontier and they could further improve their efficiency by attaining CRS (moving from the DRS (IRS) segment of the frontier to the CRS segment).

4.3. Characteristics of Acquisition Targets

In this part of the analysis we compare the efficiency characteristics of the life insurance firms in our sample that were acquired during the period 1989–1994 to those firms in the sample that were not targets of merger or acquisition activity. By virtue of the fact that the efficiency scores for each firm are constructed by comparison to other firms of roughly the same size and input or output mix, the DEA methodology we employ assures that each firm is evaluated relative to its industry peer group.

Table 5-7 compares the relevant characteristics of the target firms in our sample to those of all other firms in the industry for which efficiency estimates are available. Table 5-7 reports the values of each variable averaged over the 1989 to 1994 sample period for target firms and non-target firms, respectively. The results of t-tests for differences between the means of the target and non-target firms are also reported. This analysis reveals a number of statistically significant differences between the target firms and the non-target firms, and these differences are consistent with our predictions regarding acquisition targets in the industry.

Consistent with our hypothesis that firms characterized by non-decreasing returns to scale (NDRS) will be more attractive as acquisition targets, the proportion of acquired firms operating with NDRS is

Table 5-7. Characteristics of Acquisition Targets: 1989–1994 Averages

Variable	Target Firm Means	Non-target Firm Means	t-Test
Total Assets (millions)	1,876.14	1,904.65	*
Total Premiums (millions)	238.55	361.74	*
Capital/Total Assets	0.203	0.213	
Operating Cash Flow/Total Assets	0.029	0.087	***
Liquidity Ratio	1.606	1.348	
Percent Change in Premiums, t-1 to t	4.9	17.3	*
Percent of Constant with Non-decreasing Returns to Scale	73.3	60.3	***
Percent Unaffiliated Companies	14.0	25.1	***
Percent Mutual Companies	2.3	13.6	***
Percent of Companies with A+ Rating	15.1	29.8	***
Percent of Companies with A or A– Rating	38.4	29.9	*
Percent of Companies with B+ or B Rating	18.6	18.0	
Geographic Herfindahl for Premiums	2,890.76	3,551.32	**
Cost Efficiency Score	.384	.357	
Technical Efficiency Score	.631	.568	**
Pure Technical Efficiency Score	.681	.633	**
Allocative Efficiency Score	.622	.642	
Scale Efficiency Score	.924	.894	**
Revenue Efficiency Score	.378	.366	

Source: Authors' calculations from NAIC data.
*** Significant at the 1% level; ** Significant at the 5% level; * Significant at the 10% level.

significantly higher than the proportion of non-target firms operating with NDRS. Among target firms, 73.3% operated with NDRS, compared with only 60.3% for non-target firms. Moreover, acquisition targets exhibit significantly higher technical, pure technical, and scale efficiency than non-target firms. For example, the target firms had average technical efficiency of 63.1%, compared to 56.8% for non-target firms. Cost efficiency and revenue efficiency are also higher for target than for non-target firms, but the differences are not statistically significant. These findings are consistent with our prediction that relatively efficient firms will be more attractive acquisition targets and also consistent with the view that mergers and acquisitions are motivated by a desire to quickly achieve efficiency improvements. The significantly higher technical and pure technical efficiency of target firms underscore the importance of technology in driving consolidation within the life insurance industry.

Consistent with our hypothesis that acquisition targets may display signs of financial vulnerability, target firms have significantly lower ratios of operating cash flow to assets (0.029 as compared to 0.087 for non-target firms) and are significantly less likely to be rated A+ by the A.M. Best Company. Nonetheless, target companies are also significantly less likely to be unaffiliated single firms than the non-acquired firms, as predicted—only 14% of the target firms are unaffiliated, compared to 25.1% of the non-target firms. This finding is consistent with the idea that most acquisition activity in the industry is motivated by restructuring objectives rather than capital needs and that mangers of unaffiliated firms are resistant to takeover bids.

The target companies are also significantly less concentrated geographically than non-acquired firms, as measured by the geographical Herfindahl index, based on the distribution of total premium revenues by state. (A higher value of this index implies higher geographical concentration.) The geographical Herfindahl averages 2,891 for target firms and 3,551 for non-target firms. This suggests that acquiring firms prefer targets that are more geographically diversified. Finally, target companies are somewhat smaller in terms of both assets and premiums; and, as would be expected, mutual firms are significantly less likely to be acquired than stock firms.[6]

4.4. Efficiency Changes for Acquired Firms

The next step in the analysis is to compare the efficiency changes of firms that were acquired during the sample period to firms that experienced no merger or acquisition activity during the period. To make this comparison, we allow for two years of experience before and after the acquisition, i.e., a five-year window centered on the year of acquisition is used to measure changes in efficiency. The change in efficiency of a target firm is measured as the ratio of a firm's efficiency two years after acquisition to its efficiency two years prior to acquisition. Thus, a value of the ratio greater than 1.0 indicates efficiency gains. Efficiency ratios over the same set of five-year windows are computed for the non-target firms to provide a standard of comparison.

Multiple regression analysis is used to analyze the relationship between being an acquisition target and efficiency change. This technique measures the relationship between our dependent variable (the ratio of efficiency two years after acquisition to efficiency two years prior to acquisition) and several independent or explanatory variables. The principal explanatory variable of interest is a dummy or indicator variable set equal to 1 if the firm is acquired by another firm or group and to 0 otherwise. Also included in the equation are several other explanatory variables that we expect to be related to efficiency changes. Including these other variables in the equation allows us to measure the impact of acquisition on efficiency change while controlling for other firm characteristics that may also affect changes in efficiency.

In addition to the dummy variable set equal to 1 for target firms and to 0 for non-target firms, the explanatory variables in the regressions include size (the natural logarithm of assets), organizational form (a dummy variable equal to 1 for mutuals and 0 for stocks), ownership type (a dummy variable equal to 1 if the firm is an unaffiliated company and 0 otherwise), and business mix (the proportions of the firm's premiums in group life, group annuities, individual annuities, and accident and health insurance, with individual life insurance as the excluded category). To control for geographical concentration, we include the firm's geographical Herfindahl index, based on the proportions of premium revenues by state. Recall that a firm with a high geographical Herfindahl index has a substantial share of its business concentrated in one or a few states, while firms with lower Herfindahl indices are more geographically diversified.

The results of the multiple regression analysis are presented in table 5-8. The table shows six regression models, measuring the impact of acquisition on changes in the six different types of efficiency included in this study. As mentioned above, for acquired firms the dependent variables are defined as $E(t+2)/E(t-2)$, where $E(t+2)$ = efficiency two years after acquisition and $E(t-2)$ = efficiency two years prior to acquisition; and for non-target firms the ratios are computed similarly using the same centering years. The dependent variables thus measure the proportionate increase or decrease in efficiency from two years prior to the acquisition to two years after the acquisition. The study compares the firm's efficiency in a period when it was most likely not an acquisition target to a period when a substantial amount of the post-merger integration between the target and the acquirer would have been completed. The numbers shown in table 5-8 are the coefficients of the explanatory variables. Variables with positive coefficients tend to be associated with increases in efficiency between the pre- and post-acquisition periods, while variables with negative coefficients tend to be associated with decreases in efficiency.

The regressions shown in table 5-8 reveal that target firms experienced significantly larger gains in both cost and revenue efficiency than did non-M&A firms, based on statistically significant, positive coefficients of 0.4422

Table 5-8. Regression Models of Changes in Efficiency

Variable	Efficiency Two Years After Acquisition/Efficiency Two Years Before Acquisition					
	Cost	Technical	Allocative	Pure Technical	Scale	Revenue
Intercept	3.2757***	3.6868***	1.1701***	3.3447***	1.1955***	5.5823***
Target Company Dummy	0.4422***	0.3811***	0.0226	0.3279***	0.0145	0.8673***
Ln(Assets)	-0.0842***	-0.1080***	-0.0005	-0.0956***	-0.0058	-0.1727***
Mutual	-0.1341***	-0.0873*	-0.0753**	-0.0857**	0.0026	0.0185
Geographic Herfindahl	-0.2829***	-0.4007***	0.0131	-0.3791***	-0.0001	-0.6734***
Unaffiliated Company	-0.0872*	-0.0642	-0.0303	-0.0674*	0.0134	-0.1466
Percent Group Life Premiums	-0.5033***	-0.4004***	-0.1948***	-0.4813***	0.0433	-0.6748**
Percent Group Annuity	-0.1633	-0.1369	0.0302	-0.1257	0.0149	-0.5965*
Percent Individual Annuity Premiums	-0.0162	0.1077	-0.0986**	0.1018	-0.0103	0.2419
Percent Accumulation and Health Premiums	-0.5795***	-0.4751***	-0.0997***	-0.3920***	-0.0476**	-0.6576***
Adjusted R2	0.1104	0.1040	0.0923	0.1086	0.0213	0.0785
Number of Observations	1798	1798	1798	1798	1798	1792

Note: The dependent variables in the equations are the ratio of a firm's efficiency two years after acquisition to its efficiency two years before acquisition. Values shown are the coefficients of the independent variables.
*** Significant at 1% level; ** significant at 5% level; * significant at 10% level.

and 0.8673, respectively, on the dummy variable for being an acquisition target. The results of the other regressions in the table reveal that the larger cost efficiency gains experienced by acquired firms were primarily attributable to gains in technical efficiency. This is based on the finding that the coefficients of the dummy variable for acquisition in the technical and pure technical efficiency regressions are statistically significant, whereas the coefficients of this variable in the allocative and scale efficiency equations are not significantly different from 0. This provides further evidence of the importance of technology in the insurance industry.

The overall finding of the regression analysis is that acquisition target firms experienced larger cost and revenue efficiency gains than non-target firms, with the cost efficiency gains primarily attributable to gains in technical efficiency. Thus, acquisitions appear to have a beneficial effect on economic efficiency in the life insurance industry. The improvements in both revenue and cost efficiency suggest that acquisitions have a strong positive effect on profits for target firms. However, the argument that acquisitions enable insurers to access economies of scale, often used as the rationale for M&A activity by insurers, is not supported by our analysis.

The other explanatory variables in the regressions provide additional information about the relationship between firm characteristics and changes in efficiency. The significant negative coefficients on the firm size variables in the cost and revenue regressions (the natural logarithm of assets) reveal that larger firms experienced significantly lower efficiency changes than smaller firms. Mutual firms achieved significantly lower efficiency growth than stock firms, except for scale and revenue efficiency where there is no significant difference between stocks and mutuals. This finding is consistent with the argument that mutuals are less aggressive than stocks in minimizing costs and maximizing revenue because the mechanisms available for owners of the firm to control managers are weaker in the mutual ownership form. This finding could also imply that mutuals operate in less complex and less risky lines of business that may provide fewer opportunities for efficiency gains.[7]

The coefficients of the geographical Herfindahl indices reveal that geographically concentrated firms experienced smaller changes in technical, cost, and revenue efficiency than geographically diversified firms. A possible explanation for this finding is that technological advances in data transmission and communications may provide more opportunities for improving efficiency for firms that are relatively diversified geographically.

Firms with higher proportions of their premiums in group life insurance experienced significantly lower growth in all types of efficiency except scale efficiency. This is consistent with the view that group life insurance is a highly efficient line of business, because the opportunity for efficiency gains would be lower in a relatively efficient line. Efficiency gains were also significantly lower in the accident and health line of business, perhaps because this line is already relatively efficient due to the intensive pressure to control costs in the health care industry.

To summarize, in this section we analyze the changes in efficiency for acquisition targets over a five-year window extending from two years prior to the acquisition to two-years after the acquisition. Firms that are not involved in acquisitions are analyzed over matching five-year windows. We find that target firms experienced significantly larger increases in cost and revenue efficiency than did the non-target firms, with the cost efficiency gains primarily attributable to gains in technical efficiency. However, the results do not support the argument that acquisitions lead to significant gains in scale economies.

4.5. Efficiency of Acquiring Firms

Analyzing the effects of acquisitions on acquiring firms proved to be more difficult than for target firms. We have efficiency data for only 46 acquirers because some acquirers are not insurance companies, and hence do not appear in our data base, and several acquirers engaged in more than one transaction during the sample period. In addition, since our data base reports data by company, we lack consolidated statements for insurance groups. Nevertheless, we created efficiency scores for acquiring insurance organizations and for non-M&A insurers at the group level, calculating group efficiency scores by taking weighted averages of the efficiencies of the companies that were members of the group, with weights equal to total insurance output. We looked at the three-year window extending from the year prior to an acquisition to the year after the acquisition, matching non-M&A firms and acquirers by year.[8]

There are no statistically significant differences in efficiency between acquirers and non-M&A firms in the year prior to an acquisition, although non-M&A firms had slightly higher efficiencies than acquirers. The average efficiencies of both acquirers and non-M&A firms increased between the pre- and post-acquisition years. With the exception of scale efficiency, the efficiency gains were larger for acquirers; and acquirer efficiencies exceed those of non-M&A firms in the year following an acquisition, although only the difference in pure technical efficiency is statistically significant. Based on a regression analysis similar to that shown in table 5-8, acquirers experience significantly larger gains in cost efficiency than non-M&A firms in the three-year window surrounding the acquisition year. Thus, we also find some evidence that acquisitions have a beneficial effect on the efficiency of acquiring insurance organizations.

5. Conclusions

This chapter has examined mergers and acquisitions in the U.S. life insurance industry, with the aim of understanding the motives for this consolidation activity and its effects on life insurer efficiency. Our analysis provides support for five specific propositions about mergers and acquisitions in this industry: (1) that acquisitions lead to improvements in efficiency for the acquired firm, (2) that firms operating with non-decreasing returns to scale are more attractive acquisition targets than firms operating with decreasing returns to scale, (3) that efficient firms are more likely to be acquired than inefficient firms, (4) that unaffiliated single insurers are less likely to be acquired than insurers that are members of existing groups, and (5) that financially vulnerable firms are more likely to be acquired.

Our findings in support of the first four of these five hypotheses lends credence to the view that consolidation activity in the life insurance industry is driven largely by the increasingly competitive environment and the need to rapidly achieve strategic objectives. Our finding in support of the fifth hypothesis suggests that regulatory capital requirements, or the need for capital more generally, may also be a motivating factor for some life insurance acquisitions.

The overall conclusion of this study is that mergers and acquisitions in the life insurance industry are driven for the most part by economically viable objectives, and have had a beneficial effect on efficiency in the industry. We expect to see more consolidation in the industry in the future, as competitive pressures continue. There are still many insurers that are burdened with excessively costly and inefficient agency distribution systems that in the long run will not be able to compete with nontraditional competitors such as banks, mutual funds, and investment advisory firms.

The pressures on inefficient insurers will become even more intense if the Glass-Steagall Act is repealed. Glass-Steagall repeal also can be expected to motivate more mergers and acquisitions, as banks seek to enter the market with their own insurance subsidiaries. The competitive landscape would change even more profoundly if the federal income tax code were revised to reduce or eliminate the tax deferral on interest earnings accumulated in life insurance and annuity contracts. Moreover, although some firms have made progress technologically, there are still many firms in the industry that have not been able to effectively exploit technology to create value for shareholders and policyholders. Additional research will be needed to determine whether future restructuring is economically beneficial. It would also be useful to explore the effects of recent restructuring on the cost and revenue efficiency of the acquiring firms or of consolidated insurance groups.

Notes

* Portions of this chapter are excerpted from our paper "Consolidation and Efficiency In the U.S. Life Insurance Industry." (Cummins, Tennyson and Weiss), *Journal of Banking and Finance* 23 (1999), 325–357.

1. See Conning and Company, 1998; Lonkevich, 1995; and Farinella, 1996 for discussions of these motives in the financial press.

2. One limitation of the Conning data is that, in some cases, the data include sales of books of business only, and transactions that occur within a single insurance group; hence, the number of true acquisitions of life insurers per year may be slightly overstated. Additionally, the value of an acquisition is included in the annual total only if known, and hence the total value of life insurance acquisitions per year may be slightly understated. The sample of firms used in our regression analysis has been thoroughly checked to eliminate any such reporting problems.

3. Chapter 3 of this volume describes in more detail the construction of these variables for each firm.

4. We initially identified 317 mergers and acquisitions targets over this time period. We eliminated 59 of these firms from the sample because they were inactive, shell companies or in run-off when acquired; 68 were eliminated because they were merged or retired within two years after acquisition; 45 were eliminated because they were involved in one or more additional transactions within two years before or two years after the transaction; 8 were eliminated because the transaction could not be verified in Best's; and 31 were eliminated because sufficient data were not available to estimate efficiency scores.

5. The sample used to estimate the efficiency frontier by year consisted of approximately 750 firms per year, representing about 80% of industry assets.

6. Because mutuals are owned by their policyholders and do not issue shares of stock, mutual acquisitions are usually accomplished using "guarantee capital certificates." These are in reality debt instruments that are subordinated to insurance loss claims against the company. However, for regulatory purposes they are treated as equity. The use of these "surplus notes" is tightly regulated, and mutual acquisitions in general receive more stringent regulatory scrutiny than stock company acquisitions.

7. Evidence that mutual property-liability insurers are involved in less complex and less risky activities is provided by Mayers and Smith (1988) and Lamm-Tennant and Starks (1993).

8. We compared one rather than two years pre- and post-acquisition because the sample size for a five-year window is even more limited.

References

Chamberlain, Sandra L. and Sharon Tennyson. "Capital Shocks and Merger Activity in the Property-Liability Insurance Industry," *Journal of Risk and Insurance* 65 (1998), 563–595.

Charnes, A., W.W. Cooper, A. Lewin, and L. Seiford (eds.), *Data Envelopment Analysis: Theory, Methodology and Applications*, Boston, MA: Kluwer Academic Publishers, 1994.

Conning and Company. *Mergers and Acquisitions and Public Equity Offerings: Mid-Year 1998 Review*, Hartford, CT: Conning and Company, 1998.

Cummins, J. David. "Efficiency in the U.S. Life Insurance Industry: Are Insurers Minimizing Costs and Maximizing Revenues?," in J.D. Cummins and A. Santomero (eds.), *Changes in the Life Insurance Industry: Efficiency, Technology, and Risk Management*, 1999.

Cummins, J. David, Sharon Tennyson, and Mary A. Weiss. "Consolidation and Efficiency In the U.S. Life Insurance Industry," *Journal of Banking and Finance* 23 (1999), 325–357.

Farinella, Michael A. "Mergers and Acquisitions Drove 1995 Corporate Changes." *Best's Review: Life/Health Edition*, June 1996, 65 ff.

Lonkevich, Dan. "The Challenge Beyond Consolidation." *Best's Review: Life/Health Edition*, September 1995, 30–35.

Lamm-Tennant, J. and L. Starks. "Stock Versus Mutual Ownership Structures: The Risk Implications," *Journal of Business* 66 (1993), 29–46.

Mayers, D. and C.W. Smith, Jr. "Ownership Structure Across Lines of Property-casualty Insurance," *Journal of Law and Economics* 31 (1988), 351–378.

6 STRATEGY, HUMAN RESOURCE MANAGEMENT, AND THE PERFORMANCE OF LIFE INSURANCE FIRMS

Clint Chadwick and Peter Cappelli

1. Introduction

The U.S. life insurance industry, which has been characterized by stability fostered by government regulation (Scott, O'Shaughnessy, & Cappelli, 1994), has been experiencing great turbulence from the accelerating confluence of financial services such as banking, savings and loans, investment management, and other insurance. For example, many major investment houses are beginning to cross-license their brokers to sell insurance products to clients. Banks have been offering annuity products or close substitutes to their retail customers for some time, and the entire retirement asset market has seen competition from bank products, mutual funds, and various types of standard securities offered by full-service brokers. Indeed, the differentiation between different kinds of financial services formalized by the federal government's regulatory framework has been eroding for some time. This has created a great deal of uncertainty about appropriate strategies for financial services firms, including life insurance companies. The old sureties have disappeared and have been replaced with uncertainties.

The fact that many financial services firms are seeking growth through mergers and acquisitions underscores the lack of confident strategic thinking in the industry today. In fact, in our field interviews with representative life insurance firms, some individuals confided that they wondered whether their firm had *any* distinctive strategic capabilities. This is a pertinent question. Certainly, the persistent finding of considerable overall inefficiency and of widespread variability in firm efficiency in econometric studies of this industry (e.g., Cummins & Zi, 1999; Gardner & Grace, 1993; Yuengert, 1993; Grace & Timme, 1992; Weiss, 1986) does nothing to dispel the notion that many life insurance firms could be managed more effectively.

Our field interviews also brought out a striking discrepancy of opinion on a related subject, human resource management (HRM). High level managers in a majority of the firms we visited were quite certain that giving extra attention to HRM, particularly for back office personnel, would do little to enhance their firm's competitive advantage. In these firms, HRM is viewed as a purely administrative function, not a source of strategic leverage. However, top managers in some of the high performing firms we visited vehemently insisted that managing their back office functions effectively was crucial to their competitiveness. This strong divergence of opinions about the strategic importance of HRM within the same industry is not unusual, and it suggests that the HRM choices of life insurance firms may be an underdeveloped source of strategic leverage. But what kinds of HRM practices are most strategically effective?

Managers developing HRM strategies may look toward an expanding stream of academic research, Strategic Human Resource Management (SHRM), which is beginning to document the potential for HRM systems to markedly improve organizational performance (e.g., Ichniowski, Shaw, & Prenusshi, 1997; Huselid, 1995; MacDuffie, 1995; Arthur, 1994). These studies generally suggest that empowering workers with more autonomy and participation, organizing their work around cross-functionality and flexibility through such practices as job rotation and autonomous work teams, and investing in employees' abilities through intensive selection and training is related to greater organizational productivity (Dyer & Reeves, 1995). However, since these studies have been performed almost exclusively in heavy manufacturing industry contexts, it's unclear how well their results apply to a service industry. The study in this chapter, by contrast, centers on the life insurance industry and makes use of the broad-based industry study data reported in Chapter 2, in summary form, to investigate how human resource practices can and do affect firm productivity and efficiency.

2. Introduction to the Data Set

The data come from an extensive, Sloan foundation-sponsored study of productivity and performance in the life insurance industry. The data instruments comprised a comprehensive bundle of 10 different surveys, each intended for a different function in the typical life insurance firm, such as underwriting, marketing, human resources, and claims. We received at least one of these surveys from 70 different major U.S. life insurance companies. Restricting the sample to U.S. life insurance firms helped to control for heterogeneity driven by differences in national regulatory regimes in this industry. One advantage of this study is that our efforts to relate Human Resource systems to strategy and organizational performance are informed by the work of faculty from the risk management and insurance department at Wharton, who were part of our study team, to determine a concise, appropriate performance equation for these data (see Carr, 1997).

The survey data were matched to financial accounting data from the NAIC industry association's data base for all firms in life insurance. The efficiency scores for each firm were developed through an econometric method called data envelopment analysis (DEA). This approach is developed elsewhere in this book; see Chapter 3 (Cummins, 1999). Essentially, this procedure takes information from a group of firms and derives an "efficient frontier" for them, much like a standard macroeconomic production possibilities frontier. The most efficient firms map out the far edge of the frontier and have a DEA score of 1. Less efficient firms have lower scores that range down to 0. This measure has at least two advantages: 1) it explicitly gives a measure of the relative efficiencies of the firms in the sample, and 2) it is less subject to the biases generated by differences in formal reporting practices for financial measures of performance.

These DEA scores were developed in the population of firms offering life insurance products in the United States, over 700 companies. The DEA efficiency variable used in the third section of this chapter is skewed left and has an absolute range restriction on either end of its distribution (0 and 1), making a Tobit regression preferable to ordinary least squares regression. This DEA variable averages each firm's efficiency score from 1993 to 1995.

The 68 firms in the Sloan survey sample are a subset of all life insurance firms. Nevertheless, the mean values of various important characteristics of our sample firms, such as organizational size, form (mutual vs. stock companies), product mix, growth rates, and efficiency, do not differ from those of the larger population in ways that should cause serious concern (Carr, 1997), so sample bias does not appear to be a major issue. Table 6-1 contains descriptive statistics and a correlation matrix for the data used in the analyses in this chapter.

Table 6-1. Descriptive Statistics for Variables Used in Efficiency Regressions

	N	Mean	Standard Deviation
Basic Performance Model Variables			
Log of admitted assets excluding separate accounts	65	21.14	1.97
Ordinary individual life premiums as a fraction of total premiums	65	0.549	0.335
Group annuity premiums as a fraction of total premiums	65	0.027	0.108
Average market power index total—50 states + DC	65	0.052	0.108
Average annual growth in premium and annuity considerations, 1993–1995	65	0.055	0.805
Narrow (offers 7 or less of 15 individual life and health products; dummy)	52	0.442	0.501
Dominant distribution type is non-exclusive (dummy)	56	0.232	0.426
Interaction term between narrow and non-exclusive	52	0.346	0.48
Expert underwriting system (dummy)	49	0.225	0.422
HR Practices Variables			
Degree to which individual and organizational performance ratings determine merit increases	62	1.677	0.742
Formal performance appraisals	39	1.994	0.662
Number of applicants interviewed for a typical entry-level position	44	4.89	1.846
Promoting from within	44	3.016	0.825
Employee attitude surveys	62	0.371	0.487
Including teamwork skills in performance appraisals (dummy)	62	0.677	0.463
Percentage of pay tied to organizational performance for lower-level employees	60	1.47	4.249
General profitsharing (dummy)	62	0.274	0.45
Percentage of employees eligible for gainsharing	62	4.677	19.373
Use of tests in selection	62	2.29	1.407
Dependent Variable			
Average DEA score, 1993–1995	64	0.439	0.275

3. How Life Insurance Differs from Heavy Manufacturing

The types of work performed within the life insurance and heavy manufacturing industries are very different. First, life insurance work is more likely to be white collar and is not physically demanding (Scott, O'Shaughnessy, & Cappelli, 1994). Life insurance products are made up of different combinations of interest rates, risk protection, and payment schedules rather than physical goods. Second, services are generally distinguished by a strong degree of customer participation, or co-production, in generating the service being purchased in order to tailor it to customers' needs. For example, determining the appropriate life insurance product for a customer may require her to spend time actively evaluating a number of different policy options with an agent in order to achieve a good fit for her risk management needs. The requirement for customer participation can be partially mitigated by using standardized products (Fitzsimmons & Fitzsimmons, 1994), but these tend to be products with lower profit margins and more limited applicability. The third distinguishing characteristic of financial services is that, unlike manufactured, physical goods, services cannot be inventoried. Although the organizational capability to support a particular type of service product may be in put in place for an extended time, service transactions are created upon demand. For example, an individual's life insurance policy is only created through an interaction between an employee and a customer.

These three attributes of financial service products challenge concepts of efficiency associated with output per unit of input that are carried over from manufacturing. One response to this condition in life insurance has been to separate sales divisions from the rest of the firm that work more closely with customers and therefore are more highly impacted by these three attributes of service products. The degree to which sales is integrated with the rest of the firm therefore constitutes an organizational design question with significant strategic consequences.

Sales integration is usually confined to three different product distribution models. The *agency sales model* most clearly separates sales from other insurance functions. In the agency model, independent insurance agents handle the sales function for multiple insurance firms, which supply the products and some product support. The *branch sales model* works in much the same fashion, except that sales agents are dedicated to the products of and are employed by a single company, such as State Farm or Northwest Mutual. Even more closely integrating the sales function with the rest of the firm are the few life insurance firms that utilize *direct marketing* through employees in call centers to reach their target markets (Scott, O'Shaughnessy, & Cappelli, 1994; Lederer, 1971). These three product distribution systems can be viewed as stops on a continuum of integration between sales and the rest of the insurance firm that starts with the agency model, which is least integrated with the firm, to direct marketing, which is much more tightly coupled to other parts of the firm.

Interestingly, some companies use more than one of these sales models at the same time. An idea of the distribution of these various organizational forms comes from our sample of major life insurance firms. Sixty firms returned portions of our survey that addressed marketing and sales operations. We encouraged participating firms to report on each of the three types of product distribution systems employed by their firm (nine firms in our sample did not return any marketing and sales portion of the survey). Of these 60 reporting firms, 25 reported on marketing and sales within the branch sales (or exclusive) product distribution model, 41 reported on the agency (or non-exclusive) product distribution model, and 5 reported on the direct marketing model. Table 6-2 details the overlap among these product distribution models for our 60 responding firms. A surprisingly large proportion of our sample employ both exclusive and non-exclusive sales models, which are commonly thought within the industry to be incompatible. Direct marketing in our sample remains rather rare, either alone or in tandem with one of the other two sales models.[1] None of our sample firms uses all three distribution systems.

To restate our previous point, we suggest that insurance firms can attempt to concentrate co-produced services in their sales divisions through their choices of product distribution systems, and allow these firms to utilize more traditional notions of productivity in "back office" functions (i.e., output/input), such as underwriting and claims processing. However, while this approach may mitigate problems associated with co-production for

Table 6-2. Frequency of Product Distribution Models in Life Insurance Data

Product Distribution System	Count
Exclusive only	15
Non-exclusive only	32
Direct Marketing only	2
Exclusive & non-exclusive	8
Exclusive & direct marketing	2
Non-exclusive & direct marketing	1
Total	60

large portions of the firm, it cannot eliminate them altogether. The mis-alignments between the activities of sales divisions and the firm's other functions in this approach can create more inefficiencies than those elimi-nated by isolating co-production within sales. This issue has been investi-gated elsewhere to some degree with mixed results using the current data set. Carr (1977) found some evidence that firms with exclusive distribution systems are more efficient than firms with non-exclusive ones. However, the results reported in Chapter 4 reexamined this issue. Using a model of constant returns and allowing for added revenue efficiencies, it reversed this finding and supports the industry's perceived wisdom that exclusive distribution is more expensive and does not deliver proportionate advantages in productivity.

Another potential solution to the problems posed by service products is to routinize service transactions by defining them in minute detail. To cite a couple of common examples, this approach has been followed with great success by McDonald's in fast food and by Marriott in luxury lodging. However, given the state of uncertainty and rapid change in financial services, it's unclear how useful the widespread application of this approach would be for life insurance firms. Because this approach limits employees' flexibility in customizing service transactions to the needs of customers, it's best suited to environments where work flows and the types of work done are largely predictable—a description which may not apply very well to many of the more complex life insurance functions and products.

An alternative approach that recognizes employees as strategically important stakeholders in the organization has been suggested in the SHRM research noted above. At the minimum, this approach requires that 1) strategic issues inform choices about human resource (HR) practices; 2) cooperative relationships with employees be developed and maintained; and 3) HR systems that encourage employee flexibility, autonomy, skills development, and participation be put in place (cf. Frederiksen, Riley, & Myers, 1984). In the following sections, we utilize data from a comprehen-sive survey of major firms in the life insurance industry to evaluate each of these prescriptions.

4. Links to Strategy in Life Insurance Human Resource Systems

Issue #1: Is strategy related to HR practices in life insurance firms?

The strategic approach to HRM supports aligning HR systems with or-ganizational strategy. HR systems should support strategic objectives and enhance implementation. This relationship should magnify the performance impact of a strategic plan, whether this effect is positive or negative (e.g., Baird & Meshoulam, 1988). Therefore, the degree to which HR practices are related to organizational strategies is often seen as an indicator of how deeply management has adopted a strategic perspective toward managing its HR. Unfortunately, most of the life insurance firms we talked to confessed little understanding of how to adapt their HR systems to strategy. As a result, their HR systems were likely to be determined by piecemeal reactions to other, less strategic factors, such as changes in employment law, and by firm or industry custom, thus compromising their HR strategic coherence. In other words, there generally seems to be little strategic rationale for the sets of HR practices life insurance firms implement. This makes it more likely that different HR practices in a firm can contradict and cancel each other out, such as when employees are organized into teams but are only compensated as individuals. In this example, the compensation scheme makes it much less likely that employees in teams will work cooperatively.

Analyses of our survey data support the assertion that life insurance firms' HR systems have little strategic coherence. We attempted to link three different measures of strategy to HR practices within our sample firms: 1) Michael Porter's familiar generic strategies of cost leadership, differentiation, and focus (Porter, 1980, 1985); 2) a sophisticated operationalization of strategy, which measures the reported emphasis a firm places on various strategic initiatives relevant to life insurance firms[2]; and 3) the general compensation strategies for each firm. Table 6-3 gives the relationship of these strategies with two important organizational attributes, exclusive distribution and stock ownership (non-exclusive distribution and mutual companies are the respective omitted categories). As the correlations show, the strategies do not overlap significantly, with the exception of cost-leadership strategies and market-based compensation. Perhaps tying compensation to market rates helps some firms keep a lid on their compensation expenses. Exclusive distribution companies are more likely to have a differentiation strategy. This appears reasonable because it can be both difficult and expensive to imitate the distinguishing characteristics of exclusive distribution systems. In our sample, stock companies are more likely to use exclusive distribution.

Despite many different permutations of the analysis, the relationships between these measures of strategy and firms' HR practices were no more significant than if occurring by chance (analyses not shown). Organizational strategy does not appear to significantly influence the kinds of HR practices implemented in life insurance firms' back-office functions. As we noted

Table 6-3. Correlations of Firm Strategies, Governance Structures, and Primary Distribution Systems

	1	2	3	4	5	6	7	8	9	10
1. Cost strategy	1.00									
2. Differentiation strategy	-0.12	1.00								
3. Focus strategy	-0.19	-0.07	1.00							
4. Market-based compensation strategy	-0.34*	-0.10	0.01	1.00						
5. Internally-oriented compensation strategy	-0.02	0.15	0.11	-0.05	1.00					
6. "High service to customers and managers, wide range of product offerings and distribution, advertising and build brand awareness, and operating efficiency/cost control" strategy	-0.17	0.17	0.02	0.21	-0.28	1.00				
7. "Options in market management of funds" strategy	-0.19	-0.08	0.08	-0.03	0.01	0.00	1.00			
8. "High investment returns, lower pricing, and conservative underwriting" strategy	0.13	0.19	-0.02	-0.09	0.09	0.07	0.09	1.00		
9. Exclusive distribution	-0.21	0.32*	0.20	0.00	0.03	0.03	-0.07	0.04	1.00	
10. Stock company	0.01	-0.11	0.10	0.14	-0.09	0.06	0.12	-0.13	-0.39*	1.00

$*p < .05$

above, other factors such as reactions to changes in employment law may be more important determinants of life insurance HR systems, and relationships between HR systems and strategy might be uncovered if we controlled for these stronger influences. But that is precisely our point. If life insurance firms are to derive strategic value from their human resources, strategy must play a stronger role in policy development.

Nevertheless, individual and group performance is addressed in some interesting ways in life insurance firms' HR systems. Concerning individual performance, 97% of firms responding to the human resource portion of the survey have formal performance appraisal programs that cover both exempt and non-exempt employees. Sixty-eight percent of responding firms report including assessments of teamwork skills in formal appraisals. Moreover, many firms are experimenting with appraisals that include other raters in addition to supervisors. Forty-eight percent of our survey firms utilize appraisal input from at least one source other than the employee's immediate supervisor. Table 6-4 provides a breakdown of the degree to which different appraisal input sources are used in our sample firms.

Ties between the activities of individual employees and organizational performance also figure prominently in life insurance firms' HR practices, especially in the compensation of middle- and upper-level managers. However, compensation based on organizational performance for workers farther down in the organizational hierarchy is rare (see table 6-5, below). This becomes even clearer when considering the kinds of compensation our sample firms employ. For example, 80% of our firms report having an incentive bonus plan. However, as table 6-5 illustrates, incentive pay based on organizational performance is much more likely to be extended to upper level employees. Other types of compensation based on organizational performance, which traditionally have been more likely to include both lower and upper level employees such as non-qualified profitsharing (30%

Table 6-4.　Sources of Appraisal Input in Addition to Immediate Supervisors

Appraisal Input Source	Percentage of Sample Firms Using this Input Source
Other superiors	29
Coworkers/peers	27
Customer(s)	24
Subordinates	21
Other	11

Table 6-5.   Mix of Compensation Types by Hierarchical Level (Percent)

Compensation Type	Senior Managers	Middle Managers	Supervisors	Support Staff
Base salary	58	70	72	75
Benefits	19	20	21	21
Incentive pay	17	8	3	2
Organizational performance	7	3	2	1

Note: Due to rounding, columns may not add exactly to 100%.

of firms), employee stock ownership plans (ESOPs) (12% of firms), and gainsharing (6% of firms), are much less common in our sample.

This pattern is consistent with the work of organizational theorists, who argue that the effects of upper-level employees' actions are much more difficult to accurately attribute to individuals and should therefore be linked to organizational performance. Moreover, agency theorists argue that the actions of upper level employees have a more pronounced influence on organizational performance, making merit-based rewards for organizational performance more appropriate for upper level employees. Thus, it's not surprising to observe the above patterns in compensation and to note that 97% of our sample firms claim to adjust salaries annually based on merit considerations.

However, this approach may be shortsighted. Along with the poor links between HR practices and strategy, this pattern in compensation practices implies that life insurance firms are taking an overly quantitative, financially oriented approach to employment relationships. During this time of rapid industry change, firms are reinforcing hierarchical compensation plans rather than taking advantage of participative HR systems that encourage adaptability and innovation among lower ranking employees. Some life insurance companies are beginning to recognize the harm of such uneven compensation practices. Fifty-four percent of our sample firms give awards or recognition for team or small-group performance. These group incentives are concentrated in companies with non-exclusive rather than exclusive agents. This suggests that life insurance firms that have less direct administrative control of employees in their distribution systems are more likely to recognize the importance of integrating the efforts of their non-sales employees through teamwork. Perhaps the difficulties in exerting control over non-exclusive agents also focused the attention of these firms on coordinating their non-sales employees.

Nevertheless, it will often be difficult for insurance firms to adapt to a new, flexible competitive environment in financial services after having been comfortably ensconced in a very predictable, regulated industry for such a long time. This will be especially true for firms that only encourage flexibility within compensation schemes and ignore potential linkages between strategy and HR, which is a common approach among firms. In fact, some well-known SHRM studies find that many firms that aim for more flexibility and commitment from their employees follow the "adjust compensation only" route (Huselid & Becker, 1997). Unfortunately, these studies also document how organizational performance for firms utilizing this approach usually lags behind the performance of firms that employ more comprehensive approaches to strategically managing their human resource systems (e.g., Chadwick & Cappelli, 1998; Arthur, 1994; Ichniowski, et al., 1997). As we detail in the next section, focusing on psychological as well as financial aspects of employment relationships during times of strategic change can markedly increase organizational performance in life insurance firms.

5. Downsizing and Firm Efficiency in Life Insurance

Issue #2: Do measures which aim to preserve cooperative relationships with employees after downsizing also increase post-downsizing productivity?

Downsizing and other types of dramatic strategic renewal initiatives, such as restructuring, have swept American industry in the last two decades. We define a downsizing episode, also known as rightsizing or as a reduction in force (RIF), as a layoff in which a group of employees are asked to leave an organization, but are not discharged "for cause." This includes groups of displaced employees even if they are placed elsewhere in a related operation or in another subsidiary of the same parent organization. The essential goal of downsizing is eliminating employment positions within an organization. Consistent with the emerging consensus among downsizing researchers, our data suggest that the choices firms make in managing employees through a downsizing can be crucial to post-downsizing organizational efficiency (cf., Chadwick, Walston, & Hunter, 1998; Cameron, Freeman, & Mishra, 1991). In other words, downsizing is not inherently effective or ineffective; the performance impact of a downsizing program crucially depends on how it's carried out.

Unfortunately, the sample size of firms responding to the downsizing portion of our survey was quite small (24 firms), so our results on this issue, while provocative, are tentative. Nevertheless, the data suggest that the life insurance industry has experienced widespread and increasingly deeper downsizing episodes. Our downsizing subsample comprises 35% of the full sample of life insurance firms, and, because the downsizing supplement was optional, this proportion probably undercounts the number of sample firms that had recently downsized. Suggestive support for this contention comes from the human resource portion of the survey on a related issue, strategic restructuring, where a considerable 67% of responding firms reported having reorganized internal reporting relationships, 35% reported having consolidated lines of business, and 32% reported having consolidated activities geographically within the past three years. Of the 24 firms which returned the downsizing survey, 7 have exclusive distribution systems, 11 have non-exclusive distribution, 3 have both exclusive and non-exclusive distribution, and 3 did not respond to the marketing survey. Not surprisingly, considering the favor that Wall Street has bestowed on downsizing in recent years, 75% of these firms are stock companies rather than mutuals. The average depth of workforce reductions, measured as a percentage of a firm's total employees who have been released, grew over the study period from 4.3% of employees in 1992 to 7.1% of employees in 1995 (see figure 6-1).

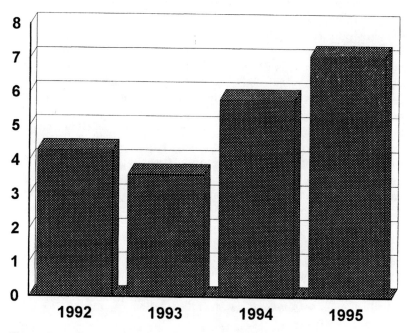

Figure 6-1. Percentage of Workers Downsized, 1992–1995

The most commonly cited factors leading to downsizing were competitive pressures, cost reduction, and changes in corporate strategy. However, the reported importance of reducing costs far outstripped the importance ascribed to the other two factors by our downsizing firms. Similarly, far and away the most *commonly cited* objective of downsizing was reducing labor costs (83% of the downsizing sample), which was also rated as the *most important* downsizing goal. Other common downsizing goals were reducing organizational layers (74%), eliminating unnecessary work (70%), and increasing productivity (65%). Nearly half of downsizing sample firms were trying to achieve all four of these goals simultaneously.

However, putting reductions in labor costs first in a downsizing program can lead to downsizing practices that ignore the psychological impact of downsizing on "survivor" (remaining) employees, undermining their commitment to the firm and their trust in management and, consequently, seriously depressing organizational performance after downsizing (Chadwick, et al., 1998; Cascio, 1993). For example, denying terminated employees a degree of dignity and respect during the downsizing process has a powerful effect on survivors, who draw inferences about the firm's opinion of their worth and of their job security from the ways in which downsized employees are treated. Thus, humiliating practices like having security escort downsized employees out of the firm can negatively affect the productivity of survivors, who become disaffected with their current jobs and begin searching for positions outside the firm. On the other hand, affirming employees through careful attention to open and fair downsizing processes and investments in outplacement assistance can help preserve survivors' commitment to the firm. Over the past decade, downsizing researchers have steadily documented the effects of such downsizing practices on individual level outcomes such as job satisfaction and commitment to the firm but, until now, they have not been able to directly link these individual level downsizing "best practices" to organizational productivity.

To realize this objective in our sample, we created a simple index of nine questions based on behavioral researchers' prescriptions for carrying out downsizing in ways that should maintain individual downsizing survivors' satisfaction and commitment to the firm. Each of the following questions was included in the life insurance downsizing supplementary survey and was scored using five-point Likert measures of respondent firms' levels of agreement (a 1 or 2 indicated disagreement, a 3 indicated neutrality, and a 4 or 5 indicated agreement):

- *Our company prepared a systematic analysis of jobs months prior to the downsizing.*

- *Middle and lower level managers were involved in identifying which individuals would be released.*
- *We carefully trained managers in procedures for counseling remaining employees.*
- *The reasons for an employee's layoff or redeployment were carefully explained to affected employees.*
- *During the course of downsizing management increased the amount and openness of communication with employees.*
- *We were successful in preserving employees dignity during the downsizing process.*
- *We have increased our investment in training current employees since downsizing.*
- *We have undertaken efforts to increase remaining employees' sense of employment security with our company.*
- *We have undertaken efforts to increase employees' confidence in the marketability of their skills.*

The downsizing index is a count of the number of times a responding firm disagreed with one of the nine statements above. These index scores ranged from 0 to 5. We trichotomized our 24 firms into three groups: low (index scores of 0 or 1), medium (index scores of 2) or high (index scores of 4 or 5). We then used nonparametric Mann-Whitney tests to examine the differences between the high and low groups (comprised of 10 and 9 firms, respectively) on various performance measures. In other words, we compare two groups of downsizing firms, with the high group being those firms that had more clearly rejected the suggestions of behavioral downsizing researchers.

We found that the high index group was significantly more likely to have higher voluntary turnover (13.8% vs. 7.8%, $p < .03$), but significantly less likely to have hired back downsized employees as contract or temporary help (mean Likert score of 1.3 vs. 2.4, $p < .001$). Both of these can be seen as negative outcomes. Voluntary turnover, of course, is often interpreted as an indicator of employee commitment, while many downsizing researchers and consultants view rehiring downsized employees as a sign that the downsizing was poorly planned and didn't really accomplish fundamental strategic change. Indeed, it's not unusual for firms to find their de facto employment levels creeping back to pre-downsizing levels in the months following a major downsizing (Cascio, 1993). Thus, these results suggest mixed implications for organizations that emphatically reject the prescriptions of behavioral downsizing researchers. The low index group is more actively externalizing employment by changing employees from full-time status to independent contractors to a greater degree than the high index group. By definition, this practice makes working relationships more contractual and less infused with loyalty to the firm. Paradoxically, these firms may reap less disaffection, reflected by lower turnover, among their surviving employees. Although these index scores were not directly related to differences in organizational productivity or financial performance in our sample, we suspect that a larger sample would have detected significant differences in the productivity of life insurance firms in our high and low index groups.[3]

We also examined all of the downsizing index questions individually to see if a few specific questions were driving these results. For voluntary turnover, firms that had prepared a systematic analysis of jobs prior to downsizing, had undertaken efforts to increase survivors' sense of employment security, and had attempted to increase employees' confidence in the marketability of their skills were especially likely to have lower turnover. This underscores the need to address survivors' concerns about their post-downsizing futures as well as the need for a well-reasoned downsizing plan. If these needs are not met, those employees with other labor market opportunities are likely to express their confidence in management by "voting with their feet": leaving the firm for other opportunities.

Some of the individual index items also shed light on the results for the rehiring of former employees as contractors or temps. Increased investment in training survivors after downsizing and efforts to increase survivors' sense of employment security were both associated with more rehiring of former employees. Perhaps this reflects a partitioning of the workforce into "core" employees who are the focus of managerial investments that reduce turnover and increase productivity while, at the same time, "peripheral" employees who hold positions that are increasingly reduced, de-skilled, or externalized. If this is true, then the high index group, which more strongly rejected behavioral researchers' prescriptions, tells an important story: These firms may be following a losing course, one in which they alien their current employees, which leads to higher turnover, yet, at the same time they are not willing to hire independent contractors or temps to fill the gaps in employment.

Thus, we have suggestive evidence that firms which, on average, are less committed to the prescriptions of behavioral downsizing researchers for keeping downsizing survivors happy may have created conditions that depress their firms' future. Nevertheless, because these data are cross-sectional, predictions are hazardous. It's possible, for example, that the increase in voluntary turnover is a temporary post-downsizing phenomenon which has no real effects on long- term organizational performance. Also, the sample is too small to dispel serious caveats about sample bias.

In spite of these concerns, these provisional results are compelling and serve as the foundation for more elaborated research on these issues in a large sample of U.S. hospitals (Chadwick, Walston, & Hunter, 1998) which is generating similar results as well as connections with organizations' financial performance. Thus, as our analysis here implies, management sensitivity to treating employees fairly and respectfully during downsizing may impact the subsequent productivity of life insurance firms. HR management can be an important complement to strategic initiatives designed to enhance organizational competitiveness, and should not be overlooked, especially during events as traumatic as downsizing and restructuring.

6. Relating Human Resource Systems to Firm Performance in Life Insurance

Issue #3: Can human resource management systems that encourage flexibility, autonomy, skills development, and participation, enhance organizational performance in life insurance?

Mark Huselid's *Academy of Management Journal* article (1995) has had one of the strongest impacts of any empirical research paper in the growing SHRM subfield. Huselid's influence came from offering credible evidence that HR can be directly related to bottom-line organizational performance measures. Using Huselid's analysis as a guide to construct strategically valuable HR systems in our life insurance data provides a plausible, previously tested framework for relating HR systems in life insurance to organizational performance. Huselid measured thirteen "high performance work practices" in a survey of senior human resource professionals from 968 firms. These firms were a subset of the population of U.S. firms with more than 100 employees. Holding companies, foreign-owned firms, and subsidiaries of larger firms were excluded from his sample. Huselid's 13 HR practices were loaded onto two factors, one of which Huselid labeled "employee skills and organizational structures" and the other he labeled "employee motivation." Huselid used these factors to argue that HR systems that concurrently attempt to motivate employees to actively bend their skills toward accomplishing organizational goals, to increase employee functionality by magnifying workers' skills, and to utilize these skills more effectively are most likely to enhance organizational performance. Because Huselid's HR systems factors received significant support in the 1995 study, we tested whether this generic logic applies to out life insurance data.

We did not have all 13 of Huselid's HR practices available for an exact replication. Nevertheless, we still wished to determine whether Huselid's general HR systems factors are appropriate for the life insurance context. Therefore, we used 10 questions in our survey that approximated Huselid's HR practices in an attempt to recreate, as closely as possible, Huselid's two HR systems factors. These HR practices encompassed the following (see table 6-1 above, for descriptive statistics): promotion from within, the inclusion of employee attitude surveys, the inclusion of teamwork skills in performance appraisals, the percentage of pay tied to organizational performance through such instruments as stock options and profitsharing for lower level employees, general profitsharing, the percentage of employees eligible for gainsharing, the use of tests in selection, the degree to which individual and organizational performance ratings determine merit increases, formal performance appraisals, and the number of applicants interviewed for a typical entry-level position.

When we performed exploratory factor analysis and cluster analysis on our 10 items, we found that our items did not load together in the same pattern that Huselid reported. In fact, both analyses implied that the best structure for these 10 items was to keep each one separate. Moreover, when we forced our 10 items to load together in the same pattern that Huselid found, operationalizing this HR systems factors as two scales, the dismal Cronbach alphas for these scales caused us to abandon the attempt. Therefore, the results we report here utilize HR practices individually, rather than in aggregated systems of HR practices. Given the strong arguments in SHRM for evaluating the effects of HR practices systemically, this result in itself is quite interesting.

Huselid matched the data for HR practices and other important organizational characteristics with financial accounting data available for these firms in the Compact Disclosure data base. His HR factors were significant in regression models in his study that predicted many of these organizational level financial outcomes. Similarly, we matched our survey data to the relative efficiency scores utilized in Carr's (1997) analysis of these data, which were derived from formally reported accounting measures of performance. We added our HR practices to the parsimonious performance model for the data that was determined in Carr (1997). The results of hierarchical Tobit regression analysis predicting relative efficiency scores appear in table 6-6.

The second regression in table 6-6 suggests that considering our 10 HR practices individually rather than as a system (such as with an index) may actually be more enlightening, because some of these practices have positive relationships with efficiency, while others have negative relationships. For example, the use of formal performance appraisals is associated with decreased organizational efficiency, but tying performance appraisals to

Table 6-6. HR Practices and Performance in Life Insurance

Dependent Variable: Average DEA (relative efficiency) score, 1993–1995

	Basic Performance Model	Performance Model + HR Practices
Intercept	−0.517	−0.592*
Basic Performance Model Variables		
Log of admitted assets excluding separate accounts	0.048**	0.044***
Ordinary individual life premiums as a fraction of total premiums	−0.158*	−0.266***
Group annuity premiums as a fraction of total premiums	0.620***	0.101
Average market power index total—50 states + DC	0.676*	3.871***
Average annual growth in premium and annuity considerations, 1993–1995	−0.557**	−0.510***
Narrow (offers 7 or less of 15 individual life and health products; dummy)	0.035	−0.136**
Dominant distribution type is non-exclusive (dummy)	0.025	−0.070
Interaction term between narrow and non-exclusive	−0.119	0.002
Expert underwriting system	−0.061	−0.260***
HR Practices Variables		
Degree to which individual and organizational performance ratings determine merit increases		0.124***
Formal performance appraisals		−0.071**
Number of applicants interviewed for a typical entry-level position		0.008
Promoting from within		0.024
Employee attitude surveys		0.015
Including teamwork skills in performance appraisals		0.138***
Percentage of pay tied to organizational performance for lower level employees		0.009**
General profitsharing		−0.167***
Percentage of employees eligible for gainsharing		−0.002**
Use of tests in selection		0.017
SCALE	0.138	0.059
N	46	32
LL	25.834	45.320
Adjusted Pseudo R^2	0.28	0.37

merit increases boosts efficiency. Assessing teamwork skills in performance appraisals significantly raises efficiency, as does tying lower level employees' compensation to organizational performance. Surprisingly, two items that are designed to increase employees' motivation and commitment to organizational goals, profitsharing and gainsharing, appear to significantly *reduce* organizational efficiency. Thus, our results suggest that HR practices that target specific employees' behaviors in performance appraisals and direct compensation are strongly related to increased efficiency, but those that aim at distributing portions of organizational financial rewards to employees are associated with lower cost efficiency. The latter practices can be interpreted as a gift exchange between workers and management, enhancing their relationship (Chadwick & Cappelli, 1998). It appears, then, that such relationship-oriented compensation practices are not as effective in this context as using compensation and appraisal, which target more specific employee behaviors.[4]

This implies that the ways in which individual workers' efforts are tied to organizational outcomes in back office functions in life insurance firms should be transparently specified and rewarded by management in its compensation and performance appraisal systems. Types of compensation in which workers share in organizational financial outcomes, such as gainsharing and profitsharing, are typically computed in arcane formulas that make their implications for employees' day-to-day activities much less obvious. Perhaps the majority of the work done in back office functions such as claims processing is fairly straightforward, making it more likely that management can successfully specify the behaviors it requires. The uncertainty about the future that plagues the industry may occur mostly at the strategic level and in the sales function; back office functions may best be occupied with efficiently implementing management's strategic decisions, rather than encouraging employees to exercise discretionary effort and autonomy in order to tailor their services to customers' needs. A corroborating piece of evidence in this regard is the high importance many life insurance firms attach to speed, accuracy, and predictability in their back office functions, as opposed to innovation.

7. Conclusion

Life insurance firms may be on the right track in linking compensation and individual performance on the individual level for lower level, back office employees, as noted in the first issue investigated in this chapter. However, it is important that those linkages be informed by organizations' strategic goals, which does not yet appear to be the case in life insurance. If life insurance firms are to effectively implement their chosen strategies, their objectives must be strategic and not merely tactical in nature.

The chapter's second issue reveals the potential pitfalls of not paying attention to strategic human resource issues, particularly those concerning the firm's relationships with employees, during a strategic change initiative such as downsizing. This is somewhat contradicted by the third area analyzed, which demonstrates the potential for back office Human Resource practices to enhance organizational efficiency to the degree that they are tied to specific objectives and behaviors. The more commitment-oriented Human Resource practices for back office functions do not have strong relationships with firm efficiency in life insurance. It may be that commitment-based Human Resource Management is more useful in conditions where the requisite behaviors are not easily specified by management, such as during times of strategic change and renewal through downsizing and restructuring. If this is true, it's a mistake to equate Systems Human Resource Management with commitment-based Human Resource Management in a universalistic, prescriptive fashion (e.g., Huselid, 1995; Pfeffer, 1994). A truly *strategic* approach to Human Resource system design would not only consider how to support a firm's intended strategies, but also the stability and specificity of the tasks required from employees. It must make reasoned choices about how the firm and its Human Resource Management will interactively react to and shape these contingencies. It may well be that, as we discussed earlier, the opportunities for commitment-based Human Resource systems emphasizing flexibility to add value in service organizations are in those parts of the firm where tasks are ambiguous and worker flexibility is required. The common approach of Systems Human Resource Management researchers in treating Human Resource systems to apply uniformly across different parts of the firm probably needs to be modified.

Future research in financial services should examine the interaction between commitment-based Human Resource systems in discrete parts of firms, the degree of integration of that function with the rest of the firm, and the degree to which some of the unique challenges in services, such as co-production of products with customer participation, are isolated within that unit. In life insurance, for example, this implies that the opportunities for commitment-based Human Resource to add value are probably in marketing and sales rather than in back office functions, and that success could depend on whether the distribution system is primarily exclusive, non-exclusive, or direct marketing.

Notes

1. Accordingly, we utilize the distinction between firms that employ either an exclusive or a non-exclusive distribution system when we explore survey data later in this chapter. We ignore direct marketing distribution systems and/or exclude firms with both exclusive and non-exclusive distribution systems for these data comparisons.

2. The list of relevant strategic initiatives was generated in field visits to representative life insurance firms during the survey design process. The labels in table 6-3 describe rather than list all the elements of these strategies. The strategies are not mutually exclusive; firms may have more than one strategy to at least some degree.

3. We tried a number of simple alternative techniques to aggregate the responses to the behavioral questions. One was to count the number of "4" or "5" Likert responses, which signified agreement with the statement in question, for each firm and create a new index. This kind of response indicates that a firm is doing what the behavioral downsizing researchers advocate, so this approach examines the positive impact of aggressively trying to do a number of these things. We again split the sample into three groups based on scores for this new index and compared the mean efficiency, absenteeism, and other outcomes of the top and bottom groups to each other, without notable results.

4. One interesting exception to this is that the use of employee attitude surveys, which did not have a significant coefficient in the regression in table 6-6, did have a significantly positive coefficient in a regression where it was the only HR practice added to the basic performance model variables. This did not occur for the other non-significant HR practices in table 6-6.

References

Arthur, J.B. "Effects of Human Resource Systems on Manufacturing Performance and Turnover," *Academy of Management Journal* 37 (1994), 670–687.

Baird, Lloyd, and Ilan Meshoulam. "Managing Two Fits of Strategic Human Resource Management," *Academy of Management Review* 13 (no. 1, 1988), 116–128.

Huselid, Mark A. and Brian E. Backer. "The Impact of High Performance Work Systems, Implementation Effectiveness, and Alignment with Strategy on Shareholder Wealth," Working Paper, New Brunswick, NJ: Rutgers University, 1997.

Cameron, Kim S., Sarah J. Freeman, and Aneil K. Mishra. "Best practices in White-collar Downsizing: Managing Contradictions," *Academy of Management Executive* 5 (no. 3, 1991), 57–73.

Carr, Roderick M. "Strategic Choices, Firm Efficiency, and Competitiveness in the U.S. Life Insurance Industry," Risk Management Dept., The Wharton School, Philadelphia, PA: University of Pennsylvania, Unpublished dissertation, 1997.

Carr, Roderick M.J. David Cummins and Laureen Regan. "Efficiency and Competitiveness in the U.S. Life Insurance Industry: Corporate, Product, and Distribution Strategies" in J.D. Cummins and A. Santomero (eds.), *Changes in the Life Insurance Industry: Efficiency, Technology and Risk Management*, 1999.

Cascio, W. "Downsizing: What do we know? What have we learned?" *Academy of Management Executive* 7 (no. 1, 1993), 95–104.

Chadwick, Clint and Peter Cappelli. "Contracts and Investments: Two Roads to High Commitment Workplaces," Presented at the 6th Bargaining Group Conference, University of Illinois at Urbana-Champaign, May 1–2, 1998.

Chadwick, Clint, Stephen Walston and Larry Hunter. "Shrinking successfully: Best Practice Downsizing and Progressive Human Resource Practices," Working Paper, Management Dept., The Wharton School, Philadelphia, PA: University of Pennsylvania, 1998.

Cummins, J.D. "Efficiency in the U.S. Life Insurance Industry: Are Insurers Minimizing Cost and Maximizing Revenues" in J.D. Cummins and A. Santomero (eds.), *Changes in the Life Insurance Industry: Efficiency, Technology and Risk Management*, 1999.

Cummins, J. David and Hongmin Zi. "Comparison of Frontier Efficiency Methods: An Application To the U.S. Life Iinsurance Industry," *Journal of Productivity Analysis* 10 (1998), 131–152.

Dyer, Lee and Todd Reeves. "Human Resource Strategies and Firm Performance: What Do We Know and Where Do We Need to Go?" *The International Journal of Human Resource Management* 6 (no. 3, 1995), 656–670.

Fitzsimmons, James A. and Mona J. Fitzsimmons. "Service Management for Competitive Advantage," New York: McGraw-Hill, 1994.

Frederiksen, Lee W., Anne W. Riley and John B. Myers. "Matching Technology and Organizational Structure: A Case Study in White Collar Productivity Improvement," *Journal of Organizational Behavior Management* 6 (nos. 3–4, 1984), 59–80.

Gardner, Lisa A and Martin F. Grace. "X-efficiency in the U.S. Life Insurance Industry" *Journal of Banking and Finance* 17 (1993), 497–510.

Grace, Martin F. and Stephen G. Timme. "An Examination of Cost Economies in the United States Life Insurance Industry," *Journal of Risk and Insurance* 59 (1992), 72–103.

Huselid, Mark A. "The Impact of Human Resource Management Practices on Turnover, Productivity, and Corporate Financial Performance," *Academy of Management Journal* 38 (no. 3, 1995), 635–672.

Ichniowski, Casey, Kathryn Shaw and Giovanna Prennushi. "The Effects of Human Resource Management Practices on Productivity: A Study of Steel Finishing Lines," *American Economic Review* 87 (no. 3, 1997), 291–313.

Lederer, R. Werner. *Home Office and Field Agency Organization—Life*, Homewood, IL: Richard D. Irwin, Inc, 1971.

MacDuffie, J.P. "Human Resource Bundles and Manufacturing Performance: Organizational Logic and Production Systems in the World Auto Industry," *Industrial and Labor Relations Review* 48 (1995), 197–221.

Pfeffer, Jeffrey. *Competitive Advantage Through People.* Boston, MA: Harvard Business School Press, 1994.

Porter, Michael E. *Competitive Advantage: Creating and Sustaining Superior Performance.* New York: The Free Press, 1985.

———. *Competitive Strategy: Techniques for Analyzing Industries and Competitors*, New York: The Free Press, 1980.

Scott, Elizabeth D., K.C. O'Shaughnessy, and Peter Cappelli. "The Changing Structure of Management Jobs in the Insurance Industry," in Paul Osterman (ed.), *White Collar Labor Markets*. New York: Oxford University Press, forthcoming, 1994.

Weiss, Mary. "Analysis of productivity at the firm level: An application to life insurers," *Journal of Risk and Insurance* 53 (1986), 49–83.

Yuengert, Andrew M. "The Measurement of Efficiency in Life Insurance: Estimates of a Normal-gamma Error Model," *Journal of Banking and Finance* 17 (1993), 483–496.

7 THE IMPACT OF INFORMATION TECHNOLOGY MANAGEMENT PRACTICES ON THE PERFORMANCE OF LIFE INSURANCE COMPANIES

Lorin M. Hitt

1. Introduction

Life insurance firms are increasingly reliant on information technology (IT) to maintain and enhance operating efficiency as well as to purse new strategies such as direct delivery, customer segmentation, and product innovation. The size of the commitment to IT by the average life insurance company is staggering: one study estimates that life insurance companies spent as much as 5% of premium income on IT in 1996 (Bell, 1998) and that IT represented over 50% of insurance company capital expenditure throughout the 1980s (Francalanci and Hossum, 1998). As one observer succinctly stated, "today you can't do anything in a life insurance company without technology" (Harnett, 1997).

While IT has been a part of insurance company operations since the general purpose stored-program computer was invented, until recently its impact was neither particularly large nor strategic. Most information systems were primarily devoted to data maintenance and accounting; initially in the financial operations arena, and later for policyholder records and service. While some insurers were able to differentiate themselves on the quality of their internal systems (for example, USAA described in Vitale, Elam and

Morrison, 1989), the vast majority of systems were hidden from customer view and were relatively standardized across the industry.

Following the invention of the personal computer in the mid-1980s, many firms began to invest more heavily in providing agents with direct electronic links to the company. These were first accomplished through personal computers in the agent offices and later through portable computers carried by agents (see e.g. Sviokla and Wong, 1991). While these experiments had mixed success in improving sales and cost efficiency (Zaheer and Venkatraman, 1994), they represented a major push in using IT for competitive advantage by redefining the way insurance products were sold. This strategy has recently been implemented on an unprecedented scale at the Prudential, which has invested over $100 mm in equipping its agent force with laptop computers (Friel, 1998).

At about the same time technology began to diffuse throughout the organization, life insurers began to offer increasingly complex products (e.g. self-directed variable annuities), in order to compete with alternative financial services providers such as banks and mutual funds. IT increased in importance simply because these complex products could not be offered (and would not have been feasible) without the systems to support them. Finally, new technologies such as image processing and automated call distribution began to emerge as a way of improving efficiency while increasing the level of customer service. Many firms began aggressively reengineering their core business processes by using these and other technologies to support greater product complexity, increase levels of service to agents and customers, and improve cost efficiency. Again, not all these efforts were successful, but some amazing results were realized (see e.g. Mutual Benefit Life, as described in Hammer, 1990).

Given the importance of IT in this industry, one would expect there to be a large and robust body of work on how IT should be managed to create business value in life insurance companies. Surprisingly, very little is known about this important issue even when the area is expanded to include the role of IT in financial services or even to consider the service industry as a whole. General management principles for IT have been discussed extensively since the 1970s, yet the economic impact of most of these practices is not fully understood.

Most previous work on the business value of IT in the service industry has focused on the so called "productivity paradox," the idea that the large investments in IT have failed to deliver an expected level of productivity improvement or profit increases. For example, Steven Roach (1988) has argued that because IT investment has dramatically increased during a time when measured service sector productivity is stagnant or declining, IT has, at best, failed to live up to its promise and, at worst, is responsible for the productivity shortfall. However, as research in this area has progressed, it is becoming increasingly possible that the productivity paradox is simply a measurement artifact. When measurement deficiencies are reduced through improved access to micro-level data (data from firms rather than industries or sectors), collection of large and more diverse samples and the application of rigorous economic models (Hitt and Brynjolfsson, 1996), research is beginning to find that IT is at least paying for itself, and may have substantial "excess" returns (Brynjolfsson and Hitt, 1998). Perhaps a more important finding of these studies is, however, that there are substantial differences across firms on the productivity of IT investments; it is not simply a matter of investing an additional dollar for an average return. Firm specific factors appear to have a substantial impact on the benefits realized from IT investments (for a survey of studies investigating this argument, see Hitt and Brynjolfsson, 1998).

Several recent studies have begun to explore the source of this variation and found that organizational practices and strategies influence the value of IT investments. For example, Brynjolfsson and Hitt (1997), and Bresnahan, Brynjolfsson and Hitt (1998) found that the internal work organization of a firm is an important determinant of the benefits of IT; firms that invest in a cluster of work practices involving greater skills, more educated staff, and greater use of delegated decision making have made larger investments in IT and have received greater benefits from these investments. Strategy also plays a role; Brynjolfsson and Hitt (1996a) found the firms that invest in IT to pursue customer focused "extroverted" strategies have higher performance than those that pursue cost cutting. The idea that organization affects IT value is not necessarily new; one reason, for example, is that it is important to reengineer processes when IT is introduced instead of "paving the cow paths" (Hammer, 1990). However, these more recent studies have begun to identify general principles for this organizational redesign and to estimate the magnitude of the economic impact of implementing these new types of organizational practices.

What is notably absent from all of these studies is the role of IT management practices. Given that these practices and their implementation in the business units and central IT group determine what investments are made, how the actual systems are designed, and the effectiveness of these systems in transforming the business, it would seen logical that IT practices would also make a substantial contribution to performance, particularly in an IT-intensive industry such as life insurance. At a minimum, more or less effective practices should at least influence the cost of IT borne by the firm. It is also quite likely that firms that have effective processes for identifying and managing IT investments have received substantial additional economic benefits above and beyond a simple cost reduction of the IT function.

Previous work in the banking industry has argued that IT staffers may have a particularly unique role on service firms in crafting operational practices. Unlike manufacturing firms where "industrial engineers" provide a company-wide perspective on the design of manufacturing processes, there is no similar role in most service firms. The closest analog is the central IT group, who is often charged with developing an overall process perspective on the business so that its members can design, implement and maintain the information infrastructure that supports these processes. In studies of banking institutions, the IT group alone could consistently describe actual work practices that spanned more than a single unit or department (Frei, Harker and Hunter, 1997; Prasad and Harker, 1997).

In this chapter, we explore the relationship between IT management practices and two outcome measures: the level of IT investment and the overall efficiency of a firm. This is accomplished by using existing measures of insurance company efficiency constructed from public financial data[1] by Cummins, Tennyson and Weiss (1998) and Cummins (1999), and combining this with survey data on work systems, IT expenditure and other organizational features collected through a detailed survey of organizational practices (Moore and Santomero, 1999). The goal is to distinguish the effects of the IT organization on cost efficiency of IT investments as well as their contribution to the efficiency of the firm as a whole. Our expectation is that adhering to best practice management principles identified in the IT management literature (see Hitt, Frei and Harker, 1998 for a survey) should lead to greater efficiency. We would also expect that IT investment should either decrease without any loss in efficiency, or increase concurrently with efficiency if IT is being effectively managed. However, we can also explore the most plausible alternative hypothesis, suggested by the productivity paradox literature, that IT is simply not effective in delivering value to life insurers or other financial services firms. By focusing on a specific high-impact and well-defined area, which is likely to have some consistency across firms, we hope to shed light on the broader issue of how to effectively manage IT investments in insurance firms.

While our results are all exploratory in nature, primarily correlational, and are constrained by the size of the sample (which includes 54 firms[2]), our analysis suggests the largest effect of IT management practices has to do with high level strategy setting. Adopting customer-focused strategies, maintaining the accountability of IT through cost allocation mechanisms, employing an educated IT staff with strong salary-based incentives—all of these appear to substantially improve efficiency. Decentralizing authority for IT management appears to decrease IT expenditure without decreasing efficiency. There is apparently less effect from applying "high performance work practices" such as teams, variable pay or group incentives, and employee screening or retention strategies in the IT function. Interestingly, the practices that are associated with higher efficiency are consistently associated with higher IS costs and staffing; this suggests that effective practices enable firms to expand the possible range of IT applications, as opposed to enabling them to simply cut IT costs.

Overall, these results suggest that management practices by which IT is created and deployed within organizations can have a substantial effect on performance (at least in an efficiency sense) above and beyond effects of particular technologies themselves. It is thus important to recognize that IT is not simply something that is purchased, but is a joint product of vendors, business people, and IS staffers that can be shaped by the effectiveness of the management process.

The remainder of this chapter is structured as follows: section 2 reviews the previous literature and synthesizes the basic arguments, section 3 describes the methods and data, section 4 contains the results, and section 5 summarizes our discussion.

2. Previous Literature

2.1. Efficiency in Life Insurance

There have been a number of studies that have examined the efficiency of the life insurance industry and the role of various factors such as organizational form (stock vs. mutual), economies of scale (size), economies of scope (product breadth), and distribution strategy (for a comprehensive review of the life insurance efficiency literature see Carr and Cummins, 1997; for recent analysis on life insurance efficiency see Cummins, 1999). Taken collectively, these results suggest that more efficient firms are larger, utilize exclusive distribution, and are organized as stock companies. In addition, there is mixed evidence on the role of scope economies. However, while there is substantial debate as to the role of these various factors, there is one unambiguous result: that most of the (in)efficiency of insurance companies is not explained by the factors that have been considered in prior work. A similar story also appears in banking where "x-efficiency" varies substantially across firms when size, scope, product mix, branching strategy, and other strategic variables are considered (Berger, Hunter, and Timme,

1993). At least in the banking context, it has been argued that one must get "inside the black box" of the firm to consider the role of organizational, strategic, and technological factors, which may be missed in studies that rely heavily on public financial data (Frei, Harker and Hunter, 1997).

2.2. Business Value of IT

Early studies of the relationship between IT and productivity or other measures of performance were generally unable to conclusively determine the value of IT. Loveman (1994) and Strassmann (1990), using different data and analytical methods, both found that the performance effects of computers were not statistically significant. Barua, Kriebel and Muhkadopadhyay (1995), using the same data as Loveman, found evidence that IT improved some internal performance metrics such as inventory turnover, but could not tie these benefits to improvements in bottom-line productivity. Although these studies has a number of disadvantages (small samples, noisy data), which yielded imprecise measures of IT effects, this lack of evidence combined with equally equivocal macroeconomic analyses by Steven Roach (1988) implicitly formed the basis for the "productivity paradox." As Robert Solow (1987) once remarked, "You can see the computer age everywhere except in the productivity statistics."

A few studies have considered the role of technology in insurance, although the results are inconclusive. Bender (1986) and Franke (1987) utilizing Life Office Management Association (LOMA) data on large life insurers, have found weak positive correlations between various measures of IT use and various performance ratios.[3] While promising, the fact that these studies cover much earlier time periods when the PC had only been recently developed and overall computer investment was an order of magnitude smaller than it is today, make it questionable that these results are relevant to current IT decisions. Moreover, these studies did not consider the organizational or strategic factors that affect the relationship between IT and performance.

More recent work has found that IT investment is a substantial contributor to firm productivity, productivity growth, and stock market valuation in a sample that contains a wide range of industries. Brynjolfsson and Hitt (1994, 1996b) and Lichtenberg (1995) found that IT investment had a positive and statistically significant contribution to firm output. Brynjolfsson and Yang (1997) found that the market valuation of IT capital was several times that of ordinary capital. Brynjolfsson and Hitt (1998) also found a strong relationship between IT and productivity growth and that this relationship grows stronger over longer time periods. Collectively, these studies suggest that there is no productivity paradox, at least when the analysis is performed across industries using firm-level data. The differences between these results and earlier studies is probably due to the use of data that was more recent (1988–1994 instead of 1982 or earlier), more comprehensive (>400 firms), and more disaggregated (firm-level rather than industry- or economy-level).

While these studies show a strong positive contribution of IT investment on average, they do not consider how this contribution (or level of investment) varies across firms. Brynjolfsson and Hitt (1995) found that "firm effects" can account for as much as half the contribution of IT found in these earlier studies. Recent results suggest that at least part of these differences can be explained by differences in organizational and strategic factors. Brynjolfsson and Hitt (1997) found that firms that use greater levels of delegated authority and teams make greater investments in IT and receive greater overall IT benefits. Bresnahan, Brynjolfsson and Hitt (1998) found a similar result for firms that have greater levels of skills and for those that make greater investments in training and preemployment screening for human capital. A recent study by Francalani and Hossam (1998) in life insurance firms found that firms that coupled increased IT expenditure with a reduction in clerical staff and an increase in professional staff (as a proportion of the total workforce) had higher performance ratios, suggesting that organizational factors do indeed influence performance. In addition, strategic factors also appear to affect the value of IT. Firms that invest in IT to create customer value (e.g. improve service, timeliness, convenience, variety) have greater performance than firms that invest in IT to reduce costs (Brynjolfsson and Hitt, 1996a).

2.3. The Role of the IT Function

A central theme in the literature on information systems management is the importance of managing the IT function and its interrelationships with business units. Historically, when IT primarily supported the accounting and finance functions of large firms, the IT function was generally treated as a cost center in the financial operations area. However, as IT has become more strategic and more widely used throughout the firm, the management strategy for IT has undergone a substantial transformation.

In the mid-1980s it was recognized that for line managers to be successful in an IT-intensive firm, they would have to play a larger role in the design and implementation of IT. As a result, coordination mechanisms were developed to provide line managers, who directly use the technology, with increased responsibility for IT investments in their areas; in other words, "the line takes the leadership" (Rockart and Crescenzi, 1984). To coordinate overall IS activities for a firm and maintain cost control for ever escalating IT budgets, IT steering committees were formed to enable senior managers to become directly involved in technology decisions, to increase financial accountability, and to ensure that IT investments in various functional "silos" were effectively integrated. Finally, firms developed complex chargeback mechanisms to ensure that business units paid their fair share of IT expenses and that resources were allocated efficiently (for an example, see McFarlan, 1991), especially in divisionalized firms where operating units had separate profit and loss statements.

While these transformations primarily affected the operating business units, a similar set of changes also were required in the IT function. The role of the IT manager changed from primarily technological duties (managing projects, designing systems) to taking a greater role in understanding the business needs of the operating areas, proposing possible technological solutions or educating end-users about the technological possibilities (Boynton, Jacobs and Zmud, 1992; Rockart, Earl and Ross, 1996). The skill set of IT personnel also changed; no longer was it sufficient to simply be technically proficient, it was also important to have a broader perspective on how the core business operated and to be able to interact effectively with end users. Close coordination of IT functions and business functions was also a central theme of the reengineering literature (Hammer, 1990; Davenport and Short, 1990; Hammer and Champy, 1993), which stressed the use of project teams mixing IT and business unit personnel and the importance of a strong senior manager as a project sponsor.

A related issue in the management of IT is the governance of IT resources; some firms maintain large central IT functions that are essentially autonomous, while others place virtually all IT staff under the control of individual operating units or departments. The economic tradeoff between these two modes of operating is similar to the tradeoffs for other shared services. Centralization provides better utilization of fixed assets (such as mainframes), the ability to have a better technically trained staff, and centralized control of cost—essentially, the standard explanations for the existence of scale economies. However, decentralization enables increased responsiveness, flexibility, and tailoring to the needs of individual business units, and may be particularly important in building close connections between IT managers and business unit managers.

A separate issue in IT governance is the question of outsourcing. Instead of providing all services in-house, a firm can contract with an outside company to provide some or all information systems services. On the one hand, vendors have many advantages over internal IT departments such as access to economies of scale, scope, or specialization (Clemons and Row, 1992). At the same time, new types of costs arise in external procurement such as "transactions costs"; these include not only the actual cost of identifying suppliers and writing contracts, but implicit costs that arise because the incentives of vendors are not necessarily aligned with the incentives of clients. For example, vendors may underperform and require undertaking costly monitoring or contractual enforcement efforts. A detailed discussion of contractual risks can be found in Clemons and Row (1992).

Overall, the management literature is mixed on whether outsourcing makes sense. Lacity and Hirsheim (1993) argue that the transaction costs dominate any gains and advocate insourcing where possible; Quinn and Hilmer (1994) argue that anything without strategic impact should be outsourced. Gurbaxani (1996) argues that outsourcing can be effective in a wide variety of settings as long as the contracts and relationships are designed properly. A similar discussion is currently running in the life insurance trade press (Youngblood, 1998; Bazinet, Kahn and Smith, 1998).

In addition to managing the effectiveness of new systems development, the IT department may indirectly influence performance and IT cost through its choice of technology. For example, the central IT department is often a key driver of the decision whether to adopt client server technology or retain existing mainframes that are less expensive to administer but provide less applications flexibility. Similarly, firms can choose whether to upgrade systems or to continue to maintain and upgrade legacy systems; the firm defers the potentially large cost of new systems development as well as the organizational disruption involved when new systems are introduced, but at the expense of reduced functionality and high maintenance costs. Finally, the role of setting and maintaining technological standards often falls on the IT department (Boynton, Jacobs and Zmud, 1992). Standards enable more efficient support and the procurement of technology through specialization, but at the cost of imposing a "one size fits all" burden on user departments. While historically choices may be limited to affecting short run IT costs, as the pace of innovation (especially IT-enabled innovation) increases in these markets, these choices increasingly affect firm strategy and ultimately affect profitability.

The work practices within the IT organization have come under increased scrutiny in recent times. Challenges such as the "Year 2000

Problem" and the shortage of IT labor have increased attention on retaining IT personnel. The shift in skill requirements for IT jobs is away from traditional mainframe and COBOL skills and toward an ability to be more involved with end users, while simultaneously coping with a more heterogeneous technology environment.

The human resources literature suggest that firms can improve productivity and reduce turnover through the use of "high performance work systems" (Huselid, 1995; Ichniowski et al., 1996). These systems generally include a greater use of incentives, particularly at the work-group or company level, increased use of teams and delegated decision authority (reduced hierarchy), and a greater emphasis on skills and training. Others have specifically linked these types of work practices to the emergence of "knowledge-based corporations" in particular (Drucker, 1988). Previous work has found that these practices at the firm overall are associated with increased demand for IT as well as a greater productivity of IT investments. In addition, since many of these practices appear to be particularly suited to white collar knowledge work (Bresnahan, 1997), it seems reasonable to believe that they could be successfully utilized in managing IT personnel to either improve performance, build needed skills, or retain employees— all of which should make the IT function (and the firm more broadly) more efficient.

To summarize, there are a number of ways in which management practices of the IT function can influence the cost efficiency of IT investments as well as overall firm efficiency: the overall strategy for IT at the company, the technology strategy, the coordination and control mechanisms that are present to manage the interrelationships between IT and the business units, and the work practices of the IS department. While survey data cannot cover all aspects of these functions, many of the major practices were included in our organizational practices survey and their impact can be examined empirically.

3. Methods and Data

3.1. Methods

The overall approach of this chapter is to develop measures for IT practices and organizational practices and relate these characteristics to IT investment and firm performance using standard approaches that have been employed in previous work. Our approach to measuring performance utilized the work by Cummins (1999) and some of the modeling approach that appears in Carr and Cummins (1997). Brynjolfsson and Hitt (1997) introduced the idea of combining demand and productivity analyses together for understanding the effect of complementary factors (e.g. organization, management practices, strategy) on the value of IT investment. These models are described in the section below, while the measures utilized to capture organizational and IT practices will be described more fully in the data description section and the results.

3.2. Performance Measurement

For performance measurement of the overall firm, we employ efficiency measures created by Cummins, Tennyson and Weiss (1999) utilizing data envelopment analysis and used for general life insurance company efficiency comparisons by Cummins (1999). For 754 insurance companies, they computed data envelopment analysis (DEA) estimates relating output in five major business lines (individual life, group life, individual annuity, group annuity, and accident and health) to three input measures (labor, financial capital, and materials). Output can be measured either as units (policies) to determine whether firms are minimizing the cost of producing output units, or as revenue (premiums and considerations) to measure the extent to which firms are maximizing their revenue per unit of input. These measures, while closely related, may have different behavior for some types of practices; to the extent that certain organizational practices enable the firm to change the quality of outputs (in ways unobserved in our data), the value of these practices may be better captured by revenue efficiency. The efficiency ratios for each input-output combination is computed and used to determine the efficient frontier—the set of firms for which no other firm is producing at least as much output on all dimensions while using less of any one input. Each firm in the sample is then compared to the firms on the efficient frontier to obtain an efficiency score ranging from 0 to 1 (1 being a firm on the frontier). The efficiency measures for the firms in our sample are then taken from this superset of all firms (our sample of organizational data includes 54 firms over three years with complete data, while the full sample of 754 insurers is used to calculate efficiency ratios). To these data, we match a single cross-section of organizational practices collected in 1995. While this imposes a fairly strong assumption that organizational practices did not change over the time period, it appears to be a reasonable given that most of the practices we describe cannot be altered quickly and require substantial adjustment costs to implement.

Utilization of DEA methods is arguably superior to other approaches in this context; they capture the multi-output, multi-input aspect of the insurance business unlike simple performance measures and do not require all firms to fit on the same theoretical production function as required by efficiency measures based on stochastic production frontiers or standard cost function estimates. In addition, use of DEA methods has a substantial foundation for the evaluation of insurance firms (see e.g. Cummins and Zi, 1994; Cummins, Tennyson and Weiss, 1999; Cummins, 1999) and for similar types of financial services firms such as banks (see references in Berger, Cummins and Weiss, 1995).[4]

Because the DEA scores are bounded above by 1, it is not optimal to estimate the relationship between performance and organizational practices utilizing ordinary least squares. We thus employ Tobit[5] analysis for regression, which accounts for the problem that the data is "censored" at an efficiency value of 1. To control for variation in efficiency that is not related to the measures we are studying, we also include control variables for scale (asset size), scope (number of products offered), distribution strategy (exclusive agency, non-exclusive agency and direct), and ownership (stock vs. mutual). These factors have been studied in previous work on this area, and many are substantial predictors of efficiency. More discussion appears in the results section.

3.3. Information Technology Demand

Given that IT practices indirectly affect the bottom line, it is useful to have an alternative metric of IT effectiveness that is more directly influenced by management practices. A reasonable measure is how well the IT organization is able to minimize resource use to service a given level of policies. To the extent that some work practices (e.g. training the IT staff) enable a firm to more effectively deliver IT services, it should be able to reduce IT expenditure. This metric also has the advantage of relating micro-level behaviors to other micro-level behaviors, making it more easily discernable using limited data.

However, as a sole metric of IT performance this is unsatisfactory for two reasons: 1) the IT organization can adopt cost-saving strategies that may not improve overall value to the firm, which leads to the illusion that IT is contributing value by reducing costs, and 2) firms may adopt strategies that expand the possible range of productive uses of IT leading them to optimally increase IT investment, which leads to the illusion that a firm is wasting IT resources. To distinguish effective versus wasteful increases (or decreases) in IT expenditure, performance comparisons should also be made. Thus, a firm that adopts a practice that decreases IT expenditure while not decreasing performance is likely to be making a good choice; similarly, a practice that increases IT expenditure while increasing performance can arguably be enabling a firm to identify additional productive uses of IT. This approach of multiple metrics has another advantage: exogenous shocks, reverse causality, and other modeling problems may affect these two types of approaches differently which makes it less likely to find spurious correlation.

In our surveys we have estimates of IT staffing (ITS) for three years (1993–1995) as well as IS budgets (ITB) for two years (1994–1995). By using two metrics we can capture different aspects of IT expenditure, although we generally expect them to be consistent in their direction and use alternative metrics primarily as a robustness test. We will predict these levels using a demand equation that relates IT staffing or spending to prices (proxied by time) and output metrics (this procedure follows that used by Brynjolfsson and Hitt (1998) and Bresnehan, Brynjolfsson and Hitt (1998)). To account for the fact that these firms produce multiple outputs, we will use three measures of outputs: number of annuity policies (group and individual-ANNPOL), number of health and accident policies (HLTHPOL), and number of life and supplementary policies (group and individual-LIFEPOL). Allowing IT demand to vary by organizational practices and taking logarithms yields:

$$\log ITB \text{ or } \log ITS = \gamma_0 + \beta_{practice} Org\_practice + \gamma_{93} YR93 + \gamma_{94} YR94 + \gamma_{Ann} \log ANNPOL + \gamma_{Health} \log HLTHPOL + \gamma_{Life} \log LIFEPOL + other\ controls + \varepsilon$$

In this specification, a positive value on $\beta_{practice}$ suggests that a particular practice leads to increase IT demand (in addition, the coefficient can be interpreted as the percentage change in IT demand, holding output constant, due to changes in an organizational practice). In the analysis, we will include various organizational practices in this equation, individually and concurrently, to explore their impact. The control variables parallel those included in the efficiency regression (scope, distribution strategy, and ownership). Scale is omitted because it is already implicitly included in the policy count measures.

3.4. Data

The unique data for this analysis comes from a survey of organizational practices administered to large insurers (see Moore and Santomero, 1998). The survey itself is over 200 pages long and includes questions on human resource (HR) practices, IT practices, strategy, distribution methods, underwriting practices, claims processing practices, customer service practices, and restructuring. Each portion of the survey is completed by the "most informed respondent" and generally requires approximately eight people per firm to complete the entire survey. Survey questions were determined through a comprehensive review of the insurance, HR and IT literature as well as consultation with insurance industry consultants and survey participants. For more details on the administration of the survey and a detailed examination of possible sample selection biases, see Carr and Cummins (1997). Summary statistics and analysis of the survey appears in Moore and Santomero (1999).

These data were linked to NAIC data on insurance company financials to obtain measures of policies issued (for the demand equations) as well as to provide the variables for the DEA analysis. Summary statistics for the regression dependent and control variables appears in table 7-1, while summary statistics for the IT management practice variables appear in tables 7-2 and 7-3.

Table 7-1.   Sample Statistics for Baseline Regression Variables

Variable	Description	Scale	Mean	Standard Deviation
Dependent Variables				
DEA Score	DEA Measure	0–1	0.42	0.26
ITS	Information Technology Staff	log(#)	3.62	1.31
ITB	Information Technology Budget	log($)	15.62	1.43
Controls				
ASSETNSA	Non-separate Account Assets	log($)	21.02	1.78
NPROD	Products Offered (out of 15)	#	8.82	2.91
RATING	A.M. Best Rating (1 = highest)	1–20	3.24	1.84
TYPEE	Exclusive Distribution	1/0	0.22	0.42
TYPED	Direct Distribution	1/0	0.08	0.27
STKCO	Stock Company	1/0	0.73	0.44
HPOL	Health & Accident Policies	log(#)	7.44	4.63
ANNPOL	Annuity Policies	log(#)	8.93	3.32
POLICY	Life Policies	log(#)	12.01	2.12

On 1–5 scales, 5 is the highest. Sample sizes vary due to missing data.

Table 7-2.   Information Technology Management Variables

Variable	Description	Scale	Mean	Standard Deviation
Information Technology Outsourcing				
OUTSRC	Outsourcing use (5-point scale)	1–5	2.35	0.96
AVGOUTSRC	Avg. of %DEV, %MAINT, %OPER	%	85.50	22.64
%DEV	Development outsourced	%	78.47	29.34
%MAINT	Maintenance outsourced	%	88.72	22.76
%OPER	Operations outsourced	%	89.32	23.12
Technology Practices				
NLEGACY	Number of systems >5 yrs old	1–7	1.95	1.77
%NEWSYS	Percent Information Technology spending on development	%	31.90	22.42
NSYSTEMS	Number of platforms supported	1–12	5.17	2.38
CLSERV	Use of client server (scale)	1–5	2.51	0.90
FUNC	Number of activities online	0–7	5.51	1.85
Information Technology Management Practices				
ITSTEER	Has a technology investment committee	1/0	0.63	0.49
CENTIS	Number of functions centralized	1–8	7.37	1.57
CHGBK	Charges technology cost to line units	1/0	0.50	0.51
SLA	Has service level agreements	1/0	0.39	0.50
ITMEAS	Has formal Information Technology measures	1/0	0.05	0.23
ITSTRAT	Avg. level of Information Technology input to business (scale)	1–5	3.09	1.73

On 1–5 scales, 5 is the highest. Sample sizes vary due to missing data.

4. Results

In this section, we examine the results for each of the four ways in which the IT function can influence IT costs and firm performance: IT strategy, management of the IT organization, IT work practices, and technological choices. For each area we examine both the overall productivity effects of the work practices as well as their influence on overall IT demand at the firm.

The baseline models are shown in table 7-4. For the efficiency regression

Table 7-3.   Information Technology Work Practice Variables

Variable	Description	Scale	Mean	Standard Deviation
Information Technology Work Practices				
INCSUBJ	Use individual subjective incentives	1/0	0.96	0.20
INCOBJ	Use other individual incentives	1/0	0.71	0.46
INCGRP	Use incentives based on Information Technology group perf.	1/0	0.25	0.44
INCCOMP	Use incentives based on company perf.	1/0	0.69	0.47
APPR	Employees receive appraisals (scale)	1–5	3.79	0.82
PAYDIFF	Ratio of highest to lowest paid employee	#	3.37	1.41
DEVCOLL	Percent of developers with college education	%	76.30	21.54
TECHCOLL	Percent of tech staff with college education	%	46.88	31.86
TENAVG	Average tenure (4 job classes)	#	36.40	16.02
TRNHIRE	Average hours of training for 4 job classes in first year	#	177.46	130.98
TRNONG	Average hours training after 1st year	#	127.40	80.61
SELECT	Number of people interviewed per hire	#	5.27	2.53
SCNED	Importance of education in hiring (scale)	1–5	4.13	1.18
SCNTEAM	Importance of team skills in hiring (scale)	1–5	2.45	1.40
TEAMS	Extent of participation in teams (scale)	1–5	1.66	1.03
LAYERS	Number of layers of management in Information Technology organization.	#	2.07	1.50

On 1–5 scales, 5 is the highest. Sample sizes vary due to missing data.

we find that scale (total assets) has a strong positive effect on efficiency and scope (number of products offered) also has a U-shaped effect, first declining and then increasing. Claims payment rating has a positive coefficient, which implies that firms with better ratings actually have lower overall

Table 7-4. Baseline Regressions for Efficiency and Information Technology Demand

Dependent Variable	Cost Efficiency (TOBIT) DEA Score	Revenue Efficiency (TOBIT) DEA Score	IT Staff Demand (OLS) log(IT Staff)	IT Budget Demand (OLS) log(IT Budget)
Assets (excl. separate account)	.121***	.110***		
log(ASSETNSA)	(.0130)	(.0146)		
Policies (not health/annuity)			.221***	.311***
log(POLICY)			(.0569)	(.0792)
Health Policies			−.0405	−.0209
log(HPOL)			(.0268)	(.0335)
Annuities Policies			.00847	.00458
log(ANNPOL)			(.0368)	(.0446)
Number of Products	−.0863***	−.0769***	−.172***	−.182
(NPROD)	(.0233)	(.0269)	(.163)	(.181)
Products—squared	.00453***	.00304*	.0247**	.0251**
(NPROD²)	(.00140)	(.00163)	(.0102)	(.0105)
A.M. Best Rating	.0542***	.0103	−.133**	−.227***
(RATING)	(.0104)	(.0110)	(.0636)	(.0747)
Exclusive Distribution	−.0220	−.00864	.207	−.154
(TYPEE)	(.0442)	(.0509)	(.297)	(.303)
Direct Distribution	.0807	.312***	−.643*	−.803
(TYPED)	(.0774)	(.0883)	(.358)	(.523)
Stock Company	.0590	.0411	.196	.640**
(STOCK)	(.0387)	(.0448)	(.279)	(.287)
1993 Dummy Variable	−.0100	.0374	.0853	n/a
(YR93)	(.0390)	(.00455)	(.243)	
1994 Dummy Variable	−.0166	.0413	.0243	.0481
(YR94)	(.0396)	(.0456)	(.239)	(.229)
R²	n/a	n/a	47.5%	57.8%
N	140	140	104	77

*** $-p < .01$, ** $-p < .05$, * $-p < .1$; standard errors in parenthesis.

efficiency. The most plausible interpretation of this coefficient is that RATING is really capturing an unmeasured difference in quality that appears as decreased efficiency since quality of outputs is not considered in the efficiency analysis. Consistent with prior work (Carr and Cummins,

1997), direct distribution is the most efficient and ownership (stock vs. mutual) has little impact on overall efficiency after considering the effect of scale and distribution strategy. The two time-dummy variables are insignificant and suggest that the relative position of the insurers that completed the organizational practices survey has not changed over time when compared to the universe of life insurance companies.

The demand equations (table 7-4, columns 3 and 4) suggest that high-rated firms and those at either extreme in number of products have the highest demand for IT per policy. Product mix (life vs. annuity and health) appears to have little incremental explanatory power, as do ownership and distribution approach. The time dummies are positive, as would be expected, and are approximately the correct magnitude at around 5%— current dollar spending on IT in the overall economy has increased by about 5% per year over the 1987–1994 time period (see e.g. Brynjolfsson and Hitt, 1996b). The signs and magnitudes of the control variables are broadly consistent whether IT is measured as staff levels or budget, which provides some confidence in the survey measures. Finally, there appears to be substantial scale economies in IT spending: a doubling of number of policies is associated with a ~20% increase in staff and approximately a 30% increase in budget.[6] However, this may partially be due to omission of relevant outputs or errors in measurement. Explanatory power of these regressions is quite high for exploratory analysis with an R^2 of 48% and 58% for the staff and budget demand equations, respectively.

4.1. IT Strategy

Brynjolfsson and Hitt (1996a) found that firms that employ "extroverted" strategies, involving IT investments to improve service, timeliness, convenience, or product variety tend to show higher performance than firms that invest in IT for cost savings. To investigate whether this is true for our sample of insurers, we measure the correlation between six measures of IT strategy (with emphasis on maintenance of existing systems, cost control, building capacity, improving agent service, improving customer service and supporting new products[7]), efficiency, and IT demand. The correlations are computed by adding these variables simultaneously to the previous baseline regressions. We drop the measure for maintenance as the reference point, so our regression coefficients represent differences from the firm average of those that focus on maintaining existing systems.

The results are summarized in the table 7-5 (control variables are not reported in these or subsequent tables because they are very consistent

Table 7-5. Effects of Information Technology Strategy on Efficiency and IT Demand

Dependent Variable	Percent of Firms (%)	Cost Efficiency (TOBIT) DEA Score	Revenue Efficiency (TOBIT) DEA Score	IT Staff Demand (OLS) log(IT Staff)	IT Budget Demand (OLS) log(IT Budg.)
IT Cost Focus	19	.0282	−.0484	.763**	1.12***
(ITCOST)		(.0472)	(.0499)	(.300)	(.343)
IT Capacity Building	8	.0685	.130*	−.209	.331
Focus (ITCAP)		(.0580)	(.0623)	(.392)	(.445)
IT Agent Service Focus	15	−.0233	−.0549	2.48***	1.37***
(ITAGENT)		(.0579)	(.0617)	(.475)	(.421)
IT Customer Focus	25	.0392	.183***	.324	.708**
(ITCUST)		(.0480)	(.0488)	(.405)	(.346)
IT New Product Focus	13	.339	.414	.398	1.22**
(ITPROD)		(.0719)	(.0795)	(.444)	(.526)

*** $-p < .01$, ** $-p < .05$, * $-p < .1$; regression coefficient at the top of each cell, standard errors in parenthesis; includes same controls as in table 7-4.

across the various regressions). Overall, firms that are primarily investing to maintain their current position (maintenance, capacity expansion) spend the least on IT but have only average efficiency. However, those that focus on customer service or introducing new products have significantly higher efficiency and spend somewhat more on IT overall. Interestingly, the effect of service is much greater for revenue efficiency than for cost efficiency, consistent with the idea that revenue efficiency captures unmeasured output quality. Firms that focus on cost reduction also spend substantially more on IT, but appear to have neutral or even slightly negative efficiency. Interestingly, despite these differences in performance, only 57% of the firms in the sample reported customer-focused strategies.

A second key component of overall IS strategy is the extent to which the company builds and maintains its systems in-house as opposed to using outside firms. Almost all firms utilize contractors for at least some portion of their systems development work.

In this sample, the vast majority of firms retain nearly all their information systems services in-house. On average, the firms in the sample insource over 85% of operations and maintenance work, and about 80% of development work. The productivity and IT demand results (table 7-6) suggest that outsourcing is primarily used to supplement existing staff; there is

Table 7-6.　Relationship Between Outsourcing Strategy, Efficiency and Information Technology Demand

Dependent Variable	Cost Efficiency (TOBIT) DEA Score	Revenue Efficiency (TOBIT) DEA Score	IT Staff Demand (OLS) log(IT Staff)	IT Budget Demand (OLS) log(IT Budget)
Overall Outsourcing Use (1–5) (OUTSRC)	−.0231 (.0199)	−.0242 (.0229)	.303* (.173)	.0466 (.130)
Average Outsourcing Percent (AVGOUTSRC)	.000100 (.000840)	.000520 (.000968)	.00258 (.00578)	.000131 (.00591)
Development Outsourced (%) (%DEV)	−.000213** (.000936)	−.000652 (.00112)	.00639 (.00569)	.0242*** (.00659)
Maintenance Outsourced (%) (%MAINT)	−.000229* (.00119)	.000504 (.00143)	−.0000664 (.00779)	−.0100 (.0839)
Operations Outsourced (%) (%OPER)	−.000493 (.000135)	.000994 (.00158)	−.00562 (.00892)	−.0194 (.00854)

*** $-p < .01$, ** $-p < .05$, * $-p < .1$; regression coefficient at the top of each cell, standard errors in parenthesis; includes same controls as in table 7-4.

minimal effect on efficiency, and the demand equations suggest that there are only slight increases in overall IT usage. This is most pronounced for outsourcing development work, an area that often utilizes outside contractors to supplement staff on a short-term basis.[8]

4.2. Technology Strategy

The previous measures capture overall IT management practices. However, IT departments and firms must also make numerous general technological choices that pervade the IT organization and the firm as a whole. Some major choices in this area are whether to emphasize the maintenance of existing systems or the development of new systems, the extent to which systems are forced to conform to standard technological platforms or whether a diversity of platforms will be supported (especially the choice between remaining on mainframes or committing to client-server architectures). Finally, the organization can have a greater or lesser commitment to overall automation of the work process—some companies may attempt to have all processing online and utilize common data bases while others selectively automate individual functions.

Overall, one would generally believe that legacy systems impose substantial costs on an organization and result in decreased efficiency. New systems development may have a mixed effect depending on whether it is part of an overall strategy (more likely) or a one-time investment that increases cost in the short run for long-term gains. Standard systems platforms are believed to decrease IT costs, although they create some degree of inflexibility, which can reduce overall efficiency of the organization. Client server architectures originally were believed to be a way of lowering costs, retaining standardization of systems, and improving flexibility although high end-user support costs may reduce much of the gains. In addition, automation of routine operations is a standard goal for many service firms that should lead to increased efficiency, but has an ambiguous effect on overall IT costs.

Taken collectively (see table 7-7), the results of systems strategy are

Table 7-7. Relationship Between Technology Strategy, Efficiency and Information Technology Demand

Dependent Variable	Cost Efficiency (TOBIT) DEA Score	Revenue Efficiency (TOBIT) DEA Score	IT Staff Demand (OLS) log(IT Staff)	IT Budget Demand (OLS) log(IT Budget)
Legacy Systems (NLEGACY)	.0140 (.0103)	.00466 (.0123)	−.0641 (.0708)	−.125 (.0760)
New Systems Development (%) (%NEWSYS)	.00176** (.00826)	.000339 (.000980)	.00524 (.00569)	.0229*** (.00573)
Systems Diversity (NSYSTEMS)	.0100 (.00891)	.0201** (.00983)	.0538 (.0603)	.0265 (.0591)
Extent of Client-Server Use (1–5) (CLSERV)	.0339 (.0224)	.000082 (.0263)	.198 (.120)	.393*** (.140)
On-line Functionality (FUNC)	−.0151 (.0108)	.00306 (.0125)	−.136 (.0828)	−.105 (.0812)

*** $-p < .01$, ** $-p < .05$, * $-p < .1$; regression coefficient at the top of each cell, standard errors in parenthesis; includes same controls as in table 7-4.

surprising in two ways. First, none of these choices appears to substantially affect efficiency; only diversity and development have any relationship to efficiency. They are barely significant ($p < .1$) and have the "wrong" sign. One interpretation is that these results reflect the earlier observation that cost reduction is less important than supporting greater levels of service and new products, hence the positive effect of diversity. The relationship between new development and efficiency might best be explained by reverse causality—more efficient firms can afford greater development costs.

In terms of IT demand, aging systems or greater diversity appear not to increase (or decrease) IT costs substantially. Client server architectures lead to increased ITB, which suggests eight that operational costs are high relative to mainframe costs, or alternatively, that investments in development or a strategy to migrate to newer architectures raise IT costs in the short run.

4.3. Managing the IT Function

Given the strong interdependencies between the IT function and the business units it serves, a key part of managing information resources is managing the interrelationships between the IT function, senior management, and line business units. On the survey, we capture these relationships by four sets of measures; these results are shown in table 7-8.

First, the existence of an IT investment committee suggests that there is an attempt to align IT spending with overall organizational strategy or at least to provide some cost control. These committees are in place in about 58% of the firms in the sample. However, while they exert a mild negative influence on overall investment levels, there is a slight positive effect on cost efficiency and virtually no effect on revenue efficiency. The relatively weak effects may be due to the fact that most IT investment is not discretionary. Another explanation comes from a study of the banking industry; Hitt, Frei and Harker (1998) found that in practice these committees act as information-gathering forums rather than decision-making bodies; almost all investment decisions are made at lower levels and are rarely changed at the steering committee level.

Second, the firm can choose to centralize or decentralize the IT function. One would generally expect the central IT department to be more efficient in using IT resources, although it runs the risk of misguided systems efforts or of rationing IT services. To measure centralization, we construct a count of the number of major systems (out of a total of 8) where decision-making authority lies outside of the department and life and annuity business unit

Table 7-8. Relationship Between Information Technology Management Practices, Efficiency and Information Technology Demand

Dependent Variable	Cost Efficiency (TOBIT) DEA Score	Revenue Efficiency (TOBIT) DEA Score	IT Staff Demand (OLS) log(IT Staff)	IT Budget Demand (OLS) log(IT Budget)
IT Steering Committees	.0762**	−.00845	−.712*	−1.17**
(ITSTEER)	(.0344)	(.0408)	(.388)	(.518)
Centralized IT	−.00157	.0195	.211***	.191***
Management	(.0218)	(.0121)	(.0669)	(.0734)
(CENTIS)				
Chargeback of IT	.133**	.157***	−.0159	.627**
Expenses	(.0413)	(.0477)	(.299)	(.291)
(CHGBK)				
Service Agreements	.0555	.0841**	.708***	.841***
(SLG)	(.0354)	(.0407)	(.242)	(.224)
IT Department	.0000654	−.103	.712*	1.17**
Measured	(.0691)	(.0772)	(.388)	(.518)
(ITMEAS)				
IT Role in Strategy	−.00386	−.00371	.0783**	.147**
(ITSTRAT)	(.00519)	(.00600)	(.0391)	(.0482)

*** $-p < .01$, ** $-p < .05$, * $-p < .1$; regression coefficient at the top of each cell, standard errors in parenthesis; includes same controls as in table 7-4.

(therefore, it is made either at the life company or holding company level). Of eight major IT decisions,[9] on average, seven are centralized for the firms in our sample. However, there is little evidence that firms are achieving the desired benefits from centralization; firms that decentralize IT functions, appear to be more cost efficient without sacrificing performance, although the lack of sample variation suggests care in interpreting this result.

Third, the firm can choose different levels of monitoring and control of the IT function, either through measurement or through chargeback mechanisms that allocate IT costs back to business units (perhaps the strongest form of accountability). Overall, both chargeback and service agreements appear to improve performance and all measures of IT control are associated with greater levels of IT investment. A reasonable interpretation is that these mechanisms are responses to higher demands for IT services, and do appear to be accomplishing their intended objective.

Finally, IT can play a greater or lesser role in formulation of business unit strategy; although the investment committee can provide some guidance on strategy, these linkages are probably strongest at the operational level. We measure the linkage between IT and business unit strategy by the extent to which the IT manager rates their input into strategy in five business units.[10] Contrary to expectation, coordinating IT and business unit strategy has no apparent effect on performance, although it is associated with higher IT demand. Thus, IT has a greater role in strategy when the firm spends more on IT, but there is no evidence that this either hurts or helps cost efficiency.

4.4. Work Systems

The survey contains extensive information about the use of various types of incentive systems (individual, subjective, group, company-level), the use of formal job appraisals, and the extent to which pay varies among individuals. Human capital investments are captured by measures of the educational composition of the IT department, measures of the amount of training given to new hires as well as existing staff, and the extent of pre-employment screening for education. Finally, the use of teams is directly measured as the percentage of personnel participating in work teams, and indirectly measured by the importance of "team skills" in pre-employment screens.

Because of the large number of measures and a multitude of scales, the results for this section report on whether they are positive (+), negative (−) or zero (0, meaning that the measure had a p-value greater than .9). These results are summarized in table 7-9.

On the one hand, many of the standard "high performance work practices" such as training and group incentives have almost no effect. Individual objective incentives are associated with greater cost efficiency but most measures alternate in sign depending on the analysis. There appears to be mixed evidence on increases in decision-making authority; work teams have some positive effect, but increased hierarchy is positively related to performance (contrary to expectation). Job tenure is also negatively related to performance but positively related to IT use.

However, two sets of measures stand out very strongly. First, differentials in pay, probably the clearest evidence of individual incentives for an organization, are strongly related to revenue efficiency, but not cost efficiency. Given that variable pay tends to be only a small component of compensation, and appears to have little effect in this sample, it appears

Table 7-9. Summary of Information Technology Work Practice Relationship to Efficiency and Information Technology Demand

Dependent Variable	Cost Efficiency (TOBIT) DEA Score	Revenue Efficiency (TOBIT) DEA Score	IT Staff Demand (OLS) log(IT Staff)	IT Budget Demand (OLS) log(IT Budget)
Incentives				
— Individual Subjective	–	+	+	–
— Individual Objective	–	+	0	+
— Group (IT division)	+	+	+	+***
— Company	+	+	–	–
— Formal Appraisal (% employ)	+	–**	–***	–***
— Pay Differentials (High/Low)	–	+***	+	+***
— Developer Pay (rel. to ind.)	–**	–***	+**	+
Human Capital				
— % Developers College Ed.	+	+***	+***	+***
— % Tech Support College Ed.	+**	–	+***	+***
— Job Tenure (average)	–**	–**	+***	+***
Training				
— At hire (average hours)	–	–	0	0
— Ongoing (average hours/year)	+	+	–	+
Hiring				
— Selectiveness of IT staff	–	–***	–	–***
— Screening for Education	+	+	+**	+**
— Screening for Teamwork	–***	–***	+	–
Work Teams				
— Participated in teams (1–5)	+**	+	–*	+*
Hierarchy				
— Management Layers in IT	+***	+**	+***	+***

*** $-p < .01$, ** $-p < .05$, * $-p < .01$; symbol represents sign of regression coefficient; includes same controls as in table 7-4.

that this results can be interpreted as variations in base salary. Because job tenure has the opposite effect (negative efficiency effect), it is reasonable to conclude that these pay differentials are merit based rather than simply reflecting seniority. Results are almost identical when tenure is included as a control variable. They also appear whether differentials are measured as the ratio of top to average pay, top to bottom (shown in the table), or average to bottom. Interestingly, higher pay relative to other insurers does not help; it has a negative effect on overall efficiency but a weak positive relationship with IT demand, which suggests that it is more important to have pay differentials within organizations rather than between them.

Second, education of the development staff has a strong positive relationship with performance. This is consistent with the importance of general rather than specific human capital in IT organizations, at least for those employees who are designing software. While this is somewhat counterintuitive given the importance of specific technical skills, the result is weaker with education of the technical support staff where, arguably, specific skills play a larger role.

Altogether, while we do not find that broadly defined high performance work practices are important, we do find a substantial role for straightforward incentive systems (variation in base pay) and general skills in the development staff.

5. Summary and Conclusion

5.1. Summary

Overall, the results suggest that high level IT management issues have an influence on both overall IT expenditure as well as firm efficiency. Firms that focus on creating customer or agent value, that utilize service agreements and chargeback mechanisms for controlling the IS function, and that have larger pay differentials and better educated IT staff utilize more IT and have greater firm efficiency. Technological factors and work systems that go beyond the individual (teams, group incentives, teamwork skills) appear to have little effect.

The fact that technological choices do not have an inordinate effect may be consistent with the nature of the decisions made. The decision to invest in (say) a particular networking technology or mainframe software system is heavily dependent on the specifics of a particular business problem. Thus, to the extent that we observe variation, it may be due more to unobserved requirements leading to near optimal choices rather than an indication of random variation. However, the practices we do find that have an influence are much more likely to be discretionary at a relatively high level in the organization and the linkages between these practices (e.g. customer value vs. cost) have a much greater uncertainty than the relative cost of a mainframe versus a PC network.

Almost all the factors that increase performance are also associated with increased expenditure on IT. This suggests that many of the management practices that leverage IT are such that they open new opportunities for IT investment rather than enabling firms to operate with lower IT costs. Despite the higher IT investment, these firms still show greater efficiency (one of the factors included is IT in the cost side) so that the net benefits of these investments appear to be positive. This is consistent with earlier work by Brynjolfsson and Hitt (1995), which found that customer-focused strategies were associated with higher IT investment and greater performance; a similar result for human capital was found by Bresnahan, Brynjolfsson and Hitt (1998). Taken collectively, these results suggest that it is critical to evaluate the effectiveness of the IT function, not solely by the ability to control IT costs, but as a comparison of the overall contributions to the business to the costs incurred. Organizations that overemphasize IT cost control may lose opportunities to enhance service quality, build customer relationships, or offer products required to effectively compete in an increasing technology-driven competitive environment.

5.2. Limitations

It is important to note that all of these results are correlational in nature so it is difficult to attribute causation solely from statistical tests. Many of the variables that have significant effects are arguably exogenous (predetermined), at least relative to efficiency, so that they can be interpreted in many cases as "causing" higher efficiency. It seems more plausible that customer-focused firms and IT chargeback mechanisms result in higher performance, rather than being the result of unexpected high earnings. Similarly, it is relatively easy to believe that higher performing firms may pay more, but it is harder to reconcile this sort of reverse causation story with greater pay differentials. However, other measures are less clear. Firms that have better earnings can afford to hire better quality workers in their IT function.

It also may be true that the various measures of IT practices are part of a larger system that includes different strategies, products, and organizational practices throughout the organization. Thus, we have not made any direct examination of the magnitude of these effects except to

say that they contribute positively to performance; a full understanding of
the magnitude of the IT effect would require the identification of the other
complementary factors as well—an effort beyond the scope of this book.
However, it would not be surprising if the other complements to these IT
practices are an order of magnitude higher in cost than the actual IT practices. Brynjolfsson and Yang (1997) and Brynjolfsson, Hitt and Yang (1998)
found that a dollar of IT investment is associated with as much as $10 of
other intangible assets (e.g. work systems, human capital) for a large sample
of firms.

5.3. Implications for Life Company Practice

Most of the phenomena identified in this chapter are not unique to particular systems or practices of the life insurance industry. However, it is
important to recognize that many of the practices that help IT lead to higher
performance do apply to life insurers. Most of the existing discussion of
technology in services has focused on the so-called productivity paradox
or on the application of distributed computing to the agent force. Little
attention has been paid to the basic management principles of effectively
utilizing IT in life insurers or for that matter, more broadly in financial
firms. Specific types of IT investments such as expert systems for life
underwriting, claims processing, or annuity recordkeeping systems can
and will have a substantial impact on the operational performance of
life insurers.

An important point of this chapter is that the positive effects of IT are
not only due to the functionality of specific systems—these systems can only
improve performance if they are chosen correctly, designed properly, implemented effectively, and integrated within the organization. The ability to
make these types of decisions and actions is highly dependent on the capabilities of the internal IT organization. It addition, much of the debate on
technological factors, which dominates the business press (e.g. mainframes
vs. client server), is only one piece of the IT management challenge.

Notes

1. Data for the calculation of firm efficiency was provided by J. David Cummins (see
Cummins, 1999 for further discussion of these data). Specifically, this study utilizes measures
constructed from the National Association of Insurance Commissioners (NAIC) annual
statements for 1993–1995.

2. This sample is a subset of the overall survey. Our analysis is restricted to firms that have complete data on IT and the relevant control variables used in our analysis.

3. Similar results are found by Harris and Katz (1991).

4. See Cummins (1999) for more discussion of the robustness and justification for utilizing these measures and Carr and Cummins (1997) for a discussion of econometric approaches to utilizing these data.

5. The Tobit analysis will be performed using the SAS LIFEREG procedure. We assume that the data are censored above by 1 and below by zero (although no observations actually reach the lower bound). The error term is assumed to be a truncated normal distribution as is commonly assumed in Tobit analysis.

6. This can approximately be calculated by summing the coefficients on the number of policy variables.

7. Supporting new products was not included in the survey, but was listed by 4 out of 5 firms who responded "other" to the IT strategy question. The other firm had incomplete data on other variables and was therefore not included in this analysis.

8. Most companies generally prefer to use in-house staff for maintenance and operations because it requires no special skills after initial training and is a long-term commitment. The only exceptions are firms that have engaged in total outsourcing, none of which appear in our sample.

9. The decisions are: mainframe operations, applications development, network standards, PC hardware procurement, PC applications software, telephone systems, technical support, client server hardware and applications.

10. The departments considered are: sales, policyholder services, investment management, underwriting, and claims management. (Average of the five is taken, which results in a scale with a Cronbach's alpha of .82—firms either have high input across all units or low input, neither of which tends to vary across business units).

References

Bazinet, G.G., S.A. Kahn, and S. Smith. "Measuring the Value of Outsourcing," *Best's Review* 98(12) (1998), 97–100.

Barua, Anitesh. Charles H. Kriebel, and Tridas Mukhopadhyay. "Information Technologies and Business Value: An Analytic and Empirical Investigation," *Information Systems Research* 6(1) (1995), 3–23.

Bell, A. "Life Insurers Spending More on Info Technology," *National Underwriter* 102 (no. 35, 1998), 3–49.

Bender, D.H. Financial Impact of Information Processing, 3 (no. 2, 1986), 22–32.

Berger, A.N. and L.J. Mester. "Inside the Black box: What Explains Differences in the Efficiencies of Financial Institutions?" *Journal of Banking and Finance* 21 (1997), 895–947.

Berger, Allen N., J. David Cummins, and Mary Weiss. "The Coexistence of Multiple Distribution Systems for Financial Services. The Case of Property-Liability Insurance" Working Paper, Wharton Financial Institutions Center, Philadelphia, 1995.

Berger, Allen N., W.C. Hunter, and J. Timme. "The Efficiency of Financial Institutions: A Review and Preview of Research Past, Present and Future," *Journal of Banking and Finance* 17 (1993), 221–250.

Boynton, A.C., G.C. Jacobs, and R.W. Zmud. "Whose Responsibility is IT Management?" *Sloan Management Review*, (Summer 1992), 32–38.

Bresnahan, T. "Computerization and Wage Dispersion: An Analytic Reinterpretation." Mimeo, Stanford University, 1997.

Bresnahan, T., E. Brynjolfsson, and L. Hitt. "Information Technology, Workplace Organization and the Demand for Skilled Labor: A Firm Level Analysis." Mimeo, MIT, Stanford University, and the Wharton School, 1998.

Brynjolfsson, E. and L. Hitt. "Information Technology and Organizational Design: Evidence from Micro-Data" Mimeo, MIT, Stanford University and the Wharton School, 1997.

Brynjolfsson, E. and L. Hitt. "Computers and Economic Growth: Firm-level Evidence," Working Paper 3714, Sloan School, Massachusetts Institute of Technology, 1994.

Brynjolfsson, E. and L. Hitt. "Information Technology as a Factor of Production: The Role of Differences Among Firms." *Economics of Innovation and New Technology* 3 (no. 4, 1995), 183–200.

Brynjolfsson, E. and L. Hitt, "The Customer Counts," *Informationweek* (September 8, 1996), 38–43.

Brynjolfsson, E. and L. Hitt. "Paradox Lost? Firm-level Evidence on the Returns to Information Systems Spending." *Management Science* 42 (no. 4, 1996), 541–558.

Brynjolfsson, E. and L. Hitt. "Computing Productivity: Are Computers Pulling Their Weight?" Mimeo, MIT and the Wharton School, 1998.

Brynjolfsson, E. and S. Yang. "The Intangible Benefits and Costs of Computer Investments: Evidence from Financial Markets," in *Proceedings of the International Conference on Information Systems*, Atlanta, GA, 1997.

Brynjolfsson, E., L. Hitt, and S.K. Yang. "Intangible Assets: How the Interaction on Information Systems and Organizational Structure Affects Stock Market Valuations", forthcoming in *the Proceedings of the International Conference on Information Systems*, Helsinki, Finland, 1998.

Carr, R. and J. David Cummins, 1997, "Strategic Choices, Firm Efficiency and Competitiveness in the Life Insurance Industry" Unpublished Doctoral Dissertation, University of Pennsylvania, Wharton School.

Clemons, E.K. and M.C. Row. "Information Technology and Industrial Cooperation: The Changing Economics of Coordination and Ownership." *Journal of Management Information Systems* 9 (no. 2, 1992), 9–28.

Cummins, J. David and Zi Hongmin. "Comparison of Frontier Efficiency Methods: An Application to the U.S. Life Insurance Industry," *Journal of Productivity Analysis* 10 (1998), 131–152.

Cummins, J. David. "Efficiency in the U.S. Life Insurance Industry: Are Insurers Minimizing Cost and Maximizing Revenues" in J.D. Cummins and A. Santomero (eds.), *Changes in the Life Insurance Industry: Efficiency, Technology and Risk Management*, 1999.

Cummins, J. David, Sharon Tennyson, and Mary Weiss. "Life Insurance Mergers and Acquisitions," in J.D. Cummins and A. Santomero (eds.), *Changes in the Life Insurance Industry: Efficiency, Technology and Risk Management*, 1999.

Cummins, J. David, Mary Weiss, and Hongmin Zi. "Organizational Form and Efficiency: An Analysis of Stock and Mutual Property-liability Insurers," *Management Science*, forthcoming 1999.

Davenport, Thomas H. and James E. Short. "The New Industrial Engineering: Information Technology and Business Process Redesign." *Sloan Management Review* 31 (no. 4, 1990), 11–27.

Drucker, Peter F. "The Coming of the New Organization." *Harvard Business Review*, (January–February, 1988), 45–53.

Francalanci, C. and G. Hossam. "Information Technology and Worker Composition: Determinants of Productivity in the Life Insurance Industry." *MIS Quarterly* 22 (no. 2, 1998), 227–241.

Franke, Richard H. "Technological Revolution and Productivity Decline: Computer Introduction in the Financial Industry," *Technological Forecasting and Social Change*, Vol. 31, 1987, 143–154.

Frei, F.X., P.T. Harker, and L.W. Hunter. "Inside the Black Box: What Makes a Bank Efficient?" Working Paper 97-20, Wharton Financial Institutions Center, The Wharton School, University of Pennsylvania Philadelphia, 1997. Also available at *http://fic.wharton.upenn.edu/fic/wfic/papers.html*

Frei, F.X., P.T. Harker, and L.W. Hunter. "Innovation in Retail Banking," in R. Landeau and D. Mowrey (eds.), *America's Industrial Resurgence*, Washington, DC, National Academy Press, 1998.

Friel, W. "Prudential Agents Now Make House Calls", *Information Week*, 738, (October 26, 1998).

Gardner, Lisa A. and Martin F. Grace. "X-efficiency in the US Life Insurance Industry", *Journal of Banking and Finance* 17 (1993), 497–510.

Grace, Martin F. and Stephen G. Timme. "An Examination of Cost Economies in the United States Life Insurance Industry", *Journal of Risk and Insurance* 59 (1992), 72–103.

Gurbaxani, V. "The New World of Information Technology Outsourcing," *Communications of the ACM* 39 (no. 7, 1996), 45–46.

Harnett, W. "Deciding How to Spend Your Technology Budget," *National Underwriter* 101 (no. 40, 1997), 14–42.

Hammer, M. "Reengineering Work: Don't Automate, Obliterate." *Harvard Business Review*, July–August, 1990, 104–112.

Hammer, M. and J. Champy. *Reengineering the Corporation*, New York: Harper Business, 1993.

Harris, S.E. and J.L. Katz. 'Organizational Performance and Information Technology Investment Intensity in the Insurance Industry," *Organizational Science* 2 (no. 3, 1991), 263–296.

Hitt, L. *Economic Analysis of Information Technology and Organization*.

Unpublished doctoral dissertation, Cambridge, MA: MIT Sloan School of Management, 1996.

Hitt, L. and E. Brynjolfsson. "Productivity, Business Profitability, and Consumer Surplus: Three Different Measures of Information Technology Value," *MIS Quarterly* 20 (no. 2, 1996), 121–142.

Hitt, L. and E. Brynjolfsson. "Information Technology and Internal Firm Organization: An Exploratory Analysis," *Journal of Management Information Systems* 14 (no. 2, 1997), 81–101.

Hitt, L. and E. Brynjolfsson. "Beyond Computation: Information Technology, Organization and Productivity," Mimeo, MIT, Stanford University and the Wharton School, 1998.

Hitt, L., Frances X. Frei, and Patrick T. Harker. "How Financial Firms Decide on Technology," Working Paper 98-34, Wharton Financial Institutions Center, The Wharton School, University of Pennsylvania, Philadelphia, Also available at http://fic.wharton.upenn.edu/fic/wfic/papers/98.html.

Huselid, Mark. "The Impact of Human Resource Management Practices on Turnover, Productivity and Corporate Financial Performance," *Academy of Management Journal* 38 (no. 3, 1995), 635–672.

Ichniowski, C., T.A. Kochan, D. Levine, C. Olson, and G. Strauss. "What Works at Work: Overview and Assessment." *Industrial Relations* 35 (no. 3, 1996), 299–333.

Lacity, M.C. and R. Hirscheim. "The Information Systems Outsourcing Bandwagon," *Sloan Management Review* 35 (no. 1, 1993), 73–86.

Lichtenberg, F.R. "The Output Contributions of Computer Equipment and Personal: A Firm-Level Analysis." *Economics of Innovation and New Technology* 3 (1995), 201–217.

Loveman, G.W. "An Assessment of the Productivity Impact of Information Technologies," in T.J. Allen and M.S. Scott Morton (eds.), *Information Technology and the Corporation of the 1990s: Research Studies*, Cambridge, MA: MIT Press, 1994. (Initial working paper published as an MIT Management in the 1990s Working Paper, 1986).

McFarlan, J. "CSC/General Dynamics: Information Systems Outsourcing," Harvard Business School Case Study," Cambridge, MA: Harvard Business School Press, 1991.

Moore, J. and A. Santomero. "The Industry Speaks: Results of the WFIC Insurance Survey", in J.D. Cummins and A. Santomero (eds.), *Changes in the Life Insurance Industry: Efficiency, Technology and Risk Management*, 1999.

Prasad, B. and P.T. Harker. "Examining the Contribution of Information Technology Toward Productivity and Profitability in U.S. Banking," Working Paper, Wharton Financial Institutions Center, The Wharton School, University of Pennsylvania, Philadelphia, 1997.

Quinn, J. and F. Hilmer. "Strategic Outsourcing," *Sloan Management Review* 35 (no. 4, 1994), 43–55.

Roach, S.S. "America's White-Collar Productivity Dilemma." *Manufacturing Engineering*, (August, 1998), 104.

Rockart, J. and A.D. Crescenzi. "Engaging Top Management in Information Technology," *Sloan Management Review*, (Summer 1984), 3–16.

Rockart, J.F. "The Line Takes the Leadership—IS Management in a Wired Society," *Sloan Management Review*, (Summer 1998), 57–64.

Rockart, J.F., M.J. Earl, and J.W. Ross. "Eight Imperatives for the New IT Organization," *Sloan Management Review* 38 (no. 1, 1996), 43–55.

Solow, R.M. "We'd Better Watch Out," *New York Times Book Review*, (July 12 1987), 36.

Strassmann, Paul E. *The Business Value of Computers*. Information New Canaan, CT: Economics Press, 1990.

Sviokla, J. and A. Wong. "Profiling at National Mutual", Harvard Business School Case 9-191-100, Cambridge, MA: Harvard Business School Press, 1991.

Vitale, M.R., J.J. Elam, and J. Morrison. "United Services Automobile Association (USAA)," Harvard Business School Case, Cambridge, MA: Harvard Business School Press, 1989.

Youngblood, T. "Outsourcing is a 'savior' for IT." *National Underwriter* 102 (no. 34, 1998), 3–11.

Zaheer, A. and N. Venkatraman. "Determinants of Electronic Integration in the Insurance Industry: An Empirical Test," *Management Science* 40 (no. 3, 1994), 549–566.

8 TOWARD A UNIFIED VALUATION MODEL FOR LIFE INSURERS

David F. Babbel* and Craig Merrill**

Recently much attention has been given to the approaches insurers undertake in valuing their liabilities and assets. For example, in 1994 the American Academy of Actuaries created a Fair Valuation of Liabilities Task Force to address the issue.[1] In 1997, the Academy established a Valuation Law Task Force and a Valuation Tools Working Group to investigate the various valuation approaches extant and to recommend the models best suited to the task. FASB and IASB have also been exploring the issue.

Much of the published work has focused on attributes of the various models, their strengths, and their shortcomings. Some of the work has addressed the larger questions, but in our view, it is useful and necessary to provide a taxonomy of approaches and evaluate them in a systematic way in accordance with how well they achieve their aims.

In this chapter we focus primarily on the economic valuation of insurance liabilities, although we do address some valuation issues for assets. In section 1 we identify the components of an insurance company's economic value. Next, in section 2, we discuss the criteria for a good economic valuation model. This is followed by a taxonomy of valuation models in section 3. In section 4, we suggest an approach for valuing insurance company liabilities that is consistent with the discussion presented in section 1. In section 5, we examine insurance liabilities in the context of our modeling taxonomy and identify the minimum requirements of an economic valuation approach that purports to adequately value them. An illustration of the application of a modern valuation model is given in section 6. We conclude in section 7 with a discussion of some of the limitations of our analysis and offer some recommendations for implementation.

1. The Components of Insurance Company Value

The market value of insurance company owners' equity is defined as the difference between the market value of assets and the market value of liabilities. For purposes of valuation, it is helpful to partition more finely the components of equity value. In this chapter, we will partition the value of insurance company owners' equity, or stock in the case of a stock company, into its four major components: franchise value, market value of tangible assets, present value of liabilities, and put option value. (See figure 8-1.)

These components have the following elements. The franchise value stems from what economists call "economic rents." It is the present value of these rents that an insurer is expected to garner because it has scarce resources, scarce capital, charter value, licenses, a distribution network, personnel, reputation, and so forth. It includes renewal business.[2] Franchise value is dependent on firm insolvency risk. The less insolvency risk there is, the more likely the firm is to stay solvent long enough to capture all the available economic rents arising from its renewal business, its distribution network, its reputation, and so forth.

The next two components can be netted together to produce what we

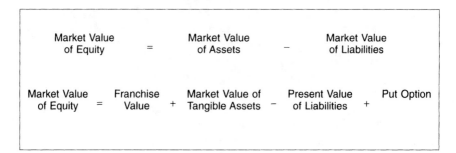

Figure 8-1.   Market Value of Insurance Equity

will call "net tangible value." This value is simply the market value of tangible assets less the present value of liabilities.[3] This net tangible value is independent of what *kind* of assets an insurer has, but does depend on the *amount* of assets the insurer holds. For instance, if the firm swaps Treasury securities worth $5 billion for junk bonds worth the same (but with higher coupons and/or face values), or swaps them for $5 billion worth of pork belly futures, the market value of tangible assets is the same. Similarly, the present value of the *promised* cash flows to insurance consumers remains the same—although the quality of the promise has changed (more will be said about this later). Therefore, the net tangible value of the firm at any given moment is unaltered by the kind of assets the firm holds. Moreover, it is completely independent of firm insolvency risk, although how this value evolves over time will depend on risk.

Put option value arises from the limited liability enjoyed by equityholders when their firm issues debt (i.e., insurance policies, the major debt of an insurance company). It is the value to equityholders of capturing the upside earnings while not incurring all the downside costs of default. The insolvency put option increases in value as the insurer takes on more risk. If the insurer faces minimal insolvency risk, there may be little benefit inuring to it from this component of value; but if it is a risky firm, the implicit insolvency put option may be of considerable value.

In what follows, we will use the more compact notation to represent the above equations:

$$MV(E) = MV(A) - MV(L) \tag{1}$$

$$MV(E) = FV + MV(TA) - PV(L) + PO \tag{2}$$

At this point it is useful to pause and consider these juxtaposed equations. It is clear that the right-hand sides of both equations must be equal to each other. It is equally clear that the market value of liabilities differs from the present value of liabilities unless the market value of assets is defined as the sum of the franchise value, market value of tangible assets, and put option (i.e., unless $MV(A) \equiv FV + MV(TA) + PO$).

But this broad definition of the market value of assets is not universally used and, therefore, neither is the associated equivalence of market value of liabilities with present value of liabilities. For instance, oftentimes people will think of the market value of liabilities as being the same thing as the market value of debt from an investor's point of view. Thus, if a bond that is subject to credit risk has been issued, its market value is reduced below that of an otherwise comparable default-free bond. Accordingly, the market value of liabilities is reduced when the debt becomes risky. This is ironic from an insurance regulatory perspective. If the insurer is likely to default on its insurance policies, it would suggest that the liabilities are worth less than they would be if they were secure. The riskier a firm is, the lower the market value of its liabilities. Therefore, were the insurer to report this market value of liabilities to regulators, the lower market value could suggest the insurer is in better financial health than if the insurer were to report a present value of liabilities that is not reduced by the prospect of insolvency.[4]

From a financial economics perspective, a firm issuing a default-prone bond has issued a combination of a default-free bond along with a default put option. The value of the bond is reduced by the value of the put. The investor is long a default-free bond and short a put.[5] The issuer is short a default-free bond and long a put. This put option would normally be on the asset side of an "economic balance sheet," although it appears nowhere on the typical accounting statement.

In figure 8-2, each of these components of value is displayed separately as a function of firm insolvency risk. When these value elements are displayed together, as in figure 8-3, we can see how the overall market value of the firm is related to its risk exposure. As the firm increases in insolvency risk, firm market value increases, and as it decreases in risk, again there is an increase in firm value. This equity market value premium over net tangible value stems either from franchise value or from put option value, or from some combination of the two. This is not merely a theoretical construct. It has been accepted wisdom in the financial institutions literature

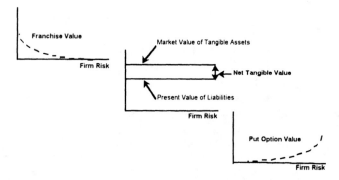

Figure 8-2.   Insolvency Risk and the Components of Equity Value

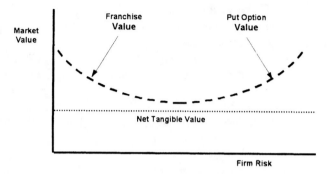

Figure 8-3.   Components of Equity Value Combined

for decades. Empirical research suggests the effect is pronounced in the case of insurance firms.[6] These insights will be helpful as we proceed to consider the valuation of insurance liabilities.

2. Criteria for a Viable Economic Valuation Model

It would be advantageous to employ a consistent valuation methodology across the various components of the insurance firm discussed above. To this end, several criteria can be identified as necessary ingredients for a viable economic valuation model. We propose the following criteria:

1. A model that purports to be an economic valuation model should produce values that are *consistent with the definition of economic value* that is being used so that it will be *relevant* and *meaningful*. This criterion is undoubtedly the most important one, and a precursor for the others. Another type of model should not be substituted for an economic valuation model simply because the former is easier to apply. If its focus is on the wrong thing, or if it simply is not designed to address adequately the dimension of economic valuation, then it should not be used for economic valuation purposes. When practitioners enlist an accounting model or some other such dubious approach to estimate economic value, it reminds us of the legendary intoxicated man who was searching under a street light for his lost keys. An approaching police officer inquired of the hapless man what he was doing, and the man explained that he had lost his

keys near a parking meter some distance away, but that it was easier to search for them under the bright light than around the location where he had dropped them.

2. A viable model should be *implementable*. It almost goes without saying that the reach of a valuation model must not exceed its (and our) grasp. The generality of the model must be tempered by our ability to implement it. While it is common among academicians in the field of financial economics to develop theoretical models that are far removed from any current application, the actuarial profession cannot afford that luxury. Actuaries require models that can be developed readily, and implemented with available computer technology. A model that fails on this front may offer future promise, but cannot hold in abeyance the valuation work that needs to be done today.

3. A viable model should produce *consistent* prices across all assets and liabilities. Many valuation models in use today are specialized for only one class of assets or liabilities. For example, an option pricing model may be used to price options, an equity valuation model may be used to price common stock, a bond pricing model may be used for bonds, and an actuarial model may be used for insurance liabilities.[7] The only consistency obtained in using such disparate models is that they render a value in dollar terms. It would be far better to have a general valuation model capable of valuing most, or all classes of assets and liabilities. This would be helpful not only for encouraging consistency of assumptions, but is also necessary for generating future economic scenarios for solvency testing and business planning. Parsimony should not be mistaken for efficiency. While it is correct that a particular financial instrument, such as a short-term default-free noncallable bond, may require only a single random factor to generate an appropriate value, that does not imply that such parsimony in modeling should be heralded as the guiding principle in model selection. A more inclusive model may incorporate additional factors that are not particularly germane to the valuation of a particular instrument, but which may allow the valuation of the financial instrument in question as well as a host of other instruments, such as callable corporate bonds, in a consistent fashion.

4. A viable model should *calibrate closely* to observable prices. Economic value is the same as market value when the financial instrument in question is tradable in an active market. The standard for a good fit, which has been widely accepted in recent years, is that the

model should closely match observed U.S. Treasury prices, particularly "on-the-run" Treasury bills, notes and bonds, and the prices of Treasury derivatives, including options on Treasury futures. These prices are important because the instruments are widely traded and very liquid. We can have confidence that reported prices are not stale, and that there is sufficient trading volume subject to the discipline of arbitrage forces to ensure that prices are at appropriate levels. The model should also calibrate reasonably well to the market prices of other financial instruments, but insofar as valuing insurance liabilities is concerned, calibration to other financial instruments may be unnecessary.[8]

5. A viable model should be *noncontroversial*. It should be based on well-established principles and accepted valuation practices. It would be unwise for any body of professionals to adopt a valuation model for reporting or managerial purposes that was based on fanciful theory and unproven technology.

6. A viable model should be *specifiable* and *auditable*. By specifiable we mean that regulators and managers ought to be able to specify a set of economic parameters to be used in the valuation for the purpose of studying the company. Of course, the best values of the parameters for valuation purposes are those that are inferred from observed market prices and the behavior over time of interest rates and other economic factors that influence value. But a viable model should also be open to a set of parametric specifications from parties who have an interest in promoting solvency and managing a company. Once the parameters are estimated or otherwise specified, the output of the model should be amenable to auditing, to ensure that it is producing scenarios and values consistent with those parameters.

7. A viable model should feature *value additivity*. By this, we mean that the values estimated for various parts of a portfolio of assets or liabilities should be equal to the value of the entire portfolio when summed together.[9] In a world that does not foster costless arbitrage, the sum of the parts may not be exactly equal to the value of the whole, but should fall within some bounds related to transaction costs.

Having discussed seven criteria needed in a viable valuation model, we next proceed to a discussion of the menu of available models, their relation one to another, and their inclusiveness of the factors that determine economic value.

3. A Taxonomy of Valuation Models

There are many seemingly different valuation models in the literature. Some examples include general equilibrium models, partial equilibrium models, contingent claims models, Black-Scholes option pricing model, Arbitrage Pricing Theory (APT), the Capital Asset Pricing Model (CAPM) and its variations, as well as a wide variety of models for pricing interest rate contingent claims. In this section, we will introduce a simple taxonomy for understanding the relationships between valuation models.

In any valuation model there will be cash flows, with their associated probabilities of occurrence, and discount rates. A key feature of financial valuation models is how they account for risk in the cash flows. There are three common methods for dealing with risk: by modifying the cash flows, the discount rate, or the probabilities.

The first method is to use a certainty-equivalent cash flow.[10] The certainty-equivalent cash flow is the cash flow that would make the investor indifferent between a certain outcome and facing a random draw on a set of risky cash flow outcomes. This approach depends on the specification of an individual's utility function. Given an assumed utility function, different individuals' risk aversion may be ranked by comparing their certainty-equivalent cash flows. This approach is not often used in security valuation models. However, it has been profitably applied to the firm's capital budgeting problem.

The second approach is to embed a risk premium in the discount rate to allow for the excess return that investors seek as compensation for bearing risk.[11] In practice, valuation models for basic securities like stocks, bonds, or projects within a firm tend to use the risk premium approach. The CAPM and APT are well-known models that have been developed specifically to estimate risk premiums.

Third, there is the risk-neutral pricing methodology employed in option pricing. In risk-neutral pricing the probability distribution is typically adjusted to compensate for risk so that cash flows can be discounted at the risk-free rate as if investors were risk neutral. Risk-neutral valuation is most commonly applied to derivative securities. It is important to keep in mind that with risk-neutral valuation, the price is determined by the absence of arbitrage. The existence of the risk-neutral measure is synonymous with the absence of arbitrage.[12] Thus, investors with widely varying levels of risk aversion can agree on the price yielded by a risk-neutral model because it represents the price that allows no arbitrage opportunities. However, there need be no inconsistencies between the models. Properly implemented, all approaches will lead to the same valuation.[13]

	Deterministic Cash Flows	*Stochastic Cash Flows*
Deterministic Interest Rates	A	B
Stochastic Interest Rates	C	D

Figure 8-4. Matrix of Valuation Model Complexity

Our framework for considering valuation models can be represented with a two-by-two matrix depicting two dimensions along which a model may be extended or simplified. This matrix is given in figure 8-4. The first column of the matrix represents models with deterministic, or known, cash flows. The second column represents models with stochastic cash flows. Similarly, the rows represent the deterministic or stochastic nature of interest rates as used in a model. Therefore, moving to the right or down in the matrix represents an increase in the complexity of the valuation model. Cell D would be the most general model, featuring both stochastic cash flows and interest rates. We will present a valuation equation for each of the four cells. Each valuation equation will be in terms of a single cash flow. Securities with multiple cash flows are treated as portfolios of single cash flows.

In our matrix, cell A represents the simplest class of models. Both the sequence of future interest rates and the future cash flows are known with certainty today, at time zero. Let x_t be a cash flow at time t. Let $r_t(n)$ represent an n-period spot rate of interest at time t. Define the short rate to be the spot rate that applies to the shortest time increment. For example, in discrete time the one-period spot rate, $r_t \equiv r_t(1)$, or more simply, r_t, would be the short rate of interest. In continuous time, the instantaneous spot rate, $r_t \equiv r_t(\Delta t)$, would be the short rate. In the equations below, we will render the continuous-time formulations.

Given these definitions, our valuation equation for cell A is

$$V_0 = x_t \exp\left(-\int_0^t r_s\, ds\right). \tag{1}$$

This equation includes the simple present value formula from introductory finance, in which interest rates are assumed constant as a special case. That is, $V_0 = x_t \exp[-r_0(t)t]$.

In cell B we assume that the cash flow is stochastic and possibly affected or determined by other stochastic factors. The cash flow is denoted by $x_t(\mathbf{y}_t)$, where $\mathbf{y}_t$ is a vector of sources of randomness. For example, payments to an auto insurance policyholder are determined by the random losses that occur during a period of coverage. The loss distribution is usually described by frequency and severity distributions. In this case the vector, $\mathbf{y}_t$, might be composed of two components: a random variable for frequency and a random variable for severity. The actual payment, $x_t(\mathbf{y}_t)$, would depend on realized losses as well as on policy provisions such as deductibles and limits of liability.

Another example can be found in option pricing. Consider an equity option-pricing model. In this case $\mathbf{y}_t$ would be a scalar representing the stock price at time t. The option's cash flows are deterministically linked to the price of the stock. Thus, $x_t(\mathbf{y}_t)$ would represent the cash flow to the option.

The valuation equation for cell B is

$$V_0 = E_y^*[x_t(y_t)]\exp\left(-\int_0^t r_s\,ds\right), \tag{2}$$

where the asterisk denotes that the expectation is being taken over the risk-neutral probability measure. The subscript on the expectations operator indicates that the expectation is being taken over the stochastic factors, $\mathbf{y}_t$, that influence or determine the cash flow, $x_t(\mathbf{y}_t)$. If we can exactly replicate the cash flows of a security using a portfolio of other securities, then the security of interest and its replicating portfolio should have the same price. Otherwise, there would be an arbitrage opportunity. As we stated above, Harrison and Pliska [1979] show that if there are no arbitrage opportunities then we can construct a probability measure under which we can price risky cash flows as if investors were risk neutral. This is the risk-neutral, or equivalent martingale, measure. The risk-neutral measure is the probability measure that sets equation (2) equal to the price of the replicating portfolio. A risk-neutral measure can be used in place of the realistic, or "true" probability distribution because with perfect replication of cash flows, the replicating portfolio and the security being valued must have the same price or else there would be an arbitrage opportunity. Thus, all investors, regardless of their level of risk aversion, will agree on the price.

Equation (2) says that the value of a stochastic future cash flow is the present value, discounting at the risk-free rate, of the risk-neutral expected cash flow. Alternatively, we could specify this valuation equation as

$$V_0 = E_y[x_t(y_t)]\exp\left(-\int_0^t [r_s + \lambda(s)]ds\right), \tag{2'}$$

where the expectation is over the true probability distribution of y_t and $\lambda(t)$ is the (possibly time varying) risk premium. In complete markets where the components of y_t are actively traded, equation (2) and (2') will yield identical valuations. For example, options could be valued using either equation. However, when the underlying source of uncertainly is not actively traded, equation (2') is more likely to be used. Thus, when valuing auto insurance where y_t would be composed of the random variables representing frequency and severity, equation (2') is used.

The market price of risk must be estimated: this is usually accomplished by specifying a utility function for a representative investor. The risk aversion associated with the assumed utility function determines the functional form of $\lambda(t)$. The market price of risk can then be determined empirically by calibrating the model to market data—that is, estimating $\lambda(t)$ to best equate model prices to market prices.

Examples of models that would fall within cell B are the CAPM, APT, Black-Scholes option pricing model, and many traditional insurance pricing models. In each case, some sort of distribution of future cash flows is assumed and the expectations of those cash flows are discounted at deterministic, and often constant, interest rates. While the CAPM and APT are referred to as pricing models, they actually determine an appropriate discount rate to compensate for risk when discounting risky cash flows. Thus, they fall within the category of risk-premium models. They would be an example of the process of determining the risk premium in equation (2'). The Black-Scholes model, on the other hand, is the classic example of equation (2). Their pricing model is derived using the absence of arbitrage between the option and a dynamically rebalanced portfolio that exactly replicates the option's potential cash flows.

In cell C, we assume that cash flows are known in advance but that interest rates are stochastic. This is the approach taken in fixed income valuation models, such as the Cox, Ingersoll and Ross (1985), Brennan and Schwartz (1979), or Hull and White (1990) models. The valuation equation in this case is

$$V_0 = x_t E_r^*\left[\exp\left(-\int_0^t r_s ds\right)\right], \tag{3}$$

where the asterisk once again represents the risk-neutral expectation operator. In this case, the expectation is being taken over the distribution of possible future short rates. If the expectation is taken over the true probability distribution and we incorporate a risk premium, then the valuation equation would be

$$V_0 = x_t E_r \left[\exp\left(-\int_0^t [r_s + \lambda(s)] ds \right) \right].$$ (3′)

The various theories of the term structure of interest rates put forth possible formulations for $\lambda(t)$.[14] It should be noted that the local expectations hypothesis (LEH) suggests that $\lambda(t) = 0$. This means that the expected return over the next period on all interest rate contingent securities is the risk-free rate. If the LEH holds, then equations (3) and (3′) are identical.

Finally, cell D is the most general case. Here, both cash flows and interest rates are treated as stochastic. In addition, cash flows may depend on or be influenced by interest rates. The valuation equation for cell D is

$$V_0 = E_{r,y}^* \left[\exp\left(-\int_0^t r_s ds \right) E_{y|r}^* [x_t(\mathbf{r}_t, \mathbf{y}_t)] \right].$$ (4)

where $\mathbf{r}_t$ denotes a vector of short rates that have occurred from time zero to time t and the subscript on the risk-neutral valuation operator indicates over which variable the expectation is being taken. The interior expectation is taken over the marginal distribution of $\mathbf{y}_t$ given the path $\mathbf{r}_t$. The exterior expectation is taken over the joint distribution. It is important to remember that the term

$$E_{y|r}^* [x_t(\mathbf{r}_t, \mathbf{y}_t)]$$

is the expected cash flow *given* a particular path of the short rate of interest at time t. Then, the expectation over the joint distribution of $\mathbf{r}$ and $\mathbf{y}$ gives the time 0 value of the (potentially interest sensitive) expected cash flow at time t.

In order to be clear about the meaning of equation (4), we will illustrate with an application. We can extend this equation to value a block of liabilities, denoted by L_0, by integrating over t:

$$L_0 = \int_0^t V_0^t dt$$

where the superscript t on V_0 emphasizes that it is the value of the time t cash flow in equation (4). We are suggesting that when valuing a block of liabilities one should first take an expectation with respect to the variables representing sources of uncertainty other than interest rates in order to determine the expected cash flows at each point in time. This expected cash flow is potentially interest sensitive and path dependent. Then, the expected cash flows for each point in time can be aggregated by integrating over the interest rate paths. Finally, if the liability has potential cash flows at multiple points in time we can integrate, or sum as appropriate, over time.

This model is the most general in the matrix. Other examples of potential applications of this formula include options on bonds, interest rate caps and floors, mortgage-backed securities, and catastrophe bonds that are used to fund reinsurance.

The analog to equation (4) that incorporates risk premiums in the discount rate is

$$V_0 = E_{r,y}\left[\exp\left(-\int_0^t [r_s + \lambda_r(s) + \lambda_y(s)]ds\right)E_{y|r}[x_t(r_t, y_t)]\right] \qquad (4')$$

where the subscript on λ denotes the risk premium relative to interest rates or the factors contained in y_t.

In reality, cells A, B, and C are just special cases of cell D, which is codified in equation (4). Therefore, we can treat equation (4) as the valuation model in almost all cases. However, in the case of pricing a simple bond, cash flows are deterministic and there is no necessity to deal with the added complexity of equation (4). We can think of equation (4) as a model with optional features that can be turned on or off as needed. When we have deterministic cash flows we can "toggle off" the stochastic cash flow portion of the model and use only what is left in cell C or equation (3). On the other hand, when we value short-lived equity options the important feature is the stochastic cash flow. Modeling stochastic interest rates just does not impact estimated value enough to justify injecting the added complexity. So we can "toggle off" the stochastic interest rate portion of (4) and use cell B or equation (2). Finally, when we teach present value, the stochastic portion of (4) can become quite confusing. So we use cell A or equations similar to (1) to teach discounting and capital budgeting. At the core, though, a very wide variety of valuation models are encompassed in cell D or equation (4).

The valuation formulae presented above can be generalized to apply to multi-factor models as well. In most multi-factor interest rate models, the additional factors relate to components of the stochastic evolution of the short rate of interest. For example, Fong and Vasicek [1991] assume that the volatility of the short rate is itself stochastic. Thus, the two factors, or sources of uncertainty, are random shocks to the short rate itself and random changes in the volatility of the short rate. Similarly, most models of the evolution of the short rate of interest incorporate mean reversion. Hull and White [1994] assume that the level to which rates revert is itself stochastic. In this case, the two sources of uncertainty are random shocks to the short rate and random shocks on the level to which the short rate reverts. Figure 8-5 provides a classification of many of the models in popular use today.

One last comment on discrete-time vs. continuous-time models is in order. The impact of changing to discrete time on the valuation equations given above is in the probability distributions and the integral over short-

	Deterministic Cash Flows	Stochastic Cash Flows
Deterministic Interest Rates	Gordon Growth Model (Gordon and Shapiro, 1956) APV—Adjusted Present Value Approach (Myers, 1974) Weighted Average Cost of Capital Approach (Miles and Ezzell, 1980)	Black Model (Black, 1976) Black-Scholes Model (Balck and Scholes, 1973) Merton Model (Merton, 1973) Quantos Model (Babbel and Eisenberg, 1993) Binomial Option Pricing (Cox, Ross and Rubinstein, 1979) CAPM (Sharpe, 1964) Arbitrage Pricing Theory (Ross, 1976) Stulz Model (Stulz, 1982) Margrabe Model (Margrabe, 1978)
Stochastic Interest Rates	CIR Model (Cox, Ingersoll and Ross, 1985) Vasicek Model (Vasicek, 1977) Longstaff-Schwartz Model (Longstaff and Schwartz, 1992) Random Volatility Model (Fong and Vasicek, 1991)	CIR Model (Cox, Ingersoll and Ross, 1985) Vasicek Model (Vasicek, 1977) Longstaff-Schwartz Model (Longstaff and Schwartz, 1992) GAT Model (Ho and Lee, 1986) Derivatives Solutions Model—BDT (Black, Derman, and Toy, 1990) Random Volatility Model (Fong and Vasicek, 1991) Ultimate Black Box (Babbel, Merrill, and Remeza, 1999)

Figure 8-5. Examples of Models in Each Cell of the Matrix of Valuation Model Complexity

rate paths. For a discrete-time model, the expectation would be over a discrete distribution and the interest rates would be for discrete periods of time. Therefore, the integral in the exponential function would have to be changed to a summation.

4. Insurance Liabilities

Given that there is extensive literature on the valuation of the asset classes usually held by an insurance company, we will turn our attention here to the valuation of insurance liabilities. A useful question to begin our valuation of liabilities is: "How much money would I need today to satisfy completely, on an expectations basis, the obligations imposed on me through the insurance policies I have written?" It turns out that this is not only a good starting point, but a strong case can be made that it is also a good ending point insofar as liability valuation is concerned. The actuarial profession can best serve insurance management, financial markets, regulators, and investors by addressing that question. It can then be left for others to argue about the value of the default put option, franchise value, and the spin-off values of certain lines of business.

If the focus is on determining the amount of assets necessary to satisfy, on an expectations basis, the obligations imposed by the liabilities, the next issue is how best to estimate that amount. We could take an indirect or a direct valuation approach. In the case of insurance companies, it becomes readily apparent that the indirect method of valuing liabilities may be quick, but it is inefficient in addressing the question posed in the previous paragraph. Under the indirect method, tangible assets are valued and the market value of owners' equity is subtracted, presumably resulting in an estimate of the market value of liabilities. The problem with this approach, as can be seen by rearranging the terms of the equations in figure 8-1, is that the equity value embraces the net value of default put options, franchise value, spin-off values, and perhaps other options, as well as the net tangible value; yet the market value of tangible assets (as distinguished from the market value of assets), omits one or more of these. Accordingly, the implied value of liabilities will be entangled with various options that are best relegated to the asset side of the balance sheet, as shown below:

$$PV(L) = FV + MV(TA) + PO - MV(E)$$
$$\neq MV(TA) - MV(E) = PV(L) - FV - PO$$

As can be seen to the right of the inequality above, subtracting the market value of equity from the market value of tangible assets will *understate* the present value of liabilities by the amount of franchise value and the default put option. While it is possible to estimate the values of the various options and add them to the value of the investment portfolio before subtracting the equity value to arrive at the present value of liabilities, this operation invokes several layers of subjective judgment and controversy that render the resulting liability calculation rather dubious. The criteria listed in section 2 lead us to conclude that a more direct method is needed.

With a more direct approach to the valuation of liabilities,[15] we can avoid a number of the pitfalls associated with the indirect approach, provided that we focus our attention on addressing the question posed in the first paragraph of this section. The present value of liabilities tells us the amount of tangible assets needed today in order to satisfy, on an expectation basis, our liabilities. (We may be able to satisfy them with fewer assets, if we get lucky, by taking interest rate, equity, or low credit quality bets, but *hope* should not be confused with *expectation*.)

This present value, properly computed by means of Treasury-rate-based lattices or simulations properly calibrated to current Treasury security and derivatives prices, takes into account any interest rate sensitivities in the cash flows. Mortality and morbidity are factored in only on an expectation basis, although interest rate sensitivities are included to the extent that, with interest-sensitive policy surrenders and lapses, adverse selection is expected. (In practice, most companies do not currently take into account interest rate sensitivities of mortality and morbidity. As more reliable data become available, we suspect that they will.) The reserves and surplus needed to cushion variations from these interest-sensitive projections are not included in the present valuation of liabilities.

In insurance parlance, our present value of liabilities measure is analogous to the "actuarially fair value" concept developed by actuaries many decades ago. The major difference is that our measure modernizes it by explicitly accounting for stochastic interest rates and the cash flows that relate to them. Because we know, through modern finance valuation principles, how the stochastic nature of interest rates impacts value, it is a natural extension to incorporate. It also provides more meaningful value estimates of liabilities than those that ignore this source of randomness. The resulting present value estimates have, in essence, stripped out any insurer-specific C-1 risk (asset default) and C-3 risk (interest rate risk). Because the valuation lattices or simulation paths are calibrated to Treasury securities and derivatives before they are applied to insurance policies, we can be assured that the resulting liability estimate can be satisfied, on an expectation basis and, in principle, along all interest rate paths, with a properly engineered portfolio of Treasury securities and derivatives on Treasury securities. C-2 risk (mispricing of mortality/morbidity risk or of other pure risks) and C-4 risk (qualitative management issues) remain and are accounted for at their expected present values.

Now, if an insurer were to set aside reserves equal to the present value of liabilities, would this be adequate under most circumstances to satisfy the liabilities? The answer is a resounding "no." This is easy to demonstrate with an example. To be concrete, consider an insurer with a closed blok of business. If assets were set aside in an amount equal to the present value of that closed block of liabilities, and the block were left in a run-off mode, these assets would usually be inadequate to fund them. This is true whether the assets are duration and convexity matched to the liabilities or mismatched, because there can always be a deviation in the timing of a claim from what is expected. More often than not, the value of insurer assets would drop below that of the liabilities before the final dollar of liabilities is paid, even though the assets were equal to the expected present value of the liabilities at the outset.[16] However, if the insurer were able to dip into surplus during those periods of shortfalls and reimburse with interest the surplus during periods of excess asset values, by the time the final dollar of liabilities is due, the insurer would have 50-50 odds of retaining sufficient assets remaining in the closed block to satisfy the final liability payment.

Clearly, a prudent insurer would need to set reserves greater than the present value of liabilities in order to have hopes of survival. Reserves, as usually computed, have a conservative bias in them designed to increase the probability of insurer solvency over time. Additionally, surplus is required in order to cushion against any shortfalls should the reserves prove to be inadequate.

In an economic sense, we need not focus on accounting concepts such as reserves, surplus, and risk-based capital. From a managerial viewpoint, these are best viewed as merely regulatory constraints. What is needed to cushion the liabilities against inadequate assets is actual money, as measured by the net tangible value—the excess market value of tangible assets over the present value of liabilities. The amount of net tangible value needed to provide an adequate cushion will depend on the amount and behavior of the present value of liabilities. A certain amount will be needed to handle actuarial risk, i.e., deviations from expected claims. More will be needed if there is model risk, i.e., the risk that experience will deviate from the functional relationships expressed as assumptions (e.g., interest-sensitive lapse functions) in our valuation models. If the insurer retains asset default risk, asset liquidity risk, and interest rate risk, additional net tangible value will be needed. Yet all of these calculations will depend on the amount and riskiness of the present value of liabilities and the desired level of insolvency risk.

Occasionally, an objection is raised against our notion of the present value of liabilities by comparing it to readily observed market values of certain insurance liabilities. This objection is handled by keeping in mind that the present value should be formulated in a context of keeping the insurance business on the primary carrier's books, and for some good reasons.[17]

Consider a situation in which an insurer has tangible assets worth $105 and a present value of liabilities of $100. Suppose that the net value of its put option to default together with its franchise value is $2, and while not carried explicitly on its balance sheet, this value enhances the market value of its assets and equity.

Now, suppose that the insurer's liabilities are all GICs, and that it can repurchase and retire them in the open market for only $98. Alternatively, if it leaves them outstanding, it will require $100, in present value, to satisfy them ultimately. If one looks only at the cash price to retire the GICs, it looks like an attractive deal. But the *full* cost includes not only the $98 cash price but also the lost value of options ($2) associated with dropping that business.

Next, suppose that the insurer can transfer the liabilities to another insurer. Again, the true cost for the insurer is not only the value of tangible assets that must be transferred to the other insurer, but also the lost value of its options. The acceding insurer may require less than the $100 of present value needed to fully satisfy the liabilities but that does not mean that it costs less than $100 to fully satisfy them on an expectation basis. The acceding insurer may charge less because it gains the value of renewals or increases the value of its own default put option. After all, the transferred business will affect the acceding insurer's franchise and default put option values differently than that of the cedant. In fact, even the interest rate sensitivity (and therefore the value) of some of the liability cash flows may itself change when the business is transferred to a new carrier with a different kind of marketing force, crediting strategy, and financial strength. The acceding insurer may charge more simply because it can get more through negotiations. Yet these factors should not be misconstrued as impacting the present value of funds required for the primary carrier to satisfy fully, on an expectation basis, the retained liabilities.

Another objection against the present-value-of-liability concept is sometimes raised that the valuation models are fashioned to be arbitrage-free, yet the insurance liabilities, because of randomness surrounding claims and lapses, cannot be subject to the forces of arbitrage. But here we are reminded that it was not long ago when the mortgage-backed securities market emerged. Pricing was not subject to the forces of arbitrage due to the uncertainty surrounding the prepayment speeds, and there were no close comparables traded in the market. Nonetheless, satisfactory pricing algorithms were eventually developed based on two-factor, stochastic interest rate models. Subsequently, option-adjusted spreads,[18] correctly calculated, have narrowed considerably and all but disappeared in some segments of that market. This suggests that even though these valuation models cannot rely on the forces of riskless arbitrage, they can still closely approximate value.

It would appear that similar pricing algorithms should be used to value insurance liabilities. These liabilities are also subject to considerable uncertainty. Some of the uncertainty, such as the incidence of lapse and surrender, devolves from the vacillation of future interest rate levels and paths. This uncertainty can be modeled in a fashion similar to mortgage-backed security prepayments. Uncertainty stemming from mortality, morbidity, accident experience, and some base levels of lapses and surrender may not be related directly to interest rates and can be reflected directly in the expected cash flows input into the valuation model.

In life insurance, there is a need to model the dividend and crediting rate practices of the insurer. These practices are often difficult to codify because a committee may declare a set of numbers to be used that is not related, through a simple formula, to the level and evolution of the stochastic Treasury rates used in the valuation models. Nonetheless, the decision process can usually be approximated by some formula tied to these interest rates. The actual process may rely more on realized portfolio yields and returns than on Treasury rates, yet on an *ex ante* basis, the stochastic Treasury rates may be used because they serve as certainty-equivalent rates of return on the portfolio subject to credit and liquidity risk. This should suffice for liability valuation purposes.[19]

It is entirely another question, albeit an interesting one, to model the optimal dividend or crediting rate strategy. If a firm is not following such optimal strategies in certain lines of its business, it might be reflected in a higher spin-off value. Another separate question is whether the insurer is following sound asset/liability management practices. The present value of an insurance liability is not dependent on what assets the insurer holds nor on how its portfolio is structured. Rather, it depends simply on how much in default-free securities would be required today to meet its expected liability payments over time. Again, the present value must account for any interest rate sensitivities in the liabilities.

It is an important, but separate issue how much in reserves and surplus is needed to ensure, with an acceptable degree of probability, that a sufficient cushion of assets is in place to handle any adverse deviations in liability payments from those expected. The amount of reserves and surplus required will, of course, depend on the structure of the investment portfolio and the probability distribution of state-contingent liability payments (where the states are defined by the levels and evolution of interest rates).

5. The Valuation Model for Insurance Liabilities

Having discussed the important issues in valuing insurance liabilities, we now turn to the task of selecting a suitable valuation model. In reviewing the taxonomy of economic valuation models presented in section 3, it appears that we must opt in favor of a model from Class D. Only models of this class are capable of producing viable estimates of economic values for financial instruments that feature stochastic cash flows that are influenced by stochastic interest rates.

We have argued elsewhere[20] that virtually all insurance company liabilities exhibit these characteristics. Accordingly, if an economic valuation of insurance liabilities is our main objective, and we wish to satisfy criterion (1) of section 2, we are relegated to use models from Class D to obtain viable values.

While it is possible to enlist a valuation model from another class for the task of valuing insurance liabilities, the gerryrigging and contorting of model parameters needed in order to approximate a proper economic value are themselves inconsistent with financial valuation principles and subject to imprecision, mischief, controversy, and a dubious end result. It would be only by accident that they produce a number which could address the question: "How much money would an insurer need today to satisfy, on a probabilistic basis across various economic states of the world, the obligations imposed on it through the insurance policies it has written?" Moreover, one could not determine whether the "values" produced by such models were close approximations to true economic values without first computing them with a Class D model.

We are fortunate indeed if we opt for an economic valuation model from that class, because it is also the best model for valuing the myriad of disparate financial assets held by most insurers. While it is true that models from Classes A, B, and C could produce viable estimates of value for some asset categories, only Class D models embrace the valuation technology that can be used with virtually all asset categories. Moreover, Class D models produce output that is *relevant* and *meaningful*. The number produced serves as a threshold above which an insurer must operate if it is to stay in business long. This is a useful number to regulators and insurers alike, who need to know how much it should take to defease fully the liabilities the insurer has underwritten. It is a number that is easily compared among insurers, and meaningfully related to the market value of assets supporting the liabilities. It also is a number that serves as a sound starting point for the analysis of the amount of net tangible value needed to maintain solvency.

Now let us revisit the remaining six criteria for a viable economic valuation model to see how well Class D models may satisfy them. Criterion (2) is met because these models are clearly *implementable*. Wall Street has been using Class D models for over a decade in the valuation of massive amounts of mortgage-backed securities. Like insurance liabilities, mortgage-backed securities are subject to a considerable amount of cash flow uncertainty, most of which devolves from fluctuating prepayment rates occasioned by changing interest rates. In the case of insurance liabilities, some of the uncertainty, such as the incidence of lapse and surrender, devolves from the vacillation of future interest rate levels and paths. This uncertainty can be modeled in a fashion similar to mortgage-backed security prepayments. To the extent that the uncertainty stemming from mortality, morbidity, accident experience, and some base levels of lapses and surrender is not related directly to interest rates, it can be reflected directly in the expected cash flows input into the valuation model.

With respect to criterion (3), Class D models are capable of producing *consistent prices* across all assets and liabilities. Of course, to achieve full consistency, one must use the same general valuation model for both assets and liabilities, and not merely any one member of the class.[21] Perhaps the greatest benefit to practitioners from using a single Class D model is in the generation of future scenarios and distributions of values. By having all liabilities and assets valued using a single model, we can be assured of consistency when it comes to modeling the effect of a change in one or more parameters on the economic well-being of the company.

Class D models calibrate well to observable market prices, where available. Thus, criterion (4) is satisfied. Not all Class D models are created equal, however. Some calibrate more closely than others. For example, single-factor models typically calibrate poorly to observable prices without relying on deterministic time-varying model parameters that are difficult to justify theoretically.[22] Additionally, they often imply perfect correlation of movements between short-term and long-term interest rates over time, which gives a very misleading picture of interest rate risk exposure. Finally, if the single-factor models do not feature time-varying parameters, they typically require substantial distortion of parameter values in order to achieve a good fit to currently observed prices, rendering them virtually useless for simulating viable future economic scenarios. On the other hand, multi-factor models can achieve a far better fit to observed prices and observed economic phenomena, without imposing perfect correlation in movements across the term structure and without distorting the parameters to unrealistic levels. Thus, while they are more complex and painstaking to run, their valuation capabilities and scope make them far more useful for financial institutions such as insurers. Indeed, we would be so bold as to say that anything less than a two-factor model is inadequate for modeling most insurance liabilities.

Class D models have been in use since 1979, and are now so ubiquitous that their use is noncontroversial from a practitioner's viewpoint. From a theoretical point of view, there are currently no valuation models which are received more favorably, despite their drawbacks. Certainly today, it is far more controversial to enlist a model from another class for valuing an insurer's assets and liabilities, because it would not capture the economic importance and valuation impact of the interplay between stochastic cash flows and stochastic interest rates. Accordingly, we can say that criterion (5) is fulfilled.

Another attractive aspect of Class D models is that they are specifiable and auditable. After a particular model has been found with a suitable set of attributes, its parameters may be estimated or otherwise specified, and the model's output is ready for audit. Once a software implementation of the model has been certified for accuracy, most of the auditing attention can be turned toward the model's inputs and assumptions. Because there is so little that is subjective in Class D models, it meets criterion (6) well. And those elements that are subjective (e.g., surrender rates as a function of interest rates) can be the focus of additional scrutiny and sensitivity testing.

Finally, we consider criterion (7), the value additivity principle. The way in which Class D models compute value for a single financial instrument is based strictly on value additivity of its component parts. Moreover, if the same general valuation model is used for a portfolio of assets or block of liabilities, value additivity is automatically assured.

6. An Illustration

To be concrete about the application of Class D models to insurance liabilities, we provide two charts. In figure 8-6, we show a lattice of short-term interest rates (i.e. "short rates") as they evolve in discrete steps over the

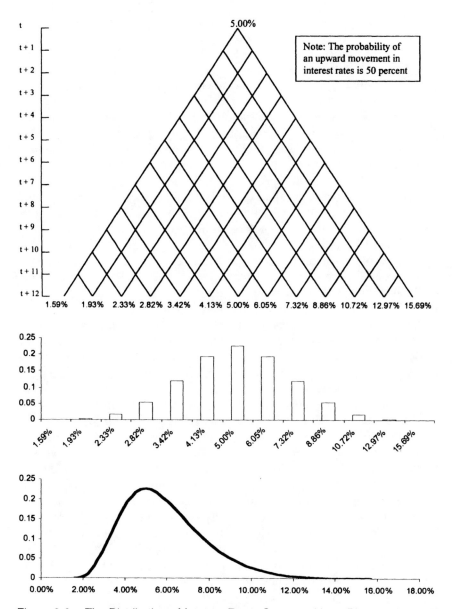

Figure 8-6. The Distribution of Interest Rates Generated by a Binomial Lattice

time period from t to $t + 12$. Each jump in interest rates is 10% either above or below its prior level. Below the lattice we show the probability distribution of interest rates at time $t + 12$, with the scale on the horizontal axis being ordinal only. At the bottom of figure 8-6, we show, using a cardinal scale, how our simple multiplicative stochastic interest rate process, when smoothed, converges to a lognormal distribution.

Figure 8-7 continues our illustration and demonstrates how to interface the insurance cash flows with the lattice of short rates. At two of the nodes, we have shown how the cash flows may be modeled using an arctangent lapse function fitted to lapse data. Depending on where along the arctangent curve the interest-rate spreads lie, we could get a different distribution of lapse rates. Nonetheless, the expected cash flows given by the arctangent function associated with each node would be used as inputs to the valuation process, and their value would be determined by applying the sequences of short rates that could give rise to those cash flows. In some models, a change of probability measure is enlisted and applied to each node to achieve arbitrage-free pricing.

What these figures show is how uncertainty arises from several sources. First, there is the uncertainty surrounding future interest rates. The economic valuation of liabilities would reflect this interest-rate risk (as captured by the arctangent function). Second, there is additional uncertainty associated with the lapse rates at each node. This residual lapse risk is not priced explicitly, but would need to be reflected in the level of net tangible value needed to maintain solvency.[23] These, and other risks may not be additive because of their correlations with one another; accordingly, the overall uncertainty should be assessed in order to determine appropriate surplus levels. Furthermore, there is additional uncertainty stemming from the use of the model itself, and the assumed distributions of interest rates and cash flows. Such uncertainty would increase the amount of surplus deemed to be prudent. Finally, by construction, the model assumes that the asset managers are fully aware of the attributes of the liabilities and have taken every effort to hedge their market risks. If, instead, the investment department has strayed from matching its assets to the needs of the liabilities, additional surplus would be needed to accommodate its choices. Yet the liability valuation model provides a useful benchmark that is a starting point for determining the level of surplus adequacy.

7. Limitations and Recommendations

In the final analysis, we can say that all of the seven listed criteria for a viable insurance valuation model are met with Class D models. Two ques-

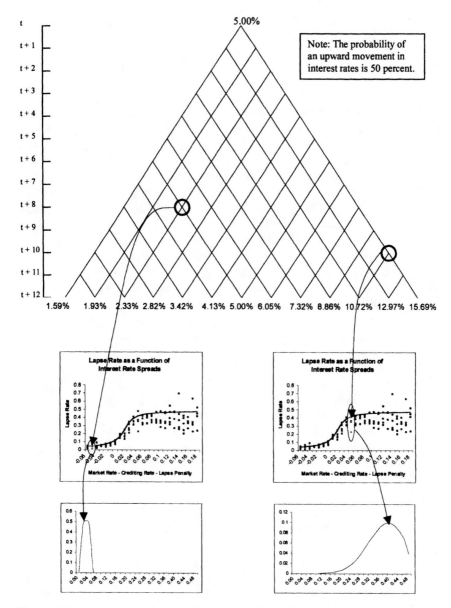

Figure 8-7.   Uncertainty Surrounding Interest Rate Contingent Cash Flows

tions remain. What are the drawbacks of using such a model, and which model is most suitable for insurers?

The major drawbacks in using such models for insurance liability valuation purposes are manifold:

1. Class D models require a higher level of analytical capability than is found at some insurance companies. However, most actuaries who are not already conversant with these models could adopt them with a little bit of directed training, because their curriculum already equips them to undertake tasks of equal complexity.

2. They elicit valuation inputs that may not be readily available, such as lapse functions and crediting rate algorithms. But these inputs are also necessary with far less sophisticated models. The only nuance is to model these inputs as (perhaps fuzzy) functions of the underlying factors (such as interest rates and inflation) that are driving the valuation.

3. The computer requirements for data analysis using stochastic methods are more extensive than those for simpler accounting models. As most insurers already have tremendous data processing capacity, we do not see this as a binding constraint.

4. Regulators may not embrace the output of these models until they become more familiar with them, and may therefore require an additional layer of scenario testing using more primitive models. Over time, however, as the comfort levels of regulators increase, the advantages and insights that can be garnered through reliance on Class D models will surely impel regulators to use them. When you have to travel from Boston to Hartford, most people would opt for the Mercedes over the roller skates, especially if the skates were never designed to go that far.

5. There are additional short-run costs when going from what has traditionally been an accounting focus to an economic focus—software costs, data assembly and modeling costs, and training costs. Yet we would suggest that in a competitive environment, the insurance companies that delay adopting an economic focus will in the end incur the greater costs due to mispricing of policies and asset/liability imbalances.

With regard to the selection of a suitable Class D model, we are reluctant here to get into a discussion of the competing "brands" of available products and those under development. Therefore, we will restrict our com-

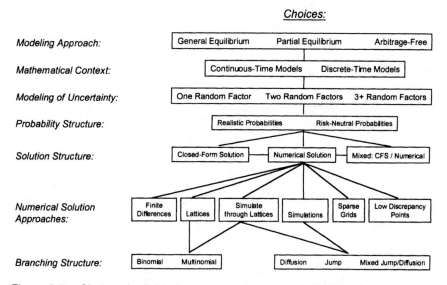

Figure 8-8. Choices Available for Implementing Class D M272odels

ments to some general observations that may help guide an insurer in its search for a suitable model for valuing its liabilities.

Numerous variants of Class D models exist. They may be distinguished one from another by the choices they make in deriving the valuation models. In figure 8-8, we list the issues that confront the insurer and the choices available. The first decision that needs to be made is whether an equilibrium approach will be used or an arbitrage-free pricing approach. The equilibrium approach begins with some assumptions and observations about the general economy, and from them, implications are derived for the behavior of the term structure of interest rates. This approach is suitable for scenario testing and "broad brush-stroke" valuation. It is especially adept at producing reasonable future scenarios that should be used in the management of insurance financial risk. However, an arbitrage-free approach is more suitable for daily trading. Yet, such an approach is less likely to produce helpful future economic scenarios for solvency testing, because the evolution of the term structure of interest over time under this kind of model often does not reflect certain stable economic relationships that are observed in practice.

Next, we feel it is important that the model be congruent with valuation of all classes of liabilities. For many insurers with predominant asset holdings that are publicly traded securities, the importance of a model to value these assets is less important, as such securities have readily observable market values. What is important, however, is that the liability valuation model be consistent with observed prices on Treasury securities and their derivatives. This feature enables assets and liabilities to be simulated harmoniously over time based on random movements in the factors that determine Treasury prices. Models that tend to accommodate these needs are most often based on discrete-time approaches.

At least two random factors are a minimum configuration for a suitable liability valuation model. Which two factors should be modeled explicitly depends on the nature of one's business. Companies with inflation-indexed pension business should opt for a model that focuses on inflation and a reference real or nominal rate of interest. This is because elements of the liabilities are strongly influenced by inflation, as well as interest rates. (Such models would also work for other types of pension plans and, but the inflation factor would be a less direct way to model nominal interest rates.) For a life insurer without pension business, it may be sufficient to have both factors focus on nominal interest rates. Available models have factors related to short-term and long-term nominal interest rates, short-term rates and the spread between short-term and long-term rates, short-term rates and random volatility, short-term rates and a random level for mean reversion, and so forth. Models incorporating more factors than two are also available.

One criterion that guides the selection of a model is whether it features closed-form solutions for Treasury bonds. For models with such capabilities, the economies in modeling and computer intensity are simply enormous, especially when running scenario analyses. While all Class D models can produce present values, either through simulation, finite differences, lattices, sparse grids, low-discrepancy points, or closed-form solutions, the advantage of a model with closed-form solutions is that it allows for the modeling of future values with little extra effort. Such models compute the entire term structure of interest rates and other asset prices at each future point in time under each simulation scenario without incurring any additional simulation runs. Without this feature, a model would need to incur many tens of millions of additional simulation runs to achieve a similar level of richness, and to provide for a rigorous and consistent depiction of asset/liability management.

While a discussion of the various numerical techniques that have been used to implement these models is beyond the scope of this chapter, there are a few points to keep in mind. There is no such thing as a "correct" numerical approach. In general, the choice of modeling approach, context, and number of factors will determine the valuation problem to be solved.

That problem may be solved in closed form or numerically. If it is to be solved numerically, then the choice of technique will be guided by trade-offs between computational speed, accuracy, and applicability to the particular problem. For example, lattices are quite easy to implement for single-factor models. However, for multi-factor models, simulations or low discrepancy points might represent a preferable mix of computational ease and accuracy.

A final element that would be useful in a valuation model is for there to be a completely open architecture. New asset and liability instruments are continually being introduced, and no valuation program without an open architecture would be useful for very long in today's dynamic economic environment.

8. Conclusion

Our narrower definition of liability values, while unlikely to produce value estimates that precisely match those market values of liabilities which are actually traded in the marketplace, nonetheless has some merit. First, it is simpler to compute for most insurance liabilities than it would be to a more expansive definition of market value, which would impound in some way the values of put options and franchise value. Second, it is less controversial to relegate some of the most troublesome areas of valuation to the other side of the balance sheet. Third, it provides a useful number as a starting point for regulators and for the insurers themselves, who need to know how much it should take to fully defease the liabilities that the insurer has underwritten. Fourth, it provides a number that is more easily compared among insurers. Fifth, it is helpful in firm risk assessment, particularly if the liabilities are valued using models that feature the same drivers of uncertainty as those used on the asset side of the economic balance sheet. Finally, it can serve as the basis for financial performance measurement.

Notes

* The Wharton School, University of Pennsylvania, Philadelphia, PA 19104-6218, babbel@wharton.upenn.edu.

** Marriott School of Management, 673 TNRB, Brigham Young University, Provo, UT 84602, merrill@byu.edu.

This chapter is based on two previous studies. See Babbel, 1999 and Babbel and Merrill, 1998. Portions of the latter work are reprinted with permission of the Society of Actuaries.

The authors received helpful comments on earlier versions of this chapter from Burt Jay, David Libbey, Arnold Dicke, David Sandberg, Kim Balls, Lone-Young Yee, and other members of the Valuation Law Task Force of the Academy of Actuaries, as well as Algis Remeza, Jeremy Gold, and Frank Fabozzi.

1. See Reitano et al (1997), Reitano (1997), Babbel (1997a, 1997b), Babbel and Merrill (1996), and Merrill (1997).

2. It is reduced (usually slightly) by the present value of payments that the solvent insurer is expected to pay to state insurance insolvency guaranty programs, to the extent that these payments are not fully offset by state and federal tax reductions.

3. Elsewhere this has been referred to as "liquidation value." However, because that expression is laden with connotations that are unhelpful in this context, we prefer to use the expression "net tangible value" here. In an actual liquidation, assets are sometimes unloaded at "fire sale" prices. This reduction in value may or may not be more than offset if the liquidator is able to extract favorable terms from assumption reinsurers, because the book of business transferred may still have some renewal value.

4. Executive Life Insurance Company of California, a $16 billion insurer that bet heavily on junk bonds until its demise in 1991, is an example of a company whose market value of liabilities (under this definition) would have been reduced far below the present value of its promised cash flows to policyholders.

5. This notion was introduced by Merton (1974, 1977).

6. Babbel and Staking (1989, 1991) and Staking and Babbel (1995, 1998).

7. Practitioners on Wall Street sometimes clumsily attempt to apply the same model for pricing U.S. Treasury and corporate bonds. Because a model which prices Treasuries well does not fit well the observed market prices of corporate bonds, practitioners often assume a different (lower) volatility of short-term Treasury rates than what is used for pricing the Treasuries themselves. While this *ad hoc* procedure may produce model price estimates that are closer to corporate bond market prices, it clearly violates the consistency standards of accepted valuation principles.

8. The reason it is unnecessary to have the model calibrate closely to market prices of other financial instruments is that only the default-free rates of interest are used in deriving the guaranteed economic value of insurance liabilities. See Babbel (1994, 1997a,b). Similarly, for non-guaranteed insurance payments, the default-free interest rates can be used in their valuation, but the cash flows are first adjusted to their certainty-equivalents. See Merrill (1998).

9. As explained in section 5, while the values must be consistent with the value additivity principle, the risks need not be additive.

10. See Robichek and Myers (1965).

11. See Robichek and Myers (1965), and Rubinstein (1976).

12. Jarrow and Turnbull (1996, p. 163) state this proposition in the context of a binomial pricing model. A more general proof is given in Harrison and Pliska (1979).

13. See Singleton (1989), and Babbel and Merrill (1996, pp. 40–44) for a more thorough discussion of the relationship between risk-neutral pricing and pricing based on a risk premium.

14. See Santomero and Babbel (1997, pp. 88–101) for a discussion of the various term structure hypotheses.

15. A good example of this approach is given by Asay, Bouyoucos, and Marciano (1993).

16. The reason that the probability of having enough assets is not simply 50-50 is that the expectation concept used in defining the present value of liabilities does not take into account the paths that the asset and liability values follow over time. Therefore, there will be many

paths that would generate adequate asset returns by the final payment date to satisfy the remaining liabilities, yet inadequate returns over many paths prior to that final date. See Buhlman (1970).

17. See Merrill (1997).

18. An option-adjusted spread is a "fudge factor" of sorts to capture in the interest rate lattices or paths the mispricing of the security based on the model price vs. the market price. See Babbel and Zenios (1992). It is common to calculate option-adjusted spreads based on some fixed level of volatility for purposes of historical charting, but when pricing the securities, the volatility assumed should relate to the future period over which the mortgages will be repaid.

19. For an application of this certainty-equivalent valuation paradigm to non-guaranteed insurance benefits in the context of stochastic interest rates, see Merrill (1998).

20. See Babbel (1990).

21. This is not to say that one cannot produce good estimates of economic values using different valuation models; rather, that it is preferable to use a unitary model capable of valuing types of financial instruments under consideration, both assets and liabilities, in order to assure consistency.

22. See, for example, Black, Derman and Toy (1990).

23. The net tangible value elicited will manifest itself, in an accounting sense, in the insurance reserves and statutory surplus that the insurer holds on its books.

References

Asay, Michael, Peter Bouyoucos, and Thomas Marciano. "On the Economic Approach to the Valuation of Single Premium Deferred Annuities," in Stavros Zenios (ed.), *Financial Optimization*, Cambridge University Press, (1993), 132–135.

Babbel, David F. "Valuation of Interest-Sensitive Cash Flows: The Need, The Technologies, The Implications," *Record of the Society of Actuaries*, v. 16 (no. 3, 1990), 125–132.

Babbel, David F. "A Perspective on Model Investment Laws for Insurers," *C.L.U. Journal*, (September 1994), 72–77.

Babbel, David F. "Financial Valuation of Insurance Liabilities," in Edward Altman and Irwin Vanderhoof (eds.), *Fair Value of Insurance Liabilities*, Irwin Press, 114–126.

Babbel, David F. "The Market Value of Insurance Liabilities," *North American Actuarial Journal*, (October 1997).

Babbel, David F. "Components of Insurance Firm Value and the Present Value of Liabilities," in D. Babbel and F. Fabozzi (eds.), *Insurance Company Investment Mangement*, New Hope, PA: Frank J. Fabozzi Associates, 1999.

Babbel, David F. and Laurence Eisenberg. "Quantity Adjusting Options and Forward Contracts," *Journal of Financial Engineering*, (June 1993), 89–126.

Babbel, David F. and Frank J. Fabozzi. *Insurance Company Investment Management*, New Hope, PA: Frank J. Fabozzi Associates, 1999.

Babbel, David F. and Craig B. Merrill. *Valuation of Interest-Sensitive Financial Instruments*, Society of Actuaries, New Hope, PA: Frank J. Fabozzi Associates, 1996.

Babbel, David F., Craig B. Merrill, and Algis Remeza. "The Ultimate Black Box: A Three-Factor Valuation Model with Closed-Form Solutions," Working Paper, The Wharton School, University of Pennsylvania, Philadlephia, 1999.

Babbel, David F. and Craig B. Merrill. "Economic Valuation Models for Insurers," *North American Actuarial Journal*, (July 1998).

Babbel, David F. and Kim Staking. "The Market Reward for Insurers that Practice Asset/Liability Management," *Financial Institutions Research*, Goldman Sachs, (November 1989), 1–13.

Babbel, David F. and Kim Staking. "It Pays to Practice A/L M" *Best's Review, Property/Casualty Edition*, (May 1991), 28–32.

Babbel, David F. and Stavros Zenios. "Pitfalls in the Analysis of Option-Adjusted Spreads," *Financial Analysts Journal*, (July/August 1992), 65–69.

Beaglehole, David and Mark Tenney. "General Solutions to some Interest Rate Contingent Claims Pricing Equations," *Journal of Fixed Income*, (September 1991).

Black, Fischer. "The Pricing of Commodity Contracts," *Journal of Financial Economics*, (January 1976), 167–179.

Black, Fischer and Myron Scholes. "The Pricing of Options and Corporate Liabilities," *Journal of Political Economy*, (May–June 1973), 637–653.

Black, Fischer, Emanuel Derman, and William Toy. "A One-Factor Model of Interest Rates and its Application to Treasury Bond Options," *Financial Analysts Journal*, (January–February 1990), 33–39.

Boyle, Phelim P. "Options: A Monte Carlo Approach," *Journal of Financial Economics*, 1997, 323–338.

Brennan, Michael J. and Eduardo S. Schwartz. "A Continuous Time Approach to the Pricing of Bonds," *Journal of Banking and Finance*, (September 1979), 135–155.

Buhlman, Hans. *Mathematical Methods of Risk Theory*, Heidelberg: Springer-Verlag, 1970.

Cox, J.C., J. Ingersoll, Jr. and S. Ross. "An Intertemporal General Equilibrium Model of Asset Prices," *Econometrica* (1985), 363–384.

Cox, J.C., J. Ingersoll, Jr. and S. Ross. "A Theory of the Term Structure of Interest Rates," *Econometrica* (1985), 385–407.

Cox, J.C., S. Ross, and M. Rubinstein. "Option Pricing: A Simplified Approach," *Journal of Financial Economics*, (September 1979), 229–263.

Fong, H. Gifford and Oldrich A. Vasicek. "Fixed-Income Volatility Management: A New Approach to Return and Risk Analyses," *Journal of Portfolio Management*, (Summer 1991), 41–46.

Gordon, Myron J. and Eli Shapiro. "Capital Equipment Analysis: The Required Rate of Profit," *Management Science*, (October 1956).

Harrison, J.M. and S. Pliska. "Martingales and Arbitrage in Multi-period Securities Markets," *Journal of Economic Theory* (1979), 381–408.

Ho, Thomas and S. Lee. "Term Structure Movements and Pricing Interest Rate Contingent Claims," *Journal of Finance*, (December 1986), 1011–1028.

Hull, John C. and Alan White. "Pricing Interest Rate Derivative Securities," *Review of Financial Studies* 3 (no. 4, 1990), 573–592.

Hull, John C. and Alan White. "Numerical Procedures for Implementing Term Structure Models: Two-Factor Models," *Journal of Derivatives*, (Winter 1994), 7–16.

Jarrow, Robert and Stuart Turnbull. *Derivative Securities*, Cincinnati, OH: South-Western College Publishing, 1996.

Longstaff, Francis A. and Eduardo S. Schwartz. "Interest Rate Volatility and the Term Structure: A Two-Factor General Equilibrium Model, *Journal of Finance*, (September 1992), 1259–1282.

Margrabe, William. "The Value of an Option to Exchange One Asset for Another," *Journal of Finance*, (March 1978), 177–186.

Merrill, Craig. "Valuation of Non-Guaranteed Insurance Benefits," LECG Working Paper, October 1998.

Merrill, Craig. "Thoughts on the Market Value of Insurance Liabilities," *North American Actuarial Journal*, (October 1997).

Merton, Robert C. "Theory of Rational Option Pricing," *Bell Journal of Economics and Management Science*, (Spring 1973), 141–183.

Merton, Robert C. "On the Pricing of Corporate Debt: The Risk Structure of Interest Rates," *Journal of Finance*, (May 1974), 449–470.

Merton, Robert C. "An Analytic Derivation of the Cost of Deposit Insurance and Loan Guarantees: An Application of Modern Option Pricing Theory," *Journal of Banking and Finance*, (June 1977), 3–11.

Miles, J. and R. Ezzell. "The Weighted Average Cost of Capital, Perfect Capital Markets and Project Life: A Clarification," *Journal of Financial and Quantitative Analysis*, (September 1980), 719–730.

Myers, S.C. "Interactions of Corporate Financing and Investment Decisions—Implications for Capital Budgeting," *Journal of Finance*, (March 1974), 1–25.

Reitano, Robert, et al. "Financial Valuation of Insurance Liabilities," in Edward Altman and Irwin Vanderhoof (eds.), *Fair Value of Insurance Liabilities*, Irwin Press, 114–126.

Reitano, Robert. "The Market Value of Insurance Liabilities," *North American Actuarial Journal*, (October 1997), 104–137.

Robichek, Alexander and Stuart Myers. *Optimal Financing Decisions*, Englewood Cliffs, N.J.: Prentice-Hall, 1965.

Ross, Stephen. "The Arbitrage Theory of Capital Asset Pricing," *Journal of Economic Theory*, (December 1976), 341–360.

Rubinstein, Mark. "The Valuation of Uncertain Income Streams and the Pricing of Options," *Bell Journal of Economics and Management Science* (1976), 407–425.

Santomero, Anthony M. and David F. Babbel. *Financial Markets, Instruments, and Institutions*, New York: McGraw-Hill Irwin, 1997.

Sharpe, William. "Capital Asset Prices: A Theory of Market Equilibrium Under Conditions of Risk," *Journal of Finance*, (September 1964), 425–442.

Singleton, Kenneth J. "Modeling the Term Structure of Interest Rates in General Equilibrium," in S. Bhattacharya and G. Constantinides (eds.), *Theory of Valuation*, Savage, MD: Rowman & Littlefield, 1989.

Staking, Kim and David F. Babbel. "The Relation between Capital Structure, Interest Rate Sensitivity, and Market Value in the Property-Liability Insurance Industry," *Journal of Risk and Insurance*, (December 1995), 690–718.

Staking, Kim and David F. Babbel. "Insurer Surplus Duration and Market Value Revisited," *Journal of Risk and Insurance*, (March 1998), 739–743.

Stulz, Rene. "Options on the Minimum or the Maximum of Two Risky Assets: Analysis and Applications," *Journal of Financial Economics*, (June 1982), 161–185.

Tilley, James A. "Valuing American Options in a Path Simulation Model," *Transactions of the Society of Actuaries* (1993), 499–520.

Vasicek, Oldrich. "An Equilibrium Characterization of the Term Structure," *Journal of Financial Economics* (1977), 177–188.

9 AN ANALYSIS OF THE FINANCIAL RISK MANAGEMENT PROCESS USED BY LIFE INSURERS*

David F. Babbel and Anthony M. Santomero

1. Introduction

The past decade has seen a dramatic rise in the number of insolvent life insurers. The ostensible causes of these insolvencies were myriad. Some of the insolvencies were precipitated by rapidly rising or declining interest rates. Others resulted from losses on assets such as junk bonds, commercial mortgages, CMOs, real estate, and derivatives. Mispricing of insurance policies hurt still others. The "churning" of policies by unscrupulous sales agents, insolvencies among the reinsurers backing the policies issued, noncompliance with insurance regulation, and malfeasance on the part of officers and directors of the insurance companies affected some as well. But despite the numerous and disparate apparent causes of these insolvencies, the underlying factor in all of them was the same: inadequate risk-management practices. In response to this, insurers almost universally have embarked upon an upgrading of their financial risk management and control systems to reduce their exposure to risk and better manage the amount they accept. In short, the industry has turned to financial risk-management techniques as a way to improve performance.

Coincidental to this activity, and, in part, because of our recognition of the industry's vulnerability to financial risk, the Wharton Financial Institutions Center, with the support of the Sloan Foundation, has been involved in an analysis of financial risk management processes in the financial sector. From 1995 through 1996, on-site visits were conducted to review and evaluate the risk-management systems and the process of risk evaluation that are in place.

In the life insurance sector, system evaluation was conducted covering a number of prominent companies, both in the United States and abroad. The information obtained on the philosophy and practice of financial risk management comes primarily through intensive interviews of domestic insurance firms, conducted by a team of researchers from the Wharton Financial Institutions Center.[1] Measured in terms of admitted assets, these firms range in size from $7 billion to well over $100 billion. They are organized as stock or mutual insurers. These visits were augmented by interviews (conducted by one of the authors) with additional large life insurance firms domiciled in Japan and Europe as well as in North America.

Our information was then supplemented by five recently published surveys. Three of these were the 1994, 1995, and 1996 "Insurer CIO Surveys," conducted by Goldman, Sachs & Co.[2] Another pair of surveys was conducted by Joan Lamm-Tennant.[3] While all of these surveys also included some companies from the property/casualty sector, the responses from only the life insurers are included in this chapter. This information was also supplemented with the analysis of actual practice that continued beyond the primary wave of WFIC interviews. The lead researchers used the first document's publication to solicit reaction and to receive feedback concerning our characterization of current practice. As more evidence was assembled and new models implemented, the state of application changed and this review reflects the advances made over the past several years.

The purpose of this chapter is to outline the results of this investigation. It reports the state of risk management techniques in the industry—questions asked, questions answered, and questions left unaddressed by respondents. This report cannot recite a litany of the approaches used within the industry, nor can it offer an evaluation of each and every approach. Rather, it reports the standard of practice and evaluates how and why it is conducted in the particular way chosen. But even the best practice employed within the industry is not good enough in some areas. Accordingly, critiques will also be offered where deemed appropriate. The chapter concludes with a list of questions that are currently unanswered, or answered rather unsatisfactorily in the current practice employed by this group of relatively sophisticated insurers. Here, we discuss the problems that the industry finds most difficult to address, shortcomings of the current methodology used to analyze risk, and the elements that are missing in the current procedures of risk management.

2. Why Manage Risk—Some Generic Answers

It seems appropriate to begin our analysis of risk-management techniques with a review of the reasons given for firm level concern over the volatility of financial performance. The finance literature on why firms manage risk at all is usually traced back to 1984. In that year Stulz (1984) first suggested a viable reason for objective function concavity, and his contribution is widely cited as the starting point of this burgeoning literature. Doherty (1985) provides the first comprehensive treatment of this topic in a finance framework. Since that time a number of alternative theories and explanations have been offered. Recently, Santomero (1995) presented a useful review of these explanations, from which we draw here.

The goal, as noted above, is to offer viable economic reasons for firm managers, who are presumed to be working on behalf of firm owners, to concern themselves with both expected profit and the distribution of firm returns around their expected value. The rationales for risk aversion can usefully be segmented into four categories:

a)   Managerial Self Interest
b)   The Non-linearity of Taxes
c)   The Cost of Financial Distress
d)   The Existence of Capital Market Imperfections

In each case, the economic decision maker is shown to face a non-linear optimization because of the reason offered, and this leads the decision maker to be concerned with the variability of returns. In the first case the objective function itself is concave, while in the others the effect of some feature of the economic environment is to lead firm managers to behave in a risk averse manner. Following is an explanation of each theory.

2.1. Managerial Self Interest

As mentioned above, this rationale is generally attributed to the work of Stulz (1984), who argued that firm managers have limited ability to diversify their own personal wealth position, those associated with stock holdings and the capitalization of their career earnings that are associated with their own employment position. Therefore, they prefer stability to volatility because, other things being equal, such stability improves their own utility at little or no expense to other stakeholders. In truth, this argument can be traced back to the literature on the theory of agency. In this area, the relationship between firm performance and managerial remuneration is clearly developed in such works as Ross (1973) and Ross (1977).

Objections have been offered, however, to this line of reasoning. Some find the theory unconvincing because it offers no reason for the manager to hedge his/her risk within the firm rather than directly in the market. According to this view, managers with highly non-linear employment contracts could enter the financial market to offset the effect of such agency agreements on their own wealth position. By taking a short position in the firm's stock, the stocks of competitors, or the market, managers could obtain any level of concentration in firm-specific profitability.

However, this argument misses at least three important features of the employment relationship. First, it is illegal for senior management to take a short position in the firm's stock and problematic for them to be seen divesting themselves or systematically diversifying the investments that are correlated with firm performance. Yet, such a public divestiture would be required to properly hedge management's personal investment profile. Moreover, in the case of mutual insurers, it is even more difficult to offset a long position in firm-specific performance risk. Second, to the extent that some outcomes, defined as financial distress, lead to termination of the contract, it may be in the best interest of managers to constrain firm-level outcome, if only to not lose the future value of the employment earnings. More will be said about this under section 3 below. Third, arguments in favor of expected value managerial decisions neglect the fact that managerial ability itself is not directly observable. Therefore, as Breeden and Viswanathan (1990) and De-Marzo and Duffie (1992) argue, observed outcomes may influence owner perception of managerial talent. This would, in turn, favor reduced volatility, or at least the protection of firm-specific market value from large negative outcomes that may be found within the distribution of possible returns. For all, or for any one of these reasons, therefore, there appears to be ample justification for the assumption that managers will behave in a manner consistent with a concave objective function.

2.2. The Non-linearity of Taxes

Beyond managerial motives, firm-level performance and market value may be directly associated with volatility for a number of other reasons. The first is the nature of the tax code, which both historically and internationally is highly non-linear. This was brought to our attention by Smith and Stulz (1985) and Gennotte and Pyle (1991). The point has recently been emphasized in Smith and Smithson (1990) and Fite and Pfleiderer (1995) as a key rationale for risk reduction. In each case, the authors indicate that, with a non-proportional tax structure, income smoothing reduces the effective tax rate and, therefore, the tax burden shouldered by the firm. By reducing the effective long-term average tax rate, activities that reduce the volatility in reported earnings will enhance shareholder value.

However, two points are worth mentioning in this context. First, with the advent of more proportional tax schedules, particularly in the United States, the arguments here are somewhat mitigated. In fact, one should observe, *ceteris paribus*, a decline in the interest in risk management by American firms over the last decade because of the reduced progressivity of U.S. tax schedules. No one, however, has suggested that such is the case. Second, the tax argument rests on reported income, not true economic profit. To the extent that accounting principles permit tax planning, this argument may favor tax motivated reporting and more careful management of the difference between book and market value of profits. For example, in the financial sector there is a long literature on tax planning that speaks to this distinction between reported and operating profit. Greenawalt and Sinkey (1988) document the existence of substantial income smoothing through the use of the loan-loss provision expense item, while Scholes, Wilson and Wolfson (1990) present evidence of portfolio selection that accomplishes the same result. However, the argument here is that real economic decisions are affected by the tax code, not just their reporting. To the extent that significant discretion exists in tax reporting, tax consideration may not motivate actual decision making nearly as much as this theory suggests. Evidence on these points for the insurance industry is provided by Lamm-Tennant and Rollins (1994).

2.3. The Cost of Financial Distress

Firms may also be concerned about volatility of earnigns because of the consequences of severely negative deviations from expected value and their implications for corporate viability. It is known that corporate debt creates a fixed cost that can be used as a competitive weapon in gaming models. (See Brander and Lewis (1986) and Maksimovic (1988), for example.) In such models, severely negative outcomes cause disruption and bankruptcy. To the extent that the bankruptcy state—or any set of specific states—is associated with a discrete increase in costs, the firm will be forced to recognize this fact in its choice calculus. In such cases, the firm behaves as if it had a concave objective function, because its payoff structure is non-linear across states.

The literature is filled with such stories. The classic paper by Warner (1977) was the first to present empirical evidence of this cost, but more recent studies, such as Weiss (1990) have continued to reinforce its importance. As a result, standard corporate finance textbooks make clear reference to the cost of bankruptcy in their analysis of the investment decision. Smith and Stulz (1985) use this same argument to justify a desire for reduced volatility.

The cost is, perhaps, more important in regulated industries, however. In these cases, large losses may be associated with license or charter withdrawal and the loss of a monopoly position. For example, in the banking literature, Marcus (1984) makes this same argument for financial firms subject to charter review by regulatory agencies and Santomero (1989), and Herring and Santomero (1990) used this story to justify corporate separation for financial services firms. Staking and Babbel (1995) provide empirical support for its application to the property/casualty insurance industry. In all cases, however, the cost of financial distress must be non-linear, as linear cost functions do not lead to the required behavior.

Yet, the authors are on firm ground here, as there is ample evidence that financial distress leads to substantially increased costs associated with bankruptcy proceedings, legal costs, and perhaps most importantly, the diversion of management attention from creating real economic value. Interested readers are referred to Smith, Smithson, and Wilford (1990) for an extended discussion of these costs.

2.4. Capital Market Imperfections

Recently the above argument has been extended in the work of Froot, Scharfstein, and Stein (1993, 1994). The theoretical core of their contribution is in the 1993 paper. Here, they accept the basic paradigm of the financial distress model above, but rationalize the cost of bad outcomes by reference to Myers' (1990) debt overhang argument. In their model, external financing is more costly than internally generated funds due to any number of capital market imperfections. These may include discrete transaction costs to obtain external financing, imperfect information as to the riskiness of the investment opportunities present in the firm, or the high cost of the potential future bankruptcy state. In the case of mutual insurers, who have little access to the capital market, this line of argument is particularly compelling.

At the same time, the firm has an investment oppportunity set that can be ordered in terms of net present value. The existence of the cost imperfections results in underinvestment in some states, where internally generated funds fall short of the amount of new investment that would be profitable in the absence of these capital market imperfections. Stated another way, the volatility of profitability causes the firm to seek external finance in order to exploit investment opportunities when profits are low. The cost of such external finance is higher than the internal funds due to the market's higher cost structure associated with the factors enumerated above. This, in turn, reduces optimal investment in low profit states.

The cost of volatility in such a model is the forgone investment in each period that the firm is forced to seek external funds. Recognizing this outcome, the firm embarks upon volatility reducing strategies, which have the effect of reducing the variability of earnings. Hence, risk management is optimal in that it allows the firm to obtain the highest expected shareholder value.

The authors can support their theory with reference to evidence offered by Fazzari, Hubbard, and Peterson (1988) and Hoshi, Kashyap, and Scharfstein (1991), who present evidence that internal cash flow is, in fact, correlated to corporate investment. In addition, Smith, Smithson, and Wilford (1990) regale us with anecdotes that further support this contention.

2.5. Summary of Rationales

Together, the stories work fairly well. Firm managers are interested in both expected profitability and the risk, or variability, or reported earnings, or market value. The latter can be rationalized by the existence of non-linear costs across the range of profit states associated with any given expected value. The non-linearity is associated with managerial incentive effects, the tax structure, the costs of crisis, and/or forgone investment opportunities. In any or all of these cases, the firm is led to treat the variability of earnings as a choice variable that it selects, subject to the usual constraints of optimization. How it proceeds to manage the risk position of its activity is the area which we deal with next.

3. Risk as a Central Ingredient in the Industry's Franchise

3.1. The Role of Insurers in the Financial Sector

Insurers are in the risk business. In the process of providing insurance and other financial services, they assume various kinds of actuarial and financial risks. Over the last decade much has been written of the role of insurers within the financial sector.[4] This literature will not be reviewed in detail here. Suffice it to say that market participants seek the services of insurers because of their ability to provide actuarial risk pooling through their major product lines of life and health insurance, pension products, annuities, and other financial instruments. At the same time, they are major providers of funds to the capital market—particularly to the fixed income sectors. In performing these roles they generally act as a principal in the transaction. As such, they use their own balance sheet to facilitate the transactions and to absorb the risks associated with them. Therefore, it is here that the discussion of risk management and the necessary procedures for risk control has centered. Accordingly, it is in this area that our review of risk-management procedures will concentrate.

3.2. What Risks Are Being Managed?

The risks contained in the insurer's product sales, i.e., those embedded in the products offered to customers to protect against actuarial risk, are not all borne directly by the insurer. In many instances the institution will eliminate or mitigate the actuarial and financial risk associated with a transaction by proper business practices; in others, it will shift the risk to other parties through a combination of reinsurance, pricing, and product design. Only those risks that are not eliminated or transferred to others are left to be managed by the firm for its own account. This happens because the insurance industry recognizes that it should not engage in business in a manner that unnecessarily imposes risk upon it, nor should it absorb risks that can be efficiently transferred to other participants. Rather, it should only manage those risks at the firm level that can be managed more efficiently by the firm than by the market itself or by their owners in their own portfolios. In short, it should accept only those risks that are uniquely a part of the insurer's array of services.

Elsewhere, it has been argued that risks facing all financial institutions can be segmented into three separable types from a management perspective.[5] These are:

a) risks that can be eliminated or avoided by standard business practices;
b) risks that can be transferred to other participants, and
c) risks that must be actively managed at the firm level.

In the first of these cases, the practice of risk avoidance involves actions to reduce the chances of idiosyncratic losses from standard insurance activity by eliminating risks that are superfluous to the institution's business purpose. Common risk-avoidance practices include at least three types of actions. The first of these is the standardization of process, insurance policies, contracts, and procedures to prevent inefficient or incorrect financial decisions. A second such action is the construction of portfolios on both sides of the balance sheet that benefit from diversification and the application of the Law of Large Numbers and Central Limit Theorem, which will reduce the effects of any one loss experience. Third, is the implementation of incentive-compatible contracts with the institution's management that require employees be held accountable. In each case, the goal is to rid the firm of risks that are not essential to the financial service provided, or to absorb only an optimal quantity of a particular kind of risk.

There are also some risks that can be eliminated, or at least substantially reduced through the technique of risk transfer. Markets exist for many of the risks borne by the insurance firm. Actuarial risk can be transferred to reinsurers. Interest rate risk can be hedged or transferred through interest-rate products such as swaps, caps, floors, futures, or other derivative products. Insurance policies and lending documents can be altered to effect a change in their duration and convexity. Equity market risk can be reduced with an appropriate futures position in equities. In addition, they can offer products that absorb some financial risks. while transferring others of these risks to the purchaser. Defined contribution pension plans and variable universal life policies are clear examples of this approach. Finally, the insurer can buy or sell financial claims and reinsurance to diversify or concentrate the risk that results from servicing its client base. To the extent that the actuarial and financial risks of the insurance policies underwritten by the firm are understood by the market, they can be sold in part or in whole at their fair value. Unless the institution has a comparative

advantage in managing the attendant risk and/or a desire for the embedded risk they contain, there is no reason for the insurer to absorb rather
than transfer such risks.

However, there are two classes of activities where the risk inherent in
the activity must and should be absorbed at the insurance firm level. In
these cases, risk management must be aggressive and good reasons exist
for using firm resources to manage insurance-level risk. The first of these
includes actuarial exposures, where the nature of the embedded risk may
be complex and difficult to communicate and transfer to third parties. For
example, Lutheran Brotherhood has a natural advantage for writing life
insurance to its clientele. A similar situation may arise on the asset side of
the business, where the insurer holds private placements and other complex,
proprietary assets that have thin, or even non-existent, secondary markets.
Communication in such cases may be more difficult or expensive than
hedging the underlying risk. Moreover, revealing information about the customer may give competitors an undue advantage. The second case includes
risk positions that central to the insurer's business purpose and are
absorbed because they are the *raison d'être* of the firm. Actuarial risk inherent in the key insurance lines, where the insurer may enjoy a competitive
advantage or a market niche, is a clear case in point. In all such circumstances, risk is absorbed and needs to be monitored and managed efficiently
by the institution. Only then will the firm systematically achieve its financial
performance goal.

3.3. How Are These Risks Managed?

In light of the above, what are the necessary procedures that must be in
place to carry out adequate risk management for those risks that are
essential ingredients to the insurer's franchise? What techniques are
employed to both limit and manage the different types of risk, and how
are they implemented in each area of risk management? We now turn to
these questions.

In general, the management of an insurance firm relies on a variety
of techniques for their risk-management systems. However, it appears
that common practice has evolved such that four elements have become
key steps to implementing a broad-based risk-management system.
These include:

a)   standards and reports
b)   underwriting authority and limits

    c)   investment guidelines or strategies, and

    d)   incentive contracts and compensation

These tools are established to measure risk exposure, define procedures to manage these exposures, limit exposures to acceptable levels, and encourage decision makers to manage risk in a manner that is consistent with the firm's goals and objectives. To understand how these four parts of basic risk management achieve these ends, we elaborate on each part of the process below. Section 5 illustrates how these techniques are applied to control each of the specific risks facing the insurance community.

3.3.1. Standards and Reports. The first of these control techniques involves two different conceptual activities, i.e., standard setting and financial reporting. They are listed together because they are the *sine qua non* of any risk management system. Underwriting standards, risk classification, and standards of review are all traditional tools of risk control. Consistent evaluation and rating of exposures of various types are essential for management to understand the risks on both sides of the balance sheet, and the extent to which these risks must be mitigated or absorbed.

The standardization of financial reporting is the next ingredient. Obviously, outside audits, regulatory reports, and ratings agency evaluations are essential for investors to gauge asset quality and firm level risk. But the types of information collected and the manner in which data are assembled and presented in statutory accounting reports are not adequate enough to manage an insurance company. For instance, it is difficult to discern the magnitude and import of options insurers have effectively written on both sides of the balance sheet, e.g., call and prepayment options and loan commitments on the asset side, lapse, loan and surrender options on the liability side, by relying solely on statutory accounting reports. It is also difficult to estimate interest rate risk and default risk from the information provided there.

The statutory accounting reports have long been standardized, for better or for worse. However, it is necessary to go beyond public reports and audited statements to provide management with information on actuarial risk, asset quality, and overall risk posture. Such internal reports need to be standardized but also need much more frequent reporting intervals, with daily, weekly, and monthly reports that substitute for the statutory quarterly accounting periods. Thus, the collection and presentation of sufficient data to adequately manage the risk exposure of a company is a starting point.

3.3.2. Underwriting Authority and Limits. A second technique for internal control of active management is the use of position limits, and/or minimum standards for participation. In terms of the latter, the domain of risk taking is restricted to only those customers or assets that pass some pre-specified quality standard. Then, even for those that are eligible, limits are imposed to cover exposures to counterparties, credits, and overall position concentrations relative to various types of risks. In general, each person who can commit capital, whether on the asset or liability side of the ledger, will have a well-defined limit. This applies to underwriters, portfolio managers, lenders, and traders. Summary reports show limits as well as current exposure by business unit on a periodic basis. In large organizations, with thousands of positions maintained, accurate and timely reporting is difficult, but even more essential.

3.3.3. Investment Guidelines or Strategies. Investment guidelines and recommended positions for the immediate future are the third technique that is commonly in use. Here, strategies are outlined in terms of concentration and commitments to particular areas of the market, the extent of desired asset/liability mismatching or exposure to interest rate risk, and the need to hedge against systematic risks of a particular type. These limits lead to passive risk avoidance and/or diversification, because managers generally operate within position limits and prescribed rules. Beyond this, guidelines offer firm level advice on the appropriate level of active management, given the state of the market and the willingness of senior management to absorb the risks implied by the aggregate portfolio. Such guidelines extend to firm level hedging and asset/liability matching. In addition, securitization and even derivative activity are rapidly growing techniques of position management that are open to participants looking to reduce their exposure to be in line with management's guidelines.

Similar guidelines are required on the liability side of the balance sheet. Underwriting standards and strategies are needed to ensure that the risks accepted conform to the parameters that the insurer is capable of and willing to accept. They also foster better pricing of products, and prevent any one underwriter from compromising the future solvency of the firm.

3.3.4. Incentive Schemes. To the extent that the firm can enter incentive compatible contracts with senior management, line managers, and sales agents and make compensation related to the risks borne by these individuals, the need for elaborate and costly controls is lessened. However, such incentive contracts must be consistent with the insurers' financial goals and require proper internal control systems. Such tools, which include underwriting risk and loss analysis, investment risk analysis, the allocation of costs, and the setting of required returns to various parts of the organization are not trivial. Notwithstanding the difficulty, well designed systems align the goals of managers with other stakeholders in a most desirable way. In fact, most financial debacles can be traced to the absence of incentive compatibility. For instance, the linkage of compensation to sales can lead to reckless and dangerous growth and poor underwriting or mispricing of risks. The linkage of managerial compensation to book earnings can lead to the acquisition of investments with negative convexity, duration mismatch risk, liquidity risk, and credit risk where book yields are higher than their expected returns.

4. Risks in Providing Insurance Services

How are these techniques of risk management employed by the insurance sector? To explain this, we must begin by enumerating the risks that the insurance industry has chosen to manage, and illustrate how the four-step procedures outlined previously in sections 3.3.1. to 3.3.4 are applied to risk control in each area.

4.1. The Actuarial View of Risks

As a starting point, most of the insurers interviewed classified their risks by adapting a framework that was proposed years ago by the Society of Actuaries' Committee on Valuation and Related Problems. The various categories of risks are dubbed C-1, C-2, C-3, and C-4, deriving these names from the Committee assigned to make recommendations on these issues.[6] Our review of the perceived risks begins with an explanation of the industry's own definitions.

C-1 risks are **asset risks**, which arise from the possibility that borrowers of insurer funds may default on their obligations to the company, or that the market value of an insurer's investment assets may decline. They include interest rate risk, credit risk, market risk, and currency risk.

C-2 risk is **pricing risk**, which stems from uncertainty about future operating results relating to items such as investment income, mortality and morbidity rates, administrative expenses, sales, and lapses. If an insurer's pricing is based on assumptions that prove inadequate, it may not be able to meet its obligations to policy owners.

C-3 risk is **asset/liability matching risk**, which springs from the impact of fluctuating interest and inflation rates on the values of assets and liabilities. If the impact of fluctuating rates is different on assets than on liabilities, the values of assets and liabilities will change by different amounts, and could expose the insurer to insolvency.

C-4 risks are **miscellaneous risks**, generally thought to be beyond the ability of insurers to predict and manage, but they nevertheless represent real risk to the company. These risks include tax and regulatory changes, product obsolescence, poor training of employees and sales agents, and malfeasance, malversation, or misconduct of managers or other employees. Also included is the risk that laws or legal interpretations will change in a way that will alter the firm's obligations *ex post*. Another manifestation of C-4 risk is that there will be an unforeseen downgrade of acquisitions that could lead to a "run" on the assets of the insurance company. One firm referred to C-4 risk as "stupidity risk"—failure to employ and retain good people.

Two firms wryly referred to a new category of risk, dubbed **C-5** risk, which is the havoc that arises when a person who has strong political ambitions or is running for higher political office is appointed to be state insurance commissioner.

The use of the Society of Actuaries' risk classification taxonomy was viewed merely as a useful point of departure by some of the insurance firms we interviewed, while others viewed it as satisfactory for their purposes. In our view, none of the risk classification schemas we saw was completely satisfactory. However, most of the conceivable risks that would impact insurers were included somewhere on the lists that we saw. In most cases, however, the industry was straining to define the inherent financial risks as part of the C1 through C4 paradigm that had been developed years ago. In addition, it appeared that most schemas had undue focus on risks in isolation, rather than on their contribution to overall firm risk.

4.2. The Financial View of Risks

As an alternative to the actuarial decomposition of risk that is unique to the insurance industry, standard financial risk definitions are increasingly being proposed in the industry. For the sector as a whole, these risks can be broken into six generic types: actuarial, systematic, credit, liquidity, operational, and legal risks. Briefly, we will discuss each of these risks facing the insurance institution; in section 5 we indicate how they are managed. Our focus will be on the financial risks, which include the first four of the risks listed below. Of course, the risks associated with the provision of insurance services differ by the type of service rendered.

Actuarial risk is the risk that arises from raising funds via the issuance of insurance policies and other liabilities. It is the risk that the firm is paying too much for the funds it receives, or alternatively, the risk that the firm has received too little for the risks it has agreed to absorb. If an insurer invests its funds in efficiently traded securities, it should expect to have, on average, a zero net present value on those assets. If the insurer pays too much for these funds, it cannot expect to earn a satisfactory profit in the long run. Another aspect of actuarial risk is that during any given time period, the underwriting losses will be in excess of those projected. This could happen for two reasons. First, the expectations themselves may be based on an inadequate knowledge of the loss distribution. Second, the losses may exceed their expectations in the normal course of business simply because losses fluctuate around their mean. The degree to which they deviate from the mean will depend, of course, on the characteristics of the loss distribution, which depend on the nature of the risks insured.

Systematic risk is the risk of asset and liability value changes associated with systematic factors. It is sometimes referred to as market risk. As such, it can be hedged but it cannot be completely diversified away. In fact, systematic risk can be thought of as undiversifiable risk. All investors assume this type of risk whenever assets owned or claims issued can change in value as a result of broad economic factors. Systematic risk comes in many different forms. For the insurance sector, however, three are of greatest concern, *viz.*, variations in the general level of interest rates, basis risk, and inflation.

Because of the insurers' dependence on these systematic factors, most try to estimate the impact of these particular systematic risks on performance, attempt to hedge against them, and thus limit the sensitivity of their financial performance to variation in these undiversifiable factors. To do so, most will both track and manage each of the major systematic risks individually. The first of these is undoubtedly *interest rate risk*. Here, they measure and manage the firm's vulnerability to interest rate variation, even though they cannot do so perfectly. At the same time, insurers with large corporate bond, mortgage, and common stock holdings closely monitor their *basis risk*. Here the concern is that yields on instruments of varying credit quality, liquidity, and maturity do not move together and expose the insurer to market value variation that is independent of liability values. In this case too, they try to manage, as well as limit, their exposure. Finally, to the extent that sales, surrenders, and asset values are influenced by *inflation risk*, expected losses will also be affected. All three of these systematic risks will be recognized as sources of performance variation.

Credit risk is the risk that a borrower will not perform in accordance with its obligations. Credit risk may arise from either an inability or an unwillingness on the part of the borrower to perform in the pre-committed contracted manner. This can affect the investor holding the bond or lender of a loan contract as well as other investors and lenders to the creditor. Therefore, the financial condition of the borrower as well as the current value of any underlying collateral is of considerable interest to an insurer who has invested in the bonds or participated in a direct loan.

The real risk from credit is the deviation of portfolio performance from its expected value. Accordingly, credit risk is diversifiable but difficult to eliminate completely, as general default rates themselves exhibit much fluctuation. This is because a portion of the default risk may, in fact, result from the systematic risk outlined above. In addition, the idiosyncratic nature of some portion of these losses remains a problem for creditors in spite of the beneficial effect of diversification on total uncertainty. This is particularly true for insurers that take on highly illiquid assets. In such cases, the credit risk is not easily transferred and accurate estimates of loss are difficult to estimate.

Liquidity risk can best be described as the risk of a funding crisis. While some would include the need to plan for growth, the risk here is more correctly seen as the potential for a funding crisis. Such a situation would inevitably be associated with an unexpected event, such as a spike in the rate of policy surrenders or a large write down of assets, a loss of confidence, or a legal crisis. Because insurers operate in markets where they may receive clustered claims due to natural catastrophes, or massive requests for policy withdrawals and surrenders due to changing interest rates, their liabilities can be said to be somewhat liquid. Their assets, however, are sometimes less liquid, particularly where they invest in private placements and real estate. Given this situation, it is important for an insurer to maintain sufficient liquidity to easily handle any demands for cash. Otherwise, an insurer that would be solvent without a sudden demand for cash may have to sell off illiquid assets at concessionary prices, leading to large losses, further demands for cash, and potential insolvency.

Operational risk is associated with the problems of accurately processing claims and accurately processing, settling, and taking or making delivery on trades in exchange for cash. It also arises in record keeping, in processing system failures, and with compliance with various regulations. As such, individual operating problems are small probability events for well-run organizations but they expose a firm to outcomes that may be quite costly.

Legal risks are endemic in financial contracting and are separate from the legal ramifications of credit and operational risks. New statutes, court opinions, and regulations can put formerly well-established transactions into contention even when all parties have previously performed adequately and are fully able to perform in the future.

Legal risk arises from the activities of an institution's management, employees, and agents. Fraud, violations of regulations or laws, and other actions can lead to massive class actions. Even a situation where the insurer legally fulfills all of its contractual obligations can result in massive litigation if some policy owners had different expectations or understandings about the performance of their policies than what was specified in the contracts.

Every insurer faces a different exposure to each of these risks, depending on its business mix. In all its activities, an insurer must decide how much business to originate, how much to finance, how much to reinsure, and how much to contract to agents. In doing so, it must weigh both the return and the risk embedded in the asset and liability portfolios. Management must measure the expected profit and evaluate the prudence of the various risks enumerated above to be sure that the result achieves the stated goal of maximizing shareholder value, in the case of a stock insurer, or of maximizing ownership interests, in the case of a mutual or reciprocal insurer. If the product's expected profit warrants the risk, then the activity is added to the insurer's balance sheet and the risk must be managed. This risk management is achieved through the four-step process outlined above. How this is implemented for each of the key financial risks also enumerated above is the focus of our next section.

5. Insurance Risk Management Systems

5.1. Actuarial Risk

The risk of paying too high a price to raise funds is an important risk, particularly in light of the fact that insurers raise few funds in the competitive capital market. Most of their debt is raised in the form of issuing insurance policies. Policies are written today in exchange for lump sum or periodic premiums, but the amounts and timing of the repayment of these funds are often unknown; repayments may occur within a month or more than 80 years later. Because the pricing of the policies reflects not only expected losses but also the yields an insurer can earn on the funds between the inception of a policy and its termination or the payment of benefits, the interest assumption used in developing insurance prices is of critical importance. Two things complicate this process. First, forward interest rates cannot be synthesized to lock in a spread, for the insurer has no way of knowing if future periodic premium payments will be forthcoming. Second, the loss distributions can undergo substantial evolution over time, as more information is revealed and as the economic environment changes.

Insurers are typically quite skilled in managing actuarial risk. The manner in which this is done is described in insurance and actuarial textbooks.[7] Therefore, here we will focus on what developments have occurred during the past decade that improve an insurer's ability to price and manage this risk.

Until recently, life insurance prices were developed using conservative static assumptions regarding loss distributions and interest rates. While this approach was satisfactory for much of the past century, it was ill-equipped to accommodate the interest rate volatility that began during the late 1970s. Life insurance policies are replete with options—settlement options, policy loan options, over-depositing privileges, and surrender or renewal privileges on the part of the insured, and discretionary dividend and crediting rate options on the part of the insurer. Indeed, some have even viewed a life insurance policy as little more than a package of options.[8] In stable interest rate environments, policy owner utilization of these options is often predicated on individual or family circumstances. Hence, in the aggregate, utilization rates are fairly steady and amenable to forecasting.

However, when interest rates are volatile, the options gain in value and their utilization rates can fluctuate wildly. Traditional actuarial methods, which depend upon stability, were incapable of correctly valuing these options; hence, many policies have been woefully underpriced.[9] Today the standard valuation methods that have been adopted by most of the sophisticated life insurers explicitly value these embedded options. Thus, insurers now can estimate the cost of the various option-like provisions of all kinds of life insurance policies. Most life insurers we interviewed were using the PTS software of SS&C, Inc. Subsequently, there has been a migration toward the new versions of software offered by Tillinghast, AQS, Milliman and Robertson, and others. Moreover, PTS developed a 1998 version of its software, which is now being marketed widely. All of these software programs use modern stochastic valuation techniques, familiar in the pricing of fixed income and mortgage-backed securities, to estimate the values of insurance policies in a manner consistent with that used to value the assets. Needless to say, this represents a big advance in the tools with which insurers can practice risk management.

So that our enthusiasm for this advance is not construed as euphoria, we hasten to add that all is not well here. First, the stochastic valuation methodology most commonly used has relied on a single stochastic factor. Most fixed-income and mortgage-backed security valuation models are based on at least two stochastic factors. Without two factors, one tends to produce model values that are too highly correlated with movements in value that are perfectly correlated. Moreover, it is unrealistic to attempt to model a prepayment feature or a call feature, which may be triggered by changes in long-term yields, while using the short-term rate paths to value the instrument. Fortunately, the newest versions of insurance valuation software are now incorporating two stochastic factors. However, the speed of the software is so slow that it is difficult to implement more than a handful of path simulations in arriving at "option-adjusted" values. A second drawback is perhaps even more serious. Most insurers have inadequate data collected and assembled with which to reliably model the interest sensitivity of policy option utilization. Accordingly, the valuation models only allow an insurer to better quantify the impact of its guesses about what those utilization functions might look like. We encountered much frustration among life insurers because even though the valuation software had taken a long time to develop, the data requirements of the valuation software still were not met. The third drawback is in how insurers interpret the data analyses provided by "black boxes." We found that in some companies, there is neither an understanding of nor an appreciation for the risk measures produced. There is often such shallow understanding of the underpinnings of the methodologies employed to measure risk that the computer output is either disregarded or uncritically accepted. Over time, as insurer personnel receive more training in stochastic methods and the meaning of the risk measures, they will be able to use the software to greater advantage in measuring and managing their risks.

Nonetheless, the availability of valuation software that is consistent with modern valuation principles is an important step forward. Software that is currently under development will remedy the shortcomings of being based on a single stochastic factor and of producing value estimates, dare we say, at a relaxed pace. With this software, actuaries can produce pricing estimates based on a dozen or so scenarios. However, they typically also test their prices using hundreds and thousands of additional scenarios, albeit not in an option-adjusted framework.

The use of reports and standards for underwriting life/health risks is routine. It is common to have dozens and sometimes over a hundred "cells" in which to classify the risks. Base rates can be related to a number of factors, such as age, gender, occupation, education, health status, and history, and so forth. While the fair premiums will be a function of interest rates, in practice the premiums charged often will not adjust to reflect current interest rates. This is because it is administratively cumbersome to alter insurance premium schedules every time the interest rates change.

Underwriting limits are commonly established. Authority is limited to a certain amount. While insurance agents may have temporary binding authority, it is a common practice to have a party who is not involved in the policy sale review the underwriting and make a determination whether the risk will ultimately be accepted and insured. Insurers are typically better at keeping track of sales commissions than in tracking losses to a particular sales agent or underwriter. However, many of the leading life/health insurers are carefully tracking the experience of their sales and underwriting personnel. If the experience falls outside the norm, it is common to place restrictions on further sales or more severe limitations on underwriting; alternatively, the activities of these sales agents and underwriters could be subject to greater oversight.

Perhaps the area of greatest concern in the area of actuarial risk is the misalignment of incentives between the owners of the insurance firm and the firm's sales and marketing staff. Much can be done to improve this situation. The typical arrangement is to pay commissions for sales of new policies, with the commissions on a multi-period contract heavily front-loaded, particularly for permanent life products. This creates a tremendous incentive for agents to sell as much business as possible, whether or not it is profitable for the company. It also creates strong incentives to replace existing policies, with commission rates that have dwindled to the low single-digit percentage range, with new policies that pay commissions ranging from 20% to 100% of first-year premiums. Sales managers and marketing personnel also often are rewarded based on volume of sales. Even senior management may sometimes have its compensation tied to sales growth.

Experience has shown that rapid growth is one of the factors most commonly associated with insolvency. It is useful to remember here that what is growing most rapidly is the accumulation of liabilities, not assets. One way to foster rapid growth is to underprice liabilities. Employees and agents whose compensation is tied to sales growth are therefore strong proponents of more "competitively-priced" insurance policies. Senior management often comes from a sales background, and is sympathetic with the notion that what is good for the insurance agents is good for the company. Pricing actuaries, who are supposed to be the watchmen and gatekeepers in this area, are often placed under tremendous pressure to alter their assumptions so that the company's products can be priced more competitively. Of course, over time it will become apparent if the insurance policies are mispriced, but that is weighed against the immediate benefits of higher commission earnings and growth.

The sales side has one powerful weapon in this battle for determining policy prices. Sales agents often work for a number of insurers and can shift new business toward them. Worse, they can take existing business away from the firm, before it breaks even from heavy initial policy costs, and direct it elsewhere if they can demonstrate satisfactorily that policy illustrations or prices appear to be more favorable elsewhere. Many firms in the insurance industry are well aware of this misalignment of interests, yet they feel thwarted by regulations about commission schedules.

In the long run, of course, insurers offering non-economic policies will go bankrupt. But the long run can take a long time to arrive; hence, an insurer that is trying to rationally price its policies faces a quandary. Does it succumb to the uneconomic pricing temporarily and hope to survive beyond the irrational players, and then restore sensible pricing, or does it choose to write very little current business and lose its distribution force? Neither choice is an attractive alternative.

5.2. Systematic Risk

5.2.1. Systematic Risk of Liabilities. No area in financial risk management of insurance has evolved as much as the analysis of systematic risk of liabilities during the past decade. This is, in large measure, due to the fact that insurers feel an increased sense of urgency in applying the tools of asset/liability management to measure and manage interest rate risk. We note that the two most recent Goldman Sachs surveys of life insurance chief investment officers (CIOs) ranked asset/liability management (ALM) at the top of the list of their concerns, whereas the topic did not surface in the top four rankings in their earlier surveys.

The increased importance given to ALM was echoed in the 1995 and 1996 surveys of Lamm-Tennant, who found it near the top of the factors that influence investment policy. Her findings are notable because they cover companies that are much smaller than those in the Goldman Sachs surveys. When contrasted with the earlier surveys of Babbel and Lamm-Tennant (1987), Babbel and Klock (1988), Lamm-Tennant (1989), and Bouyoucos and Siegel (1992), the increased importance of interest rate risk and ALM during the past few years is remarkable. All of the life/health insurers we interviewed perceived this source of risk to be crucial to understand, measure, and manage. However, the insurers we interviewed ran the gamut from naive to very sophisticated when it came to measuring interest rate risk.

On the liability side of the balance sheet, most of the life insurers were using PTS software developed by Chalke, Inc. to measure the effective duration and convexity of their liabilities.[10] The others were using TAS from Tillinghast, or some internally developed software. Most of the life insurers who were using the commercially available software packages had implemented some of their own customized enhancements to better meet their needs, capabilities, focus, and concerns.

The use of effective duration and convexity measures represents a quantum leap from what the practice was only a few years earlier. Prior to 1992, virtually none of the insurers had access to a commercially available software package that could compute measures of effective duration and convexity for their liabilities. Even the PTS, TAS, and Milliman and Robertson software packages available at that time would not produce measures of effective duration and convexity. Rather, the duration numbers, in those cases where they were produced, were simple modified or Macaulay measures, which assume that all cash flows are fixed, even though liabilities are virtually all interest sensitive to some degree. The traditional duration measures produce errors so large as to lead to reckless investment decisions, while imbuing such decisions with a veneer of analytical and quantitative credibility.[11] Back then, insurers who were concerned about interest rate risk relied heavily upon simulations. Indeed, duration estimations were considered so primitive that they were generally eschewed in favor of simulations, and rightfully so in our opinion. This is because many of the duration estimates that we saw then did not fully incorporate the interest rate sensitivity of cash flows for either assets or liabilities.

Today, convexity measures are produced by PTS-98, TAS-98, AQS, and other software that is most commonly used. We found that insurers placed less confidence in the convexity numbers produced than in the duration numbers. This is because convexity numbers are much more sensitive to lapse assumptions than are duration numbers; while a misspecification of the interest rate sensitivity of lapses and other options can cause a large error in effective duration estimates, it will cause an even greater error in the estimates of convexity. Most insurers feel that they do not have enough reliable data on which to specify the relation of lapses and policy surrenders to interest rate movements. The lack of confidence they have in this crucial input to convexity estimates translates into a lack of confidence in the convexity estimates themselves. However, most companies did pay some attention to convexity estimates, but placed wide ranges around those estimates. The most common way to grasp the impact of convexity was in toggling the lapse/surrender sensitivity parameters in numerous simulations. The standard among the companies we interviewed was to perform simulations of between 500 and 10,000 paths to capture the impact of changing interest rate levels on policy lapses/surrenders.

While life insurers have more interest than confidence in the convexity estimates, they have progressed a long way over the past few years. Prior to 1992, the commercially available software did not even produce convexity estimates for life insurance liabilities. Instead, firms relied almost entirely on simulations. Many firms used only the seven highly artificial scenarios required of New York's Regulation 126. Prior to its passage, some insurers did not use the simulation method at all. Rather, they relied simply on their "best point estimates" and static lapse assumptions. Even today, there are insurers who use nothing more than the seven scenarios required under Regulation 126 to assess their exposure to interest rate risk.

5.2.2. Systematic Risk of Assets.   Insurers are concerned with interest rate risk more than other systematic risk factors, and rightly so. Over the past two decades, it has been the source of much of the fluctuation in the value of fixed income assets, which constitute the majority of their assets. However, while it is the crucial systematic risk on the life insurance liability side, it is prominent but less dominating on the asset side of the balance sheet. This is because asset values are perceived to be affected not only by general interest rate levels, but also by basis risk, default risk, liquidity risk, call risk, prepayment risk, extension risk, sinking fund options, convertibility, and real estate and equity risk. Yet, several of these risks are simply different manifestations of interest rate risk, making accurate measurement of paramount importance.

The measurement of interest rate risk on the asset side of the balance sheet is generally well done, although some insurers have a long way to go. Many insurers use the actuarial software mentioned earlier to estimate the durations and convexities of their investments. Some use software and pricing services like GAT and Bloomberg that are oriented strictly toward the asset side of the balance sheet. Several have developed their own, more sophisticated in-house programs for estimating values of both sides of the balance sheet. We noted that it was common to use more than a single source to assess the duration and convexity of assets. One stated reason for this was the divergence of opinion between the various programs and pricing services.

5.2.3. Asset/Liability Management.   Asset/liability management typically did not go far beyond an assessment of the impact of interest rate movements on the value of the firm. Other systematic risks were usually dealt with in a more piecemeal fashion. The standard practice is to produce estimates of liability durations and convexities for each line of business as well as for each asset class. These estimates are then weighted by the fair value of liabilities, or market value of assets, to arrive at overall asset and liability duration and convexity estimates. After factoring in leverage, the insurers are able to obtain measures of surplus duration and convexity. Examples of product level and firm level analyses are given in tables 9-1 and 9-2.

The frequency for providing analysis of interest rate risk varies widely. Some firms provided weekly summaries of their asset durations and convexities, and monthly or quarterly summaries of their liabilities. In the case of interest rate futures and options, reports were more frequent, owing to their tremendous impact on overall interest rate risk. Some firms assessed their liability interest rate risks only on an annual basis.

Many companies coupled this kind of analysis with one that shows the distribution of the future market value, or more typically, book value of surplus, based on hundreds of scenarios. (See figure 9-1.) This approach is conceptually fine, although we caution that when looking at distant future values of surplus, the values produced are extremely sensitive to slight variations in assumed yield spreads, which can get compounded for 30 years, and often are overly optimistic. Rarely are these approaches implemented with sufficient skill to account for the various correlations and patterns that can be observed in practice.

Although many firms use the same general frameworks for analysis, when it comes to implementation we begin to see divergence in the quality of inputs and practice. By relying on a number of outside sources to provide the estimates of interest rate sensitivity for assets and liabilities, a number of insurers have injected another risk into the mix: divergent technologies and assumptions. We believe that for the purposes of asset/liability management, it is a misdirected effort to obtain the most credible measures of interest sensitivity of certain assets or liabilities. It is far more important to get measures of interest rate sensitivity that are calibrated similarly. After all, the absolute values are of less importance here than their relative values and the implication these have for the volatility of equity.

We saw a number of practices that invite problems. One prominent insurer used effective duration and convexity estimates for the liability side of the balance sheet, and Modified Macaulay duration measures for the asset side. Another insurer did exactly the opposite. Some insurers base their aggregate duration and convexity numbers on book-value weights, rather than market-value weights. More than one insurer was frustrated that its actuarial departments relied entirely on simulations and provided no duration or convexity measures whatsoever. The actuarial scenarios run were based on completely random interest rate paths, inconsistent with any financial theory or history of interest rates. Several insurers relied on liability duration estimates based

Table 9-1. Option Adjusted Duration/convexity

Life Product XX

Interest Rate Shift (b.p.)	Assets			Liabilities			Surplus		
	Option-Adjusted Value	Effective Duration	Convexity	Option-Adjusted Value	Effective Duration	Convexity	Option-Adjusted Value	Effective Duration	Convexity
-200	1,600	2.9	N/A	1,545	4.1	N/A	55	-30.8	N/A
-150	1,500	3.0	-66	1,405	2.9	60	95	4.5	-3,000
-100	1,400	3.1	-85	1,330	2.1	450	70	22.1	-25
-50	1,300	3.3	-176	1,243	1.8	700	57	36.0	-125
0	1,200	3.5	-190	1,151	1.5	680	49	50.5	-10,000
50	1,100	3.8	-121	1,061	1.4	390	39	69.1	-8,555
100	1,000	4.2	-50	975	1.2	85	25	121.2	-6,000
150	900	5.0	0	901	1.1	20	-1	-3,508.9	100
200	800	5.9	N/A	845	1.0	N/A	-45	-86.1	N/A

Table 9-2. XYZ Insurance Company

Surplus Duration Analysis

Asset Class	Market Value	Effective Duration	Liabilities	Fair Value	Effective Duration	Economic Surplus	Effective Duration
Bonds	10,000,000	6.5	SPDA 1	8,500,000	3.2		
Mortgage-backed Securities	5,000,000	4.2	SPDA 2	4,000,000	2.0		
Preferred Stock	200,000	8.1	Universal Life	400,000	7.9		
Common Stock	3,000,000	2.1	Term Life	300,000	1.3		
Mortgage Loans	6,000,000	5.7	Whole Life	12,000,000	6.8		
Equity Real Estate	2,000,000	1.0	Endowment	500,000	8.5		
Short-term and Cash	1,500,000	0.8					
Totals	27,700,000	4.74		25,700,000	4.85	2,000,000	3.36

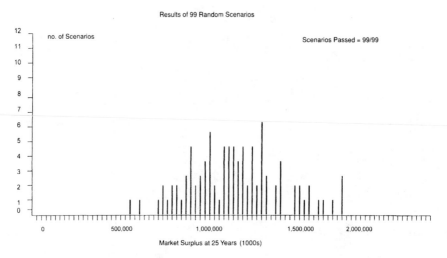

Figure 9-1.   Distribution of Surplus Accumulation

on only one interest rate factor, but on asset duration estimates based on two factors. Some insurers used duration measures for corporate bonds and mortgage-backed securities supplied by Wall Street that were based on different volatility parameters and processes than those used for other asset and liability categories. Some estimates were based on lattice models, while others were based on simulation models, or simulating through lattices. Only one insurer we know of is attempting to correct the duration measures on corporate bonds for the basis risk between corporate and government bonds.[12] Some insurers took the basis risk between movements in long-term vs. short-term interest rates into account, but many did not. Some took into account all kinds of potential twists in the yield curve, while others allowed only for parallel shifts.

In setting limits on the amount of systematic risk the company desires to retain, a common approach is the one used by a leading multi-line insurer. The company places limits on its desired portfolio structure to reflect the variety of risks to which it is exposed. Limits are set on individual asset holdings, on industry concentration, and on asset type including mortgage-backed securities and collateralized mortgage obligations, all in a risk-based capital context. However, nowhere did we observe a methodology to derive such limits, or even a standardized approach across business lines.

For the balance sheet as a whole, limits are employed in two different ways. One approach is to impose a limit on the amount of duration mismatch allowed, either for particular product lines or for aggregating across all assets and liabilities. For instance, one company applies these restrictions on a product segmentation basis, allowing up to a year duration mismatch on participating whole life products, but only one-tenth of a year on GICs. Another company does not place restrictions on duration mismatches on a product-by-product basis, but on an aggregate portfolio basis. In our view, although most companies we interviewed used some sort of product segmentation approach, it is not necessary to do so. The advantage of a segmentation approach is the discipline it imposes on the pricing process, so that long-term yields do not get used for pricing short-term liabilities, and so forth. However, if this same discipline can be achieved in the pricing of insurance policies without a segmentation of assets into various product groupings, it seems that advantage would disappear. On the other hand, valuable resources would not be consumed in notionally dividing up the general account into the various segments, and it could be managed on an aggregate basis. This would avoid the costly duplication of efforts, where one product manager is selling an asset and another is buying the same or a similar asset, incurring transaction costs. Some firms simply transfer the assets between portfolio segments and use some sort of internal transfer pricing mechanism. Assets are acquired by the firm and then allocated to each product group according to perceived needs. This is done to foster a better sense of accountability and for use in performance evaluation. But to reward a product group for producing net profits between liability costs and rates of return on assets for which they had no responsibility in acquiring or divesting seems to be rewarding them for risks over which they had no control. While we appreciate the need for pricing discipline and control, we feel this could be achieved more simply and that the asset portfolios can be better managed on an aggregate basis.

The other limit is a restriction on the amount of scenarios that are allowed to reveal losses due to asset/liability mismatches. These limits are typically placed not only on the distribution of final simulated results, but also on the evolution of solvency over time associated with the simulations. One firm has almost no tolerance for scenarios showing negative profitability due to interest rate risk exposure. Because it is persuaded that interest rates are virtually impossible to forecast, and over which it has no control, the firm has decided to avoid interest rate risk of any kind, to the extent possible.

At the aforementioned firm, portfolio managers are not rewarded in any way for taking interest rate risk and trying to "time" the market. Indeed, their jobs could be lost if they stray outside narrow boundaries. Some firms purport to eschew interest rate risk, yet reward their investment department personnel if they achieve investment income or total rates of return above some benchmark level. By measuring only periodically the interest rate risk of assets, this invites the portfolio managers to "game" the system and attempt to improve their returns by incurring interest rate risk for brief periods of time. Some firms have duration targets but ignore convexity, leading portfolio managers to try barbell, ladder, or bullet maturity approaches to achieve higher investment income, depending on the shape of the term structure.

But by and large, the major difference between investment practices that we saw during this study, compared to what was occurring less than a decade ago, was that there was far less emphasis on yield and more on total rate of return. As recently as five years ago a survey of the American Council of Life Insurance revealed that two-thirds of chief investment officers did not even consider total rate of return as an investment objective. Yield was the primary focus. This impediment to effective asset/liability management is beginning to dwindle. Nonetheless, we observed more concern with book yield than we feel is appropriate, given its lack of importance to the true economic performance of the firm.

5.3. Credit Risk

In addition to the credit risk that reveals itself as basis risk in the systematic risk factors listed above, there is also the risk of default on significant firm investments. While it may be idiosyncratic risk to the market as a whole, it is not idiosyncratic risk to the insurer maintaining a significant position in an asset that goes into default.

Insurance firms are generally very focused on credit risk, as are rating agencies and regulatory authorities. They produce weekly and monthly reports that monitor the credit risk of their assets. They rely on outside rating agencies, such as Moody's, Standard and Poor's, Duff and Phelps, and Dunn and Bradstreet. In addition, virtually all of their investments are assigned credit ratings by the Securities Valuation Office of the NAIC, which are used for statutory reporting purposes. These ratings are not always viewed as sufficient measures of credit risk for those insurers who feel that absorbing credit risk is an important part of their franchise. Many insurers have their own due diligence requirements to meet before they will take on an investment that has credit risk. They undertake internal credit risk ratings, in some ways quite similar to those of Moody's or Standard and Poor's, although with different weightings on the risk factors. Moreover, they are prone to update their internal credit risk ratings promptly as important information bearing on the creditworthiness of a major investment position is revealed.

Insurers produce "watch lists" of firms they feel are in financial jeopardy, likely to be downsized or to become insolvent. They often have a dual-track credit risk assessment, one for the asset itself, and another for the underlying collateral. They place limits on the portfolio exposure by industry, by geographic region, by business (e.g., real estate prohibited), and by company. They also have lists of approved counterparties for brokerage, settlement, and swaps.

In figures 9-2 and 9-3, we provide an example of one set of investment guidelines, with general and specific authorizations and limits that we feel are representative of the industry. However, there is substantial variation in the practices that we have seen. Perhaps the poorest approach we saw was a firm that used Moody's ratings, and assigned numerical values to each rating class. For instance, 1.0 was assigned to a rating of Aaa, 2.0 was assigned to Aa, 3.0 to A, 4.0 to Baa, 5.0 to Ba, 6.0 to B, 7.0 to Caa, 8.0 to Ca, 9.0 to C, and 10.0 to D. Adjustments are made to accommodate the modifiers of 1, 2, and 3 that Moody's often uses to designate relative quality within a ranking class. The company then has a target number of 3.0 to achieve in its overall credit risk plan. One problem with this approach, which they recognize, is that default rates and volatility of default rates do not grow linearly as rating is decreased step by step. Coupled with an incentive structure that rewards portfolio managers for the investment yields they book, this system leads to a credit barbell approach, as shown in figure 9-4, because the portfolio manager can achieve superior yields by doing so.

The best approach we saw included a more refined ranking of credit risk, not by letter but by default probability coupled with standard deviation of defaults for each ranking. Covariance of asset returns was also taken into account, and the entire credit risk problem was cast in a surplus oriented mean-variance model. Diversification guidelines were incorporated through constraints on the optimization. Liquidity risk was reflected by reducing the expected returns by a number of basis points that was deemed appropriate from historical experience.

5.4. Liquidity Risk

Although insurance companies are faced with liquidity risk, most of the insurers we interviewed were only a little concerned. Only one was concerned about having too little liquidity, and one was concerned about having

General Authorizations

These general authorizations are to remain in effect until January 1997, unless modified or canceled.

> The total investment in any one credit (total of bonds, preferred stock, convertible securities, and common stock) is limited to 1% of net admitted assets, with the exception of direct U.S. Treasury and full faith and credit obligations and U.S. government-sponsored enterprise obligations, as further specified below.

The following authorizations specify which transactions the Investment Officers of the Company are authorized to conduct at their discretion.

Fixed Income Securities—Non Convertible[13]

A.   Purchase U.S. Treasury and full faith and credit obligations in unlimited amounts.

B.   Purchase U.S. Government-sponsored enterprise obligations. Such purchases to be limited to 3% of net admitted assets per enterprise, and an aggregate limitation of 10%.

C.   Purchase corporate, municipal, or foreign bonds denominated in U.S. dollars, which are rated in the Baa category or better; purchase private placement issues rated in the Baa category or better, or its equivalent.

D.   Purchase mortgage-backed securities and collateralized mortgage obligations consistent with Investment Committee limitations and the Specific Authorizations.

E.   Purchase asset-backed securities consistent with Investment Committee limitations and Specific Authorizations.

F.   Purchase preferred stocks of companies with bonds or preferred stocks that are rated in the Baa category or better, or its equivalent.

Short Term Fixed Income

H.   Purchase commercial paper (with maturities not exceeding 270 days), certificates of deposit or bankers acceptances, which are rated with A-1 or better by Standard & Poor's or P-1 by Moody's.

Such purchases to be limited to 1% of net admitted assets per credit.

Repurchase Agreements

I.   Repurchase agreements may be purchased with banks or security dealers as designated in the Specific Authorizations with the following characteristics: at least 102% collateralized by U.S. Treasury or Agency obligations; for periods not exceeding 60 days.

Total amount outstanding is limited overall to 5% of net admitted assets and per counter party to 2%.

Reverse Repurchase Agreements

J.   Reverse repurchase agreements may be transacted with banks or security dealers by Specific Authorization.

Total amount outstanding to be limited to 5% of net admitted assets and per counter party to 2%.

Figure 9-2.   Investment Guidelines

R. Purchase convertible preferred stocks under the limits specified for non-convertible with issues rated Baa or better, or of companies with lower or non-rated issues according to the following schedule:

Moody's (or S&P) Rating	Authorized Limit per Issuer as Percentage of the Convertible Portfolio
Ba1 (BB+) to Ba3 (BB–)	2.0
B1 (B+) to B3 (B–)	1.0
No Rating	1.0
Caa (CCC+) to C (D)	0.5

Common Stocks

S. The Investment Officers are authorized to purchase common stocks of any U.S. or Canadian corporation or any foreign corporation whose shares are included in the S&P Common Stock Index in amounts consistent with the Investment Policy Statements as approved by the Committee subject to these additional restrictions. Specifically, the Investment Officers may not:

1. Invest in the equity securities of closed end funds, investment companies, limited partnerships or real estate investment trusts without specific authorizations

2. Make any purchase of common stock which would result in more than 5% of the value of the common stock portfolio being invested in the securities of one issuer

3. Purchase a common stock if as a result thereof more than 25% of the assets of the common stock portfolio will be invested in a particular industry

4. Purchase a common stock if as a result more than the authorized limit of the assets of the common stock portfolio will be invested in common stock of that particular issuer. The authorized limit per issuer will be a function of the issuer's common stock market capitalization in accordance with the following schedule:

Market Capitalization of Issuer of Common Stock	Authorized Limit per Issuer as % of the overall Common Stock Portfolio
$0–$25 million	0
$26–$50 million	0.25
$51–$100 million	0.50
$101–$200 million	1.00
$201–$500 million	2.00
$501–$1,000 million	3.00
$1,001–$2,000 million	4.00
more than $2,000 million	5.00

Furthermore, the Investment Officers will make a quarterly presentation to the Investment Committee on the performance of the common stock portfolio and its risk characteristics in relation to appropriate benchmarks.

T. The Investment Officers are authorized to use stock index futures and options contracts (exchange traded and over-the-counter) to reduce stock market risk exposure.

Real Estate / Commercial Mortgages

U. The Investment Officers are authorized to:

1. Commercial Mortgages and Real Estate Equity

Consummate transactions for the purchase, sale, exchange, and disposition of real estate loans or equities, up to $2.5 million with the approval of any three of the following officers of the Company:

Chairman of the Board, President, Chief Investment Officer, and Senior Real Estate Investment Officer.

All transactions completed under this authority will be reported to the Real Estate Subcommittee of the Investment Committee of the Board of Directors

Figure 9-2. *Continued*

Dollar Rolls

K. Enter into dollar roll transactions with banks or security dealers designated in the Specific Authorizations.

Total amount outstanding to be limited to 5% of net admitted assets and per counter party to 2%.

Other

L. Enter into CMO residual commitments as specified in the Specific Authorizations.

M. Use financial futures contracts and interest rate options (exchange traded and over-the-counter) to reduce interest rate risk exposure.

N. Sell securities held in the portfolio. Any purchaser or transfer agent of such a security need not inquire into the authority for such sale upon the Secretary's certification that it is made under this subdivision "N".

Convertible Securities[14]

O. Under the limits specified for non-convertible bonds, purchase convertible bonds of companies with issues rated in the Baa category or better, or of companies with lower or non-rated issues according to the following schedule:

Moody's (or S&P) Rating	Authorized Limit per Issuer as Percentage of the Convertible Portfolio
Ba1 (BB+) to Ba3 (BB−)	2.0
B1 (B+) to B3 (B−)	1.0
No Rating	1.0
Caa (CCC+) to C (D)	0.5

Purchases must not cause the aggregate statement value of convertible debt rated less than 2 by the NAIC to exceed the following percentages of the convertible debt portfolio:

NAIC Rating	Restrictions
3 3Z 6 6Z	60.0
4 4Z 6 6Z	40.0
5 5Z 6 6Z	7.5
6 6Z	2.5

P. Purchase of medium or lower grade bonds must not cause the aggregate statement value of bonds, including convertible debt, rated less than 2 by the NAIC to exceed the following percentages of net admitted assets:

NAIC Rating	Restrictions
3 3Z 6 6Z	10.0
4 4Z 6 6Z	5.0
5 5Z 6 6Z	3.0
6 6Z	1.0

Q. No more than 25% of the portfolio's bonds rated less than 2 by the NAIC can be companies within a single industry nor should these issues in aggregate conduct business within one narrow geographic region. The duration of these issues as a group should be viewed in the context of the total bond portfolio.

Figure 9-2.   *Continued*

Specific Authorizations

The following specific authorizations for the purchase of securities to be executed at the discretion of the Officers of the Company were renewed by the Committee:

1. Bonds, Short-term Investments, Convertibles Subordinated Debentures
   None

2. Common Stocks
   a. Domestic
      None

		Authorization Percent
b.	Foreign Companies	
	DeBeers Consolidated Mines (ADR)	1.0
	Sea Containers Ltd.	1.0

3. Convertible Preferred Stock

Sea Containers Ltd.	1.0

4. Repurchase Agreements, Reverse Repurchase Agreements, and Dollar Roll Transactions

   There is a list of banks and security dealers authorized for repurchase agreements and reverse repurchase agreements and dollar roll transactions.

5. Hedging Transactions
   A. The following officers of the Investment Department are hereby authorized to execute hedging transactions in accordance with the guidelines:
      Executive Vice President & Chief Investment Officer
      Senior Vice President; Vice President; and Second Vice President, Equity Securities
      Senior Vice President; Vice President; and Second Vice President, Fixed Income
      Assistant Vice President, Equity Trader

   B. There is a list of banks and brokerage firms approved for the establishment of futures trading accounts.

   C. Maximum amount which may be hedged is 5% of admitted assets.

6. Residual Commitments

   The maximum amount of CMO Residual commitments is limited to $100 million.

7. Mortgage-backed Securities Commitments

   In the aggregate, the maximum amount of FHLMC, FNMA, and whole loan commitments is limited to $750 million at book value.

8. Asset-backed Securities

   In the aggregate, the maximum amount of ABS is limited to $250 million at book value.

9. Short-term Borrowing

   Up to a maximum amount of $100 million, such maximum amount not to exceed $50 million with any one bank or financial institution

Figure 9-3.   Investment Guidelines

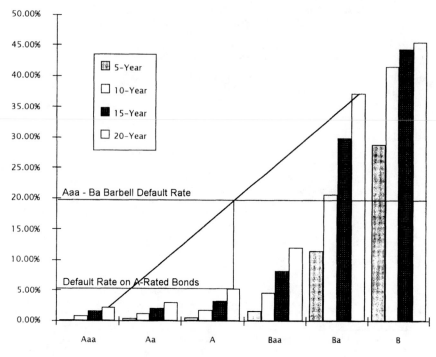

Figure 9-4. Cumulative Default Rates: 1970–1995 (for 5, 10, 15, and 20 years)

too much liquidity. The others did not seem to be concerned, believing their situation to be well managed.

Liquidity is not as big a concern with many insurance firms as it is in other financial institutions for one good reason: most of their policies are less liquid than their assets. Life insurance companies issue policies that commonly feature high surrender charges. These charges are either explicitly stated, or implicit in the schedule of cash build-up. For example, a single premium deferred annuity, with annual crediting rate reset and a seven-year maturity, may feature surrender charges beginning at 7%–10% during the first year, and declining in steps toward 0 at maturity. Similarly, universal life and whole life products often have very low surrender values during the first year or two of a policy, and begin building up rapidly after that point. Other policies, such as variable universal life, have surrender provisions that act much like a mutual fund, where the amount received depends on the value of the underlying fund.

A decade or so ago, the problem of illiquidity was more pronounced. Policy surrenders for some companies approached a 60% rate, and massive amounts of policy loans were withdrawn. The industry has managed this problem in two ways. First, much of the new business written is sensitive to market rates of interest, so that there is not as wide a divergence between crediting rates on life policies and annuities vs. market rates of interest. Thus, the incentive to surrender a policy is lessened. Second, policy loans are now offered mostly at variable rates that track market rates of interest, rather than the fixed policy loan rates of yore. An alternative to the variable rates charged on loans is a process known as "direct recognition," whereby the schedule of cash value build-up is altered if policy loans are incurred. The tax environment has also changed, and interest paid on policy loans is now no longer a tax-deductible expense. Thus, the interest rate arbitrage incentive has virtually disappeared.

Not long ago, however, several well-known life insurance companies, such as First Capital Life, Fidelity Bankers Life, Executive Life of California, Executive Life of New York, and Mutual Benefit experienced severe liquidity problems. But in each of these cases, there were other factors that precipitated a "run on the bank" phenomenon. The run in each case was caused, in part, by well publicized investment performance problems. In the case of the first four of the aforementioned companies, there were vast sums of policies in force with minimal, and even zero surrender charges. Some of the policies had been marketed through Wall Street brokerages, and were therefore of the "hot money" variety. Although the first four of these companies had large amounts of liquid assets, the withdrawal rates were so high that even these liquid resources were strained. Generally, however, life insurers are managed in such a way as to avoid these runs on the bank, either through policy design, sales channel, investment policy, or level of surplus.

Another problem that was more prevalent a decade ago was that all bonds were essentially reported at amortized book values. If a bond was sold prior to maturity, any capital gain or loss would need to be recognized. Many insurers, particularly during the early 1980s, could not afford to have the large capital losses appear on their books and impact their surplus. Today, however, a large portion of fixed income holdings are placed in accounts available for sale or trading, and are therefore already marked to be sold. Therefore, whether they are sold or not does not impact the reported values or the surplus as much.

We provide some tables that are representative of the practice of liquidity risk measurement and management. The company defines liquidity risk as the risk of having inadequate net cash flows to meet expenses, benefits, withdrawals, and loan payments. It views product liquidity risk as the fluctuations in cash flows outside of the ranges that are expected. It first ranks assets by relative liquidity. It then projects its cash flows over a multiple-year horizon on both sides of the balance sheet using a form like figure 9-5. For those firms that maintain segmented accounts by product line, these liquidity reports are generated by product, as in the case of figure 9-6.

A company's asset/liability committee is typically responsible for measuring and managing liquidity risk. Despite the lack of concern regarding this risk, there is still a large amount of analysis that is done to guard against illiquidity. In this regard, liquidity risk decisions are part of the analytics and scenario testing used by the company. In its investment plan, management of liquidity risk is twofold. First, the company uses corporate- and Regulation 126-modeling to measure net cash flow under various interest rate scenarios. Second, control is achieved by imposing constraints on investment. One such constraint includes ensuring that over 50% of the assets are held in "marketable securities."

Many companies use PTS, TAS, or AQS for most of their analysis and stress testing. The scenario testing includes about 50 to 100 scenarios that shift the yield curve, both parallel and slope changes. For each path created by the scenario, net cash flows must be positive. Solvency of the company is also determined along each path. Reports are used for each product, and

Life Product XXX Projected Cash Flows

Period	Asset Cash Flow	Liability Cash Flow	Net Cash Flow
1996			
1997			
1998			
1999			
2000			
2001			
2002			
2003			
2004			
2005			
2006			
2007			
2008			
2009			
2010			
2011			
2012			
2013			
2014			
2015			

Figure 9-5. Liquidity Report

Life Product XXX

Liabilities				
	Current Quarter	Prior Quarter-1	Prior Quarter-2	Prior Quarter-3
Level 1 Liquidity				
Level 2 Liquidity				
Level 3 Liquidity				
Level 4 Liquidity				
(Levels 1 + 2) ÷ Total				

*Liabilities are net of Policy Loans

Assets				
	Current Quarter	Prior Quarter-1	Prior Quarter-2	Prior Quarter-3
Level 1 Liquidity				
Level 2 Liquidity				
Level 3 Liquidity				
Level 4 Liquidity				
(Levels 1 + 2) ÷ Total				

Summary				
	Current Quarter	Prior Quarter-1	Prior Quarter-2	Prior Quarter-3
Level 1 (Assets) ÷ Level 1 (Liabilities)				
Level 1–2 (Assets) ÷ Level 1–2 (Liabilities)				
Guideline				
Level 1–3 (Assets) ÷ Level 1–3 (Liabilities)				

Note:	Level 1	Level 2	Level 3	Level 4
Liabilities Surrender is at:	Book SChg < 2%	Int Grnty Expires + Scheduled Ann Paymts, Next 12 months	Market; Market & SChg; Book, SChg > 2%	Now Allowed
Assets	Cash, STI Inv Grade Bonds with aggregate market loss < IMR; Other	Mtg amort NII over Next 12 months	Inv Grade Bonds with aggregate market loss in excess of IMR	Mtg.; Below Inv Grade Bonds; Affil; VC: Other

Figure 9-6.   Relative Liquidity of Assets and Liabilities

cash flows are projected out for about 30 years under each of the scenarios. By aggregating across products for each scenario, the company has an idea of the distribution of liquidity at the firm level.

After all the scenario tests, the results have little impact on immediate decisions. For instance, if net cash flows were negative for a large portion of the stress tests, this would not imply that asset composition would change immediately. Suggestions would of course be made, but there is no guarantee that the portfolio would change immediately. Similarly, concentrations are not altered unless there are modifications to limits that would only occur quarterly or annually.

In addition to running these scenario tests, there is also a "worst-case scenario." This includes cash outflows of over 300% over a two- to three-year period and a lapse rate of 45%. For comparison, the highest lapse rate the company has ever experienced is 18%, when it decided to decrease significantly dividends after a long history of either increasing or maintaining dividend payments.

There are no managers at the companies studied whose performance is based on the management of liquidity risk. Although it would be difficult to base everyday compensation on unlikely events, the company may benefit in the future from having a clearer line of responsibility with regard to liquidity management. The general procedure is that any ongoing problems with liquidity would be brought to the attention of the chief financial officer. Any changes to the company's credit ratings which could potentially affect liquidity demands are very much a concern of the auditing group.

5.5. Other Risks Considered But Not Modeled

Beyond the basic four financial risks, *viz.*, actuarial, systematic, credit, and liquidity, insurers have a host of other concerns, as was indicated above. Some of these, like operating risk, are a natural outgrowth of business and insurers employ standard risk avoidance techniques to mitigate them. Standard business judgment is used in this area to measure the costs and benefits of both risk reduction expenditures and system designs, as well as operational redundancy. While generally referred to as risk management, this activity is substantially different from the management of financial risk addressed here.

Yet there are still other risks, somewhat more amorphous, but no less important. In this latter category are legal, regulatory, reputational, and environmental risk. In each of these risk areas substantial time and resources are devoted to protecting the firm's franchise value from erosion. As these risks are less amenable to *a priori* financial measurement, they are generally not addressed in any formal, structured way. However, they are not ignored at the senior management level of the insurance firm.

In passing from this topic it is worthwhile and timely to pause to consider one of the legal risks now encroaching upon the life industry. During the course of our interviews, a number of firms had been sued in the area of misrepresentation of insurance products by insurance agents. At the time of this writing, over 100 class actions had been filed against firms for their so-called "vanishing premium" policies, whose premiums did not vanish, as illustrated, owing to a prolonged decline in market interest-rate levels. The damages claimed are staggering for some of the companies.

The manner in which insurers are responding to these lawsuits ranges from attempts to gain a quick and comprehensive settlement to attempts to have the arguments heard in court. Some insurers are merely biding their time to see how other firms fare in the struggle. But more interesting is how insurers are acting to avoid future problems stemming from alleged agent misrepresentation. One of the firms has established a very large department of compliance to train and monitor the behavior of its sales agents. All of its sales and promotional literature is undergoing careful scrutiny by the legal department.

Another firm has created an auditing division to oversee compliance from a central location, which computerizes each transaction. Management is concerned with five components of compliance: customer satisfaction, new products, stable earnings, expansion capabilities, and corporate miscellaneous. Controls are being built into the centralized computer system. Should an agent exceed the allotted number of address changes, disbursements, lapses, or sales, the computer will not process the policy until the auditing department has had a chance to investigate further. These stop measures are not announced to either the customer or the sales agent. The director of auditing indicated that this system is intended to prevent problems rather than to react to them.

A compliance division has been introduced to complement the role of the internal audit group. This division is responsible for insuring the field force and also for providing training to sales agents so they will be able to better represent the company's products. This division is currently sending out surveys to its customers to find out if they really understand the products they now hold. It is hoped that these measures will mitigate any class action suits in the future.

6. Areas Where Further Work Will Improve Methodology

Thus far, the techniques used to measure, report, limit, and manage individual risks have been presented. In each of these cases, a process has been developed, or at least has evolved, to measure the risk considered and techniques have been deployed to control each of them.

The insurance industry is clearly evolving to a higher level of risk management techniques and approaches than has been in place in the past. Yet, as this review indicates, there is significant room for improvement. Before the areas of potential value added are reviewed, however, it is worthwhile to reiterate an earlier point. The risk management techniques reviewed here are not the average, but are techniques used by firms at the higher end of the market. The risk management approaches at smaller institutions, as well as larger but relatively less-sophisticated ones, are less precise and significantly less analytical. In some cases, they would need substantial upgrading to reach the level reported here. Accordingly, our review should be viewed as a glimpse at best practice, not at average practices. Nonetheless, the techniques employed by those that define the industry standard could use some improvement. By category, recommended areas where additional analytic work would be desirable are listed below.

6.1. Actuarial Risk

There remains too much disagreement in the most fundamental area of actuarial science—namely, what discount rate or rates does one use to value insurance liabilities.[15] With such broad disagreement about what insurance is worth, or what it will cost the insurer, it is little wonder that we encounter difficulties when it comes to managing risk. On the bright side, it must be acknowledged that there is a flurry of activity directed toward solving this conundrum. In our opinion, as the scope of what exactly is being valued is more carefully defined, there is convergence in the estimates produced by the alternative valuation methods.[16]

During the past decade, tools have been developed that can take into account the interest rate sensitivity of policy cash flows. However, many insurers have not employed these tools. Among those who have, there is a severe problem with the data inputs that are necessary to produce useful output. Insurers have not tracked or organized their lapse, surrender, and claims data in a manner that allows them to accurately model their interest rate sensitivity. While the models are capable of accommodating virtually any functional form of this behavior, including the effects of policy seasoning, channel of distribution, and so forth, little data exist to estimate the functional form. Of course, this was also the case regarding the modeling of mortgage-backed securities prepayment a decade ago, but since that time data have been collected and analyzed, permitting the enlightened application of the valuation tools that we see today in that sector. We expect that the same will be true for insurers in a few more years.

Another area where we expect to see rapid improvement is in the versatility of the actuarial software and its speed. Currently, single-factor stochastic models are being used most widely for valuing liabilities, although this is changing. This results in output that is inconsistent with the other side of the balance sheet, where two or more factors are typically used. Moreover, the speed of processing is so slow that insurers make undesirable compromises when it comes to fully modeling their products. Emerging computer technology undoubtedly will remove this impediment to better policy pricing and risk analysis.

6.2. Systematic Risk

Tremendous progress has already been made over the past five years in this arena. Most of it has been directed toward interest-rate risk management, which is appropriate given its importance to insurers. An important area for further development is the incorporation of basis risk and equity risk. Another important advance will be a consistent valuation methodology for both sides of the balance sheet.

While simulation studies have substantially improved over the past few years, the use of book value accounting measures and cash flow losses continues to be problematic. Movements to improve this methodology, such as the Unified Valuation System currently being developed by the Valuation Task Force of the American Academy of Actuaries, will require increased emphasis on market-based accounting. Such a reporting mechanism must be employed on both sides of the balance sheet, however, not just with the asset portfolio.

The simulations also need to incorporate the advances in dynamic hedging that are used in complex fixed-income pricing models. As it stands, these simulations tend to be rather simplistic, and scenario testing is rather limited.

6.3. Credit Risk

The evaluation of credit rating continues to be an imprecise process. We note divergence between the NAIC ratings assigned to particular public and private placements vs. the ratings assigned by the Wall Street ratings agencies. We should never expect to see a complete convergence here, as there is no single set of weights to apply to the risk factors across all industries and firms. However, we do expect to see less divergence over time, as more becomes known about the factors that lead to default.

We also expect to see more enlightened practices when it comes to aggregating credit risks. A sensible aggregation scheme would take into account default rates, default losses, and the shape of the distribution of losses across all ratings categories. In time, we may even see a move toward market-based default measures, at least on publicly traded debt instruments. We anticipate that credit risks will soon be evaluated in a framework consistent with other financial risks. Some insurers are already moving in this direction.

6.4. Liquidity Risk

Life insurers regard liquidy risk as one of the least of their major financial risks. Most companies are doing a satisfactory job of managing this risk. With the advent of mark-to-market accounting, the problems for liquidity caused by the fiction of book accounting will gradually subside. Most life insurers model this risk well. If liquidity is to be better managed, the price of illiquidity must be defined and built into illiquid positions. While this logic has been adopted by some institutions, this pricing of liquidity is not commonplace.

6.5. Risk Aggregation and Knowledge of Total Firm Exposure

The quest for an estimate of aggregate firm risk has been a stumbling block for the insurance industry. The extent of the differences across risks of different types is quite striking. Actuarial risk is carefully modeled, but reported at infrequent intervals. There is often a lack of follow-up to see whether, based on the insurer's experience, the actuarial assumptions have been appropriate. Systematic risk, particularly interest rate risk, is typically measured by life insurers on both sides of the balance sheet. Interest rate risk exposure is discerned using measures of effective duration and convexity, scenario simulations, or a combination of the two. For assets, it may be reported as often as weekly or monthly, but for liabilities it is generally reported only quarterly or annually. The credit risk process is a qualitative review of the performance potential of different bonds and borrowers. It results in a rating, periodic re-evaluation at reasonable intervals through time, and ongoing monitoring of various types or measures of exposure. Liquidity risk, on the other hand, more often than not, is dealt with as a planning exercise, although some reasonable work is done to analyze the effect of adverse events that affect the firm.

The analytical approaches that are subsumed in each of these analyses are complex, difficult and not easily communicated to non-specialists in the risk considered. The insurer, however, must select appropriate levels for each risk and select, or at least articulate, an appropriate level of risk for the organization as a whole. How is this achieved?

The simple answer is "not very well." Senior management often is presented with myriad reports on individual exposures, such as specific credits, and complex summaries of the individual risks, outlined above. The risks are not dimensioned in similar ways, and management's technical expertise to appreciate the true nature of both the risks themselves and the analyses conducted to illustrate the insurer's exposure to them is limited. Accordingly, over time, the managers of specific risks have gained increased authority and autonomy. In light of recent losses, however, things are beginning to change.

At the organizational level, overall risk management is being centralized into a risk management committee, headed by someone designated as the senior risk manager. The purpose of this institutional response is to empower one individual, or group, with the responsibility to evaluate overall firm-level risk, and determine the best interest of the company as a whole. At the same time, this group is holding line officers more accountable for the risks under their control, and the performance of the institution in that risk area. Activity and sales incentives are being replaced by performance compensation that is based, not on business volume, but on overall profitability.

At the analytical level, aggregate risk exposure is receiving increased scrutiny. To do so, however, requires the summation of the different types of risks outlined above. This is accomplished in two distinct but related ways. In the first approach, risk is measured in terms of variability of outcome. Where possible, a frequency distribution of net returns is estimated, from historical data, and the standard deviation of this distribution is estimated. Capital is allocated to activities as a function of this risk or volatility measure. Then, the risky position is required to carry an expected rate of return on allocated capital, which compensates the firm for the associated incremental risk. By dimensioning all risk in terms of loss distributions, and allocating capital by the volatility of the proposed activity, risk is aggregated and priced in one and the same exercise.

The second approach is similar to the first, but depends less on a capital allocation scheme and more on cash flow or earnings effects of the implied risky position. This approach can be used to analyze total firm level risk in a similar manner to the first approach. Again, a frequency distribution of net returns from any one type of risk can be estimated from historical data. Extreme outcomes can then be estimated from the tail of the distribution. Either a worst-case historical example is used for this purpose, or a three- or four-standard deviation outcome is considered. Given the downside outcome associated with any risk position, the firm restricts its exposure so that, in the worst-case scenario, the insurer does not lose more than a certain percentage of its surplus or current income. Therefore, rather than moving from volatility of equity value through capital, this approach goes directly to the current earnings implications from a risky position. The approach, however, has two very obvious shortcomings. It is cash-flow based, rather than market-value driven; and it does not necessarily directly measure the total variability of potential outcomes through *a priori* distribution specification. Rather, it depends upon a subjectively pre-specified range of the risky environments to drive the worst-case scenario.

Both measures attempt to treat the issue of tradeoffs among risks using a common methodology to transform the specific risks to firm-level exposure. In addition, both can examine the correlation of different risks and the extent to which they can, or should, be viewed as offsetting. As a practical matter, however, only two of the insurers interviewed that were using these approaches viewed the array of risks as a standard portfolio problem. The others would separately evaluate each risk and aggregate total exposure by simple addition. As a result, much is lost in the aggregation. Perhaps over time this crucial issue will be more widely addressed.

The ability of insurance companies to estimate and manage firm level risk is a long way off. To reach this goal requires much more precision in the estimation and management of the individual risks within the firm. Aggregation only has meaning to the extent that the individual elements can be aggregated. This presumes that they are measured correctly, dimensioned in a similar manner, and incorporated in a unified framework of risk. When this is accomplished, risks of different types will be contrasted and compared, and tradeoffs will become possible. However, to achieve this a significant amount of work on the individual risks within the industry is required before any reasonable aggregation can transpire.

Notes

*This chapter is a revised version of "Financial Risk Management by Insurers: An Analysis of the Process," *Journal of Risk and Insurance* 64 (1997, no. 2): 231–270. Copyright American Risk and Insurance Association, used with permission.

1. Members of the team included Anthony Santomero (leader), David Babbel, Yuval Bar-Or, Richard Herring, Paul Hoffman, Susan Kerr, Spencer Martin, Steve Pilloff, Jeffrey Trester, and Sri Zaheer.

2. See Alexander et al (1994), and Siegel, Millette and Pouraghabagher (1995).

3. See Lamm-Tennant (1995) and Lamm-Tennant and Gattis (1996).

4. See, for example, Merton (1989, especially pp. 242–258).

5. See Oldfield and Santomero (1997).

6. Our discussion of these risks follows that of Black and Skipper (1994).

7. See Black and Skipper (1994) and Beard, Pentikäinen, and Pesonen (1984), Gerber (1979), and Cummins and Derrig (1989).

8. See M. Smith (1982).

9. The value of the policy loan option by itself could account for 20%–45% of the present value of all future insurance premiums, if the option were used optimally. When factoring in the suboptimal utilization of this option, he estimated that the cost to an insurer of providing this option was in the 8%–12% range. Yet insurers had historically charged *nothing* for this option. Indeed, it was simply mandated that insurers begin to offer this option.

10. Measures of interest rate sensitivity that take into account the interest-sensitive cash flows of an asset or liability stream are referred to as "effective duration and convexity," or alternatively, "option-adjusted duration and convexity." Measures of interest rate sensitivity that assume all cash flows are fixed, or at least insensitive to movements in interest rates, include "modified duration and convexity" and "Macaulay duration."

11. For example, we estimated the duration on a block of participating whole life policies for one mutual company. Its Macaulay duration was around 22 years, while its effective duration was approximately 5.6. See Lamm-Tennant (1989) for a revealing survey of the level of sophistication in understanding and applying duration and Babbel (1994) for a discussion of the pitfalls in using the older duration measures.

12. See Babbel, Merrill and Panning (1997) for an explanation of the correction procedure.

13. "Baa category" should be interpreted to mean having a rating no lower than either Baa3 (by Moody's) or BBB- (by Standard & Poor's).

14. At market value: includes debentures and preferreds.

15. See Altman and Vanderhoof (1998), and Babbel and Merrill (1999).

16. See Babbel (1998).

References

Altman, E. and I. Vanderhoof (eds.), *Fair Value of Insurance Liabilities*, Norwell, MA: Kluwer, 1998.

Alexander, J., P. Bouyoucos, M. Siegel, and A. Gola. "The Goldman Sachs Insurer CIO Survey," *Industry Resource Group*, (May 1994).

Babbel, D. "A Perspective on Model Investment Laws for Insurers," *C.L.U. Journal*, (September 1994).

Babbel, D. "Financial Valuation of Insurance Liabilities," in E. Altman and I. Vanderhoof (eds.), *Fair Value of Insurance Liabilities*, Norwell, MA: Kluwer, 1998.

Babbel, D. and C. Merrill. "Toward a Unified Valuation Model for Life Insurers," in D. Cummins and A. Santomero (eds.), *Changes in the Life Insurance Industry: Efficiency, Technology and Risk Management*, 1999.

Babbel, D. "Asset-Liability Matching in the Life Insurance Industry," in E. Altman and I. Vanderhoof (eds.), *The Financial Dynamics of the Insurance Industry*, Irwin Press, 1994.

Babbel, D. and D. Klock. "Insurance Pedagogy: Executive Opinions and Priorities," *Journal of Risk and Insurance*, (December 1988).

Babbel, D. and J. Lamm-Tennant. "Trends in Asset/Liability Management for Life Insurers," *Insurance Perspectives*, Goldman Sachs, (November 1987).

Babbel, D., C. Merrill, and W. Panning. "Default Risk and the Effective Duration of Bonds," *Financial Analysts Journal*, (January/February 1997).

Babbel, D., R. Stricker, and I. Vanderhoof. "A Modern Approach to Performance Measurement for Insurers," in R.L. D'Ecclesia and S.A. Zenios (eds.), *Operations Research Models in Quantitative Finance*, Physica-Verlag, 1994.

Barton, E., G. Bodnar, and A. Kaul. "Exchange Rate Variability and the Riskiness of U.S. Multinational Firms: Evidence from the Breakdown of the Bretton Woods System," Working Paper 94–6, Wharton Weiss Center, 1994.

Beard, R., T. Pentikäinen, and E. Pesonen. *Risk Theory*, 3rd ed., New York: Chapman and Hall, 1984.

Beaver, W. and G. Parker. *Risk Management, Problems and Solutions*, New York: McGraw Hill, 1995.

Black, K. Jr. and H. Skipper, Jr. *Life Insurance*, 12th ed., Englewood Cliffs, N.J.: Prentice Hall, 1994.

Bouyoucos, P. and M. Siegel. "The Goldman Sachs Insurer CIO Survey," *Industry Resource Group*, (October 1992).

Brander, J. and T. Lewis. "Oligopoly and Financial Structure: The Limited Liability Effect," *American Economic Review*, (December 1986).

Breeden, D. and S. Viswanathan. "Why Do Firms Hedge? An Asymmetric Information Model," Working Paper, Duke University, 1990.

Campbell, T. and W. Kracaw. *Financial Risk Management: Fixed Income and Foreign Exchange*, New York: Harper Collins, 1993.

Campbell, T. and W. Kracaw. "Information Production, Market Signaling and the Theory of Financial Intermediation," *Journal of Finance*, 1980.

Cummins, J. and R. Derrig. *Financial Models of Insurance Solvency*, Norwell, MA: Kluwer Academic Publishers, 1989.

DeMarzo, P. and D. Duffie. "Corporate Incentives for Hedging and Hedge Accounting," Working Paper, Northwestern University, 1992.

Doherty, N. *Corporate Risk Management: A Financial Exposition*, New York: McGraw Hill, 1985.

Fazzari, S., R. Hubbard, and B. Petersen. "Financial Constraints and Corporate Investment," *Brookings Papers on Economic Activity*, 1988.

Fite, D. and P. Pfleiderer. "Should Firms Use Derivatives to Manage Risk?" in Beaver and Parker (eds.), *Risk Management Problems and Solutions*, New York: McGraw Hill, 1995.

Froot, K., D. Scharfstein, and J. Stein. "A Framework for Risk Management," *Harvard Business Review*, (November 1994).

Froot, K., D. Scharfstein, and J. Stein. "Risk Management: Coordinating Investment and Financing Policies," *Journal of Finance*, (December 1993).

Geezy, D., B. Minton, and C. Schrand. "Why Firms Hedge: Distinguishing Among Existing Theories," Working Paper, 1995.

Gennotte, G. and D. Pyle. "Capital Controls and Bank Risk," *Journal of Banking and Finance*, (September 1991).

Gerber, H. *An Introduction to Mathematical Risk Theory*, Homewood, IL: Richard D. Irwin, Inc., 1979.

Greenawalt, M. and J. Sinkey. "Bank Loan Loss Provisions and the Income Smoothing Hypothesis: An Empirical Analysis," *Journal of Financial Services Research*, (December 1988).

Helfat, C. and D. Teece. "Vertical Integration and Risk Reduction," *Journal of Law, Economics and Organization*, (Spring 1987).

Herring, R. and A. Santomero. "The Corporate Structure of Financial Conglomerates," *Journal of Financial Services Research*, (December 1990).

Hoshi, T., A. Kashyap, and D. Scharfstein. "Corporate Structure, Liquidity, and Investment: Evidence from Japanese Industrial Groups," *Quarterly Journal of Economics*, 1991.

Jorion, P. "The Pricing of Exchange Rate Risk in the U.S. Equity Markets," *Journal of Financial and Quantitative Analysis*, (July 1991).

Lamm-Tennant, J. "Asset/Liability Management for the Life Insurer: Situation Analysis and Strategy Formulation," *Journal of Risk and Insurance*, (September 1989).

——. "Survey and Commentary on Investment Policies and Practices of the U.S. Insurance Industry," Chantilly, VA: Chalke Incorporated, 1995.

Lamm-Tennant, J. and D. Gattis. "Survey and Commentary on Investment Policies and Practices of the U.S. Insurance Industry," Bloomfield, CT: SS&C, 1996.

Lamm-Tennant, J. and T. Rollins. "Incentives for Discretionary Accounting Practices: Ownership Structure, Earnings and Taxation," *Journal of Risk and Insurance*, (September 1994).

Litterman, R. and K. Winkelmann. "Managing Market Exposure," *Risk Management Series*, New York: Goldman, Sachs & Co., (January 1996).

Marcus, A. "Deregulation and Bank Financial Policy," *Journal of Banking and Finance*, (December 1984).

Maksimovic, V. "Capital Structure in Reported Oligopolies," (*Rand Journal of Economics*, Autumn) 1988.

Merton, R. "Financial Innovation and the Management and Regulation of Financial Institutions," *Journal of Banking and Finance*, (June 1995).

——. "On the Application of the Continuous-Time Theory of Finance to Financial Intermediation and Insurance," *Geneva Papers on Risk and Insurance*, (July 1989).

Millette, M., A. Levinson, and J. Oleinick. "The Goldman Sachs Insurer CIO Survey," Industry Resource Group, (June 1996).

Moody's Investor Services. *Moody's Credit Ratings and Research*, Moody's 1995.

Myers, S., "Determinants of Corporate Borrowing," *Journal of Financial Economics*, 1990.

Nance, D., C. Smith, and C. Smithson. "On the Determinants of Corporate Hedging," *Journal of Finance*, 1993.

Oldfield, G. and A. Santomero. "The Place of Risk Management in Financial Institutions," *Sloan Management Review*, (Fall 1997).

Ross, S. "The Determination of Financial Structure: The Incentive Signaling Approach," *Bell Journal of Economics*, (Spring 1977).

Ross, S. "The Economic Theory of Agency: The Principal's Problem," *American Economic Review*, (May 1973).

Santomero, A. "Financial Risk Management: The Whys and Hows," *Financial Markets, Institutions, and Investments*, (December 1995).

Santomero, A. "Commercial Bank Risk Management: An Analysis of the Process," *Journal of Financial Services Research*, (October/December 1997).

——. "The Changing Structure of Financial Institutions: A Review Essay," *Journal of Monetary Economics*, 1989.

Scholes, M., G. Wilson, and M. Wolfson. "Tax Planning, Regulatory Capital Planning and Financial Reporting Strategy for Commercial Banks," *Review of Financial Studies*, 1990.

Siegel, M., M. Millette, and D. Pouraghabagher. "The Goldman Sachs Insurer CIO Survey," *Industry Resource Group*, (April 1995).

Smith, C. and R. Stulz. "The Determinants of Firm's Hedging Policies," *Journal of Financial and Quantitative Analysis*, 1985.

Smith, C., C. Smithson, and D. Wilford. *Strategic Risk Management*, New York: Harper and Row, 1990.

Smith, M. "The Life Insurance Policy as an Options Package," *Journal of Risk and Insurance*, (September 1982).

Staking, K. and D. Babbel. "The Relation between Capital Structure, Interest Rate Sensitivity, and Market Value in the Property-Liability Insurance Industry," *Journal of Risk and Insurance*, (December 1995).

Stulz, R. "Optimal Hedging Policies," *Journal of Financial and Quantitative Analysis*, 1984.

Warner, J. "Bankruptcy Costs: Some Evidence," *Journal of Finance*, (May 1977).

Weiss, L. "Bankruptcy Resolution: Direct Costs and Violation of Priority Claims," *Journal of Finance and Economics*, 1990.

10 CHALLENGES AND ISSUES FOR GROWTH IN THE LIFE INDUSTRY

Michael R. Tuohy

1. Introduction

It is obvious that the entire financial services industry is in the midst of a period of massive transition. Regulatory barriers are falling even as the market restructures in anticipation of the new environment. Life insurers are facing much tougher competition, with nontraditional players redefining what is needed to succeed in the marketplace. As customers gain access to more information, they are becoming more demanding and are increasingly willing to turn to alternative products to satisfy their financial needs. Distribution channels continue to be rationalized, realigned, and redefined in response to these competitive pressures and customer demands.

This chapter has three objectives. First, it is intended to recap several of the major trends that have been shaping the life insurance landscape, including:

- Convergence and consolidation of financial services
- Rise of investment-oriented insurance products
- Evolution of insurance distribution

- Restructuring of mutual insurance company entities
- Moving beyond market-conduct issues.

Some of these trends were presented in Chapter 1. This discussion is intended to provide a high level, concise description of the major forces and lay the groundwork for a discussion of the future; it is not, however, an in-depth analysis.

The second objective is to summarize the top concerns and priorities of life insurance chief economic officers (CEOs), based on a recent Tillinghast–Towers Perrin CEO survey, thus providing insight into the strategic thinking of the executives who are leading the industry through these turbulent times. The third objective is to comment on where the industry may be headed in the coming years.

The discussion in this chapter is focused on the individual (i.e., retail) life insurance industry in the United States.

2. Key Trends

2.1. Convergence and Consolidation of Financial Services

For years, there has been talk of industry consolidation and restructuring. It has now become a reality. Large, integrated financial service organizations that combine elements of the previously "siloed" insurance, brokerage, investment management, and banking sectors are being created.

The competitive landscape of financial services has changed in fundamental ways over the past two decades, as shown in figure 10-1. Twenty years ago, the financial services industry consisted of three distinct sectors. Insurance companies sold traditional insurance products (life insurance and annuities) to the mass market through their agents. Insurers' competitive advantages resulted from their products and unique customer-agent relationships. Banks sold transaction-oriented products, such as deposit accounts and certificates of deposit (CDs), to the mass market through branches. The banks' competitive advantages included convenience, security, and a protected geographic franchise. The third major sector, securities/brokerage firms, sold investment products through brokers. Their competitive advantages came from the products they provided and their knowledge of the customer, as well as investment research, advice, and transaction capabilities.

Today, the financial services industry is increasingly comprised of an integrated group of providers competing to serve customers through multiple

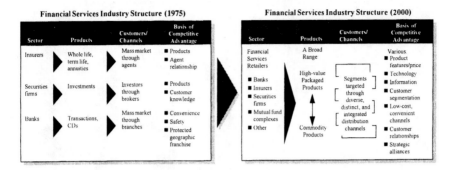

Figure 10-1. The Changing Financial Services Industry

distribution channels. Financial services retailers—including banks, insurers, securities firms and mutual fund companies—offer a spectrum of products ranging from high-value packaged products to commodity items. As the authors pointed out in Chapter 1, distinctions are blurring as to which type of company offers which product. Banks are selling annuities and, to a lesser extent life insurance, insurance companies are beginning to offer bank-like products, and many insurers own mutual fund and asset management companies. All financial service companies now seek to target customers through distinct and integrated distribution channels. Perceived competitive advantages stem from product features, price, technology, information, customer segmentation, distribution channel efficiency, customer relationships, and strategic alliances. A provider no longer enjoys a unique (or protected) competitive advantage by virtue of the financial services sector from which it emerged.

Partly in response to the challenges from other financial service sectors, the life insurance industry is consolidating. Consolidation is being spurred by a combination of slow revenue growth, overcapacity, the need for cost reduction and the desire to achieve economies of scale. However, companies are also seeking access to critical capabilities (such as distribution, asset management, and technology), complementary product lines, and risk diversification. The number of publicly announced acquisitions of life/health companies has been steadily increasing through the decade (as depicted in figure 10-2) and the level of merger and acquisition activity shows no signs of abating. Selected significant transactions for the year 1998 are listed in figure 10-3.

This convergence and consolidation is occurring in the context of an increasingly deregulated environment—the legal barriers that have traditionally differentiated and protected the different sectors are breaking down.

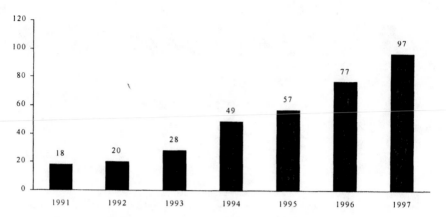

Figure 10-2.   Publicly Announced Life/Health Acquisitions*

*Includes acquisitions of companies as well as major blocks of business (e.g., Lincoln National's acquisition of CIGNA's life insurance business).
Source: *The Actuarial Digest.*

Acquirer	Acquired Entity	Announce-ment Date	Transaction	Amount (US$M)
Citicorp	Travelers	4/98	Merger	$70,000
AIG	SunAmerica	8/98	Acquisition	18,000
Conseco	Green Tree Financial Corp.	4/98	Acquisition	7,600
Swiss Re	Life Re	8/98	Acquisition	1,800
Nationwide Life	Allied Mutual Insurance Co.	*9/98	Merger	1,600
Lincoln National	CIGNA (individual life and annuity business)	*1Q 98	Acquisition	1,400
Lincoln National	Aetna (individual life business)	6/98	Acquisition	1,000
Northwestern Mutual	Frank Russell Co.	8/98	Acquisition	1,000
Fortis	John Alden	3/98	Acquisition	600

Figure 10-3.   Selected Significant 1998 Transactions
* Transaction date.

Although banks are still generally prohibited from directly underwriting mortality risk, many bank holding companies have created insurance subsidiaries or entered into partnerships or agreements to distribute insurers' products. Similarly, insurance companies may now engage in selective non-insurance-related activities, including brokerage, mutual funds, institutional asset management and financial planning. For example, a number of life insurers have applied for (or obtained) thrift licenses, primarily in order to offer trust-related services. The ultimate regulatory development may well be the eventual repeal of Glass-Steagall, the decades-old legislation that keeps apart the different financial service sectors.

Perhaps the most dramatic example of convergence through consolidation is the recent merger of Citicorp and Travelers to form a true financial conglomerate, CitiGroup (discussed in Chapter 1). Other mega-mergers can be expected as competitive pressures accelerate the trend toward convergence.

If the CitiGroup merger is the most obvious example of the converging paths, many subtler signposts exist. One such signpost is the general migration of executive talent into the insurance industry from other financial service sectors. For example, the CEOs of the two largest U.S. life insurance companies have come from other sectors of the financial world. Art Ryan, CEO of The Prudential Insurance Company of America, spent most of his career at Chase Manhattan Bank, while Robert Benmosche of Metropolitan Life Insurance Company came from Paine Webber. Non-insurance executives now populate the executive ranks of such high profile insurers as Equitable, New York Life, Aetna, Manulife, and others.

Clearly, the competitive environment has intensified and it shows no signs of abating. Insurers are facing competition from both traditional and nontraditional sources. For example, traditional life insurance distribution has lost ground relative to other financial services sectors, particularly with respect to asset accumulation products (e.g., annuities). Banks have been very successful with annuities, but still have a long way to go when it comes to life insurance. Mutual fund complexes pose a serious threat to insurers because of their large scale, advanced technology platforms, efficient operations, and brand recognition. Finally, brokerage firms are gaining ground, particularly in the current bull market.

The direct results of continued convergence, consolidation, and intense competition will be increased market share concentration among fewer, larger companies and the further growth of nontraditional competitors. What are the implications for life insurers, and who will emerge as "winners" in the new marketplace? It appears likely that the winners will be large national and multi-national companies, as well as the niche players

who are able to capitalize on a particular market need and exploit strategic advantage. Many insurers with large customer bases, powerful distribution franchises, and a well-defined market focus are well positioned to
succeed in the new environment. Small and medium insurers, who lack scale
and the capital to invest in important new technologies and who lack
leveragable capabilities, will likely be less successful.

2.2. Rise of Investment-oriented Products

Over the past few decades, the balance of power in the U.S. financial services industry has shifted. Not only have nontraditional financial service
competitors been encroaching on each others' territories, but the share of
personal financial assets held by intermediaries has also changed dramatically. As figure 10-4 shows, thrifts and commercial banks have been the
primary victims of this shift, as they have found themselves increasingly dis-
intermediated. In contrast, mutual fund complexes and money market managers have grown dramatically. Insurers experienced a slow but steady
decline from a 20% share of personal assets in 1970 to about 10% in 1986.
Around 1986, the decline ended and life insurers began gaining share, albeit
at a slow rate.

The shift in market share reflects a fundamental shift in the balance sheet

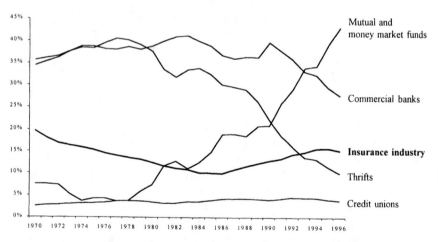

Figure 10-4.   United States Market Share of Personal Assets Held by
Intermediaries

Source: Tillinghast–Towers Perrin.

of the U.S. household toward increasing risk since the early 1980s. This increased risk has resulted from a growing interest in (and tolerance for) participating in the financial markets, either through direct purchases of debt and equity securities or, more commonly, through purchases of packaged products such as mutual funds. In addition, as defined benefit retirement plans have become less common, defined contribution plans have grown to be significant sources of consumer participation in the financial market(s).

These factors have made it increasingly difficult for life insurers to attract savings dollars from consumers. As figure 10-5 shows, between 1981 and 1995 only traditional bank products have grown more slowly than life insurance reserves (7%) among the major categories of financial assets on the U.S. household balance sheet.

However, life insurers have realized some benefit from consumers' increasing appetite for investment-oriented financial products as suggested by figure 10-6, which presents detail of the life insurer trend line shown in figure 10-4. The trend line is composed of two elements: life insurance (of which the majority is traditional protection-oriented products) and annuities (fixed, variable and equity indexed). Clearly, the annuity business has

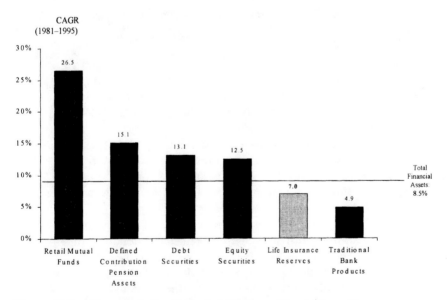

Figure 10-5. Changes in the Household Balance Sheet (Percent)
Sources: Federal Reserve Board, FDIC, ICI, Bernstein Research.

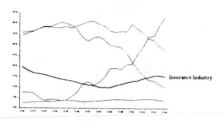

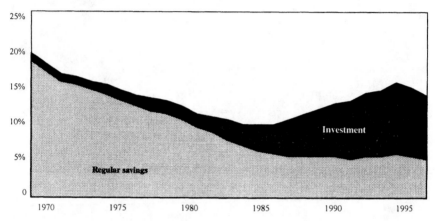

Figure 10-6.   United States Market Share of Personal Assets Held by Insurance Companies

Source: Tillinghast–Towers Perrin.

accounted for the growth in the life insurance industry over the past 10 years. While individual life policy sales have dropped roughly 35% since 1975, annuity deposits have nearly tripled in the last decade. This product shift (and the associated differential in commissions) has dramatically impacted the economic viability of traditional insurance distribution.

Figure 10-7 shows the growth in annuity sales in recent years. Most recently, variable annuity sales have far exceeded both those of fixed annuities and those of the newer equity-indexed annuities (which share elements of both fixed and variable products). Not surprisingly, the strong performance of the U.S. stock market has drawn consumers toward variable annuities while the low interest rate environment has generally dampened the appeal of fixed annuities.

Looking ahead, demographic changes (some of which were discussed in the first chapter) will continue to shape demand for investment-oriented life insurance and other financial products. Two dynamics in particular are likely to have a significant impact: the expected pattern of intergenerational

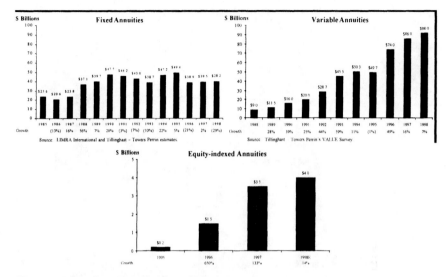

Figure 10-7. Growth in Annuity Sales
Source: LIMRA International and Tillinghast–Towers Perrin estimates.
Source: Tillinghast–Towers Perrin's VALUE Survey.
Source: Tillinghast–Towers Perrin's ELITE Survey.

wealth transfer over the next two decades and the growth in the population of the "highest saving" 45- to 64-year-old age group (see figure 10-8). The increasing intergenerational wealth transfer should enhance *long-term* demand for estate planning life insurance products. It will also, ultimately, generate future dollars available for investment. In the *near term*, however, the aging of the U.S. population is likely to fuel further demand for investment-oriented (and retirement) products at the expense of traditional life insurance products.

2.3. Evolution of Insurance Distribution

Within the insurance industry, distribution effectiveness is a critical driver of company performance. Over the past decades, the nature and structure of distribution has evolved—in part, responding to marketplace changes and, in part, contributing to them.

The first stage (Stage 1) of retail life insurance distribution, the "traditional agency distribution model," prospered through the 1970s and into the

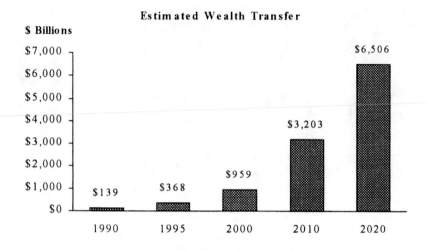

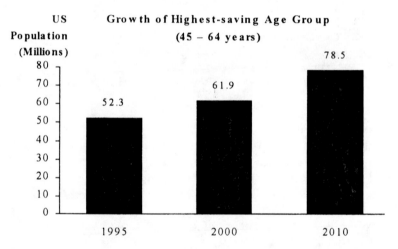

Figure 10-8.

Sources: US Department of Commerce, Bureau of the Census, Bernstein Research, Cornell University, Towers Perrin analysis.

early 1980s. Whole life insurance was the focus and selling was agent-driven using a personalized, needs-based approach. The industry and market were relatively stable. The business economics focused management's attention on the "top line" (i.e., the company with the most agents garnered the most growth and gained market share). Absent close competition from non-insurance products, the whole life product's pricing carried all of the distribution costs and companies enjoyed profitable growth. Through the 1970s, term insurance remained something of a niche product, while annuities and mutual funds were insignificant. Career agency companies dominated and competed fiercely with each other to attract and retain agents.

The second stage (Stage 2) of evolution (early 1980s to early 1990s) began as life companies responded to the emerging competition of money market funds, which experienced explosive growth because of unprecedented high interest rates in the late 1970s and early 1980s. The slogan "buy term insurance and invest the difference" became a driving force. Career agency systems continued to dominate life insurance distribution, but the product mix shifted. Whole life gradually gave way to universal life (UL) and, eventually, variable life and variable universal life. Also, term insurance gained a share of new sales. While agent distribution dominated, agents' sales approaches increasingly focused on policy illustrations and interest rates—investment features tended to supplant the protection orientation that prevailed in Stage 1.

Given management's continued focus on increasing new sales, the industry appeared to prosper during the 1980s. However, with the benefit of hindsight, many of these "new" sales were merely the replacement of more profitable, in-force, whole life policies by new UL policies. The cost of these new product sales, especially distribution costs and the higher costs of administering new, flexible premium products, tended to exceed pricing allowances and squeeze profit margins. Stage 2 was also the beginning of the convergence of previously distinct financial service sectors. Towards the end of Stage 2, fixed annuities experienced significant growth, reinforcing the shift in emphasis towards interest rates and investment returns, as well as the start of many agents' shift towards investment products.

Stage 3, which began in the early to mid-1990s, was marked by the emergence of distribution productivity as the life industry's primary challenge. Increased scrutiny by rating agencies and investors obliged management to focus on expenses, capital management and the bottom line. New life insurance sales dropped for many companies. As management's attention focused increasingly on the financial bottom-line, the requirements, challenges and potential benefits of distribution have become far more apparent. Encouraged by the realization that consumers were increasingly responsible for anticipating and managing their retirement needs, the market has shifted towards increasing demand for investment products and services. This, in turn, has accelerated the convergence of the financial services industry, and brought a variety of traditional and nontraditional distribution approaches together in a more integrated marketplace.

With flexible premium products having replaced much of the in-force whole life business, new policy sales are declining; investment products (i.e., variable annuities) are experiencing significant growth, paralleling the interest in and performance of equity markets. Stage 3 is characterized by increased competition, diminished new business profitability, rapid maturing of permanent insurance, decline in new life sales and a significant shift of product mix to investment products. As a result, the industry is rethinking approaches to distribution. For many, the old Stage 1 or Stage 2 model of distribution is no longer relevant or viable. Perhaps the straw on the camel's back has been the scrutiny focused on sales practices from the 1980s onward. The financial consequences, as well as the damage to reputation, of market conduct litigation has reinforced management's desire to get right its future approach to distribution.

In Stage 3, we are witnessing management posing fundamental questions about their companies' distribution future, the extent to which they will focus on the retail distribution business and, if so, what approach to distribution will work best for them. In essence, Stage 3 marks the point at which the value of distribution as a business has begun to be recognized, reinforced by the willingness of independent manufacturers to pay high fees to access the more powerful distribution franchises. There is an increasing amount of experimentation, with companies establishing additional and different channels of distribution as they find new ways to grow (as the authors discussed in Chapter 1). Distribution is seen as an integral part of the entire customer value proposition, and as one of the few means of sustaining competitive advantage in retail financial services—if one can get it right. Some companies are rethinking their approach to distribution and trying to become much more customer focused, including more disciplined and active efforts to understand distribution economics and customer segmentation and profitability. The industry has shifted from "life insurance distribution" to "company distribution" of a varied array of products. For many companies, counselor-selling remains core but also a focus on a broader range of consumer needs.

The future of distribution, Stage 4, is likely to be a quite varied picture. As with the maturing of any market, financial institutions will focus their efforts on identifying distinct market segments or niches for which a number of specific product-distribution approaches will be tailored. Thus "distribution" will evolve from a few, simple, and nearly universal models to a diversity of distribution-product-market segment approaches based on distinct market segment opportunities, management interests, and company capabilities.

2.4. Mutual Company Restructuring

Primarily in response to the changing insurance and financial services environment, mutual life insurance companies are restructuring at an increasing rate. Intensifying competition, a desire to increase access to capital, a need to overcome slow growth, and a desire to instill the financial discipline imposed by financial markets have all contributed significantly to the pace of this restructuring.

As the financial services industry continues to converge, spurring a flurry of merger and acquisition activity, mutual insurers may find it difficult to participate. By restructuring, the insurance company has the opportunity to use its stock as acquisition "currency." Another advantage of having stock is that it can be used as a form of compensation (typically through stock options); this is increasingly important for insurers who are attempting to attract top talent in a highly competitive financial services labor market.

Mutual company restructuring is a complex and highly regulated process, and it typically requires 18 to 36 months to complete. Mutual company restructuring can take several forms. The two primary forms are full demutualizations and conversions to a mutual holding company, both of which require approval from the insurer's board of directors, policyholders, and regulators.

Under a full demutualization, a mutual company undergoes an outright conversion to a stock company. Policyholder membership rights are exchanged for consideration, which could be in the form of common stock in the resulting stock company, cash, or additional benefits. The company may also choose to raise additional capital by offering shares of the company to the public through an initial public offering.

The formation of a mutual holding company creates an ownership structure in which the company is converted into a mutual holding company with a stock life insurance company subsidiary. Shares in the stock company may be issued to the public, but more than 50% of the shares must be owned by the holding company. This structure provides access to capital without ceding control to shareholders and ensures that the entity cannot be taken over in a hostile bid. However, some find the mutual holding company structure objectionable because existing policyholders do not realize as much value in the near term for the restructuring as they would under a full demutualization.

Other possible avenues of mutual restructuring are mergers among mutual insurers, and the formation of a downstream stock company. Figure 10-9 elaborates on the advantages and disadvantages of various restructuring options, including the option of maintaining the status quo.

Option	Pros	Cons

Status Quo	■ Retain advantages of mutual structure and approach
	  ■ Long-term perspective
	  ■ Singular focus on policyholders
	  ■ Marketplace "story"
	■ Preserve independence—no outside takeover threat
		■ Retain disadvantages of mutual structure
		  ■ Capital access/flexibility
		  ■ No stock acquisition currency
		  ■ Ability to attract/retain top management talent over the long term
		■ Continuing pressure to act over time—last mutual standing?

Mutual-to-Mutual Merger	■ Same as above, plus whatever benefits (scale, capital strength, distribution access) accrue from the merger	■ Scarcity of eligible/desirable partners ■ Does not resolve capital access, acquisition and executive compensation issues
Mutual Holding Company	■ Retain mutual structure, but with stockholder company benefits ■ Less expensive and time-consuming process (as compared to full demutualization) ■ Long-term flexibility to change structure at later date ■ Maintain independence without outside takeover threat	■ Strong negative sentiment in the press and public concerning the structure; ability to pass MHC legislation in New York doubtful ■ Increasing pressure from full demutualization as policyholders receive current value ■ Some constraint on ability to raise equity capital
Downstream Stock Company	■ Ability to realize value of subsidiary companies ■ Raise capital quickly ■ Relatively inexpensive form of restructuring ■ Retain mutual structure at parent company level—preserve independence ■ Gain some degree of stock currency for acquisitions	■ Cannot unlock full value of company—scope limited to non-par insurance and all non-insurance businesses ■ Subsidiary IPOs, while attractive, may not offer enough scale and therefore acquisition currency is limited ■ Structural complexity and potential conflict regarding future reorganization
Full Demutuali-zation	■ Complete transfer of value to existing policyholders ■ Maximum flexibility with respect to capital access, acquisitions, etc. ■ Favorably viewed by key constituencies (rating agencies, capital markets) ■ Provides for greater financial management discipline	■ Time-consuming and x costly process ■ Requires give-up of (deeply ingrained) mutual philosophy and culture ■ Potential displacement of long-term focus ■ Greatest degree of change ■ Risk of takeover

Figure 10-9.   Advantages and Disadvantages of Restructuring Options

The restructuring trend in the United States is still in a relatively early stage compared with countries such as Australia and the United Kingdom. UNUM's demutualization in 1986 and Equitable's in 1992 were among the first in the United States. Lately, though, many prominent mutual companies have initiated or announced plans to restructure (see figure 10-10). The MONY Group (previously Mutual of New York) completed its demutualization in November 1998 and Prudential, MetLife, and John Hancock are in the process of restructuring through a full demutualization. Companies that have completed mutual holding company restructuring include AmerUs, Pacific Life, Principal Life, and General American; others are pending, including National Life, Provident Mutual, and Security Benefit. Some companies considering restructuring plans, such as New York Life, have been vocal in their support for mutual holding company legislation.

The restructuring of a significant number of mutual life insurers will likely have a profound impact on the competitive landscape. Today's largest U.S. life insurers are mutual companies that are constrained in how they raise capital and in how they form partnerships and alliances. As these

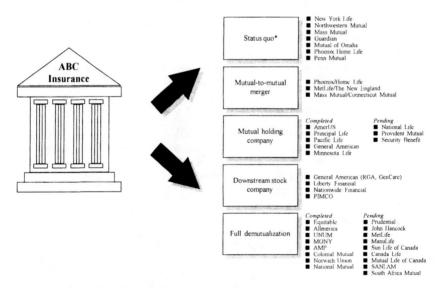

Figure 10-10.   Examples of Selected Restructuring Options

Note: Faded names indicate non-U.S. insurers.

*As of November 1998. Many of these companies are considering restructuring plans.

companies shed their mutual ownership structure, they will be presented with new opportunities. Provided they can sustain the level of performance expected of public companies, these insurers will emerge as major new competitors. In addition, they will be free to seek mergers with other public companies and form alliances that had previously been impossible. The result may be financial giants competing in arenas from which they had been *de facto* excluded until now.

2.5. Market Conduct and Compliance

As a result of the aggressive pursuit of sales and revenue growth in the 1980s and early 1990s, many companies face legal action resulting from allegedly questionable sales practices. Market conduct and compliance issues have become more visible and costly over the past few years despite the wish of life insurance companies to downplay them. Expected settlements of related litigation are estimated in the billions of dollars. As a result, the industry's image has suffered, and future revenue may be affected. These market conduct issues are costly to settle, can damage a company's reputation, and can be a significant distraction to management.

Insurers are responding to compliance and market conduct issues in a variety of ways. Most companies are strengthening their compliance function to ensure adherence to stated policies and procedures. Most major companies are also participating in the Insurance Marketplace Standards Association (IMSA), (discussed below) and are improving their agent training. Other responses include assuming greater control of sales activities in the home office, imposing greater sanctions on agents for noncompliance and more aggressively auditing new business cases.

IMSA is a self-regulating body created in 1997 to address sales and marketing practices. Its purpose is to facilitate, advance and promote ethical market conduct in the life insurance industry and, by doing so, to stave off looming state and federal regulation. IMSA's scope covers sales and marketing practices for individually sold life insurance and annuity policies, through all distribution channels of U.S. operations. Membership in IMSA is voluntary and conditional on a certified assessment.

What might be the next reaction to these market conduct issues? One possibility is regulatory action, which may range from minor regulations governing promotional materials and illustrations, to sweeping regulatory changes such as establishing a compulsory nationwide code of conduct. Another possibility is the adoption of commission disclosure, a practice adopted in the United Kingdom in 1995 and in Australia in 1994. In the near term, this change would force a rethinking of point-of-sale presentation by agents and companies. Over the longer term, sales may also shift toward low-load and no-load products.

Opinions are split as to whether the industry's compliance problems are behind it or whether the worst is yet to come. While many believe that the majority of issues are behind them, others expect several more years of negative publicity, class-action lawsuits, and other issues to arise.

3. Concerns and Priorities of Life Insurance CEOs

Against a backdrop of major industry restructuring and within the context of the trends just discussed, Tillinghast–Towers Perrin undertook a survey of life insurance CEOs to explore how industry executives are addressing these challenges. The findings presented here provide insight into the industry's response to this dynamic competitive environment from the viewpoint of the executives at the helm. Many of the key findings are consistent with those of the WFIC Insurance Survey discussed in Chapter 2. In addition, both surveys seemed to highlight the diversity of CEOs' responses—there does not appear to be one commonly recognized model for success.

Tillinghast–Towers Perrin surveyed CEOs of approximately 300 of the largest life insurers in the United States and Canada. The findings are based on confidential responses received from 90 of them, a 30% response rate. The respondents, both stock and mutual companies, have individual life and annuity reserves ranging from less than $500 million to well over $20 billion.

3.1. CEOs' Top Concerns

CEOs are most concerned with distribution channel productivity, increased competition, and changing market/customer demands, as shown in figure 10-11. These issues are closely linked. Solving the distribution dilemma will be critical to maintaining or improving competitive position within the industry. The entry of a new and more cost-efficient set of competitors is forcing insurers to act quickly and decisively. Winners will be those insurers who are able to find ways to meet customers' demands for greater value, while maintaining adequate profitability and satisfying the needs of their distribution systems. Those with an undisciplined or tentative approach to change are likely to fall by the wayside.

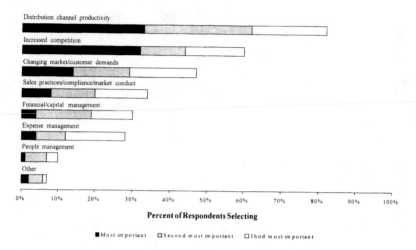

Figure 10-11. Key Strategic Issues Facing Life Insurers

Source: Tillinghast–Towers Perrin 1997 Life Insurance Industry CEO Survey Report.

Distribution channel productivity is CEOs' number-one concern. While executives acknowledge the need to address the symptoms—high costs/low productivity and agent recruiting, retention and training—they are most concerned with the root causes. CEOs believe the alignment of customer, agent, and company interests is the primary distribution challenge facing their companies. They seem to recognize that without this alignment, they may be paying too much for things that neither they nor their customers value.

Increased competition is CEOs' second greatest concern. Nearly all CEOs expect dramatic changes in the competitive landscape over the next five years. Life insurance executives expect the merger and acquisition wave that has swept the financial services landscape (from insurers to banks to brokerage firms to asset management companies) to accelerate and intensify. CEOs are nearly unanimous in their conviction that the industry will see an increase in nontraditional competitors.

CEOs are also concerned about changing market/customer demands. To satisfy an increasingly demanding customer, executives believe their companies need to provide better customer service and make greater use of technology to distribute and service products. They also believe that they need to find ways to improve their acquisition and use of customer/household information. Executives recognize that the industry's historically loose connection with its customer base cannot continue.

Most chief executives are also not satisfied that their companies have effectively leveraged their existing customer/household relationships, in terms of growing either their protection or asset accumulation/investment businesses. Most believe that their customer base represents a significant untapped asset that must be more effectively cultivated. Consumers have more and more options available to satisfy their savings and protection needs. Many of these options are easier to understand and access, and less expensive than existing life insurance products. Insurers are responding by more finely segmenting the market and focusing on profitable niches.

3.2. Company Responses to Top Concerns

3.2.1. Distribution Productivity. Insurers are taking aggressive action to address their top challenge, distribution productivity (see figure 10-12). They are looking to technology, alternative distribution methods and strengthened compliance procedures. The most popular strategy is to increase their use of technology. Companies are using technology both to improve the productivity of their agents (e.g., expert underwriting, access to better information) and to explore alternative distribution approaches (e.g., Internet, kiosks).

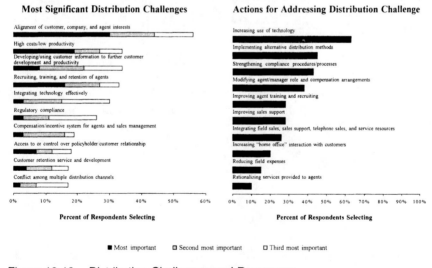

Figure 10-12.   Distribution Challenges and Responses

Source: Tillinghast–Towers Perrin 1997 Life Insurance Industry CEO Survey Report.

Many companies are also implementing alternative distribution methods. These alternative channels include banks, direct response (e.g., direct mail, telemarketing, Internet), broker-dealers, joint ventures/alliances with other companies, and fee-based approaches. Interest in financial planning seems to have increased, both as a tool for wrapping around the customer relationship and as a channel of distribution, whether fee-based, fee-only, or commission-oriented. The big issue is how to implement alternative channels without disrupting current channels. As companies begin to distribute through multiple channels, the issue of channel conflict will become increasingly important. As in the WFIC Insurance Survey, CEOs seem to think that there will be fairly dramatic changes in how life insurance products are distributed.

Companies are also strengthening their compliance processes/procedures in an attempt to address distribution challenges. In the past, CEOs seemed to focus on more traditional approaches to improving distribution productivity, including improving agent training and recruiting and modifying compensation arrangements.

The strategies companies are using to respond to distribution challenges vary by size and type of company. Large companies are much more likely to be increasing the use of technology than small companies, probably reflecting the ability to amortize the higher cost of technological improvements over a larger customer and capital base. They are also much more likely to be modifying agent/management compensation arrangements. Small companies, however, are more likely to be improving sales support. Finally, mutual companies are much more likely than stock companies to be improving agent training and recruiting.

With alternative distribution methods becoming more popular, it is important to understand what forms of distribution CEOs believe to be most effective for the distribution of individual life products and annuity products. For life insurance, traditional methods are still favored. CEOs believe PPGA to be most effective, followed by insurance brokers and general agency. For annuities, CEOs overwhelmingly favor alternative distribution methods, and their popularity is increasing. This reflects the success insurers have had in selling both fixed and variable annuities through non-agency channels. Most CEOs believe that banks are the most effective form of distribution for annuities. Many also favor securities brokers. Very few CEOs believe the branch/managerial agency system is the most effective distribution method for annuity products.

CEOs believe that banks will be the fastest-growing form of distribution for both life insurance and annuities. For life insurance, CEOs also think that direct response, fee-based financial planners, the Internet, and securities brokers will grow quickly. For annuities, CEOs think securities brokers and the Internet will become more important. CEOs seem to be much more positive about the growth prospects of the Internet than they have been in the past. Internet-related technology has greatly advanced over the past few years, and executives are recognizing that the Internet may have the potential to become an effective marketing and selling vehicle. Considerable debate still exists among executives, however, about whether the Internet will ultimately be an effective commercial channel for insurance products and services or, rather, more of a servicing medium.

3.2.2. Increased Competition.   Nearly all CEOs believe that the growth of nontraditional competitors will increase over the next five years. This is in line with CEOs' views that banks and securities brokers will be among the fastest-growing forms of distribution. Figure 10-13 lists other views on the most likely changes to the competitive structure of the industry.

The desire to achieve critical mass and scale economies and broaden distribution access will likely drive an increase in the number of mergers, acquisitions, joint ventures, and strategic alliances. Many CEOs are predicting significant increase in these activities. Some CEOs offer cautions

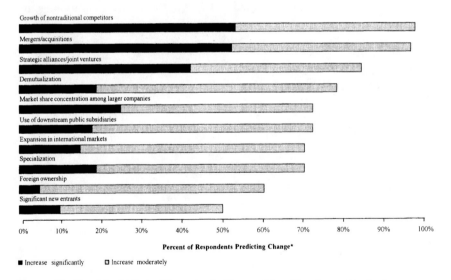

Figure 10-13.   Most Likely Changes to Competitive Structure of Industry

*Balance of respondents (to total 100%) said these items would stay the same or decrease.

Source: Tillinghast–Towers Perrin 1997 Life Insurance Industry CEO Survey Report.

about the economic success of these alliances, but seem to think they are necessary to gain market access, round out product offerings, and build critical mass. Given the predicted level of restructuring activity, it is not surprising that CEOs expect increased market share concentration over the next few years.

Chief executives also predict increased specialization as companies move away from the generalist models of today and increasingly pick and choose the market segments in which they will compete, relying on niche marketing to target the most attractive and profitable segments. One CEO predicting a significant increase in specialization commented, "As companies begin to focus on core competencies, it is logical that they narrow their focus to areas where they can be excellent."

According to CEOs, expansion into international markets will increase as companies attempt to find less mature markets that offer more attractive growth prospects. However, they believe the level of diversification by insurers will stay the same or decrease over the next five years. Nevertheless, for most companies, the need for greater focus/specialization continues to vie with the need to redeploy capital to potentially more attractive product/market segments, like asset management.

CEOs are taking a variety of actions to improve their companies' competitive positions, as shown in figure 10-14. In a new twist, companies are

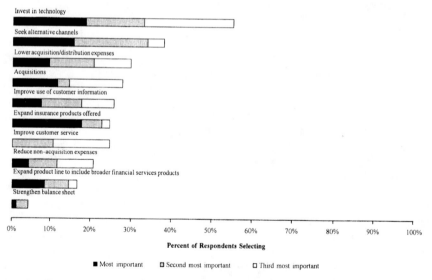

Figure 10-14.   Top Competitive Strategies
Source: Tillinghast 1997 Life Insurance Industry CEO Survey Report.

investing in technology as their primary competitive weapon. In fact, the role of technology in supporting customer acquisition, distribution productivity, and overall operations/expense improvement emerges as a major thrust among insurers across multiple functions and all lines of business. Again, this is consistent with the WFIC Insurance Survey, where the rapid and efficient harnessing of technology was thought to be important for survival and growth.

However, some CEOs expressed skepticism about the ability of insurers to compete with other financial institutions in terms of technology, particularly in the back office. They point to the huge investments in technology made by some of the large financial service players and their significant head start on the insurance industry. These CEOs question whether insurers, especially smaller ones, have the resources and ability to compete. This is particularly true in the asset accumulation business, where technology and scale are critical to profitability.

The second most popular competitive strategy is to seek alternative distribution channels. CEOs understand that if they are to reduce costs, improve productivity, participate in growth, and tap new market segments they need to find new methods of delivering their products and services.

A number of companies are also focusing on lowering their acquisition/distribution expenses, acquiring companies or blocks of business, improving their use of customer information, expanding their insurance product offering, and improving customer service. Few companies are expanding their product line to include broader financial services products or strengthening their balance sheet as their key competitive strategies.

3.2.3. Changing Market/Customer Demands.

CEOs believe that customers want greater use of technology, multiple points of access, and simpler products. These views imply that customers are looking for greater ease of use, both in the types of products they buy and how they buy them. To meet those needs, insurers are challenged to simplify what have historically been very complex products and sales processes.

CEOs also believe that customers are seeking more value from their products and services in the form of lower prices or increased benefits. However, this may be a difficult demand to meet in an environment where margins already do not provide attractive returns on investment for many companies.

Overall, CEOs feel their companies are at least somewhat prepared to meet customer demands. They are fairly confident in their ability to provide simpler products and maintain a strong surplus position/financial rating. However, they are far less comfortable with their preparedness in addressing issues of service, technology, and customer relationship management.

Most CEOs are planning to make some adjustments in their target market focus over the next three years, either broadening or narrowing it depending on company strategy. A number of companies are also tailoring distribution channels to different target market segments and developing product bundles to fit individual channels and their customers. One CEO said that while his company is broadening its target market focus overall, it is narrowing it for its agency system. Another CEO commented that his company will eventually narrow its target market focus because middle-income consumers will likely be lost to the banks.

As noted, certain CEOs are generally dissatisfied with how well their companies have leveraged their existing customer/household relationships in terms of protection needs and investable assets. However, the industry has not yet developed effective strategies for maximizing the value of its customer relationships.

3.3. Secondary Concerns

CEOs are also concerned about market conduct issues, financial/capital management, expense management and people management, albeit to a lesser extent than the issues described thus far.

CEOs remain concerned about sales practices/compliance/market conduct. They believe the recent negative publicity about the alleged market conduct practices of some life insurers has had a definite impact on how their companies are distributing products. Companies are responding by strengthening the compliance function. They are also participating in Insurance Marketplace Standards Association; however, they view it more as a competitive requirement (similar to getting good policyholder security ratings) rather than a competitive advantage. Companies prefer to make voluntary changes rather than waiting to see what regulators will impose. CEOs are evenly split on whether there will be additional regulations governing disclosure of agent commissions, promotional materials, and sales illustrations.

Financial/capital management is also a secondary concern of CEOs. Most executives are moderately satisfied with their company's profit margins, but still see room for improvement. New business margins are particularly problematic. A fair number of chief executives are dissatisfied with new business profitability, and most expect future margins to remain the same or decline moderately. Companies feel that many of the actions they are taking to address distribution productivity issues will go a long way to improve new business profitability.

Although expense management is still a concern for many CEOs, it is not their most pressing issue. These views are in sync with those expressed in the WFIC Insurance Survey, where insurers did not convey an urgency to address costs, nor a consistent vision of how to do so. While most executives believe that their cost structures need to be lowered, top line revenue growth is generally viewed as a higher priority. An overwhelming majority of executives do not think that expenses have been reduced to the lowest reasonable level, either in the home office or in the field. Expenses are still high even though a significant number of these companies have undertaken formal cost reduction programs and cut expenses by over 10 percent. Despite their views, less than half of the CEOs plan to undertake additional cost-cutting efforts in the near future. A number of CEOs view these programs as ineffective, too disruptive, or less critical than efforts to increase top-line growth.

Very few CEOs think that people management is a key strategic issue for life insurers. Although CEOs are concerned about the quality of their companies' management/leadership skills, the ability to change or adapt their companies' culture to new requirements and the ability of their workforces to adapt to change other issues take precedence.

3.4. Company Preparedness

While most CEOs are fairly confident in their ability to deal with these issues, those that feel well prepared are definitely in the minority. Most CEOs believe their companies are somewhat prepared to address their key strategic concerns. Figure 10-15 shows the percent of respondents who felt "well prepared" to respond to key strategic issues. CEOs feel most prepared to address financial/capital management and expense management issues.

In general, CEOs of mutual companies believe that they are less prepared than those of stock companies to respond to the top strategic issues. Perhaps this reflects the degree to which many stock companies that have generally been leaders in the retirement and investment markets have already addressed many of these strategic challenges.

Analysis of views by size of company yields some interesting findings. CEOs of mid-sized companies expressed the greatest confidence in their ability to respond to sales practices/compliance/market conduct. Small companies feel least prepared. Companies' preparedness to address distribution channel productivity seems to increase with company size, with large companies believing they are best prepared.

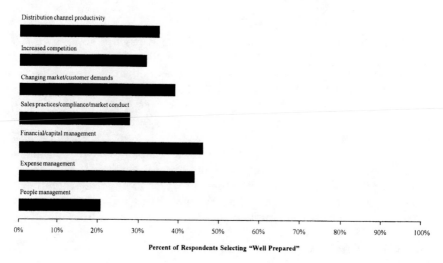

Figure 10-15.   Ability to Respond to Key Strategic Issues

Source: Tillinghast 1997 Life Insurance Industry CEO Survey Report.

4. Where the Industry Is Headed

Although the transformation of the financial services industry is often characterized as *revolutionary*, it is really an *evolutionary* process. Thus, the
significant trends that have been shaping the industry in the recent past will
continue to do so for the foreseeable future. In turn, the same underlying external factors that have influenced these trends will continue to influence the ongoing evolution of the industry. These underlying external
factors include:

- Customer requirements/demographics
- Taxation
- Regulation
- Technology
- Financial market behavior.

A number of these were touched on in Chapter 1, including changing
demographics and technology. Although these factors are largely outside
the control of insurers, it is important not to underestimate the degree to
which they will drive the future.

So, what will the future look like? Obviously, no one can predict exactly
what the future will hold. However, extrapolating from the past and using

our experience as consultants to the industry, we have developed a view of the insurance industry's future in broad brush strokes. Our discussion will focus on the likely changes to the industry in terms of industry structure, distribution, and product.

4.1. Industry Structure

Consolidation within the life insurance industry will continue at an ever-increasing pace. Scale requirements will be large compared to what they are today. Therefore, some insurers will look to acquire or consolidate in-force blocks of business to achieve the scale they need to operate efficiently. To date, the consolidation that has been occurring in the industry has largely been among stock insurers. As mutual insurance companies restructure, which currently represent about half of the industry by some measures, the level of consolidation activity will increase sharply. Many insurers that go through a demutualization are unlikely to remain independent for a significant time after they emerge from the protection period. They will likely be involved in some sort of deal, whether it be a merger, an acquisition or a joint venture—either as the initiator or as the target.

Insurers will also continue the process of disaggregating distribution from manufacturing (although this process does not necessarily preclude the existence of some integrated systems). Already, this disaggregation is an emerging trend within integrated companies, as the tension grows between independent advice and proprietary solutions. This trend is likely to play out in the form of increased open architecture on the part of distributors, particularly for investment products, and broader access to distribution on the part of product manufacturers. As companies increase their focus on areas where they have a source of competitive advantage, outsourcing will increase across a broader array of functions in which companies do not have a capability or cost advantage. That is, outsourcing will not be limited to traditional activities such as marketing and selling—it will also increasingly include functions such as administration, servicing, underwriting, claims, and investment and will likely vary by product line. As companies look to outsource various activities, they will be seeking "superior providers" that have unique capabilities in a given function, enabling insurers to focus on what they do best. The fast growing variable annuity marketplace may provide a glimpse into the future, as many companies are outsourcing key functions such as investment management, administration, and distribution as they look for other ways to add value. Similarly, many companies have "outsourced" the manufacturing of disability income products. Importantly, the outsourcing decisions will need to carefully balance the potential advantage of outsourcing with its inherent risks (e.g., acquisition of outsourcing provider by a competitor). And, needless to say, while outsourcing can be a viable strategy, the company itself must perform or provide something of value to justify its continued existence. That "something" could be as varied as a superior marketing engine or a loyal customer base. This environment will spell opportunity for many companies, particularly those that can excel in one particular niche activity.

Consolidation of the broader financial services industry will also continue. Companies will seek to amalgamate businesses across sectors (e.g., insurance, banking, mutual funds). As a result, in some instances insurance will become a product line rather than a business. The speed of this consolidation will be heavily influenced by the regulatory environment, but it is quite likely that the seminal regulatory changes required to truly eliminate remaining sector barriers will occur within the next three to five years. The Citibank/Travelers merger may act as the immediate impetus for this regulatory change and serve to challenge existing regulations that would require CitiGroup to divest its insurance business within the next few years. As regulatory barriers between sectors fall, a tremendous amount of activity will ensue. We will witness the formation of huge financial conglomerates combining banking, insurance, and asset management. The large banks will be seeking to buy life insurance companies; at the same time, leading life insurance companies will be looking to strike deals with banks.

Within this context, the globalization of financial services will likely play out in the U.S. marketplace and elsewhere. Foreign insurers will play a significant role in the U.S. insurance marketplace as they look for additional opportunities. Large multinational companies will be important players in the future consolidation, acquiring banks and money managers as well as growing their existing insurance operations. Conversely, U.S. insurers will continue to seek new untapped markets to expend their business.

4.2. Distribution

The future of distribution is likely to be a quite varied picture. As one might expect with the maturing of any market, financial institutions will focus their efforts on identifying distinct market segments or niches for which a number of specific product-distribution approaches will be tailored. Thus, distribution will evolve from a few, simple, and nearly universal models to a diversity of distribution-product-market segment approaches.

The role of advice will remain a key driver of insurance product distribution in the foreseeable future. While there are increasing opportunities to go direct (Internet, mail telephone, ATM, etc.), the proliferation and access to information will increase the value of advice. Within the advice-seeking segment, the agency system in its current form is unlikely to thrive as a dominant distribution channel. Current levels of cost and profitability make this an untenable distribution proposition. The industry will increasingly move to open-architecture (non-proprietary) systems. Distribution channels, including hybrid models of distribution, will proliferate (e.g., combinations of direct mail, telephone-based selling and servicing, Internet-based communication, and face-to-face interactions). Self-service distribution (i.e., Web-based) will increase in popularity for certain segments of the population and for simple product types. If direct distribution is at one end of the spectrum and intermediary distribution is at the other, there will be many different models in between. In addition, the lines between direct and intermediary distribution will become increasingly blurred as new technology enables previously unheard of combinations. However, for these channels to have value, they must have some tie to a natural customer base or brand.

Another likely area of growth is worksite distribution. Worksite will likely grow in importance both as a medium of education and as the deliverer of financial service products. For example, many mutual fund customers were introduced and educated to mutual funds through 401(k) plans and the replication of this model to other financial service products (e.g., group benefits) is likely to take place, though more slowly.

In general, these distribution changes will be driven and enabled by a shift in management's thinking. In the past, most companies have tended to concentrate on the life product and a simple, "push the product" business focus. In the future, many companies will begin to focus on serving a defined set of needs for a distinct segment of customers with whatever products and distribution approaches work. Alternatively, they may serve a set of independent retailers' own product and related distribution needs (whether that independent retailer is another financial institution or "merchant" retailer, such as Nordstrom's, L. L. Bean, Intuit, or amazon.com).

With the maturing of both the market and the business, the opportunities for achieving competitive advantage, for many companies, will be in the distribution realm. The opportunities for achieving and sustaining real advantage through product, technology, or investment management have become quite limited or fleeting. Brand, knowledge of specific customer segments, the ability to act on customer information, the ability to create productive (i.e., profitable) product-service-distribution combinations and, ultimately, the ability to craft a profitable distribution business will be the key.

4.3. Product

As described earlier, investment-oriented products will continue to dominate demand for financial products. These and other successful products will continue to be influenced significantly by tax structure and regulations. Products will be tax efficient and will likely be manufactured by the institution that has the greatest tax advantages, whether that be a bank, an insurer, or a mutual fund company. The winners will be those companies that can react quickly to take advantage of changes in the tax, regulatory, and economic environment.

While financial products are becoming increasingly complex, in the future they are likely also to be more transparent (i.e., understandable) to the customer. They will be tailored for specific needs and packaged as a compelling bundle. Those companies that are innovative in developing products that appear simple, but that combine aspects of various financial products, will emerge as winners. For example, the recent appearance in the United States of mutual funds with guaranteed minimum death benefits and "universal policies" (U.K.) that permit policyholders to carry debt balances against collateralized assets such as home mortgages illustrate how such aspects may be combined. In addition, some product innovation will likely revolve around the integration of advice and product, such as wrap accounts and integration of financial planning and unified account type products.

In addition, in the future product performance and individual risk management will assume greater importance. As customers become more informed and sophisticated about financial products, they will become more discriminating in the selection of products to meet their changing financial needs. This change will be accompanied by the assumption of greater personal responsibility for long-term financial/retirement well-being (for large segments of the population). Financial product providers, in turn, will need to offer the flexibility that enables individuals to address their needs in accordance with their individual tolerance for risk.

4.4. Implications for Insurers

What does this mean for insurers? As with any industry, there is no single strategy, no magic bullet that ensures success. The success of such varied companies as USAA, American Express Financial Advisors, Hartford Life, and Northwestern Mutual is a testament to this fact. Whatever strategy and business model insurers choose to adopt requires *focus*. Insurers must focus to create a point of strategic differentiation—in other words, they must choose what they want to be. Then, they need to evaluate their current situation and determine what strategy best fits the intersection of their capabilities, consumers' needs, and competitors' threats.

A company's future strategy must be built on its strengths. Moreover, these strengths must be real and not simply asserted; they must provide the insurers with sustainable competitive advantage. For example, if an insurer is extremely efficient at manufacturing and wholesaling products, it could logically pursue a low-cost, product manufacturing-oriented strategy. Alternatively, if a company has unique skills and capabilities in building deep multi-product customer relationships, it could pursue a value-added retailer strategy. These are just two possible strategies among many. For instance, in certain circumstances a company could choose to be an integrated manufacturer/distributor of a focused niche player (e.g., worksite selling).

4.3.1. Product Manufacturer. An insurer could choose to become a high volume manufacturer, and provide product on a wholesale basis through multiple distribution outlets. Such a strategy is likely to include the following:

- Maximum distribution access
- Ongoing product development and innovation
- Investments in technology to maximize manufacturing efficiency and distributor servicing
- Selective acquisition of blocks of business to increase scale.

4.3.2. Customer Relationship Manager. An insurer could also choose to focus on building broad-based multi-product customer relationships. Such relationships can either be direct (like USAA) or through an advisor (like American Express Financial Advisors). Companies pursing such strategies seek to maximize customer share-of-wallet rather than distributor share-of-shelf (as in the manufacturing strategy). One such strategy is likely to include the following:

- Offering a wide array of financial products (proprietary and non-proprietary) to meet consumer needs
- Significant technology investment in customer knowledge/-customer information
- Focus on high value-added customer service with linkage to sales function
- A defined process and/or vehicle for wrapping around the customer relationship (financial plan, unified account, etc.)
- Investment in building a brand to attract and retain customers.

The imperative for insurers in implementing a strategy is to align its business model, operations, and investments. Too often, there is a disconnect between an insurer's strategic intent and its actions. The bottom line for these and other possible strategies is that execution is everything. There are many potential models for success. Winning companies will be distinguished by visionary management that can engineer individualized strategies from the marketplace back into the company's manufacturing and distribution approaches.

INDEX